高等院校基于工作过程的校企合作系列教材

商务翻译实务

（第三版）

A Practical Coursebook on Business Translation

(Third Edition)

主　　编　袁　洪　王济华
副 主 编　钱立武　赵继荣
编　　者　陈　岚　郝俊杰　何　芸　潘小波
　　　　　吴端明
企业顾问　李泳忠　赵震锋　李巨均　江　南

对外经济贸易大学出版社
中国 · 北京

图书在版编目（CIP）数据

商务翻译实务 / 袁洪，王济华主编. --3 版.
北京：对外经济贸易大学出版社，2024. 6.（2025. 6 重印）--（高等院校基于工作过程的校企合作系列教材）. --ISBN 978-7-5663-2604-1

Ⅰ. F7

中国国家版本馆 CIP 数据核字第 2024ER6746 号

商务翻译实务（第三版）

A Practical Coursebook on Business Translation (Third Edition)

袁 洪 王济华 **主编**

责任编辑： 谭利彬

出版发行：对外经济贸易大学出版社
社　　址：北京市朝阳区惠新东街 10 号
网　　址：www.uibep.com
资源网址：www.uibepresources.com
邮政编码：100029
邮购电话：010－64492338
发行部电话：010－64492342
E-mail：uibep@126.com

成品尺寸：185mm×260mm
印　　张：20
字　　数：462 千字
ISBN 978-7-5663-2604-1
印　　刷：三河市少明印务有限公司
版　　次：2024 年 6 月北京第 3 版
印　　次：2025 年 6 月第 2 次印刷
定　　价：68.00 元

出 版 说 明

党的二十大擘画了以中国式现代化推进中华民族伟大复兴的宏伟蓝图，发出了为全面建设社会主义现代化国家、全面推进中华民族伟大复兴而团结奋斗的伟大号召。习近平总书记在党的二十大报告中强调，要“推进职普融通、产教融合、科教融汇”，为我国未来职业教育的发展指明了方向。报告指出，“教育、科技、人才是全面建设社会主义现代化国家的基础性、战略性支撑”，而我们与之相对应的课程开发方式和课程内容的改革模式是“与行业企业共同开发紧密结合生产实际的实训教材，并确保优质教材进课堂”。“高等院校基于工作过程的校企合作系列教材”正是对外经济贸易大学出版社在高等职业教育课程建设领域的最新研究成果。

本系列教材适用于全国高等院校**应用型本科**商务英语专业和国际经济与贸易、贸易经济、国际商务、工商管理、市场营销等经济与贸易类和工商管理类专业的学生；同时适用于全国**高职高专院校**商务英语、应用英语、旅游英语等语言类专业以及国际贸易实务、国际经济与贸易、国际商务等财经商贸大类专业的学生。

本系列教材主要呈现以下特点：

1. 体现“基于工作过程”

在我国高等职业教育新一轮课程改革中，我们学习、引进并发展了德国职业教育的一种新的课程模式——基于工作过程的课程模式。该模式指“为完成一件工作任务并获得工作成果而进行的一个完整的工作程序”建立起来的课程体系。

2. 突出“校企合作”

课程体系的“校企合作”以教师和企业人员参与为主体，是“校企合作，工学结合”的人才培养模式发展的必然产物，旨在提高学生的综合能力，尤其是实践能力和就业能力，实现学校教学与工作实践的零距离。

“高等院校基于工作过程的校企合作系列教材”的课程方案与传统的课程方案相比，打破了高等职业教育学科系统化的课程体系，在分析典型职业活动工作过程的前提下，按照工作过程中的需要来设计课程，以突出工作过程在课程框架中的主线地位，整合优化了理论知识与实践活动。在教材编写过程中，教师结合自身的教学实践、调研论证和外贸专家对工作岗位的实际要求来安排课程结构和内容，而这形成了具有特色的基于工作过程的校企合作系列教材体系。

本套教材涵盖三大模块：语言技能类、专业英语类和专业知识类。作者都是本专业的“双师型”教师，不仅具有丰富的语言教学经验，而且具备企业第一线的工作经历，还主持或参与过多项国家或省市级相关科研项目。他们为本套教材的编写质量提供了有力的保证。

本系列教材包括：

语言技能类

商务英语听说
实用商务英语口语教程（第三版）
国际商务英语口语实训（第二版）
致用商务英语阅读（上册）
致用商务英语阅读（下册）
新编商务英语应用文写作
商务英语函电
外贸函电与单证实训教程（第二版）
商务翻译实务（第三版）
经贸英语口译实训教程（第二版）
英语语法实训教程

专业英语类

会展实务英语（第三版）
商务礼仪实务英语（第二版）
外事接待实务英语（第三版）
中英文酒店服务实训教程
旅游实务英语多模态教程
中英文导游实训教程
涉外酒店前厅服务技能实训教程

专业知识类

外贸跟单实务（第二版）
外贸单证实务
国际贸易单证操作实务
进出口报关实务（第二版）
报检实务（第二版）
国际市场营销实务
涉外企业管理实务（英文版）
生产物流运作实务
集装箱运输实务
国际贸易实务（双语版）
商务英语谈判
国际结算（英文版）

值得注意的是，本系列教材不是封闭的，它随着教学模式和课程设置的变化，将不断推出新的内容，以丰富整个体系。

同时，本套教材均配有 PPT 课件等立体化教学资源，供教师教学参考（下载网址：http://www.uibepresources.com）。

对外经济贸易大学出版社
2024 年 1 月

前　言

当前，世界百年未有之大变局加速演进，全球经济增速下行并步入中低速增长轨道。中国将继续成为全球经济增长的主要贡献者。截至 2023 年，中国连续 7 年保持货物贸易第一大国地位。

本书贯彻党的二十大报告精神，落实立德树人根本任务，落细“一体、两翼、五重点”工作。本书的编写理念之基础在于“译中学”。翻译不是吸收性、输入性的，而是表达性和输出性的，传统的翻译教程恰恰忽略了这一点。传统教程企图通过一系列的讲解教会学生翻译，重视输入而忽视输出，与课程性质背道而驰，这正如想教会学生游泳而只是给他们看一些书籍和讲一些理论，显然于事无补。因此，本书强调学生在“译中学”，强调学生的产出而不是输入，这符合翻译的学习规律。从逻辑上讲，翻译教学宜采用“归纳法”，因为学生只有通过翻译实践，从中归纳提升有关技巧和理论，才能实现翻译能力的升华。

无论是商务英语还是商务英语翻译都必须服务于国际经济与国际贸易活动，这两大领域也是商务英语专业学生的就业岗位所在。它包括在外事，外贸，外企和商务管理公司承担外贸跟单、商务管理、商务翻译、外贸洽谈、外贸业务员、驻外商务代理、涉外文秘等工作。因此，商务翻译教程应该基于国际贸易工作过程设计编写思路和编写内容。我们把商务翻译内容根据国际贸易过程分解为四大模块：建立关系、订立合同、执行合同和售后服务。基于这些模块，我们把国际贸易过程分解为十五个单元，这些单元串起来正好是国际贸易的全部过程。掌握了本书这些单元，也就掌握了国际经济和国际贸易过程中需要的商务翻译能力。本书具有以下两大特点：

第一，实践性强。本教程每章开始都编写了与现实密切相关的思考题或课前准备要求，预留学生思考的时间和空间，其应用性不言而喻，所有内容都与工作内容密切相关，贴近现实，贴近工作。实践性表现为重视对翻译过程的描述而非翻译结果的核对，表现为教材设计以学生各种翻译活动为中心，教师的作用不是主讲，而是起引导和指导作用。读者要学习的不是翻译的结果，而是翻译的思维过程，这才是翻译教程的亮点和卖点所在；读者在翻译之后进行反思，在反思之中提高翻译能力。

第二，翻译练习设计的多样性和开放性。商务翻译内容浩如烟海，其形式也多种多样，练习设计也应不落俗套，不拘一格而有所创新。除传统的句子和段落翻译外，编者设计了改错题、选择题、填空题、赏析题、比较分析题，这样更能引起学生的兴趣。翻译练习根据翻译过程设计理解、转换、翻译优化等题目。此外，题目内容直接与工作过程的现实结合起来，例如商务单证翻译内容来自贸易过程中的单证处理内容。

本书适合于应用型本科院校和高职高专院校的商务英语、国际贸易实务、国际商务、商务文秘等专业学生，适用于从事商务活动的专业人士，也适合对商务翻译感兴趣的自学人员或者外贸工作者。本书第一版出版后，一方面得到有关院校师生的好评；另一方面，新事物如移动支付（mobile payment）、共享经济（shared economy）层出不穷。因此，编者进行了修订，修订时更新了有关教学材料，也增加了“亚投行”“一带一路”等有关内容。由于读者可以参考已经发布的《公共服务领域译写规范》或者网上有关合同范本等，限于版面，不再列出附录。

本书由袁洪教授负责设计全书体例，王济华副教授对全书进行统稿，钱立武副教授、赵继荣老师对全书进行了审校。参加编写人员如下：袁洪教授编写第一、第七、第八、第九、第十五单元，郝俊杰副教授编写第二单元，王济华副教授编写第三、第十四单元，吴端明副教授编写第四单元，赵继荣老师编写第五、第十单元，潘小波副教授编写第六单元，陈岚老师编写第十一单元，钱立武副教授编写第十二单元，何芸老师编写第十三单元。

本书编写及修订过程中吸收了国内外专家学者的研究成果及中国期刊网的有关论文，虽尽量列出所有文献，但难免挂一漏万，特此致谢！

鉴于编写人员水平有限，时间仓促，疏漏和错误在所难免，均由编者负责，敬请各位专家学者批评指教。

编　者

2024 年 3 月于广州

Contents

第一单元

商务翻译概论

Unit One An Introduction to Business Translation

剑桥商务英语（BEC）考试大纲中把商务英语定义为：Business English is for business people who need to, or will soon need to, use English in their work. It may also be used by adult students who will be entering the world of business at the end of their course of studies.（商务英语是从事或将要从事商务活动的人所使用的语言；也是行将毕业、即将进入商界的大学生们将要使用的语言。）商务英语（Business English）就其语言本质而言，是在商务领域内经常使用的，反映这一领域专业活动的英语词汇、句型、文体等的有机总和，是专门针对商务和商务活动的专业英语（李太志，2006：7—8）。“商务”指商务工作人员所从事的商务活动和商务环节的总称；“英语”是进行此类商务活动时交流沟通的媒介。从整体上来说，商务英语不仅包括英语语音、语法、词汇、语篇和跨文化知识等通用英语（English for General Purposes, EGP）所包含的基础知识，还包括与商务有关的国际货物贸易、国际服务贸易、国际技术贸易、国际投资融资、国际合作等商务知识，是一种专门用途英语（English for Special Purposes, ESP）（贺雪娟，2007：9）。它是在商务活动环境中使用的功能性很强的专业英语。本单元介绍商务英语的语言特征及商务翻译的有关标准。

教学目标

1. 了解商务英语有关背景知识；
2. 了解商务英语的语言特点；
3. 掌握商务英语的翻译标准。

PART ONE
认识商务英语及商务翻译

Task 阅读下列商务英语的有关段落，体会商务英语（Business English）与通用英语（English for General Purposes）的区别。

1. Digitalization is another pillar for expansion, which will double the company's revenue in five years.
2. McDonald's announced the Sichuan's return last week, describing it as a "really, really limited release" to special locations in the US.
3. The kinds of trade nations engage in are varied and complex, a mixture of visible and invisible trade. Most nations are more dependent on exports than on any other activity. The earnings from exports pay for the imports that they need and want. A nation's balance of payment is a record of these complex transactions. By reflecting all of these transactions in monetary terms, a nation is able to combine the income it receives, for example, from exports, tourism expenditures, and immigrant remittances. This combined income is then spent on such items as manufactured goods from other countries, travel for its citizens to other countries, and the hiring of construction engineers.

从上述例子可以看出，商务英语句式比较复杂，专业词汇较多。有些词汇虽然简单，但其在商务英语中的含义与通用英语有很大差别。此外，缩略语是商务英语的一大特点，熟悉并理解商务缩略语对商务英语翻译至关重要。

PART TWO
商务翻译热身练习

Task I 把下列缩略语的全称及译文填写在横线上。

1. CBD ____________________
2. PPP ____________________
3. CIF ____________________
4. FOB ____________________
5. FDI ____________________
6. B/L ____________________
7. CPI ____________________
8. GDP ____________________

9. QS ____________________

10. WFOE ____________________

Task II　把下列句子翻译成汉语。

1. We are sorry to inform you that your price has been found uncompetitive, but we are still interested in doing business with you if you can bring down your price to be in line with the international market price.

   ____

2. After thorough investigation of the damages, we found out that the B/L showed that when the shipping company received the goods, they were in apparent good condition. The liability is certainly not on our side.

   ____

3. A firm offer is a kind of offer which is made to a specific person or persons to express or imply a definite intention of the offeror to make a contract under a clear, complete and final trade terms.

   ____

4. As the marketplace becomes truly global, as barriers of distance, time, language and regulation diminish through the new communication technologies, the level of competition among market participants has never been higher.

   ____

PART THREE
商务英语语言特点

Task I　阅读下列短语，体会商务英语的语言特点。

1. clean bill of lading
2. packing list
3. shipping advice
4. shipping instruction
5. marketing mix

____

Task II　阅读下列句子，从语言规范方面讨论商务英语的语言特点。

1. This simply means that the company continues indefinitely, that the death or withdrawal of a shareholder does not terminate the company existence, and that a shareholder does not have the power to compel or force dissolution.
2. Marketing occurs when people decide to satisfy needs and wants through exchange. Exchange is the act of obtaining a desired object from someone by offering something in

return. Exchange is only one of many ways people can obtain a desired object.

3. As prices continue to rise and consumers search for affordable ways to sustain the transitional economy, nearly 80 percent of U.S. households are shopping at Walmart. Consumers across various income brackets are now taking advantage of Walmart's one-stop shopping convenience to purchase a wide assortment of consumer packaged goods at low prices.
4. At your request, we have effected insurance on this consignment against All Risks and War Risk for US$ 50,000 on June 1, 2022.

Task III 阅读下列句子，从语言结构稳定性方面讨论商务英语的语言特点。

1. It would be appreciated if you could quote your best prices of CIF London for Christmas decorations, and also let us know the earliest possible date you can make shipment.
2. This contract is made in a spirit of friendship and cooperation by and between Party A and Party B, whereby Party A shall invite Party B as an English teacher on the terms and conditions stipulated as follows.
3. Neither party shall be held responsible for failure or delay to perform all or any part of this Contract due to flood, fire, earthquake, snowstorm, hailstorm, hurricane, war, government prohibition or any other events that are unforeseeable at the time of the execution of this Contract and could not be controlled, avoided or overcome by such party.

Task IV 阅读下列短语并翻译，讨论商务英语的语言特点。

1. CT: cable transfer
2. POD: pay on delivery
3. BOT: balance of trade
4. SO: shipping order
5. VAX: value added tax
6. BRIC: Brazil, Russia, India, China
7. BRI: Belt and Road Initiative
8. AIIB: Asian Infrastructure Investment Bank

Task V 阅读下列句子，注意数字与词汇的精确度，讨论商务英语的语言特点。

1. Party A shall be able to supply the goods in the contract on or before Sept. 10 so that they may reach the US before Christmas rush season.
2. Party A shall pay Party B a monthly salary of US$ 5,000 (SAY FIVE THOUSAND US DOLLARS ONLY).

3. Generally, in a sales contract, the insured amount is 110% or 120% of the contracted prices of the consignment.
4. Within 30 days after the signing and coming into effect of this contract, the Buyer shall proceed to pay the price for the goods to the Seller by opening a confirmed irrevocable L/C for the full amount of US$ 880,000 in favor of the Seller through a bank at export port.

____

Task VI　阅读下列句子，讨论商务英语的语言特征，注意斜体词汇的特征。

1. In general, when disputes arise between exporter and importer, it can be settled through friendly consultation, litigation or arbitration. Friendly negotiation or mediation is the best method of all and beneficial to both parties. The majority of the disputes are settled by this way and friendly business relations are thus *maintained* between importers and exporters. If the disputes cannot be settled through *amicable* negotiation or mediation, arbitration will be the next best *alternative*, as the litigation is usually costly and time-consuming.
2. We *hereby certify* that this invoice is true and correct, and in accordance with our books, also that the goods shipped are produced in Guangzhou, China and comply with Rules of Origin of the People's Republic of China.

____

PART FOUR
商务英语翻译标准

Task I　翻译下列句子或段落，讨论商务英语翻译的标准。

1. Over 50,000 tons of freight are being landed each day at the Port of London.

____

2. As the goods are urgently needed by our customers, they must be delivered as soon as possible by air freight.

____

3. Much of the fish sold in England is freighted overland from Scotland.

____

4. Many of the machine parts are now made of plastics instead of metals so that their weight may be decreased.

____

Task II　请翻译下列段落，讨论商务翻译的其他标准。

1. An important social impact stems from advertising's financial support of the mass media: it provides about two-thirds of print revenue and virtually all broadcast revenue. Media

operators thus see the public not as their primary audience, but as mere bait for attracting advertisers; media content, by and large, is designed to attract those citizens whose spending power is great.

____

____

2. China's digital economy logged rapid expansion in recent years, with its scale increasing from 11 trillion yuan in 2012 to over 45 trillion yuan in 2021, according to the Ministry of Industry and Information Technology. The proportion of the digital economy in China's GDP rose from 21.6 percent to 39.8 percent in the period.

____

____

PART FIVE

商务翻译标准再讨论

讨论：通过上述翻译任务，你认为商务翻译有哪些标准?

本单元讨论了商务英语的语言特征，归纳起来就是“三化三性”：“三化”即专业化、规范化和程式化；“三性”即简洁性、准确性和正式性。基于商务英语的语言特点，本单元讨论商务英语的翻译过程及翻译标准。忠实（Faithfulness）、统一（Consistency）和连贯（Coherence）是商务翻译的三大标准。忠实，就是把原文的信息尽可能完整地传递到目的语中，使目的语读者得到与原文读者一样的信息。统一，就是必须对所有的专业术语、人名、地名等专有名词进行检查，保持高度一致。连贯，就是目的语必须符合语法，表达流畅，表意清楚。商务翻译在做到忠实、统一和连贯的基础上，还应尽量做到地道，即符合目的语的语言特点和表达习惯。比如，众所周知，英语名词化程度相当高，在英汉翻译过程中，需要把英语中的名词、动名词、动词不定式等翻译成动词。如下例中的斜体单词都翻译成动词：

原文：The *adoption* of euro banknotes and coins as the legal tender in Europe will bring opportunities as well as challenges to Hong Kong exporters. The *introduction* of euro has resulted in greater price transparency, as well as a *reduction* in transaction costs and foreign exchange risks in the euro zone. The higher transparency would benefit consumers as it would be more convenient for them to compare prices and they would eventually get the best buy.

译文：欧洲**利用**欧元作为法定货币为香港出口商既带来了机遇，也带来了挑战。**使用**欧元提高了价格透明度，**降低**了欧元区交易成本和外汇风险。消费者将会受益于较高的价格透明度，因为他们更方便比较价格，最终购买更合算的产品。

关于商务翻译的标准，许多专家学者进行了探讨和研究，现概括如下，以供参考：

关于翻译标准，最耳熟能详的莫过于严复老先生提出的信（Faithfulness）、达

(Expressiveness)、雅(Elegance),至今对翻译实践仍具有一定的指导意义。鲁迅先生认为,翻译一方面要求其易解,另一方面需要保存原作的丰姿。傅雷先生和钱钟书先生分别提出了“神似”说(Similarity in Spirit)和“化境”说(Sublimation)。所有这些标准主要是基于文学翻译而不是商务翻译提出来的,尽管其对商务翻译具有一定的指导作用。

刘法公(1999:59)提出了商务翻译忠实、地道、统一的标准。“所谓‘忠实’,即译文所传递的信息同原文所传递的信息要保持一致,或者说要保持信息等值。所谓‘地道’,即是指译文的语言和行文方式都要符合商务文献的语言规范和行文规范,也就是说译者所给出的译文读起来应该像是内行的人用译语写作的文章,其中的术语、表达等都应该符合商务文献的要求。所谓‘统一’,即是指在商务英语翻译过程中所采用的译名、概念、术语等在任何时候都应该保持统一,不允许将同一概念或术语随意变换译名。”翻译中确实存在不少统一性问题。如右图所示,某省会城市的宾馆外卖店两侧都有相同的公示语,但把“桃源外卖部”分别翻译成“Tao yuan Hotel Take away”和“DELIVERY DEPARTMENT OF TAOYUAN HOTEL”,姑且不论本身翻译不当,大小写混乱不堪就可看出译者马虎草率。其实,我们可以直接将其翻译成“Take-away Service of Taoyuan Hotel”就可以了。

常玉田提出了非常实用的商务翻译标准:平民化标准,也就是“一看对不对,二看好不好”(常玉田,2005:7)。“对不对”指译文必须正确,符合原文意义。“好不好”指从读者的角度判断译文的表达,指译者翻译过程中应当意识到自己是在提供服务,意识到译文读者的阅读成本,比如把“US$ 100”翻译成“100 美元”是对的,但翻译成“100 美元(约合 670 元人民币)”就更好了。

PART SIX

商务翻译实践

Task I 请将下列短语翻译成中文。

1. terms of payment ________	2. payment advice ________
3. working capital ________	4. fixed capital ________
5. digital economy ________	6. monetary policy ________
7. commercial invoice ________	8. business hour ________
9. commodity inventory ________	10. business status ________
11. wholesale distributor ________	12. quality control ________

Task II 翻译下列句子，注意句子中斜体单词的翻译。

1. The Chinese government on Wednesday stressed the importance for the country to step up efforts to develop *emerging industries* of strategic importance.

____

____

2. In an address to the 2010 Global City Informatization Forum, China's Minister of Science and Technology Wan Gang said the priority for information technology service will be given to rural areas. "The '*digital gap*' between urban and rural China needs to be further bridged," he said.

____

____

3. A new policy allowing overseas tourists traveling in a group to get *visas upon arrival* in East China's Zhejiang Province may greatly boost local tourism, local authorities said on Sunday.

____

____

4. *Inclusive growth* in India and China made these two countries become the major players in world economy. India and China both succeeded in attaining the attention of the world by promoting inclusive growth in the fields like labor regulations, agricultural technology and infrastructure. The inclusive growth also includes plans like assisting lagging regions of the country and empowering the poor through proactive policies so that they can take part in the market on equitable terms.

____

____

Task III 翻译下列段落，注意商务英语的翻译标准。

1. The development of e-business had close links to the development of the Internet as suppliers and customers realized the cost and time benefits of online transactions. It became more efficient to do business when online systems were used throughout an organization's supply channels. The real challenge of e-business was providing customers with the latest data through every sales channel.

____

____

2. In a digital economy, you must be ready for a future of continual change. Change your vision for the future, work closely with your staff, suppliers, and partners to make changes, and learn to view your organization as the customers view it. The focus of e-business must always be on the customers. You have to use your knowledge of your market to consider how customer expectations will change in the future.

____

____

3. The golden rule of e-business is that the customer is king. In the days when your customers shopped on the high street, or purchased by telephone or mail order, their opportunity for direct comparison of price was limited. The Internet allows individual or business customers to make comparisons easily and complete their purchases from their own home or office. Many websites now exist for the purpose of comparison shopping. You should understand the power lies in the hands of the customer and you must put their needs at the center of your business.

____

____

PART SEVEN
学习参考

1. 金焕荣. 商务英语翻译［M］. 苏州：苏州大学出版社，2022.
2. 吕和发，任林静，等. 全球化商务翻译［M］. 北京：外文出版社，2011.
3. 何少庆，余姗姗. 商务英语翻译实务［M］. 北京：中国人民大学出版社，2017.
4. 中国日报网站：http://language.chinadaily.com.cn/vocabulary.shtml
5. 北京周刊网站：http://www.bjreview.com.cn/

PART EIGHT
单元预告与实训任务

1. 下一单元，我们将讲述名片翻译，请你收集各种名片，最好是双语名片。
2. 中国进出口商品交易会即将来临，为做好交易会实践准备工作，请为自己制作双语名片一张。

第二单元

名片翻译

Unit Two Translating Business Cards

名片是人类交往带来的产物。名片在中国古代又称谒、名刺、门状、名帖，是拜访他人时表明自己身份，并起介绍作用的文书。古代名片的内容及所用的材料都与现代差别甚大。在中国，最初的名片即"谒"通常刻在竹片或木片上，而后来的门状、名帖则是纸质的。现代名片由西方传来，是商业交际活动的产物。现代的名片不仅制作精美，内容丰富，语言也由过去的单一语言变为多种语言。在现代商业活动日趋国际化的大潮下，名片的双语化、多语化是大势所趋，这就要求我们了解名片的翻译。

教学目标

1. 了解名片的内容及其背景知识；
2. 了解名片的语言特点；
3. 掌握名片翻译的定译、音译和零翻译；
4. 掌握名片翻译中姓名、头衔、职务和地址的翻译策略。

PART ONE

认识名片与名片翻译

Task I 请于课前收集 10 张中英文对照的名片，观察并讨论：名片是什么？名片由什么构成？它有什么特征和功能？

Task II　比较中英文名片的异同，思考现代名片发展的趋势。

名片是表明一个人身份的卡片，根据其持有者不同的交际意图，英语中可分为 visiting card，calling card，name card，或一律称为 card（胡晓姣，2006）。名片的内容一般包括个人的姓名、头衔、单位、联系方式等。在一般的社交和商务场合中，交际双方交换名片是一项基本礼仪。

名片虽小，作用却非常大。名片以非常精练的形式概述个人的基本情况。交际双方通过交换名片，可以迅速了解对方的身份和职务。名片上还有个人的联系方式，方便交际双方的联络。对于某些职业，比如销售员、译员、演员等，一张精美的名片相当于无声的广告。

I. 名片的分类

名片可以从不同角度来分类。从制作材料来看，名片可以分为纸质名片、塑料名片、电子名片等；从印刷面数来看，可以分为单面印刷名片和双面印刷名片；从名片色彩来看，可以分为单色名片、双色名片和彩色名片。从交际功能来看，名片可以分为以下三种：

1. 商业名片：它是公司或企业进行业务活动时使用的名片，其使用大多以营利为目的。商业名片的主要特点为：名片常使用企业标志、注册商标，常印有企业业务范围；大公司的名片印刷格式统一，使用高档纸张；名片没有私人家庭信息，主要用于商业活动。

2. 公用名片：它是政府或社会团体在对外交往中所使用的名片，其使用不是以营利为目的。公用名片的主要特点为：名片常使用标志，部分印有对外服务范围，没有统一的名片印刷格式，名片印刷力求简单适用，注重个人头衔和职称，名片内没有私人家庭信息，主要用于对外交往与服务。

3. 个人名片：它是朋友间交流感情，结识新朋友时所使用的名片。个人名片的主要特点为：名片不使用标志，名片设计个性化，可自由发挥；常印有个人照片、爱好、头衔和职业；名片中含有私人家庭信息，主要用于朋友交往。在这一单元中，我们侧重讲述商业名片和公用名片的翻译。

II. 名片的特点

随着时代的变化，名片也在不断发展变化。现在的名片设计更精美、信息更全面、功能更多样化。总之，现代名片有如下特点：

1. 语言多样化。中外文对照，尤其是中英对照名片流行于世。随着对外交往的增多以及跨国公司的兴起，做一张中外文对照的名片越来越迫切。英语作为一种国际语言，在传递信息方面具有得天独厚的优势。因此，中英文对照的名片最为常见。

2. 内容丰富化。如今的名片可以包括很多内容。比如说身兼数职的人可以将若干职务都印在名片上；有些名片上还附有公司的标志、口号与广告词；联络方式也趋向于多渠道，除了传统的地址和联系电话，还有电子邮箱、网页地址、MSN、QQ 号码、微信号等。

3. 交际功能明确化。当今的名片拥有明确的交际功能。名片反映了其所有者几乎全部的社会职能和主要的社会关系。因此，名片的交际功能越发凸显出来。

4. 设计个性化。虽然名片包含的内容基本类似，但名片的设计却千差万别。有些设计精美的名片堪称艺术品，让人赏心悦目，给人以美的享受。有些企业给员工设计的名片图文并茂，别具匠心，体现出企业的文化底蕴本身就是对企业最好的宣传。

名片反映着文化。不同文化背景的人，其名片也有不同的特色。欧美人士的名片中名在前，姓在后，有些还有中间名；而中国人的名片姓在前，名在后，没有中间名。这是欧美国家人名与中国人名的重要区别。欧美国家重实际、轻名分，因此他们的名片比较简单，通常是姓名加上一两个实际职务，然后就是地址和联系方式了（项红梅，何小群，2007）。中国人的名片相对复杂。常言“名不正则言不顺”，我们习惯把所有的头衔、职务都写上去，甚至包含过去曾担任的职务以及享受的待遇。名片的新特点和中西名片的差异给名片翻译带来了许多难题。这也是名片翻译要重点研究和解决的问题。

PART TWO

热身练习

Task I 请你将课前收集的十张名片翻译成中文或英文。如果你的名片已经是中英对照的，请在自行翻译后与之比较，并讨论翻译时应注意哪些事项。

Task II 请为下列人名选择合适的翻译，并总结翻译人名的规则。

1. 张大民（　　）
   A. ZHANG DA MIN　　B. Zhangdamin
   C. Zhangda Min　　D. Zhang Damin
2. 李宝安（　　）
   A. LI baoan　　B. Li Bao’an
   C. Li Bao An　　D. Baoan Li
3. 牛智慧（　　）
   A. Niu Zhihui　　B. Niu, zhihui
   C. Cow Smart　　D. Niu Zhi Hui
4. M. A. K. Halliday（　　）
   A. 哈里德　　B. 韩礼德
   C. 马可・哈里代　　D. M.A.K. 韩李德
5. Bill Gates（　　）
   A. 比尔盖茨　　B. 比尔・改瓷
   C. 比尔・盖茨　　D. 碧儿・盖丝

Task III 请将下面的英文和译文搭配起来，将适当的代号填入英语后面的括号中。

1. Room	(　　)	A. 单元
2. Unit	(　　)	B. 省
3. Building No.	(　　)	C. 路
4. Street	(　　)	D. 区
5. Road	(　　)	E. 县

6. District ( ) F. 街
7. County ( ) G. 楼房号
8. Municipality ( ) H. 镇
9. Town ( ) I. 直辖市
10. City ( ) J. 市
11. Province ( ) K. 室
12. Autonomous Region ( ) L. 自治区

PART THREE
名片翻译技巧

Task I 请翻译以下姓名，并总结姓名的翻译原则和翻译技巧。

1. 马龙翔 ________
2. 李云飞 ________
3. 司马相如 ________
4. 王洪祥 ________
5. 文树安 ________
6. 李安 ________
7. 陆克文 ________
8. 梁朝伟 ________
9. 孔子 ________
10. 李小龙 ________

Task II 请翻译以下头衔和职务，并总结头衔和职务的翻译技巧。

第一组 政府公职类

1. 部长 ________
2. 司长 ________
3. 局长 ________
4. 省长 ________
5. 县长 ________
6. 镇长 ________
7. 秘书长 ________
8. 办公厅主任 ________
9. 处长 ________
10. 科长 ________
11. 科员 ________
12. 发言人 ________
13. 顾问 ________
14. 巡视员 ________
15. 特派员 ________
16. 总领事 ________
17. 审判长 ________
18. 警督 ________
19. 法医 ________
20. 领事 ________

第二组 社会团体类

1. 会长 ________
2. 主席 ________
3. 名誉顾问 ________
4. 理事 ________
5. 总干事 ________
6. 总监 ________
7. 董事长 ________
8. 总裁 ________
9. 总经理 ________
10. 财务主管 ________
11. 公关部经理 ________
12. 营业部经理 ________
13. 销售部经理 ________
14. 出纳员 ________

15. 车间主任 ________
16. 采购员 ________
17. 技师 ________
18. 领班 ________
19. 仓库管理员 ________
20. 审计员 ________

第三组 专业技术类

1. 高级工程师 ________
2. 教授 ________
3. 建筑师 ________
4. 设计师 ________
5. 机械师 ________
6. 化验员 ________
7. 质检员 ________
8. 农业技术员 ________
9. 外科主治医师 ________
10. 主治医师 ________
11. 总编辑 ________
12. 记者 ________
13. 助理翻译 ________
14. 录音师 ________
15. 舞蹈编剧 ________
16. 美工师 ________
17. 化妆师 ________
18. 舞台监督 ________
19. 摄影师 ________
20. 电视主持人 ________

Task III 请将下列公司名称翻译成英文。

1. 美的集团 ________
2. 恒生银行 ________
3. 中国建设银行 ________
4. 宁波奥克斯空调有限公司 ________
5. 青岛啤酒股份有限公司 ________
6. 中国外运股份有限公司 ________
7. 广州铁路集团公司 ________
8. 中国南方电网公司 ________
9. 华为技术有限公司 ________
10. 深圳市海光国际物流有限公司 ________

Task IV 请将下列机构或团体名称翻译成英文。

1. 国际武术联合会 ________
2. 国际移民组织 ________
3. 绿色和平组织 ________
4. 中国书法家协会 ________
5. 中国野生动物保护协会 ________
6. 中国志愿者保护藏羚羊协会 ________
7. 中国翻译工作者协会 ________
8. 中山市家具商会 ________
9. 中国可持续发展研究会 ________
10. 北京市新能源与可再生能源协会 ________

Task V　请将下列公司部门翻译成英文。

1. 总公司	________	2. 分公司	________
3. 总务部	________	4. 人事部	________
5. 财务部	________	6. 销售部	________
7. 国际部	________	8. 出口部	________
9. 进口部	________	10. 公共关系部	________
11. 广告部	________	12. 企划部	________
13. 培训部	________	14. 质量控制部	________
15. 董事会	________	16. 营销部	________
17. 物流部	________	18. 工程部	________
19. 研发部	________	20. 售后服务部	________

Task VI　请将以下中文地址翻译成英文。

1. 上海市乌鲁木齐中路 12 号
____
2. 北京市东城区海运仓胡同一号京东宾馆会议中心一层
____
3. 北京市西城区珠市口东大街 3 号楼四层
____
4. 北京市东城区美术馆后街 23 号
____
5. 广州海珠区阅江中路 380 号
____
6. 广州市天河北路 233 号中信广场 7201—7202 室
____
7. 广州市黄埔大道西 66 号
____
8. 武汉市江汉路步行街 126 号长盛大厦 4—5 楼
____
9. 武汉市武昌区武珞路阅马场云鹤大厦 1102 室
____
10. 北京市东城区朝阳门北大街 8 号富华大厦 A 座首层
____

PART FOUR

讨论：通过上述翻译任务，你认为翻译名片还要注意哪些事项？

I. 名片翻译总结

名片的翻译原则与翻译技巧，见表 2-1。

表 2-1　　名片的翻译原则与翻译技巧

名片的翻译原则	准确性：名片的翻译要忠实于原文的信息
	简约性：名片的翻译要考虑到名片的篇幅
	交际性：名片的翻译要以社会交际为目的
名片的翻译技巧	定译法：适用于已经有固定或通用译法的人名、地名、机构名或其他专有名词
	音译法：适用于音译的人名或其他专有名词
	零译法：适用于某些常用，并广为人知的缩略语、简写等

II. 名片翻译余论

1. 名片中缩略语的翻译

名片中普遍使用缩略语和简写形式。这是由于名片篇幅有限，简写可以节省空间。一些简写和缩略语因为使用频繁，早已深入人心，形成了一种惯例，比如说 Tel 代表电话，Fax 代表传真。在名片翻译中，我们一方面要了解各种缩略语和简写，以便能正确识别和翻译它们；另一方面，要善于在翻译中使用这些缩略语和简写。当然，前提是这些缩略语和简写不能带来歧义和疑惑。以下是一些常用英文简写的中英对照形式：

中文	英文简写	英文全称
电话	TEL	Telephone
传真	FAX	Facsimile
电子邮箱	E-Mail	Electronic Mail
地址	Add.	Address
手机	Cell/Mob	Mobile Phone/Cell Phone
分机	Ext.	Extension
路	Rd.	Road
邮政编码	P. C.	Post Code
胡同	Al.	Alley
公寓	Apt.	Apartment
街道	Ave./Av.	Avenue
广场	Sq.	Square
街	St.	Street

区	Distr.	District
楼层	Fl./F.	Floor
部门	Dept.	Department
公司	Co./Corp.	Company/Corporation
有限公司	Co. Ltd.	Company Limited

2. 职务职称的翻译

名片中体现个人职务职称词汇的翻译非常重要，它关系到名片能否准确地传达原有的信息。由于汉语称谓丰富多样，头衔更是名目繁多，要做到准确再现原称谓名的含义是十分困难的。在实际翻译过程中，我们主要参照英语国家既有的名称进行对照翻译。我国许多职业称呼和行政职务在英语里都有国际通用的功能等值词（胡晓妏，2006）。对于这些词，可以采用定译的方法。如：教授（Professor），省长（Governor），总经理（General Manager），大学校长（President）等；还有一些职务的翻译则见仁见智，比如局长，有人译成 Bureau Director，有人译成 Bureau Chief，还有人译成 Bureau Manager。

对于那些没有对应英语职务职称的词汇，我们首先要仔细查证单位和行政职务的级别，再酌情选择合适的英语词汇来翻译。比如“局长”一词，国家市场监督管理总局局长和河南省濮阳市教育局局长虽然同为局长称呼，但从级别上来讲，前者是部级单位，后者是处级单位。那么在翻译中，总局的局长要翻译成 Minister，市教育局的局长适合翻译成 Director。

英语中表示副职的词有 associate, assistant, vice, deputy 等。翻译时，应该根据不同的职位选择不同的用词。举例如下：

副省长 vice/deputy governor

副主席 vice chairman

副教授 associate professor

副经理 assistant manager

PART FIVE

译技点津：翻译技巧之专有名词的翻译

I. 姓名的翻译

人名属于专有名词，它是一个人在社会上的称呼，是一种符号，指代特定的人。中国人名习惯姓在前，名在后；这与英语国家的名在前，姓在后正好相反。无论中外，一个人的名字通常都具有深刻的含义。父母给孩子起的名字都是深思熟虑的结果。比如，英文中 Gabriel 代表上帝派来的使者，Jerome 让人联想到有趣、聪明又体贴的男孩，Eric 代表永远的领导者。中文名字的内涵显而易见，比如李红忠，“红”就代表着根正苗红，“忠”代表着忠于国家和人民；又如刘翔，说明父母希望他能“展翅飞翔”。

人名的翻译一般采取“名从主人”的原则，就是说人名的翻译要按照名字主人的叫法。中文人名的英译基本采取音译法，按照中国人的习惯，姓在前，名在后。姓和名的第一个字母大写，姓与名之间留出一个空格。比如张大民，就可以译成 Zhang Damin；复姓如西门或司马，虽然是两个字，但拼音之间没有空格，不可分开。复姓的翻译中，仍然只是姓的第一个字母大写，其他字母采用小写。比如司马相如，就可以翻译成 Sima Xiangru。有些人在翻译中为了突出自己的姓氏，也采用将姓全部大写，比如张海东，可以翻译为 ZHANG Haidong。

采用拼音翻译还要注意一点，就是当 a，o，e 开头的音节接在其他音节之后时，要加隔音符号隔开，以免产生误读。如李汉奥就要翻译成 Li Han'ao，不然就有可能被误读为 Li Ha'nao。

根据“名从主人”的原则，如果一个人本身就取了英文名，我们就要按照他的英文名来翻译，而不能采取拼音翻译法。原因有二，其一出于尊重他人，尊重他们对自己姓名的选择；其二是这样才能够做到标准统一。比如说，刘德华的英文名叫 Andy Lau，名是欧美习惯，姓则采用威妥玛-翟理斯拼音法。大家已经习惯了刘德华这个英文名，如果硬要翻译成 Liu Dehua，反而让人不知道是谁，显得不伦不类。

II. 地址的翻译

中英文地址的写法不同，中文的写法是从大到小，英文则是从小到大。比如地址“广州市东风西路 187 号时代国际大厦 1206 室”，对应的英文应该是“Room 1206, Times International Building, No. 187, Dongfeng Road (West), Guangzhou”。再看下面几个例子：

［例 1］原文：北京市东城区天坛南里西区 20 号楼 3 单元 101

译文：Room 101, Unit 3, Building No. 20, Tiantannanli West Area, Dongcheng District, Beijing City, China

［例 2］原文：江苏省扬州市宝应县泰山东村 102 栋 204 室

译文：Room 204, Building No. 102, East Taishan Village, Baoyin County, Yangzhou City, Jiangsu Province, China

［例 3］原文：中国上海市浦东新区浦东大道 2000 号阳光世界大厦 22 层 H 座

译文：Suite H, 22F, Sunshine World Tower, No. 2000, Pudong Av., Pudong New District, Shanghai, China

［例 4］原文：福建省厦门市莲花五村龙昌里 34 号 601 室

译文：Room 601, No. 34, Longchangli, Lianhuawu Village, Xiamen, Fujian, China

［例 5］原文：广东中山市东区亨达花园 7 栋 702

译文：Room 702, Building No. 7, Hengda Fenced Residential Quarter, East District, Zhongshan, China

从上面的翻译中我们可以总结出地址翻译的几点注意事项：

第一，中文地址翻译成英文时，次序要颠倒过来，由从大到小变成由小到大。第二，英文中每个分级地名要大写首字母，且分级地名之间要用逗号隔开。第三，可以使用简写形式，比如说 Number 简写为 No.，Road 可以简写为 Rd.，Room 可以简写为 Rm.。第四，对于本身已有中英对照名称的建筑物或地点要采用它本身的叫法，这也可以说是定译法。比如时代国际大厦，本身就有英文名 Times International Building，这种情况下就不适合采用音译法。这种例子还有很多，比如香港 Chungking Mansion，中文叫重庆大厦，它本身就是中英对照的。如果不明就里把它翻译成 Chungking Building 或者 Chongqing Building 都是不合适的。可以采用定译法的地名还有很多，举例如下：

香格里拉大酒店	Shangri-La Hotel	天河城	TeeMall
上海东方之珠	The Oriental Pearl	故宫	The Forbidden City
长城	The Great Wall	广百百货	Grand Buy Department Store
香港	Hong Kong	澳门	Macao
拉萨	Lhasa	内蒙古	Inner Mongolia
呼和浩特	Hohhot	乌鲁木齐	Urumqi
哈尔滨	Harbin		
新疆维吾尔自治区	Xinjiang Uygur Autonomous Region		

第五，对于路名、街道名的翻译，如果没有约定俗成的英文名和译名，基本可以采取音译法，后面再加上 Road 或 Street。比如王府井大街，可以译成 Wangfujing Street，东风西路可以译成 Dongfeng Road (West)。

PART SIX
名片翻译实践

Task I 请将以下职务翻译成英文。

第一组

1. 技术总监 ________	2. 信息技术经理 ________
3. 信息技术主管 ________	4. 信息技术专员 ________
5. 项目主管 ________	6. 信息安全工程师 ________
7. 软件测试工程师 ________	8. 硬件测试工程师 ________
9. 测试员 ________	10. 网站营运经理 ________
11. 客户服务经理 ________	12. 客户服务主管 ________

第二组

1. 销售总监 ________	2. 销售经理 ________
3. 区域销售经理 ________	4. 客户经理 ________
5. 渠道/分销经理 ________	6. 渠道主管 ________
7. 销售工程师 ________	8. 销售助理 ________
9. 销售行政经理 ________	10. 销售行政主管 ________
11. 代理经理 ________	12. 董事长兼总经理 ________

Task II 请将以下职务翻译成中文。

1. Plant/Factory Manager ________
2. Chief Engineer ________
3. Project Manager ________
4. Project Engineer ________
5. Operations Manager ________
6. Operations Supervisor ________

7. Production Manager ________________
8. Workshop Supervisor ________________
9. Production Planning Officer ________________
10. Production Supervisor ________________
11. Technical/Industrial Design Manager ________________
12. Technical/Industrial Design Engineer ________________
13. Lab Manager/Engineer ________________
14. Facility Manager ________________
15. Engineering/Facility Supervisor ________________
16. Facility Engineer ________________
17. Electrical Engineer ________________
18. Mechanical Engineer ________________
19. Maintenance Engineer ________________
20. Safety Manager/Supervisor ________________

Task III　请翻译以下名片。

1.

Ausnow
澳雪国际

刘根旺
业务主管

澳雪国际（中国）营销中心
中山市嘉丹婷日用品有限公司
地址：中国广东省中山市小榄东区深涌第三工业大厦
电话：+86-752-588888
传真：+86-752-588886
手机：19888888888
网址：www.ausnow.cn

2.

特达贸易有限公司

刘月如
业务经理
19342255555

地址：广州市东风西路 187 号时代国际大厦 1308 室
电话：020-96668888　96668889
传真：020-96668885
E-mail: tessteps_trading@126.com

3.

TOYOTA
FINANCIAL SERVICES

丰田汽车金融（中国）有限公司

市场部　经理
刘根宝

中国北京市建国门外大街 1 号国贸大厦 1 座 8 层 818 室　邮编：100004
TEL:（010）65055557　转 500　　FAX:（010）65058765
手机：19999893123　　E-mail：abcd@tischina.com.cn
公司网址：http://www.tischina.com.cn

4.

LEXUS
FINANCIAL SERVICES

丰田汽车金融（中国）有限公司

业务发展部　项目经理
白红星

中国北京市建国门外大街 1 号国贸大厦 1 座 8 层 818 室　邮编：100004
TEL:（010）65055557 转 123　　FAX:（010）65058765
手机：19999893188　　E-mail：abcd@tischina.com.cn
公司网址：http://www.tischina.com.cn

5.

中国医药工业有限公司
商务部

中国医药集团

王镇伟

地址：北京市海淀区北四环西路 9 号银星大厦 19 层
电话：010-82008500-8302
手机：19998888888
传真：010-88880000 88880001
电子邮箱：wangzhenwei@cnpic.com.cn
邮编：100080

PART SEVEN
学习参考

1. 名片网：http://www.mingpian.com/
2. 中国名片网：http://www.mingpian.org/
3. 中国在线翻译网：http://www.chinafanyi.com/b_c_dict/b_t_techtitle.htm

PART EIGHT
单元预告与实训任务

1. 下一单元我们将讲述公示语的翻译，涉及国内外各种类型的常见公示语。
2. 留意你身边的公示语，搜集不少于十条中英文对照的公示语，比较其中文和英文。

第三单元

公示语翻译

Unit Three　Translating Public Signs

随着中国国际地位的提升和中国经济的持续发展，中国正日益成为世界的焦点。在党的二十大精神指引下，中国不仅强调开放的经济发展模式，更注重文化自信与文化交流的深化。这种文化自信和开放的姿态使得与中国及中国人民打交道的国家和国际组织越来越多，到中国经商、旅游、学习的国际友人也与日俱增。近年来，中国先后成功举办了 2016 年 G20 杭州峰会、2021 年中国—中东欧国家领导人会晤，以及 2022 年北京冬奥会等活动，都展现了中国作为全球负责任大国的形象和能力。

在这样的大背景下，公示语作为外国人了解中国的一个重要途径，其翻译的准确性和规范性尤为重要。党的二十大报告强调要推动构建人类命运共同体，这要求我们不仅要在经济领域展现开放和包容，也要在文化交流中展现中国的文化自信和友好姿态。公示语不仅为公众提供信息服务，也是城市和国家形象的一部分，其翻译水平直接影响到外国友人对中国文明水平的认知和理解。2017 年，《公共服务领域英文译写规范》的发布，是我国在规范公示语翻译方面迈出的重要一步，体现了提升国家形象，优化语言环境的决心和行动。

探讨公示语翻译不仅有助于提升城市形象，同时也对语言教育有着重要的推动作用。通过标准化、系统化的翻译实践，我们不仅能够改善中国的语言环境，更能在全球化的背景下促进跨文化的交流与理解，展示一个开放、自信、文明、和谐的中国形象。

教学目标

1. 了解公示语的含义及其背景知识；
2. 了解公示语的语言特点；
3. 掌握公示语的翻译技巧；
4. 掌握商务翻译中的词类转换技巧。

PART ONE

认识公示语与公示语翻译

Task I 请将课前收集的 10 条公示语与同学分享，探讨你对目前公示语及公示语翻译的看法。

Task II 阅读下列公示语并思考：什么是公示语？公示语由什么构成？

公示语即“公开和面对公众，告示、指示、提示、显示、警示、标示与其生活、生产、生命、生态、生业休戚相关的文字及图形信息”(《汉英公示语词典》)。公示语又称为“标志语”“标识语”“标示语”“标语”等。国际图形标志委员会对公示语的定义是：“Signs are anything from a simplest way finding or information ‘marker’ to the technically sophisticated communication of a message（公示语包括简单的道路指引或信息‘标记’，也包括技术层面的复杂的信息交流)”。公示语主要由文字、图案、符号和数字等构成，图文并茂，文字与图案表意一致，达到向公众传递信息的目的。

公示语与人们的日常生活息息相关，所有的公示语都是为公众服务的，都是为公众提供相关信息的载体。公示语的使用范围非常广泛，包括旅游景区、公共设施、公共交通、公共机构、商业、体育、文化活动场所等，常见的标识、指示牌、标语、公告、告示、警示等都属于公示语范畴。根据公示语的语言风格和语气特征，公示语可以分为：

1. 指示性公示语（Directive Public Signs)：指示性公示语体现了公共场所对公众的信息服务水平，对公众没有限制、警示和强制意义，主要起到为公众指示方位、地点、服务等作用，比如：急救（First Aid)、旅游服务（Travel Service)、售票处（Ticket Office）等。

2. 提示性公示语（Informatory Public Signs)：提示性公示语为公众提供有关告知性信息，比如：油漆未干（Wet Paint)、此货暂缺（Out of Stock)、正在维修（Under Repair)、保留车位（Reserved）等。

3. 警示性公示语（Cautionary Public Signs)：警示性公示语起警醒提示作用，提醒公众需要注意的问题，如：小心轻放（Handle with Care)、小心地滑（Caution! Wet Floor!)、前方有学校（School Ahead)、当心滚石（Falling Rocks）等。

4. 限制性公示语（Restrictive Public Signs)：限制性公示语限制、约束公众的有关行为，特别强调公众应当注意的事项，起告知和提醒的双重作用，比如：残疾人设施（Disabled Only)、限高 3 米（Restricted Height 3 M)、限速 60～80 千米（Speed Limit 80 Minimum 60 Kilometers）等。

5. 强制性公示语（Mandatory Public Signs)：强制性公示语要求公众必须采取或者不能采取某种行为，语言应用直白、强硬，毫无商量余地，多用祈使句，起警示、强制作用；违反者往往受到一定的处罚或者制裁，这类公示语旨在约束公众行为、维护社会正常秩序与公众安全方面起作用。比如禁止摆卖（Vendors Prohibited)、严禁超车（Overtaking Prohibited)、禁扔废弃物（No Littering）等。

6. 宣传性公示语（Public Slogans)：宣传性公示语向公众传递信息或者对某一特定事件进行宣传，比如：一起向未来（Together for a Shared Future)、点燃你的激情（Live Your Passion)、城市，让生活更美好（Better City, Better Life)、Welcome Home（欢迎回家）(2004 年雅典奥运会的宣传口号。这是因为 1896 年首届现代奥运会是在希腊举办的)。

PART TWO

热身练习

Task I 选出下列公示语的翻译，并将其相应的编号填入括号中。

1. Staff Only	(　　)	A. 消防通道
2. No Parking	(　　)	B. 非公莫入/员工通道
3. Bicycle Parking	(　　)	C. 疏散通道
4. Cargo Lift	(　　)	D. 加油站
5. Sightseeing Elevator/Lift	(　　)	E. 货梯
6. Filling/Gas Station	(　　)	F. 禁止停车
7. Evacuation Route	(　　)	G. 观光梯
8. Fire Engine Access	(　　)	H. 自行车停放处

Task II 请翻译下列公示语。

1. Detour. Maintenance in Progress. ________________
2. Wait. Maintenance in Progress. ________________
3. Escalator Out of Service ________________
4. Horn Prohibited ________________
5. Service Area ________________
6. Service & Complaint Hotline ________________
7. Ticket Check ________________
8. Ticket Office/Tickets ________________

Task III 下列双语图片中的译文是否有待改进？如需改进，请修改并说明理由。

1. 原文：芳草萋萋，踏之何忍？

   原译：Please help us protect the grass for more people to enjoy!

   改译：________________________________

2. 原文：芳草茵茵，踏之何忍

   原译：TENDER FRAGRANT GRASS　HOW HARDHEARTED TO TRAMPLE THEM

   改译：________________________________

3. 原文：小草微微笑，请您旁边绕

   原译：THE GRASS IS SMILING AT YOU　PLEASE DETOUR

   改译：________________________________

4. 原文：宾客止步

   原译：Guest go no further

   改译：________________________________

5. 原文：严禁向窗外抛扔物品

   原译：Strictly forbid toward window to throw to throw a product

   改译：________________________________

6. 原文：请小心保管财物！

   原译：Keep your Valuables in view

   改译：________________________________

PART THREE

公示语翻译技巧

Task I　请阅读下列公示语，并说明公示语的语言特征。

1. 从词类角度讨论下列公示语的语言特征：

   （1）Conference Center（会议中心），Registration（注册登记），Information（咨询服务）

   （2）No Stopping（请勿停留），No Smoking（禁止吸烟），No Spitting（禁止吐痰）

   （3）Keep Silence（保持安静），Slow Down（减速慢行），Sold Out（售完）

   （4）F&B（Food and Beverage，餐饮服务），VIP Suite（Very Important Person Suite，贵宾室），ENT Department（Ear, Nose, Throat Department 耳鼻喉科），BRT（Bus Rapid Transit，快速公交系统）

2. 从句型方面讨论公示语的语言特征：

   （1）Don't Drive When Tired.（严禁疲劳驾驶。）

   （2）Please Don't Push or Lean Against the Door.（请勿挤靠车门。）

   （3）Please Use Handrail.（请站好扶稳。）

3. 从时态方面讨论公示语的语言特征：

   （1）The shopping cart is for store-use only.（购物车仅限超市购物使用。）

   （2）Value our lives and keep away from drugs.（远离毒品，珍爱生命。）

Task II 请翻译下列公示语，并归纳公示语的翻译原则。

1. 翻译下列英语公示语。

（1）Attention: Swimming is not advised at this time. ____________

（2）Buckle up: it's the law. ____________

（3）Winding Road Ahead ____________

（4）Do Not Extinguish With Water ____________

（5）This sign has sharp edges. Do not touch the edges of this sign. ____________

2. 翻译下列汉语公示语。

（1）老弱病残孕者专座 ____________

（2）注意：请勿攀爬墙体 ____________

（3）果皮、纸屑、酒瓶等废弃物请扔进垃圾箱 ____________

（4）小心试穿，避免口红蹭在衣服上 ____________

（5）夜间有事，请按此铃 ____________

3. 翻译下列公示语，说明汉语相同而译文不同的原因。

（1）清华大学 ____________

清华南路 ____________

（2）中山大学 ____________

中山装专卖店 ____________

中山二路 ____________

Task III 翻译下列公示语。

1. Buy One and Get One Free ____________
2. Please Do Not Feed the Goats ____________
3. No U Turn ____________
4. Road Work Ahead ____________
5. Gift Wrap ____________
6. No Horn Blowing Except for Danger ____________
7. Beware Pedestrian ____________
8. No Trespassing ____________
9. Toll Gate ____________
10. Lost and Found ____________
11. 同一个世界，同一个梦想 ____________
12. 禁止排放污水 ____________
13. 殿内请勿烧香 ____________
14. 一米以下儿童须家长陪同乘坐 ____________
15. 票已售出，概不退换 ____________

Task IV　翻译下列公示语，并讨论你使用了直译法还是意译法。

1. 内部停车场　________________
2. 减肥茶　________________
3. 长途汽车站　________________
4. 美好时光婚姻介绍所　________________
5. 你我共做绿化卫士！　________________

Task V　翻译下列公示语，并从语义的肯定和否定方面讨论翻译技巧。

1. 汽车行驶中请勿站立　________________
2. 注意安全，请勿靠近　________________
3. 请勿携带外食进入（麦当劳餐厅）　________________
4. 严禁非本部门人员入内　________________
5. 防洪通道，请勿占用　________________
6. 非机动车禁止入内　________________
7. 请勿触摸展品　________________
8. 请勿将手臂伸出车外　________________

Task VI　翻译下列公示语，并从意义的增减方面讨论翻译技巧。

1. 本厕有自动冲洗设备，用后免冲　________________
2. 实行三包　________________
3. 有您的参与，垃圾不会无家可归　________________
4. 注意归还日期，按时还书　________________
5. 免费卫生纸，请珍惜使用　________________
6. 正在售票，售完为止　________________

PART FOUR

讨论：通过上述翻译任务，你认为翻译公示语还可以采用哪些策略？公示语翻译需要注意哪些事项？

I. 公示语翻译总结

本单元从公示语的含义谈起，讲述了公示语的语言特征、翻译原则和翻译技巧。现将公示语的翻译原则与翻译技巧归纳如下（见表 3-1）：

公示语的翻译除了遵循上述原则之外，还需要注意统一性原则：即一个城市、一个部门、某个特定场所的公示语翻译应当尽量保持统一。但是，翻译不统一的问题普遍存在，如广州陈家祠站的出口信息牌、地铁语音报站、地铁出口处对“陈家祠”的翻译就不统一，分别译成了“Chen Clan Academy; Guangdong Folk Arts Museum; Chengjiaci Square”，这些都需要进行修正，使其保持统一。第一，从形式上看，要么所有公示语采用大写字母，要么按照标题格式，实词首字母大写，双音节介词大写，其余情况小写；

如果某公示语只有一个单词，为了醒目起见，一般可以全部大写，如“EXIT”“DANGER”；组织机构的翻译按约定俗成或者官方译法，如“中国银行（Bank of China）”；形式的统一还包括词性的统一，如“厕所无人（Vacancy）”和“厕所有人（Occupied）”两者词性不统一，需要改进，可分别翻译为“Vacant”和“Occupied”。另外，译者还应特别留意缩写形式，比如“Road”缩写为“Rd.”，“East”缩写为“E.”即可。第二，从译名标准化看，要么采用国家的统一标准，要么按照官方的统一译法。比如“万绿湖”就可以从河源市官方网站旅游部分查找，其译文为“Lake Wanlühu”。总之，“信息准确、行文简练、语法规范”（潘文国，2010），这是公示语翻译的基本准则，公示语翻译可以参照《公共服务领域英文译写规范》。

表 3-1　公示语的翻译原则与翻译技巧

公示语的翻译原则	忠实性原则：尽量贴近原语含义，表达原语意义
	简洁性原则：删繁就简，尽量简洁，表述清楚
	新旧有别原则：保留传统
	内外有别原则：有些特定读者对象为中国人的公示语就不必翻译
公示语的翻译技巧	直译法：多数公示语可以按字面意思直接翻译
	意译法：根据公示语含义而不是字字对译
	视角转移法：对肯定句和否定句进行适当转换
	增译法：增加适当的词语进行阐释
	减译法：根据简洁性原则，删去不必要的信息或冗余信息
	零翻译：用于那些具有特别针对性或者无须外国人了解的公示语

II. 公示语翻译余论

1. 汉英公示语翻译错误的原因

纵观各种公示语翻译的问题，除语法错误和拼写错误外，问题主要在于机械对译，或望文生义，“翻译即译意”在公示语翻译中无法贯彻执行，比如把“公交售票员（Conductor）”翻译成“Busboy”，殊不知“Busboy”意为餐馆工或餐馆助理，差之千里。又如把“环保果皮箱”翻译成“Environment-friendly Trash Box”，其实环保果皮箱就是垃圾箱，这样翻译让读者误以为该果皮箱是环境友好产品，不会对环境造成影响。翻译即译意，在公示语翻译中，翻译不仅译意，有时甚至译意图。比如“小区卫生，人人有责”，如果直译，确实不好译，“小区”本身具有中国特色，没有完全对等的英文，由于读者看到该公示语时肯定身处公示语所在场所，不必一定译出“小区”，所以翻译该公示语时只需抓住公示语作者的创作意图：即保持卫生，所以可以翻译成“Keep It Clean and Tidy”，简洁易懂，达到了传递作者意图的目的。再如：

原文：The last one is delicious. Bring me another!

译文：鳄鱼伤人　禁止入水（方梦之，2008：7）；

如果译者不考虑场合和其语用意义而直截了当地直译为“上一个很好吃，再来一个”，显得莫名其妙，难以理解。这原本是位于鳄鱼池边的一条警示语，西式幽默尽显其中，直译已无法起到原本应该具有的警告作用，所以只能意译出原文的语用意图，即警告人们，不要靠近或者进入鳄鱼池，谨防鳄鱼伤人。又如，“If you want to eat breakfast in bed, please sleep in the kitchen.”以幽默的口吻告诉人们，请勿在床上吃早餐。

2. 文化意识在公示语翻译中的作用

文化与翻译如影随形，由于文化传统、文明程度等差别，翻译时就必须考虑文化因素。比如，中国公路上常有公示语“严禁酒后驾车”，即使如此，还是屡禁不止，如果翻译成英语“Driving after drinking is strictly prohibited”就显得语气过重，英语习惯使用“Don't drive when you drink”，对西方人而言，完全可以达到禁止酒后驾车的目的。再如，许多酒店住宿须知规定：“贵重物品、现金请交服务台保管，否则后果自负。”如果翻译成“Valuable articles and cash shall be handed to General Service Desk for safekeeping. Otherwise, the owner shall be responsible for the consequence.”从文化方面考虑，“后果自负”对中国人而言，不会觉得不舒服；而如果直译为英语，就显得语气生硬，让人难以接受，显得多此一举，所以不妨删掉其英语译文。

3. 英式英语和美式英语的差异

虽然目前没有人特别注意英式英语和美式英语的区别，但是由于一国语言的影响力同该国的经济实力有一定的关联性，所以很多人认为美式英语在世界上的影响力更大，也更为人们所熟悉。美式英语和英式英语存在一定的差异，比如，在河流名称的写法上，英式英语常把 river 一词放在河流名称之前，而美式英语则相反，如英式英语“the River Thames”，而美式英语“the Mississippi River”。虽然公示语翻译没有规定一定要使用英式英语或者美式英语，但是许多译者翻译时也采用了美式英语的说法，如“长江（the Yangtz River）”“黄河（the Yellow River）”等。因此，很多时候我们更倾向于美式英语的说法。英式英语与美式英语的差异举例如下（见表 3-2）：

表 3-2 英式英语与美式英语的差异举例

举例	英式英语	美式英语
地铁	Underground	Subway
邮资已付	Post-Free	Postpaid
药房	Chemist's Shop	Pharmacy
脚下留神	Mind Your Step	Watch Your Step
垃圾箱	Rubbish Bin	Garbage Can
外语学院	Faculty of Foreign Languages	School of Foreign Languages
面包店	Bakery	Baker's Shop
请勿疲劳驾驶	Tiredness Kills, Take a Break	Stay Alert, Stay Alive

PART FIVE

译技点津：商务翻译技巧之词类转换

英语和汉语分属两个不同的语系，无论是读音还是书写方面都差别甚大。连淑能（1993）在《英汉对比研究》一书的序言中，把英汉语言的差异归纳为十组相互参照对比的特征：综合与分析，聚集与流散，形合与意合，繁复与简短，物称与人称，被动与主动，静态与动态，抽象与具体，间接与直接，替换与重复。由于语言特征的种种差别，把一种语言翻译为另一种语言时就需要进行各种转换，其中包括词类转换。

I. 名词与动词的转换

众所周知，名词表示静态，而动词表示动态。R. Quirk（Quirk et al, 1973：48）等人认为，广义而言，名词用于指稳定的实体时，自然而然可以当成是“静态”的，无论是具体的（物质的）如房子、桌子、纸张，还是抽象的（心理的），如希望、植物学、长度等。另一方面，动词表达动作、活动，暂时的或者变化的状况时，自然而然是“动态”的。英语语言特色之一就是名词化（nominalization），即英语中大量使用名词，其中包括一些具有名词功能的词，比如：动名词、动词不定式等；而汉语则使用相对较多的动词，在英汉双语转换过程中，就需要注意名词与动词之间的相互转换。

[例 1] 原文：钱款当面**点清**，**离**柜概不负责

译文：Complete *Transaction* Before *Leaving* the Counter

[例 2] 原文：前方**修路**

译文：*Road Work* Ahead

[例 3] 原文：**停止服务**

译文：*Out of Service*

[例 4] 原文：免费**送货**服务

译文：Free *Delivery* Service

[例 5] 原文：正在**检修**，请您稍候

译文：Please Wait. *Maintenance* in Progress.

从以上例子可以看出，汉语中多用动词，而翻译成英语时可以转换成名词或者名词性词语，反之亦然。如例 1 中将“离”翻译成动名词“leaving”，例 2 中“修路”翻译成“road work”，其他例子也是如此。商务翻译中名词、动词间的转换比比皆是，又如：

[例 6] 原文：We have been *in correspondence with* suppliers in Australia and were informed that they could provide us with similar goods at more attractive prices.

译文：我们已与澳大利亚供货商**取得联系**，并得知他们能够以更优惠的价格提供类似的货物。

[例 7] 原文：China’s *entry* into World Trade Organization has further resulted in even more foreign direct investment.

译文：中国**加入**世界贸易组织后吸引了更多的外商直接投资。

［例 8］原文：The *optimization* of economic structure has become one of the most important tasks in this newly-established special economic zone.

译文：**优化**经济结构已经成为这个新建经济特区的重要任务之一。

［例 9］原文：Specifically, China's *exports to* other RCEP members reached RMB6 trillion, up by 17.7%, in the first 11 months of 2022.

译文：2022 年前 11 个月，中国对《区域全面经济伙伴关系协定》其他成员**出口**达人民币 60 000 亿元，增长 17.7%。

上述例子显示，商务英语中许多名词或者名词性短语翻译成汉语时，需要进行词类转换，主要转换成动词，反之亦然，比如：

［例 10］原文：过去五年，改革开放带来了许多新变化，工人收入大幅**增加**，乡镇企业**异军突起**。

译文：In the past five years, reform and opening up brought about many new changes, which were *characterized by* a substantial *increase* in workers' income and the *rise* of township enterprises as a new force.

例 10 中的"新变化"有两层意思，这里增加了概括性短语"characterized by"把这两层意思概括起来，另外，"增加""异军突起"全部翻译成了名词，对词类进行了转换。尽管英汉翻译时多数情况是将英语中的名词转换为汉语的动词，但是也有特殊情况，需要将英语的动词转换成汉语的名词，比如：

［例 11］原文：The products of IBM are chiefly *characterized by* their fine workmanship, durability and portability.

译文：IBM 公司产品的主要**特点**是工艺精湛，经久耐用，携带方便。

［例 12］原文：The design *aims at* simple structure, easy maintenance and high productivity.

译文：该设计是为了实现结构简单，维修方便，生产率高的**目的**。

II. 形容词词类转换

形容词也是英语中非常活跃的一种词类。在商务英语翻译中，译者应根据实际情况进行调整和转换，以符合译文的行文习惯和表达方式。

［例 13］原文：We are *confident* that a trial order of these leather shoes would convince you that, at the price quoted, the goods we are offering are excellent value for money.

译文：我们**相信**，以我方报价试订这种皮鞋后，你会认为物有所值的。

［例 14］原文：He is very *familiar* with various water quality analysis instruments and has rich experience in instrument installation and maintenance.

译文：他**熟悉**各类水质分析仪器，对仪器安装和维护有丰富的经验。

［例 15］原文：Chinese silk products are very *popular* among European customers in recent years.

译文：近年来，中国丝绸产品深受欧洲客户**欢迎**。（近年来，欧洲客户非常**喜欢**中国丝绸产品。）

［例 16］原文：We would be very *grateful* if you could give us an early offer.

译文：如蒙早日报盘，不胜**感激**。

［例 17］原文：The survey found that men were more task *focused* and *concentrated* on getting the job done rather than dealing with relationships.

译文：调查发现，与女性管理者相比，男性更**关注**工作本身，他们更**专注**于搞好工作而不是忙于处理各种关系。

［例 18］原文：Men in Britain are less *engaged* in their work compared with women until the final years of employment when they get a late surge of enthusiasm, according to a survey.

译文：据调查，英国男性的工作**热情**不如女性，直到退休时他们才会迸发出一股迟来的热情。

例 13、例 14、例 15 和例 16 中的形容词表示主语的态度、情感等，可以转换成动词。例 17 中，把动词过去分词作为形容词，此时也转换成了动词。例 18 中“engaged”原意为“忙碌的”，但是，如果直译为“忙碌”，就与下文“迸发热情”不符合，所以根据上下文，转化为名词“热情”，使上下文语义连贯。

III. 介词词类转换

介词是英语中非常活跃的词类，其应用也特别灵活，意义千变万化，翻译时需要根据不同的语境确定其含义。

［例 19］原文：The manager insisted that it was *beyond* his ability to complete such a large order at such short notice.

译文：经理坚持认为，时间如此紧迫，他**没有**能力完成如此大的订单。

例 19 中“beyond”可以翻译成“没有”或者“超出”。

PART SIX

公示语翻译实践

Task I 请为下列汉语公示语选择恰当的英语译文，并将其编号填在括号里。

1. 警告：恶犬出没！ (　　) A. Beware of Pickpockets
2. 不要闯红灯 (　　) B. Do Not Crush
3. 补票处 (　　) C. Inflammable Solid
4. 大宗购物处 (　　) D. Don't Dash through the Stop Light!
5. 当心扒手 (　　) E. Warning: Bad Dogs!
6. 请使用旋转门 (　　) F. Do Not Overtake
7. 禁止超车 (　　) G. Bulk Purchase Reception
8. 切勿挤压 (　　) H. Please Use the Revolving Door
9. 压缩气体 (　　) I. Fare Adjustment/Pay Upon Arrival
10. 易燃固体 (　　) J. Compressed Gas

Task II　请翻译下列公示语。

No smoking

1. ______________

Smoking and naked flames forbidden

2. ______________

No access for pedestrians

3. ______________

Do not extinguish with water

4. ______________

Not drinkable

5. ______________

No access for unauthorised persons

6. ______________

Task III　请将下列英语公示语翻译成汉语。

1. Visitor Parking

____

2. Unauthorized Vehicles Will be Towed Away at Owners' Expenses

____

3. Army Facilities, No Trespassing

____

4. To Cross Street, Push Button, Wait for Walk Signal

____

5. Thank You for Keeping Your Voices Down

____

6. Watch for Pedestrians

____

7. Hard Hat Required at All Times

____

8. Three Minutes Parking, Drivers Must Remain in Vehicle

____

9. For Use Only in Case of Fire

____

10. Danger: High Speed Trains, Do Not Enter

____

Task IV 请将下列汉语公示语翻译成英语，注意使用视角转换翻译技巧。

1. 禁止向未成年人售烟 ____________________
2. 未经许可车辆不得入内 ____________________
3. 油漆未干 ____________________
4. 切勿近火 ____________________
5. 请您带好随身物品 ____________________
6. 禁止未成年人进入 ____________________
7. 禁止开窗 ____________________
8. 机房重地，非公莫入 ____________________
9. 请勿倒置 ____________________
10. 不要靠近 ____________________
11. 顾客止步 ____________________
12. 贵重物品，随身携带 ____________________
13. 送客止步 ____________________
14. 顾客专用，请勿载货（商场） ____________________
15. 演出进行中，请勿大声喧哗或随意走动。 ____________________

Task V 请将下列公示语翻译成英语。

1. 一慢二看三通过 ____________________
2. 请勿打扰 ____________________
3. 正在检修，请绕行 ____________________
4. 伸手出水 ____________________
5. 禁止超载 ____________________
6. 请看管好孩子 ____________________
7. 请爱护公共设施 ____________________
8. 清仓大甩卖 ____________________
9. 降下车窗　换换空气 ____________________
10. 此处发现鲨鱼 ____________________
11. 严禁夜间停车 ____________________
12. 不准张贴 ____________________
13. 置于阴凉处 ____________________
14. 避光保存 ____________________
15. 防潮 ____________________
16. 意见箱 ____________________
17. 禁止长时间占用超车道 ____________________
18. 严禁携带易燃易爆等危险品 ____________________
19. 保护环境减少使用购物袋 ____________________
20. 儿童搭乘扶梯需由家人陪同 ____________________

Task VI 下列公示语为现实生活中的双语公示语，存在各种各样的问题（译文保留原来错误），请阅读并改进其译文。

1. 原文：欢迎您再来！
   原译：Welcome you to come again! （南宁某休闲会所）
   改译：________________________
2. 原文：水深危险 请勿下水游玩 （深圳某水池）
   原译：Taking care to deep water, not to take water please.
   改译：________________________
3. 原文：小草正在长，踏入想一想（广州某公园）
   原译：Don’t interrupt when little grass is growing.
   改译：________________________
4. 原文：青青绿草，请勿践踏
   原译：Please don’t path on the green grass.
   改译：________________________
5. 原文：垃圾在此投放（火车公示语）
   原译：The garbage throws in here
   改译：________________________
6. 原文：请您带好随身物品
   原译：Please take good personal luggage
   改译：________________________
7. 原文：万绿湖景区由此购票，游览（广东河源万绿湖）
   原译：Scenic area of the Wanlühu buy the ticket from here, tour
   改译：________________________
8. 原文：小心行走，以免摔倒
   原译：Fall Down Carefully
   改译：________________________
9. 原文：请自觉购票（白云山售票说明）
   原译：Please buy your tickets consciously.
   改译：________________________
10. 原文：施工给您带来不便，请原谅
    原译：Building, please forgive us
    改译：________________________
11. 原文：请您保留好购物凭证
    原译：Please keep the receipt as proof of purchase and your guarantee
    改译：________________________
12. 原文：人类的净土，靠你我共同维护。（广东增城白水寨）
    原译：Pure land of mankind depends on the mutual preservation of people
    改译：________________________

13. 原文：禁止携带托运易燃及易爆物品（广西某国际机场）
    原译：Carrying Flammable, Explosive Materials Prohibited
    改译：____
14. 原文：云山是我家，你我爱护她（白云山）
    原译：Baiyun Mountain is Our Home We Should Love Her
    改译：____
15. 原文：非欧咪基食品饮料，请勿在本餐厅进食!
    原译：Please don’t take any food or drink which not belong to Omic in this dining-room.
    改译：____
16. 原文：保护环境从我做起
    原译：Protect Circumstance begin with me
    改译：____

Task VII 请阅读下列中英文双语公示语，并改进其译文。

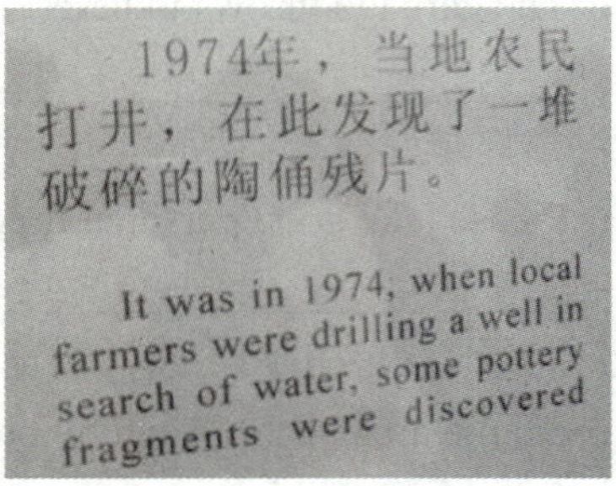

1. ____________________
   ____

2. ____________________
   ____

3. ____________________
   ____

4. ____________________
   ____

Task VIII 请翻译下列句子，注意使用词类转换翻译技巧。

1. Our company is *entitled* to lodge a claim for the losses caused by improper packing against the seller.

____

2. He was unfortunately dismissed though he has more than ten years of loyal *employment* with the company.

____

3. The best *cure* for the national economy would be economy. (Ashoey Cooper)

____

4. Experts said this new study is more *evidence* that physical exercise can help protect the person's health.

____

5. For professionals such as doctors, the computer may have more functions than we can ever imagine. It is a far more *careful and industrious inspector* than human being.

____

6. China's vast size and abundant resources, her extraordinary economic *progress* over recent years, have made her an increasingly important player in the modern international economy.

____

7. In *consideration* of the mutual covenants and agreement herein contained, the parties agree as follows.

____

8. In case of *shortage* of iron and steel, China's industry would undergo extreme difficulties in its *development*.

____

9. We just signed a contract that is *advantageous* to our company.

____

10. It is our firm conviction that a step *forward* has been taken.

____

PART SEVEN
学习参考

1. 吕和发，单丽萍. 汉英公示语词典［Z］. 北京：商务印书馆，2015.
2. 万永坤. 公示语汉英翻译探究［M］. 昆明：云南大学出版社，2015.
3. 谢丹. 变译在公示语汉英翻译中的应用［M］. 成都：西南交通大学出版社，2017.
4. 中华人民共和国国家标准公共服务领域英文译写规范［M］. 北京：中国标准出版社，2017.
5. 任丽萍. 旅游公示语汉英翻译教程［M］. 北京：旅游教育出版社，2022.

PART EIGHT
单元预告与实训任务

1. 下一单元我们将讲述组织机构的翻译。
2. 请你搜集 10 条有关政府机构、公司、社会组织的名称及翻译。

第四单元

组织机构翻译

Unit Four Translating Organization Names

组织是指按照一定的目的、任务和系统建立起来的集体，它是由若干人员结合而成的单位，如各个层次的经济实体，政府间带有具体职能的协作系统，政府的职能部门组织、军事组织、党团组织、企业等。它们是社会的基本单位，是社会的基础。如今，组织机构分类日益细致，数量规模庞大，而根据卡斯特（Fremont E. Kast）和罗森茨韦克（James E. Rosenzweig）对未来组织的预测：组织将面临波涛汹涌的变化，它们必须进行不断的改变和调整；未来的组织规模日益复杂，部门的划分将会更细，各部门的专业化程度也将更高。此外，某一特定组织的名称是专有名词，它是特定的、唯一的和权威的名称。组织的复杂性和唯一性要求翻译这一类名称时必须慎重、严谨。目前，工商局要求企业注册时需要提供企业的中英文名称。可见，企业及其他组织机构的翻译在商务活动中占据重要的地位。

教学目标

1. 了解组织机构的含义和分类；
2. 了解组织机构的语言特点；
3. 掌握组织机构的翻译方法；
4. 掌握缩略语的语言特点和翻译策略。

PART ONE

认识组织机构与组织机构翻译

Task 阅读下列组织机构图标并思考：你认识这些组织机构吗？它们代表着哪些群体？它们发挥着什么作用？

常见的组织机构可分为五大类：国际组织、国家机关、事业单位、社会或民间团体、企业。

国际组织是具有国际性行为特征的组织，包括政府间国际组织和非政府间国际组织。国际组织在功能、成员以及成员的标准上有区别。某些国际组织（全球性国际组织）是允许所有国家加入的，如联合国以及它的下属机构、世界贸易组织等。还有一些国际组织接受世界上某一地区的成员加入，像欧盟、非盟、东盟等。常见的组织名如联盟（Union, Federation）、组织（Organization）、咨询委员会（Advisory Committee）等；组织名称中显示其功能的如共同市场（Common Market）、贸易区（Trade Area）、基金（Fund）等。

国家机关是指从事国家管理和行使国家权力的机关，包括权力机关和行政机关、审判机关、军事机关、金融机关等。按照级别和划分的层次不同，国家机关可以分为：部（Department, Ministry）、局（Bureau, Authority）、委（Committee）、司（Department）、厅（Department, General Office）、署（Administration）、处（Division）等。

事业单位是指国家为了社会公益目的，由国家机关举办或者其他组织利用国有资产举办，从事教育、科技、文化、卫生等活动的社会服务组织。如科技机构方面的科学院（Academy）、学部（Division）、研究院（Academy, Institute）、实验室（Laboratory）、设计室（Studio）；教育机构方面的大学（University）、师范大学（Normal University）、函授学校（Correspondence School）、培训中心（Training Center）；医疗保健机构方面的医院（Hospital）、防疫站（Epidemic Prevention Station）、疗养所（Sanatorium）；文化机构方面的广播电台（Broadcasting Station）等。

社会或民间团体是指以推广文化、学术、医疗、卫生、宗教、慈善、体育、联谊、社会服务或其他以公益为目的，由个人或团体组成的团体。常见的社团组织如协会（Association）、学会（Academic Society）、联合会（Federation, Confederation）、促进会（Promotion Council）、商会（Chamber）、救济会（Relief Institute）、论坛（Forum）等。

企业是最常见的组织机构，它从事生产、流通、服务等经济活动，以生产或服务满足社会需要，是一种营利性的经济组织。企业的名称一般由几部分构成：所属地域、商号、从事行业或生产产品、公司类型等。其中，单单表示公司的词语就有很多，如 company, corporation, firm, agency, enterprise, group, holdings, office，等等。具体使用哪个词语还需要根据企业所属的行业和公司的规模来确定。

PART TWO
热身练习

Task I　请翻译下列组织机构名称并尝试总结翻译技巧。

1. World Bank Group ________________
2. International Energy Agency ________________
3. International Organization for Standardization ________________
4. World Health Organization ________________
5. 国家税务总局 ________________
6. 中华人民共和国外交部 ________________
7. 海关总署 ________________
8. 中国人民银行 ________________

Task II　下列缩略语的全称是什么？请写出全称。

1. NATO ________________
2. WTO ________________
3. IMF ________________
4. CIA ________________
5. IAEA ________________
6. G20 ________________
7. EU ________________
8. FIFA ________________

Task III　你知道以下企业机构吗？请写出它们的译名。

1. Exxon Mobil ________________　　2. Sinopec ________________
3. HSBC Holdings ________________　　4. Peugeot ________________

5. 微软 ________ 6. 联邦快递 ________
7. 百事公司 ________ 8. 波音 ________

PART THREE
组织机构翻译技巧

Task I 组织机构的翻译原则

1. 请阅读下列组织机构名。这些名称还有其他的说法吗？为什么？
（1）International Committee of the Red Cross
（2）International Olympic Committee
（3）International Criminal Police Organization
（4）Federal Bureau of Investigation
（5）Ministry of Commerce
（6）Ministry of Culture and Tourism
（7）SUN YAT-SEN UNIVERSITY
（8）Shanghai Jiaotong University

____

2. 阅读下列机构全称，思考其缩略方式，并尝试指出其中的规律。
（1）World Health Organization ________
（2）New York Stock Exchange ________
（3）Organization of Petroleum Exporting Countries ________
（4）International Labor Organization ________
（5）Industrial and Commercial Bank of China ________
（6）China Council for the Promotion of International Trade ________

____

3. 朗读下列企业名称，试总结其语音特征。
AT&T　Coca-Cola　Fedex
康佳　美的　贝亲　娃哈哈

____

4. 阅读下列企业名称，讨论其语义特征。
Haier　Triumph　Lenovo　Goodyear
好日子　强生　周大福　喜多

____

Task II 组织机构的翻译技巧。

1. 观察下列机构名称，总结其语序特点和构成特点。
Asia-Pacific Economic Cooperation　European Union
European Free Trade Association
Ministry of Foreign Affairs of the People's Republic of China
中国法律咨询中心　中国翻译协会
石油输出国组织　国务院港澳事务办公室

____

2. 观察下列机构名称，总结其介词用法，思考其中文译名。

(1) European Association *for* Artificial Intelligence

(2) International Chamber *of* Commerce

(3) International Court *of* Justice

(4) United Nations Conference *on* Trade and Development

(5) American Council *on* Education

3. 翻译下列几组企业名称，并讨论相应的翻译方法。

(1) Nike	Louis Vuitton	Sony	六福	大宝	娃哈哈
(2) Fedex	eBay	BP	熊猫	光明	钻石
(3) Unilever	Goldlion	Starbucks	美的	乐百氏	格力

PART FOUR

讨论：通过上述翻译任务，你认为翻译组织机构还可以采用哪些策略？组织机构翻译需要注意哪些事项？

I. 组织机构翻译总结

本单元从组织机构的含义和分类谈起，讲述了组织机构的语言特征、翻译原则及翻译技巧。现将相关组织机构的语言特点与翻译技巧归纳如下（见表 4-1）：

表 4-1　组织机构的语言特点与翻译技巧

组织机构名称的语言特点	专词专用：属于专有名词，有固定的表达方式或习惯表达法
	简洁性：很多组织机构名称有对应的缩略语，简单明了
	文化适应性：迎合译入语民族的心理特征和审美情趣
组织机构名称的翻译技巧	定译法：注重法定依据和权威依据
	专词专用：尊重其习惯的组合方式，包括语序和虚词使用
组织机构名称的翻译方法	音译法：利用最贴近原语语音的译语进行翻译
	意译法：挖掘原语的意义，体现企业名称特点和品质
	音意结合法：注重原语和译语读音的协调一致，更强调译文对企业名称特点的描述

II. 组织机构翻译余论

1. 政府部门翻译规则

关于组织机构的翻译，如果译者各行其是，无视译名原则和国家译名标准，疏于考证，则会导致译名混乱。就组织机构的英译名，学界普遍同意应遵循的原则是“名从源主”：译者从“源头”上完全服从最权威部门公布的译名或者名称主人早有的、已确定的译名。源头可分为三类：（1）组织机构的最高上级部门确定公布的译名；（2）省市政府明文规定的组织机构译名或省市组织自定且使用已久的译名；（3）由译名主人自创的独一无二的译名。在翻译单位名称时，应首先查阅有关资料，确定是否有普遍接受的定译。

考虑到这个原则，同时由于国家机关本身内涵的确定性及严肃性，所以在英译时更要注重查核权威依据。国务院办公厅秘书局2008年印发的《国务院各部委、各直属机构英文译名》最新修订本，应属最权威的译名。当然，机构改革后会出现新的机构和译名。未包含在上述修订本内的有关机构，则尽量采用该机构的官方自选英文名作为标准定译，如找不到标准定译，则转而根据“新华社”或“中国日报”等权威媒体采用的英译，如果仍然没有，则可在充分参考英美等国同等机构的基础上予以翻译。

组织机构翻译具体操作时应注意，组织部门名称由于在英语中属于专有名词范畴，要求做到专词专用，所以一个单位只能使用一种译名，包括词序，缩写形式都具有唯一性，如“中华人民共和国工业和信息化部”，英译：Ministry of Industry and Information Technology of the People's Republic of China，而不能作任何更改。

按照英语语法，专有名词的词首字母应大写，但是像of、the、and等虚词一般小写，如“天河区人民政府”，英译：the People's Government of Tianhe District。

2.“公司”的英译

“公司”最常见的英译是：Company（简写：Co.）和Corporation（简写：Corp.）。这两个词之间没有明确的界限，但侧重点有所不同。一般来说，Corporation 在企业规模上比Company要大，但这并不是普遍适用的，世界上很多大企业也使用Company，如The Boeing Company（波音公司）、Shell International Petroleum Company Limited（壳牌国际石油有限公司）。在我国的企业中，国有大企业使用Corporation的居多，但是绝大多数企业，特别是中小企业仍然偏爱Company。“公司”也绝非只用company或corporation，其他名词如lines，agency等也是名正言顺的“公司”的说法。“公司”名称翻译，见表4-2。

表4-2　“公司”名称翻译

名称	特定含义	例　　子
agency	公司，代理行	Centaline Property Agency Limited 中原地产代理有限公司 NTD Patent and Trademark Agency Limited NTD知识产权法律代理
airline(s)/line(s)	（轮船、航空、航运等）公司	Shanghai Airlines　上海航空公司 China Southern Airlines 中国南方航空公司
associates	（联合）公司	Nuclear Associates Ltd. 核子联合有限公司 John and Smith Associates Ltd. 约翰史密斯联合有限公司
enterprises	企业，实业	Coca-Cola Enterprises 可口可乐企业公司
firm	指两人或两人以上合办的公司，也可以指提供服务为主的公司	Ernst&Young Accounting Firm 安永会计师事务所 Law Firm 律师事务所
service(s)	（服务）公司	U.S. Postal Service 美国邮政服务公司
store(s)	百货公司	Walmart Stores 沃尔玛百货公司
system	系统公司	Electronic Data Systems 电子数据公司（美） Malaysian Airline System 马来西亚航空公司

3. 企业名称中行业和经营内容的翻译

由于企业所从事的行业或经营特点不同，所以他们的名称也各有特色，按中文字面直译即可，如东荣金属制品有限公司英译为：Dong Rong Metal Products Co., Ltd.，中国茶叶进出口有限公司英译为：China Tea Import and Export Co., Ltd.。

在企业名称中写上主营项目，可以使人一目了然地了解企业产品信息，起到很好的广告作用，缺点是使得名称过于冗长，违反了企业名称应简洁易记的原则，尤其是当企业名称译成英文后，本来简简单单的名称，可能啰嗦而让人难以忍受。

美英等国的企业名称很多都相当简洁，有些企业会把经营内容包括在名称当中，比如 General Electric（通用电气），Lucent Technologies（朗讯科技），有些公司则并不喜欢将主营项目写进名称，如：Pepsico Inc（百事公司），就不能从名字看出它的经营项目。

4. 中国高校校名英译

中国大部分的高校校名语义结构组合类型可以归纳为两大类：地区名/特色名/+学校性质类别；地区名+学科名+学校性质类别。在组合中，各个元素的翻译有所讲究，同时语序和构成也有一些规律可循。

首先，就学校性质类别而言，一般综合性大学可以译为 university。而随着中国高等教育的飞速发展，一些高校前身可能是某一学科的专门研究机构，或是现在仍以这一学科为最强、最有优势的学科，但学校的办学规模已经成为一个多科综合协调发展的高校，也可被称为 university。

和“大学”相比，“学院”则有不少对应的词汇可选择，如 college, institute, academy 等。从国际惯例来看，college 多指综合性的学院，而 institute 多用于科技和理工之类的院校。

校名不同组合类型的翻译，列表整理如下（见表 4-3）：

表 4-3

高校名的不同组合类型	翻译策略	例子
特色名+学校性质类别	直接对应翻译，不需调整词序	Harvard University/ Tongji University
地区名+学校性质类别	University of +地区名/ 地区名+University	University of Chicago/ New York University
地区名+学科名+ 学校性质类别	地区名+学科名+ University/College/Academy	Texas Tech University
	学科名+University/ College of+地区名	Polytechnic University of NewYork
	地区名+Institute/College of +学科名	Baylor College of Medicine

PART FIVE

译技点津：商务翻译之缩略语翻译

I. 缩略语含义与发展

缩略语由于其简约、便捷的特点经常可见于各种各样的商务文本中。据统计，1943年前，英语缩略语的数量还屈指可数。50多年后，它已发展成数量达到数百万的大军（余富林，2002：1）。而汉语的缩略语数量也随着社会发展有所增加。缩略语的数量反映了时代的变迁与发展，它的内容本身也反映了时代的变化。在电子商务方面，可以见到如B2B（Business to Business，企业对企业，指企业间的电子商务交易模式），B2C（Business to Consumer，企业对消费者，指企业与消费者之间的电子商务交易模式），O2O（Online to Offline，线上到线下，指线上与线下业务结合的电子商务模式）。在商务经济方面，有KOL（Key Opinion Leader，关键意见领袖，指在某个领域有影响力的人），KOC（Key Opinion Consumer，关键意见消费者，指能影响周围人消费决策的消费者）。商务发展，引起企业系统架构的变化和职务的变化，于是我们看到了CEO（Chief Executive Officer，首席执行官），CFO（Chief Financial Officer，财务总监），COO（Chief Operating Officer，生产主管），Exec（Executive，主管），GM（General Manager，总经理），HR（Human Resources，人力资源）。随着人工智能的爆发式大发展，以下这些缩略语越来越为我们熟悉：AI（Artificial Intelligence，人工智能），ML（Machine Learning，机器学习），VR（Virtual Reality，虚拟现实）。财务方面，简单的缩略语也为中西通用，如FY（Fiscal Year，财政年度），IPO（Initial Pubic Offering，首次公开募股）。

汉语的缩略语往往浓缩性很强，具有很强的表意能力，如“外企”“转轨”“创收”“清欠”等。很多缩略语因为经常使用，以至它的全称反而不那么为人们所熟悉，组织机构如“亚太经合组织”“质检总局”“证监会”“广交会”“国资委”，企业名如“和黄”“长实”等。汉语缩略语也有其活泼的一面，如“白骨精”（白领骨干精英）等。

II. 缩略语的词形特点

英语常见缩略语的构词形式主要有三种，包括首字母缩略语（Initialism），如：UNESCO，WHO，HP；截短词（Clipped Words），如phone（telephone），memo（memorandum）；合成词（Compound）如high-tech（high technology），newscast（news broadcast），faction（fact fiction）。

汉语缩略语的构词形式有如下两种：一种为压缩词，如“经适房”“特首”“早教”等；另一种为归纳词，如“三个代表”等。

III. 缩略语的翻译技巧

音译法：根据英语发音译成外来语。音译法简单可行，容易为人们所接受（见表4-4）。

意译法：先将英语缩略语还原为源语，将其翻译成为对应的汉语全称，然后再将全译通过压缩的方法简化为汉译缩略语（见表4-5）。这种方法多见于组织机构简称的翻译。

表 4-4　　缩略语音译法举例

译语	英语缩略语	语　源	语　义
托福	TOEFL	Test of English as a Foreign Language	把英语作为外语的考试
丁克	DINK	Double Income No Kids	双收入没小孩的家庭
艾滋	AIDS	Acquired Immune Deficiency Syndrome	获得性免疫缺陷综合征
雅思	IELTS	International English Language Testing System	国际英语语言测试系统

表 4-5　　缩略语意译法举例

原　语	英语缩略语	目的语	英语缩略语汉译
World Trade Organization	WTO	世界贸易组织	世贸
North Atlantic Treaty Organization	NATO	北大西洋公约组织	北约
International Olympic Committee	IOC	国际奥林匹克运动委员会	国际奥委会

零翻译法：零翻译法可理解为原本应该翻译，但是由于某些原因而没有翻译，使得某种语言直接进入另一语言的情况，如“MTV”“MP4”“GPRS”“WiFi”“3D”等。目前，英语缩略语的零翻译正以惊人的速度进入汉语领域，而且从它的发展势头看，大有超越意译的趋势。

汉语缩略语的翻译方式：汉语商务缩略语可先还原为源语，将其翻译成对应的英语全译，然后再将全译通过首字母缩略的方式简化为英译缩略语。这种方法常见于组织机构简称的翻译，如央视（CCTV），全国人大（NPC），中国人保（PICC）等。

汉语商务缩略语有时也会译为英语全称，为的是更能准确地表达意义。如国企可译为 state-owned enterprises，工商联可译为 Federation of Industry and Commerce。

此外，由于汉语缩略语有较高的凝练效果，如果采取字对字的直译方式，译成英语就很难理解。这种情况下，可先列出缩略语，然后再加以注释。

PART SIX

组织机构翻译实践

Task I　请将下列组织机构名称的英语译文编号填入括号中。

1. 国际民用航空组织　(　　)　A. Organization of American States
2. 国际原子能机构　(　　)　B. International Civil Aviation Organization
3. 美洲国家组织　(　　)　C. World Bank
4. 加勒比共同市场　(　　)　D. London Stock Exchange
5. 伦敦证券交易所　(　　)　E. International Atomic Energy Agency
6. 世界银行　(　　)　F. Universal Postal Union
7. 国际商会　(　　)　G. Caribbean Common Market
8. 万国邮政联盟　(　　)　H. International Chamber of Commerce

Task II 请翻译下列组织机构名称。

1. 自然资源部 ____________________
2. 中国科学院 ____________________
3. 生态环境部 ____________________
4. 审计署 ____________________
5. 国家卫生健康委员会 ____________________
6. State Administration of Foreign Exchange ____________________
7. Ministry of Science and Technology ____________________
8. National Development and Reform Commission ____________________
9. Ministry of Transport ____________________
10. State Post Bureau ____________________

Task III 请翻译下列高校名称。

1. Massachusetts Institute of Technology ____________________
2. University of Pennsylvania ____________________
3. Northwest University ____________________
4. University of California, Los Angeles ____________________
5. London School of Economics and Political Science ____________________
6. 新加坡国立大学 ____________________
7. 香港大学 ____________________
8. 华南师范大学 ____________________
9. 中山大学 ____________________
10. 广东外语外贸大学 ____________________

Task IV 请写出下列缩略语全称。

1. WWW ____________ 2. DOB ____________
3. FYI ____________ 4. AI ____________
5. B2B ____________ 6. FIFA ____________
7. VIP ____________ 8. SOHO ____________
9. EMS ____________ 10. OA ____________

Task V 下列缩略语经常出现在招聘广告中，请写出全称。

1. admin ____________ 2. P/T ____________
3. loc ____________ 4. bkgd ____________
5. bus ____________ 6. mech ____________
7. pos ____________ 8. div ____________
9. refs ____________ 10. F/T ____________

Task VI　请根据缩略语提示和中文提示写出对应的国际贸易电讯常用语全称。

1. ABB（缩写）	______________	2. A/W（实际重量）	______________
3. APRV（认可，证明）	______________	4. B/S（资产负债表）	______________
5. BEF（在……之前）	______________	6. B/L （提单）	______________
7. COD（货到付款）	______________	8. DWP（深水港）	______________
9. ED（出口申报）	______________	10. FP（全部付讫）	______________
11. GOV（政府）	______________	12. GP（集团）	______________
13. GRWT（毛重）	______________	14. HR（小时）	______________
15. I/B（散装，大批）	______________	16. IDC（在适当时候）	______________
17. MTIME（同时）	______________	18. O/B（船上，已装船）	______________
19. PKG（包装）	______________	20. P/A（预付款）	______________

PART SEVEN
学习参考

1. 中华人民共和国外交部网站：https://www.mfa.gov.cn/web/gjhdq_676201/gjhdqzz_681964/
2. 中华人民共和国中央人民政府网站：https:// www.gov.cn
3. 中国日报网站：https:// www. chinadaily.com.cn

PART EIGHT
单元预告与实训任务

1. 下一单元我们将讲述企业简介的翻译，涉及公司形象的树立和推广。
2. 请思考企业简介中应该包括哪些内容，其语言应该有什么样的特点？

第五单元

企业简介翻译

Unit Five Translating Company Introductions

随着全球经济一体化的日益加强，企业作为经济活动中最主要的主体，需要更快更好地走向世界市场，在激烈的国际竞争中求得生存空间。企业简介是企业对外宣传以树立企业国际形象的重要手段，也是让市场充分了解自己，以便赢得信任的重要途径。作为企业在国际市场上的一张名片，企业简介是企业拓展国际市场的“门面”，在企业走出国门、走向国际市场的进程中起着重要作用。每年，参加中国进出口商品交易会的企业都会把自己的企业简介翻译成英语或者其他外语，但译文良莠不齐。实际上，高质量的外语企业简介有助于企业树立良好的国际形象、展示企业实力、助力企业产品顺利进入国际市场。因此，做好企业简介的翻译就显得尤其重要。

教学目标

1. 了解企业简介的基本知识；
2. 了解企业简介的语言特点；
3. 掌握企业简介翻译中常用的翻译技巧及注意事项；
4. 掌握商务翻译中的直译与意译。

PART ONE
认识企业简介

Task 阅读下列两则企业简介并思考：

企业简介包括什么内容？企业简介有哪些功能？中文和英文的企业简介各有什么样的特点？

1. 广州酒家始建于1935年，总店坐落于广州市文昌南路与下九路交汇处，以经营传统粤菜驰名，素有“食在广州第一家”之美誉。广州酒家从早期一间仅有40多万元资产的老酒家通过自身积累发展到现时拥有多间酒家、一个大型食品生产基地及遍布全市的数十间连锁食品商场，企业员工3 000人，总资产10亿元。企业先后被评为“中国十大餐饮品牌企业”“中华老字号”“国家特级酒家”“全国十佳酒家”“中华餐饮名店”“国际餐饮名店”“中国餐饮业著名品牌”“中国餐饮百强企业”“全国用户满意服务企业”“全国精神文明建设先进单位”，获“全国五一劳动奖章”。广州酒家将秉承“服务于大众，诚暖顾客心”的服务宗旨与企业精神，以品牌优势和技术优势为依托，致力于走多元化经营、多功能服务的发展道路，不断发展规模，创造新的业绩。

2. OSRAM Profile

OSRAM is one of the two largest lighting manufacturers in the world and has 46 factories in 17 countries. This global player has its headquarters in Munich and employs more than 39,000 people throughout the world. In the 2009 fiscal year sales amounted to EUR 4 billion. OSRAM generates over 66 percent of sales from energy-efficient products. OSRAM is the world's number one supplier of automotive lamps and LED for vehicles and one of the market leaders in the field of electronic control gear (ECG) for lamps. The OSRAM brand name was registered way back in 1906 and is one of the oldest trade names still recognized throughout the world.

企业简介有多种表达方式，包括 Company（Corporate/Enterprise）Introduction（Profile/Overview/Information）等。它是对企业基本情况的介绍，内容一般包括企业的经营性质和目的、股东情况、注册资金、从业人员和厂房占地面积、产品或服务介绍和联系方式等。

一份企业简介，除概要性地介绍企业的情况外，对其产品尤其是拳头产品也会做一些宣传。因此，企业简介也属于企业宣传材料的一种。所谓企业宣传材料，就是企业为树立其自身形象、推广其产品或服务，对自己的现状、历史、组成、业务范围等进行介绍，从而达到宣传自己、顺利进入国际市场目的的书面材料。

企业简介的社会功能主要是介绍、宣传、提高企业知名度和诱导消费者消费。随着中国与世界各国的经济交往越来越密切，中国有更多的机会加入国际市场，参与国际竞争。在国际交往的大环境下，无论是买方还是卖方都需要对彼此有足够的了解才能促进商业关系的建立和买卖交易的完成。因此，以树立公司形象、让对方充分了解自己以便赢得信任为目的的企业简介就显得尤为重要。由于文化上存在偏差，中西方国家在进行公司简介写作时也在思维方式、描述重点和语言表达等方面存在较大差异。因此，如何做好公司简介的翻译也成了一个重要课题。

由于英汉两种语言属于不同的语言结构体系，两种语言在文化、风俗习惯、思维模式和审美意识上也有很大差异。英汉企业简介在内容、语言及行文结构上也有所区别。

第一，从内容上看，英语企业简介注重突出公司的形象及产品，充分表述事实，传输真实信息，用事实说话。而汉语企业简介，则表现为平铺直叙，引经据典，长篇大论，文中喜欢用概念式描述性套话，喜欢罗列权威机构的认证及企业所获得的各种奖项。

第二，从语言上看，英语企业简介倾向于“白”，即语调平实、措辞简洁，通俗易懂；用词新颖、善用修辞富有表现力；不乏行业术语，整体语气正式而平和，简单易懂的语言比较容易亲近读者，吸引潜在的合作伙伴和消费者。而汉语倾向于“雅”，辞藻华丽，描述性强；讲究工整对仗，多用排比结构，同时喜欢用一些程式化用语和标语口号式文字；整体语气正式，更具渲染性和号召力。

第三，从行文结构上看，由于英语是一种重形合的语言，在行文上具有高度的形式化和严密的逻辑性，使用明显的形式标记来表现逻辑关系；而汉语重意合，句子各成分之间的逻辑关系靠上下文和事理顺序来显示。

PART TWO

热身练习

Task I　翻译下列企业简介中的常见表达。

1. general asset ______	2. joint venture ______
3. operating income ______	4. state-owned enterprise ______
5. manufacturing business ______	6. 业务组合 ______
7. 公司股东 ______	8. 合伙企业 ______
9. 管理水平 ______	10. 经营理念 ______

Task II　检查并分析下列企业简介的翻译，看看是否有需要改进的地方？如何改进？

1. 原文：本公司全体同仁竭诚为各界服务。

　原译：The whole colleagues of our corporation will whole-heartedly serve for various circles.

　改译：______

2. 原文：四川省房地产开发总公司系经四川省政府批准成立。

　原译：Approving by Sichuan provincial government, Sichuan Real Estate Development Corporation came into being.

　改译：______

3. 原文：公司年产 150 万至 180 万双鞋，远销美国、俄罗斯、加拿大、欧洲、中南美洲、中东地区、东南亚等 40 多个国家和地区。

原译：Annually the company produces 1.5-1.8 million pairs and have been well sold to America, Russian, Canada, European countries, the middle south African, the Southeast Asia and any other countries and areas.

改译：________________

4. 原文：The company has been in the manufacturing business since 1950, adopting the corporate name of GUMOTEX in 1952.

原译：本公司自 1950 年进入制造业，1952 年采用 GUMOTEX 作为公司名称。

改译：________________

5. 译文：Reliability, security and customer proximity is included in the philosophy of PostBus Switzerland.

原译：瑞士邮政巴士旅游局的哲学是可靠性、安全性和顾客亲近性。

改译：________________

Task III 请在中国进出口商品交易会期间搜集企业简介 5 份，或者查看 5 个以上你熟悉的企业网站，仔细阅读其企业简介及翻译，思考其译文使用了哪些翻译技巧？译文是否需要改进？如何改进？

____

PART THREE
企业简介翻译技巧

Task I 分析企业简介的语言特征：观察并比较下列四组企业简介，讨论并说明汉语和英语企业简介的语言特征。

[例 1] A. "四联"（美发美容中心）的迁京，带来了先进的理发设备和高超的理发技艺，并将南派理发细腻、时尚与北派理发朴实、庄重的艺术风格相融合，创作出的发型美而不艳、秀丽清新，在京城享有很高的声誉。

B. Metrostav is one of the thriving leaders among Central European construction companies, characterized by sustainable growth of production performance and market value, with management levels meeting EU standards.

[例 2] A. 中国中铁股份有限公司是由中国铁路工程总公司以整体重组、独家发起方式设立的股份有限公司。其前身是成立于 1950 年的铁道部工程总局和设计总局。公司是集基建建设、勘察设计与咨询服务、工程设备和零部件制造、房地产开发和其他业务于一体的特大型企业集团，成立于 2007 年 9 月 12 日，注册资本 128 亿元人民币。

B. OSRAM is the world's number one supplier of automotive lamps and LED for vehicles. OSRAM is also one of the market leaders in the field of electronic control gear (ECG) for lamps. Business with optical semiconductors is growing rapidly and has taken on major strategic importance. The special display-optic lamp sector is also characterized by a high rate of innovation.

［例 3］A. 从“中餐百强企业”“中国企业 500 强”再到新加坡特许经营与授权组织（Franchising & Licensing Association of Singapore）授予的“年度国际特许经营大奖”“25 大典范品牌”……小肥羊用十年的耕耘，取得了令人欣慰的成就，也为中餐标准化、品牌化、国际化探索树立了典型。小肥羊将继续以天然、健康的品质，快乐、共享的理念，弘扬中华餐饮文化，强壮人类健康体魄，努力成长为世界级的中餐品牌，朝着打造“百年老店”的战略目标奋进。

B. Lamps and lighting systems from OSRAM provide the basis for a beautiful view of things, and ensure safety and comfort, allowing for the efficient use of resources. For more than 100 years, OSRAM has been "passionate about intelligent light". As a globally operating company, we also explicitly encourage socially and environmentally responsible policies around the world—as well as sponsoring art and culture at home and abroad.

［例 4］A. 诞生于 20 世纪末的虎豹集团，信守孜孜以求、永不言退的发展理念，在市场经济的大潮中，任凭浊浪排空，惊涛拍岸，独有胜似闲庭信步的自信，处变不惊，运筹帷幄。尽握无限商机于掌间，渐显王者之气于天地。

B. We (P&G) will provide branded products and services of superior quality and value that improves the lives of the world's consumers, now and generations to come. As a result, customers will reward us with leadership sales, profit and value creation, allowing our people, our shareholders and the communities in which we live and work to prosper.

Task II 企业简介的翻译原则：下列企业简介的翻译均有错误，思考、讨论翻译得不妥当的地方并进行修改，尝试探讨企业简介翻译的原则。

1. 原文：咸阳纺织集团有限公司是一家大型国有企业，成立于 2012 年，占地 43.5 公顷，注册资本 4 亿元人民币。

   原译：Xianyang Textiles Group Co., Ltd is a national enterprise. It was founded in 2002 and occupies 43.5 hectares. It has registered assets 400 million RMB yuan.

   改译：____

2. 原文：虎豹人以其特有的灵气，极目一流，精益求精，集世界顶尖服装生产技术装备之大成。裁天上彩虹，绣人间缤纷，开设计之先河，臻质量之高峰，领导服装潮流，尽显领袖风采。

   原译：Hubao people will walk on with their special spirit of trying to be No. 1, and the advanced manufacturing facilities and equipment. With sky as its cloth and rainbow as its colors, Hubao will innovate in design and promise customers the best-quality products, which makes it the leading enterprise in fashion world.

改译：________________

3. 原文：A world leader in mobile communications, the company has established itself as the leading manufacturer in the whole mobile industry. Backed by its experience, innovation, user-friendliness and secure solutions, it is the world's leading supplier of mobile phones, fixed broadband and IP networks.

原译：作为全球移动通信业的领导者，公司现已成为全球最大的移动电话生产商。凭借其经验、创新、操作及安全解决方案，本公司是全世界移动电话、固定宽频及 IP 网络方面的领先供应商。

改译：________________

4. 原文：东鹏产品被广泛应用于天安门城楼、国务院办公楼、国家大剧院等全国上万个政府工程，成为消费者和装饰行业人士推崇的品牌。

原译：Dongpeng products have been widely applied in more than ten thousands of key projects of the State such as Tian'anmen rostrum, Administration Building of State Department, and State Opera House etc., and thus become the top priority of consumers and decoration trade.

改译：________________

5. 原文：经过十多年的发展壮大，ABC 公司已成为中国油画行业的龙头企业。

原译：After more than ten years' development, ABC Company has become a dragon head enterprise in China's oil painting industry.

改译：________________

Task III 企业简介翻译技巧：观察下列三个企业简介片段及其翻译，讨论并总结各题中企业简介翻译所采用的翻译技巧。

1. 原文：诞生于 20 世纪末的虎豹集团，信守孜孜以求、永不言退的发展理念，在市场经济的大潮中，任凭浊浪排空，惊涛拍岸，独有胜似闲庭信步的自信，处变不惊，运筹帷幄。尽握无限商机于掌间，渐显王者之气于天地。

译文：Founded in the late 20th century, Hubao Group has its philosophy of seizing business opportunities and achieving its brilliance in the ever-changing and competitive market.

2. 原文：With a belief that superior customer service and outstanding reliability is what the market demands, MAXIMUS' philosophy is rooted in offering its customers responsive, most practical and cost-effective solutions, which combine a personal approach with innovative customer service.

译文：由于坚信一流的客户服务和卓越的可靠性是真正的市场需求，MAXIMUS 将其经营理念植根于为客户提供及时的、最实用也最实惠的解决方案，将个性化建议与创新性客户服务完美结合。

3. 原文：成立于 1991 年的珠海格力电器股份有限公司是目前全球最大的集研发、生产、销售、服务于一体的专业化空调企业。2021 年营业总收入 1 896 亿元，连续 3 年上榜美国《财富》杂志“世界五百强”榜单。

译文：Founded in 1991, Gree Electric Appliances Inc. of Zhuhai is now one of the “Global 500” ranked by *Fortune* for 3 consecutive years. It has become the world’s largest specialized air conditioner manufacturer integrating R&D, manufacture, sales and service. In 2021, the gross business revenue reached RMB 189.6 billion.

PART FOUR

讨论：通过上述翻译任务，你认为翻译企业简介还可以采用哪些策略？企业简介的翻译需要注意哪些事项？

I. 企业简介翻译总结

本单元从企业简介的内容和功能谈起，讲述了企业简介的语言特征、企业简介翻译的原则和翻译技巧。现将企业简介的翻译原则与翻译技巧归纳如下（见表 5-1）：

表 5-1　　企业简介的翻译原则与翻译技巧

企业简介的翻译原则	忠实性：翻译必须忠实于原文，译文要准确地传达原文信息
	信息性：翻译要遵循传达主要信息的原则
	流畅性：译文语言必须通顺易懂，符合译入语的语言习惯
	宣传性：译文必须尽量保留作为宣传资料的语气
	统一性：文中的概念、术语始终保持统一，不随意变换译名
	文化适应性：迎合译入语民族的心理和审美，避免文化鸿沟
企业简介的翻译技巧	省译法：提取并传达主要信息，省略文化层面上的冗余信息
	增译法：根据实际弥补译文中宣传语气或文化信息的缺失
	结构拆译（结构整合与重组）：为了理清逻辑关系，对原文进行结构上的整合或重组，以符合译入语读者的逻辑思维习惯

II. 企业简介翻译余论

外宣资料英译译者应具备的基本素质

企业简介的翻译实属外宣资料的翻译，外宣资料的英译工作意义重大，关系到国家的形象和企业的命运。因此，外宣翻译工作对译者的素质也提出了较高的要求。作为一名合格的外宣资料译者，应具备三个方面的基本素质。

1. 扎实的语言功底和娴熟的翻译技巧

外宣资料的目的是塑造国家和企业的形象，因此特别要求语言准确，这就对外宣资料译者提出了扎实语言功底的要求——只有译者拥有扎实的语言功底和娴熟的翻译技巧，才能准确地传达完整的信息；同时，外宣资料一般比较注重语言的渲染性和美感，在翻译时，译者也需要充分领悟这种美感，再尽力向目的语读者传达。由于中英两种语言和文化的区别，就需要译者对两种语言有较高的驾驭能力，对两种文化有较好的领会能力。此外，外宣资料中还经常出现许多涉及法律法规和政策方面的内容和表述，这些都是原文中的重要部分，其句式结构和词汇组成往往也比较复杂。对此，译者必须格外谨慎，避免遗漏甚至歪曲原文的主旨，给企业和国家造成不必要的损失。

2. 严谨的治学态度和良好的职业道德

随着中国的国际影响力进一步扩大，外宣资料的翻译工作也与日俱增。外宣翻译是一个国家对外交流水平和人文环境建设的具体体现，做好外宣翻译工作，首先需要翻译工作者的自觉自律和这一团队整体素质的提高。市场上出现的劣质翻译，一部分属于译者的职业水平问题，即有些企业在翻译外宣资料的时候随便找个会英语的人来做，导致翻译质量不过关，有的甚至错误百出，贻笑大方；而另外一部分的劣质翻译，是由于译者缺乏良好的职业道德，急功近利，马虎草率造成的。合格的外宣翻译工作者必须有认真负责、一丝不苟的治学态度和良好的职业道德，必须摈弃任何马虎草率的态度和做法，必须杜绝不认真不严肃的主观态度和急功近利的心态。译者应该严于律己，有严格的治学态度和良好的职业道德。

3. “内外有别” 的意识

外宣资料翻译的另外一个误区在于原文的许多话本来是说给国人的，翻译时却不知不觉原封不动地搬到了英文里，这就是所谓的“内稿外用”，这就说明译者的跨文化意识淡薄。作为外宣资料的译者，要有良好的跨文化意识，做到内知国情、外知世界，充分了解中西文化的差异，熟知外国语言习俗，并设法使译文符合目标受众的审美情趣和心理诉求。黄友义（2006）提出要坚持“外宣三贴近”原则，即贴近中国发展的实际，贴近国外受众对中国信息的需求，贴近国外受众的思维习惯。翻译的时候，尤其是翻译具有强烈中国特色的外宣资料时，要注意思维方式的转换，遵循“内外有别”，不能按照中国人的习惯直接翻译，否则事倍功半。

PART FIVE

译技点津：商务翻译技巧之直译与意译

在翻译方法上，向来有直译（Literal Translation）与意译（Free Translation）之分，但它们各有优势。翻译方法是否适宜，直接影响着译文质量的高低。

I. 直译

所谓直译，就是在转达原文意思的时候，尽可能多地使译文的表达形式或句法结构同原文保持一致，译文既保持原文的内容，又不改变其修辞或措辞特点，如保留原文所使用的比喻、形象、民族特色等，使读者从译文中获得与原文大致相同的感受。直译的方法一方面有助于保留原文的风格，另一方面又有助于从国外引进一些新鲜的词语和表达方法，可以丰富目的语民族的语言和文化。但直译并不是不顾目的语的表达习惯而采用同原文的语言形式亦步亦趋的翻译方法，即死译（Rigid Translation），也允许有一定的变通。例如：

［例 1］原文：pillar industry
译文：支柱产业

［例 2］原文：the open-door policy

译文：门户开放政策

［例 3］原文：Considering the friendly business relationship between our two banks, we decided not to charge you the overdue interest.

译文：鉴于贵我两行之间的友好业务关系，我行决定不收取贵行的过期利息。

［例 4］原文：每个人都有一天会变老，如果人们确信老年时生活一定幸福、安康，就会全力以赴地投入工作。

译文：For everyone gets old some day, and when people feel perfectly secure of a happy and comfortable life in old age, they will devote themselves wholeheartedly to work.

II. 意译

意译是指在正确理解原文的基础上，不拘泥于原文的表达形式，用规范的译入语传达出原文的内容。如果依照原文的表层意义无法将原文的真实信息表达出来，那就应该借助意译法来打破原文的语言外壳，将其中的隐含意义表达出来，即“取其意，舍其形”。然而，意译并不等于随心所欲地偏离原文，造成过度意译甚至乱译。简单来说，意译只是用不同的译文形式，表达与原文相同的内容。例如：

［例 5］原文：a *Napoleon* of finance

译文：**金融巨头**

［例 6］原文：**五湖四海**

译文：*all corners of the country*

［例 7］原文：Exporting to a certain number of countries is made difficult by the quantity of *red tape*.

译文：政府部门的**繁文缛节**使得向某些国家的出口贸易困难重重。

［例 8］原文：现在合同已经签了，真是**木已成舟**，生米煮成了熟饭，只好如此了。

译文：As the contract has been signed, *what's done is done and can't be undone*.

例 5 中，Napoleon 一词本是家喻户晓的人名——拿破仑，但在语言运用中常使用其引申义“巨头，很强大的人或集团”。例 6 中的“五湖四海”一词在汉语中具有“湖”和“海”的形象，意思为“全国各地”或“世界各地”，翻译成英语并没有直接保留其“湖”和“海”的形象，而是采取了意译的方法，将其意思直接表达出来。例 7 中的“red tape”不能直译为“红带子”，意译为“繁文缛节”，缘起英国的律师和政府官员习惯用红带子捆扎文件，后来就将“red tape”引申为公事手续上的形式主义。例 8 中采取了“what's done is done and can't be undone”一句习语来意译“木已成舟”和“生米煮成熟饭”，既精炼，又达意。

III. 商务翻译中直译和意译的恰当使用

直译和意译既有区别，又紧密联系，它们之间没有优劣之分、高下之别，两种方法的目的都是要使译文通顺、地道，能让读者理解原文内容和意义。到底应该直译还是应该意译往往要考虑到上下文、语言特点、文体、读者和文化等因素，它们就好像是翻译实践的两个车轮，缺一不可，相得益彰。一般来说，遇到语言的共相、语言特有的文化元素、科技及专业术语时，多以直译为主；遇到语言的文化差异，则多以意译为主（宋天锡，2009：38）。例如：

［例 9］原文：In some automated plants, electronic computers control the entire production line.

译文：在某些自动化工厂，电子计算机控制整个生产线。（直译）

［例 10］原文：Earnings per share have mushroomed at a 34% annual compounded rate.

译文：若以复利计算，则每股的利益每年激增了 34%。（意译，mushroom 一词作动词，比喻像蘑菇般迅速增长，在中文中也有“雨后春笋”的表达与此相近，此处意译为“激增”。）

由上例可见，在商务英语翻译中，直译与意译的运用都非常普遍。商务英语材料的专业性、严密性、规范性决定了商务英语翻译常常采用直译，但商务英语还具有交际性强、语言复杂灵活的特点，这就决定了意译法在商务英语翻译中也起着重要的作用。译者要灵活思考，在翻译过程中需要根据实际情况采用不同的翻译方法，但不管运用哪一种方法，都必须运用适度，把握尺度，让它们充分发挥各自的最大优势。

PART SIX 企业简介翻译实践

Task I 请将下列英文企业简介的句子翻译成中文。

1. SF, established in Shunde, Guangdong Province in 1993, is now the largest integrated logistics service provider in China and the fourth largest in the world.

2. Our purpose is to improve people's health and well-being through meaningful innovation. We innovate with one consistent belief: there's always a way to make life better.

3. Royal Philips Electronics is the tenth on *Fortune*'s list of global top electronics corporations. We are active in more than 60 businesses, varying from consumer electronics to domestic appliance and from security system to semiconductors.

4. Leaders in automotive lighting for over a century, we are the suppliers of choice to more than 100 car makers today. We are committed to offering best-in-class products and services for the entire automotive aftermarket. Our proven ability to innovate brings the latest technological advances to automotive lighting, maximizing safety and driving comfort for all road-users.

Task II　请将下列中文企业简介的句子翻译成英文。

1. 本公司成立于 2012 年，是一家集研发、设计、生产、销售于一体的全球科技消费电子知名企业。

2. 该厂已经通过了 ISO9002 和 SQ9000 国际质量体系认证。

3. “快速反应，马上行动，质量第一，信誉至上”是公司的宗旨。我们将以客户的需求为发展动力，为用户提供满意的产品及优质的服务。

4. 小牛翻译云平台（NiuTrans Cloud Platform）创建于 2017 年，致力于为企业用户提供机器翻译解决方案，坚持以提供高品质的机器翻译为宗旨，依托深厚的机器翻译自主研发背景，为国内外众多用户解决跨语言沟通障碍。

Task III　以小组为单位，挑选一家企业，观察其企业简介的中英文版本，思考并讨论：

1. 中文版本和英文版本在语言表达上有什么不同？译者为什么做出这样的调整和修改？这样做好吗？为什么？
2. 翻译是否有需要改进的地方？如何改进？将讨论结果进行总结和整理，在课堂上展示小组思考和讨论的成果。

PART SEVEN

学习参考

1. 小牛翻译企业简介：https://niutrans.com/platform
2. 珠海格力电器企业简介：https://global.gree.com/channels/101.html
3. 华润（集团）有限公司简介：https://en.crc.com.cn/whoweare/companyataglance/
4. 飞利浦（照明）简介：
   https://www.lighting.philips.com.cn/home?remember_customer_type=professional
5. 欧司朗企业简介：https://www.osram.com/cb/about-us/index.jsp

PART EIGHT

单元预告与实训任务

1. 下一单元我们将讲述企业网站的翻译，涉及企业宣传资料各个部分的有关翻译。
2. 你觉得企业网站的翻译与企业简介的翻译有何异同？需要注意哪些问题？

第六单元

企业网站翻译

Unit Six　Translating Company Websites

在以信息技术高速发展为基本特征的“全球化”和“地球村”时代，整个世界变得越来越开放，信息共享已经成为全球范围内企业进行资源合理配置的重要途径。对于众多涉外企业来说，信息甚至已经成为生死存亡的生产要素，尤其是在当今数字贸易日新月异的时代，如何获取信息以及如何传播信息已经成为企业发展的重大议题。通过建立企业网站并进行翻译是企业对外宣传的有效方法。准确、地道的企业网站翻译，可以很好地宣传企业的概况、文化、产品、服务以及最新动态等方面的内容，从而达到树立企业良好形象，推销企业产品，扩大企业服务范围，提高企业竞争力，并最终达到盈利的目的。

教学目标

1. 了解企业网站的构成及功能，熟悉华为、柳工、苹果等国内外知名企业网站翻译特点，并能进行对比分析；
2. 掌握企业网站在数字化、智能化背景下的跨文化传播特点及相应翻译技巧；
3. 掌握企业网站翻译的编译技巧。

PART ONE
认识企业网站及其翻译

Task I　访问自己熟悉的企业网站并思考：企业网站一般包括哪些内容？有什么作用？

1. 企业网站的构成

在进行企业网站的建设和翻译前，我们要清楚网站的服务对象——潜在顾客。但由于潜在顾客的时间和精力相当有限，如何让企业的重要信息被轻松获取是网站建设者要深入研究的问题。处处尊重顾客，以顾客为导向来设计网站是成功的关键。但是，国内的一些企业网站，其目标读者模糊不清，塞满了企业的名称和标志，大幅的企业领导照片及介绍，冗长的企业荣誉报道等，这些其实没有必要，大部分潜在顾客并不关心这些内容。一般来说，网站信息一般应包括以下几个方面：

（1）企业概况（Who We Are, Company Information, About Us）

企业概况包括企业背景、发展历史、经营规模、组织结构以及下属子公司等。如果是上市公司，提供公司的股票代码或者专门财经网站的链接，有助于顾客了解企业的实力。让顾客对企业的情况有一个基本的轮廓，并对该企业产生兴趣，这是企业网络营销战略成功的第一步。

（2）合作伙伴（Partners, Investors, Investor Relations）

合作伙伴包括整个产业链上游的原材料供应商和生产设备制造商，以及下游的经销商甚至是同行业的竞争伙伴。企业还可以在网站的合作伙伴栏目里，公布相关的合作计划，吸引投资和技术的告示或者所要寻求投资的产业，也可以提供一些友情链接和相关资源链接等信息。

（3）企业产品或业务介绍（Products, Services）

企业产品或业务介绍包括企业开展的各种产品或业务简介、市场销售情况、特殊业务的专业许可证、营销网络的建设现状以及各地的代理商等。提供企业产品和服务的目录，方便顾客在网上查看。企业可以根据需要决定资料的详略程度，或者配以图片、视频、音频资料、二维码、链接等，还可以在网上公布产品价格信息表或者价格查询数据库，以供顾客购买时参考。

（4）新闻中心（News, Media Center, Latest News, Hot News）

企业可以鼓励员工或其专职人员及时报道企业内部的重大事件，也可结合企业公关部门，报道企业所实施的公益事业和承担的社会责任，以此提升企业形象。企业网站还可以将外界媒体报道的与企业相关的信息转载到网站上来。

（5）招聘信息（Jobs, Job Opportunities, Careers）

企业网站通常会设置人才招聘栏目。在该栏目下，企业会介绍其空缺职位、招聘要求、人才理念及企业精神等。有的企业还会公布员工福利和各种待遇，对高级人才的吸引策略等。

（6）联系方式（Contact Us）

企业应当在自己的网站提供详细的联系方式，以便与顾客交流。通常包括公众号、平台链接、电子邮箱、电话、传真、联系地址和邮编等。对于有分支机构的企业，同时还应提供各分支机构的联系方式，方便顾客查询。

（7）服务信息（Services）

企业还要在网站上公布有关质量保证条款和售后服务措施，公开企业的售后服务热线，各营销机构电话等。具有网络销售功能的网站，应当详细公布自己的服务承诺和违约责任等，明确提示顾客相关法律条款。具有注册或者 Cookie 功能（This Site Uses Cookies）的企业网站，还需要公布自己的隐私条约（Read Our Private Policy）以便让顾客有安全感。网站还应设有使用说明或者 FAQ（Frequently Asked Questions，常见问题解答），以便于帮助顾客顺利操作网站的各项服务。

（8）专题信息（Features）

企业网站还可以就其产品和服务做一个专题信息栏目，让顾客来阅读或观看。比如日用化妆品企业的网站，可以开设一个化妆常识的专栏；汽车制造和销售企业的网站，可以制作一个发布汽车驾驶、保养及维修的专栏；电脑企业可以建设一个关于电脑使用和常见问题解决的专题信息栏目，一般还会提供相关硬件驱动程序的下载链接等。

2. 企业网站的功能

（1）宣传企业，树立数字化时代企业完美形象。通过企业的网站，顾客可以更便捷地了解企业。据调查，超过 30%的人通过上网查询企业的电话和地址，这一比例和通过 114 查询的比例相接近，可见企业网站已成为许多人首次接触企业、了解相关信息的选择。同时，利用新出现的信息技术，例如 VR（Virtual Reality），企业可以向客户展示产品、技术、经营理念、企业文化、企业形象，树立现代企业形象，增值企业无形资产。

（2）加强顾客沟通，宣传企业产品。企业可以通过网站建立与顾客沟通的便捷渠道，全面展示企业的所有产品。如今的科技足以令产品与品牌形象更加立体地呈现在用户面前，比传统的宣传模式更加多姿多彩，更容易发布与传播，更为经济与环保。

（3）丰富营销手段，扩大产品销售渠道。随着数字贸易，尤其是跨境电子商务的发展，企业网站销售所占的份额有逐渐扩大之势，而且可以减少销售环节，减少人员，节约费用，降低成本，有利于提高营销效率。

（4）有利于了解顾客意见，掌握顾客需求。在不干扰顾客正常工作和生活的条件下，企业通过网站上的调查表、留言簿、定制服务、电子邮箱等手段可以了解顾客的意见，倾听顾客的心声，加强企业与顾客间的联系，建立良好的顾客关系。

（5）有利于改善服务，提高企业服务质量。利用网站，通过电子沟通方式，企业开展的在线服务是传统的沟通方式（如电话、传真）不可比拟的。在线服务能够更加及时准确地掌握顾客的需求，通过网站的交互式服务使得被动提供和主动获得统一起来，从而实现售前、售中、售后全过程和全方位的服务。

（6）可以突破时空限制，时时处处服务顾客。企业网站是企业对外宣传的窗口，也是企业与顾客交流，获取顾客反馈信息的一种途径。它能一年 365 天、一天 24 小时，忠实服务世界各地的顾客。

Task II 访问华为中文网站（http://www.huawei.com/cn/），并从公司主页进入其美国网站（http://www.huawei.com/us/），比较其中英文网站的相同和不同之处。

访问中国工商银行的中文网站（http://www.icbc.com.cn），并从主页进入其英文网站（http://www.icbc.com.cn/ICBC/EN/default.htm），比较其中英文网站的相同和不同之处。

思考：这对于企业网站翻译来说有什么启示？

访问华为的中英文网站（2022 年 8 月 1 日）可以看出：两个网站的风格非常相似，均有大幅的广告图片放在显眼位置，同时提供搜索引擎，可以找到华为所有业务及产品，体现了以业务推广与营销为侧重点的特征。网站布局都比较简洁、清晰、明了，顾客可以一目了然地找到相关的栏目信息。例如，中文的主要栏目很醒目地放在网页上方，包括：个人及家庭产品、商用产品及方案、服务支持、服务伙伴与开发者、关于华为、在线购买、集团网站、选择区域/语言等。特别值得一提的是，在线购买栏目可以直接进入华为商城和华为云，将顾客最常见的产品和服务需求都清楚地列出，标明价格和促销信息，随时在线下单，体现了顾客至上的服务精神。选择区域/语言栏目主要是提供本土化语言和服务，点击进入之后可以发现华为已经为全球 32 个国家和地区设置了不同语种的专门网站，很好地体现了华为的实力及其全球化战略。美国网站的主要栏目也很醒目地放在网页上方，包括：Our Business，About Huawei，News & Events，Explore More，Corporate，United States [Change]等。其总体风格、布局、功能以及栏目、内容等方面与中文网站类似。但显然，中文网站的个人及家庭产品、商用产品及方案在美国网站中被合并成了 Our Business。美国网站还专门设置了 Explore More 栏目，提供华为技术、博客、出版物等更多信息。另外，点击进入具体栏目，我们发现个人及家庭产品翻译成了 Consumer Products，而不是 Personal and Household Products；商用产品及方案翻译成了 Enterprise Products，而不是 Commercial Products and Solutions；技术支持翻译成了 Support，而不是 Technology Support；网站左下角展会活动翻译成了 Events。事实上，这样的不完全对应从功能上说非常符合美国文化。如 Consumer Products 和 Support 均比 Personal and Household Products 和 Technology Support 简洁；而 Events 则是英文网站常用的单词，更加容易被美国顾客接受。因此，这些翻译体现了以顾客为中心的服务方向。

与华为不同的是，中国工商银行的中文网站和英文网站（2022 年 8 月 1 日）风格差异相对较大。中文网站的栏目非常多，除了一般的银行业务和服务栏目之外，还有智服务、投资理财、惠生活、生活缴费、留学服务等众多栏目/子栏目，可以说是琳琅满目、丰富多彩。但是其英文网站却相对简洁，Personal Banking, Corporate Banking, About Us Customer Service 等主要栏目很醒目地放在了主页的上方。事实上，我们访问了花旗银行、渣打银行等国际上著名的银行，它们的英文网页也都非常简洁，功能区域一目了然。因此，工商银行的英文网站布局是与国际接轨的。

通过以上比较可以看出，企业采取的中英文网站布局有可能风格相同，也有可能风格相异，关键要看企业所服务的对象及其偏好。例如华为网站以营销和服务为主，就应该让顾客轻松地找到相关产品和服务信息，所以与营销相关的栏目非常突出、简洁、清晰。工商银行的中文网站内容较多，主要是考虑到中国人的需求。事实上，随着中国人民生活水平的提高，消费、留学、生活缴费等已经成为中国人的生活之必需，工商银行在主页上提供这些信息是符合中国国情的，而其英文版的网站跟其他的银行一样，并没有设置这些栏目，这符合国外的文化习惯。

以上中英文网站的对比涉及本章的主题：企业网站翻译。其内容包括网站名称的翻译、网站宣传标语的翻译、网站栏目名称的翻译、网站栏目具体内容的翻译等。不管如何，企业网站必须方便顾客浏览，强调“读者第一”，译者应以实现译文预期功能或目的为宗旨，使用经济简明同时又符合目标读者的文化观念、阅读心理、认知能力、语言习惯的表达方式进行灵活翻译。

PART TWO

热身练习

Task I　请根据例子翻译下列网站名称，并尝试总结网站名称的构成。

例：www.sina.com.cn，翻译成“新浪网”，“新”强调与众不同，“浪”则包含网上冲浪、自由自在的意思。

1. www.google.com ____________________
2. www.soufun.com ____________________
3. www.alimama.com ____________________
4. www.shundecity.com ____________________
5. www.china.com ____________________
6. www.gzbookcenter.com ____________________
7. www.netease.com ____________________
8. www.jd.com ____________________
9. www.2797.com ____________________
10. www.made-in-china.com ____________________

Task II 试将下面网站宣传标语翻译成英文。

1. 永不止步。 （安踏） ______________________________
2. 一起向未来。 （北京冬奥会） ______________________________
3. 速度，责任，领先。 （长青集团） ______________________________

Task III 试将下列网站各栏目名称翻译成英文。

1. 关于我们 ______________________________
2. 联系我们 ______________________________
3. 站点导航 ______________________________
4. 免责申明 ______________________________
5. 诚聘英才 ______________________________
6. 指南 ______________________________
7. 友情链接 ______________________________
8. 网上论坛 ______________________________
9. 股票市值 ______________________________
10. 注册 ______________________________
11. 用户登录 ______________________________
12. 搜索 ______________________________

Task IV 试分析下面一段宣传文字的英译。如果要挂在企业网站上，你会选择哪个译文？为什么？并讨论企业英文网站的语言特征。

[原文] 广州手表厂是广州轻工工贸集团有限公司属下大中型国有企业。该厂 1958 年筹建，次年正式投产，是我国最早兴建的几家手表厂之一，是中国实力最强的机械自动表生产基地。厂址现坐落在广州市海珠区石榴岗路 14 号，与广州国际会展中心相邻，稳坐商业聚财之地，地铁相连，四通八达，环境优雅，现有员工 600 多人，其中有众多高级设计工程师、高级工艺装配师、高级品质控制师。

[译文 1] Guangzhou Watch Factory is a state-owned enterprise subordinate to Guangzhou Light Industry and Trade Group CO., Ltd. The factory was founded in 1958 and officially went into production the next year. The factory is one of the most early established watch factories in our country and becomes the leading production basis of manufacturing automatic mechanical watches in China. Adjacent to Guangzhou International Convention Center, Guangzhou Watch Factory is located at No. 14 Shiliugang Road of Guangzhou Haizhu District. The graceful environment surrounded and the convenient transportation make it stand in a favorable position to develop business. There are more than 600 staff members now, including a number of senior design engineers, senior craft assembling engineers, and senior quality control technicians.

［译文 2］Guangzhou Watch Factory (GWF), a state-owned enterprise founded in 1958 in Guangzhou, is one of the longest established watch factories and the biggest production base of automatic mechanical watches in China. GWF enjoys a prime location, adjacent to Guangzhou International Convention Center and can be easily accessed by subway.

____

PART THREE
企业网站翻译技巧

Task I　请将下列网站名称翻译成中文，并尝试总结网站名称翻译的技巧。

1. www.amazon.com ____________
2. www.boaoforum.org ____________
3. www.baosteel.com ____________
4. www.eastday.com ____________
5. www.yidaiyilu.gov.cn ____________
6. www.realtor.com ____________
7. www.pconline.com.cn ____________
8. www.xinhuanet.com ____________
9. www.people.com.cn ____________
10. www.51fanli.com ____________

Task II　试将下面网站宣传标语翻译成英文，并结合热身练习部分 Task II，思考翻译后的标语放在网站哪个位置合适，为什么？

1. 幸福生活原来是真。（华帝燃具） ____________________
2. 原来生活可以更美的。（美的集团） ____________________
3. 一心做好，始终如一。（渣打银行） ____________________

Task III　试分析下列北京同仁堂和华帝燃具网站各栏目的英译，看看哪些栏目的翻译是较好的翻译，哪些翻译可以改进？如何改进？并尝试总结其翻译技巧。

A：北京同仁堂

1. 首页（Home）
2. 走进同仁堂（About TRT）
3. 新闻中心（News）
4. 同仁堂旗下（Subsidiary）
5. 全球分布（Global distribution）

B：华帝燃具

1. 认识华帝（Recognition of Vatti）
2. 品牌中心（Brand Center）
3. 厨卫精品（Products）
4. 服务专区（Special Service Area）
5. 公益华帝（Public-welfare Vatti）

Task IV 分析下面一段企业宣传文字的原译，看看有何问题，并进行改译。

原文：面对新的百年，青岛啤酒公司将不断创新，打造学习型企业，提高核心竞争力，创建国际化的大公司，做国际市场的价值专家、中国啤酒市场的领导者和超级明星，谱写新百年的辉煌！

原译：Facing the new century, Tsingtao Brewery Co., Ltd. will continuously innovate to build up a learning type enterprise. It will promote its nuclear competitiveness, to build up an internationalized large company, a value expert on the international market and a leader and super star on the domestic beer market and to write a new history of brilliance in the new century.（www.tsingtao.com.cn）

改译：______________________________

____

Task V 请将下面一段企业宣传文字翻译成英文。

华为创立于 1987 年，是全球领先的 ICT（信息与通信）基础设施和智能终端提供商。目前华为约有 19.5 万名员工，业务遍及 170 多个国家和地区，服务全球 30 多亿人口。华为致力于把数字世界带入每个人、每个家庭、每个组织，构建万物互联的智能世界：让无处不在的连接，成为人人平等的权利，成为智能世界的前提和基础；为世界提供多样性算力，让云无处不在，让智能无所不及；所有的行业和组织，因强大的数字平台而变得敏捷、高效、生机勃勃；通过 AI 重新定义体验，让消费者在家居、出行、办公、影音娱乐、运动健康等全场景获得极致的个性化智慧体验。

____

____

____

PART FOUR

讨论：通过上述翻译任务，你对企业网站翻译有什么新的认识？企业网站翻译需要注意哪些事项？

I. 企业网站翻译总结

企业网站翻译有很大的灵活性，并不是原语网页有什么内容就翻译什么内容，需要根据网站的有关功能在语言和形式上适当进行调整。一般来说，我们需要注意以下几点：

首先，网站翻译必须考虑企业网站的功能。我们要了解网站的主要功能是什么，例如销售、服务还是互动。例如苹果公司英文网页（www.apple.com），其主要功能是宣传、销售产品，因此其首页正中间利用大幅图片宣传主打产品，并配上对应的“Your new superpower”等广告语，非常显眼，引人注目。而其中文网页（www.apple. com.cn）与英文网页如出一辙，首页正中间利用大幅图片宣传主打产品，配上了“解锁超能力”等广告语。而苹果公司中英文网站的其他栏目如 Site Map（网站地图），Job

Opportunities（工作机会），Supplier Responsibility（供应商责任）等则放在右下角，并不突出。在了解了网站主要功能之后，要将原语恰当地翻译成目的语。例如，中国工商银行的"个人网上银行"翻译成"Personal Banking"，"指南"翻译成"FAQs（Frequently Asked Questions）"。谷歌公司的"I'm feeling lucky"翻译成"手气不错"，"Google Search"翻译成"Google 搜索"等，都是与网站功能相一致的、恰当的翻译。

其次，翻译要以网站服务对象为中心。要考虑到服务对象是谁，根据服务对象的文化、知识背景、语言习惯等来考虑如何翻译，做到准确用词、恰当用句、避免歧义、简练至上。例如，阿里巴巴英文网页中的 search，中文网页的对应语为"找一下"，而不是其他很多网站中用的"搜索"，这体现了网站服务对象——商人的语言特征，无形中拉近了网站与客户的距离；又如阿里巴巴中文网站中的"免费注册"，其英文网站翻译成"Join Free Today"，用祈使句非常简练地表达出很强的劝说意图。

再次，要注意网站信息的摆放位置。应该把重要的栏目放在显眼的位置，如左上角，因为这是访问者注意力的关键位置之一。例如中国工商银行的中英文网站都把用户登录（User Login）放在左上角，这体现了其为储户服务的意识。而其他不重要的栏目可以放在次要位置，甚至可以根据需要不用翻译。当然，翻译出来的译文在网页上的位置也并不一定中英对应，这同样要考虑服务对象的需求。例如谷歌公司的英文版主页左上角栏目 Gmail，但是中文版的主页上却没有，主要原因是中国使用 Gmail 邮箱的人并不多。

最后，翻译后的网站排版要简洁、美观。网站是给服务对象访问的，简洁、美观是对服务对象的尊重。例如，华为、海尔集团、青岛啤酒、苹果、谷歌等企业网站均是简洁、美观的典型代表。特别是谷歌，其搜索标志（谷歌称之为"节日徽标"）会根据不同的节日来变换，给人一种新鲜感，又有一定的纪念意义。当然，企业中英文网站的维护人员不同，布局设计等会针对用户的不同而有所区别。但是整体上都要有达到简洁、美观、吸引用户眼球的目的。

（谷歌节日徽标——地球日）

（谷歌节日徽标——梵高诞辰）

II. 网站翻译注意事项

国内众多涉外企业都拥有自己的英文网站。遗憾的是，这些英文网站仍然有不少翻译"硬伤"。例如，这些网站英译按照汉语的字面意思和语序结构，用"对号入座"和"亦步亦趋"的方法进行生硬的"死译"，产生了大量不规范的英文，其中不乏拼写错误、词汇误译、句法及文化误译等问题，一定程度上阻碍了有效的跨文化交际，影响到企业的经济效益。

1. 拼写规范问题

要避免企业网站翻译中出现拼写错误、标点符号滥用以及大小写不分的问题。这些问题反映了个别企业态度上的不严谨和服务上的不细致。特别要注意企业网站的大小写要统一。例如，浙江某药业公司英文翻译中就曾出现“forget password Please click here!”“user name”“Password”等大小写混乱的情况。要注意除非有特殊的理由（例如用小写字体的艺术字让网站更美观），否则要坚决杜绝这种大小写不分的情况。

2. 词汇误译问题

正确翻译词汇是网站翻译的基础。目前有些网站上的翻译令人费解，甚至完全错误。例如，有网站把“物流（logistics）”翻译成 material flowing，把“公司占地面积 3 000 亩（the company occupies an area of 494.2 acres）”翻译成 total land area of 3,000 acres，“企业精神（corporate values）”翻译成 enterprise spirit 等，“新闻动态（latest news, news）”翻译成 news information。

3. 句法问题

在句法上要注意中英文的众多不同之处，翻译时可以采用包括语态调整、结构重组等方法进行恰当处理。请看例 1：

[例 1] 原文：目前，亚太药业的产品已经销售到国内 24 个省、市、自治区，在全国设有 50 多个办事处，并力争远销多个国家和地区。

原译：At present, the Asia-Pacific Pharmaceutical products already sold 24 domestic provinces, municipalities, autonomous regions and provinces in the country with over 50 offices, and strive to exported to many countries and regions.（www.ytyaoye.com）

改译：At present, our products have been sold in 24 Chinese provinces, municipalities, autonomous regions with over 50 offices nationwide and we are trying to further export to more countries and regions.

分析：“产品”和“销售”是被动关系，而非主动关系，既然前面用了“at present”，后面就不能用过去式了，这里最好用现在完成时；不定式“to”后面也只能用动词原形。

4. 文化误译

受众的文化背景是企业外宣翻译中需要考虑的一个重要因素。不同的文化背景导致不同民族所共有的文化知识也有所不同。因此，在翻译此类文化背景知识时，必须考虑中西文化差异带来的影响，把中文翻译成英文时，只需简要地说明即可。请看下例：

[例 2] 原文：该企业先后获得“省级先进企业”“市文明企业”“市质量管理奖”“市质量效益型先进企业”“全国轻工优秀企业”“国家二级企业”等称号。（广州百花香料股份有限公司）

原译：Baihua has been entitled “Provincial Advanced Enterprise with Outstanding Quality and Profits” “Municipal Civilized Enterprise” “Municipal Excellent Enterprise for Management” “Municipal Excellent Enterprise for Outstanding Quality and Profits” “National Excellent Light Industrial Enterprise” “National Second Grade Enterprise” etc.

改译：Baihua has received a dozen of honorary and professional titles conferred by national and provincial and city authorities due to its high-quality products, advanced management, and outstanding profits.

分析：译文将原文中企业所获奖项一个不漏地翻译出来，意在显示该企业获奖无数，说明企业的良好效益，在市、省，乃至全国都是一家优秀的企业。然而，这些在中国人眼里值得炫耀的荣誉，在海外受众看来，也许就是“语焉不详的套话”。由于缺乏和我们相同的文化背景，他们不一定会知道这些称号到底指的是什么。直译出来，不仅不会加深他们对这家企业的印象，反而会因为这些重复累赘的文字让他们觉得企业的效率低，作风拖沓，而无法达到预定的宣传效果。因此，应尽量简化，表达出这些奖项的内在意思即可，即产品质量好、企业管理水平高、效益好。

PART FIVE

译技点津：商务翻译技巧之编译

编译是翻译中一种独特的信息处理方式，通俗地说就是对原文进行编辑之后再翻译，其编辑方法包括增减、合并、调序等。编译可以用凝练的语言和较小的篇幅介绍鸿篇巨制的中心内容，也可以在较短的时间内完成译介大量材料的工作，速度快、效率高、实用性强。其具体操作步骤为：

第一步：领悟原文，抓住关键信息。先要分清原文的主题，再按照与主题的远近关系，对作者的观点和论据进行归纳、排序，然后根据观点和论据之间的联系，把握文本的内在逻辑。文本的整体语言风格和语言特色要能了然于胸。

第二步：对原文内容和结构进行增减、合并与调序。删减的内容大多是那些与原文主题关系疏远或关系不大、重复啰嗦、模棱两可的内容，或者是会产生文化冲突的内容。增加的是加强原作主旨以及逻辑纽带的词句；合并的是原作中松散的词、句、段；调整的是原文中不能直接翻译成目的语的语篇结构。所有这些具体的编辑工作的目的在于创造一个内容完整、主题明确、条理清晰的编译作品。

第三步：将第二步编辑后的内容翻译成目的语。

编译是企业网站翻译的常用技巧之一。中文版和英文版的企业网站服务对象不同，所关注的内容也不同。在中文版中出现的内容未必在英文版中出现，即使是同样的内容在表达方法上也会有差异。因此，在企业网站翻译中，编译不可或缺。

请看下面广西柳工机械股份有限公司的网站翻译：

[例 1] 原文：广西柳工机械股份有限公司（以下简称柳工）是中国制造业 500 强企业——柳工集团的核心企业，作为国内工程机械行业和广西第一家上市公司，柳工被誉为“中国工程机械行业的排头兵”。通过 20 世纪 90 年代及近年的大规模技术改造，公司配置了诸如机器人自动焊接线、树脂砂工艺铸造生产线、大型加工中心等一批世界水平的生产设备，并通过三位一体的 ISO 管理体系（质量、环境、职业健康安全）持续优化业务流程，使柳工产品享

有高品质、高可靠性、高效率的美誉。柳工各类产品先后荣获国家级和原机械部十余项荣誉，“柳工”牌装载机于 2004 年荣获“中国名牌产品”称号，荣获“2005 年度中国企业信息化 500 强”等荣誉和称号。柳工产品研发部门被评定为国家级的企业技术中心，建立了博士后工作站，拥有 500 多名工程技术人员从事产品设计及制造技术研究工作，使产品研发水平和技术性能始终保持行业领先地位。

译文：

- A leader in China's Construction Equipment Industry;
- Liugong Group is one of China's Top 500 Manufacturers;
- Guangxi Liugong Machinery Co., Ltd. is the first listed company in the Industry and the first listed company in Guangxi Autonomous Region;
- An integrated ISO system in Quality, Environment and Occupation Health & Safety;
- Liugong Wheel Loader-Awarded China's Top Brand;
- Informationalized Top 500 company in China;
- A state-level globally synergized R&D center.

分析：这是广西柳工机械股份有限公司真实使用过的译文，采用了编译法，经济简明，适合网站浏览。首先，译者在内容上进行了编译。把翻译的焦点放在传达最能体现柳工实力和特点的核心信息上，提纲挈领地表明了柳工的行业地位、研发实力、管理体系、市场状况和公司形象等信息。编译时舍弃了一些次要信息，或者外商并不怎么关心或不需要了解的信息。其次，译者在形式上进行了编译。原文是以篇章的形式来介绍柳工概况的，而译文是用名词词组或者简单句提纲式地列出重要的信息，很好地体现了为顾客服务的意识。

随着国家对企业诚信、工匠精神、产品质量、智能制造等方面的重视，柳工的最新网站（www.liugong.com，2022 年 8 月 1 日）翻译有所调整，将获奖记录单独设置了一个栏目，突出其实力和行业影响力。中文栏目“柳工获奖记录”如下：

世界工程机械 50 强企业
2017 年中国机械工业百强
2017 中国年度影响力品牌
最具全球竞争力中国公司 50 强
最具投资价值上市公司
企业信用评价 AAA 级企业
全国安全文化建设示范企业
国家智能制造试点示范
亚洲卓越质量奖
全国质量奖

对应英文栏目“Liugong Awards”如下：

A Top 50 Global Construction Machinery Enterprise
A Top 100 China Machinery Industry Enterprise in 2017
2017 Annual Influential Brand in China
Top 50 Chinese Companies in Global Competitive Power
Most Valuable Listed Company
Enterprise Credit Rating, AAA Grade Credit Enterprise
National Demonstration Enterprise of Safety Culture Building
National Pilot Demonstration of Intelligent Manufacturing
Asia Excellence Quality Award
National Quality Award

请再看下面阿里巴巴网站关于其价值观的翻译：

［例 2］原文：阿里巴巴的价值观

客户第一	关注客户的关注点，为客户提供建议和资讯，帮助客户成长
团队合作	共享共担，以小我完成大我
拥抱变化	突破自我，迎接变化
诚信	诚实正直，信守承诺
激情	永不言弃，乐观向上
敬业	以专业的态度和平常的心态做非凡的事情

译文：

Mission：To make it easy to do business anywhere.

Customer First	The interests of our community of users and paying members must be our first priority.
Team Work	We expect our employees to collaborate as a team. We encourage input from our employees in the decision-making process, and expect every employee to commit to the team's objectives.
Embrace Change	We operate in a fast-evolving industry. We ask our employees to maintain flexibility, continue to innovate and adapt to new business conditions and practice.
Integrity	Integrity is at the heart of our business as trust is an essential element of a marketplace. We expect our employees to uphold the highest standards of integrity and to deliver on their commitments.
Passion	Our employees are encouraged to act with passion whether it is serving customers or developing new services and products.
Commitment	Our employees have a dedicated focus and commitment to

understanding and delivering on the needs of Chinese and global small and medium-sized enterprises.

分析：这是阿里巴巴公司真实使用过的译文，同样采用了编译的方法。跟上例柳工的编译法不同的是，本例在原文的基础上增添了部分内容。例如标题栏就增加了其中文网站中“我们的使命（To make it easy to do business anywhere）”，这对于客户来说一定是振奋人心的，因为“只要加入阿里巴巴，生意就不再难做”。另外，我们逐栏对照中英文的价值观，可以发现中文版相当简洁，而英文版在中文版基础上增加了较为详细的解释，这些解释也就是具体编译中所增加的内容。这似乎与网站翻译经济简明的要求背道而驰，但是，我们仔细分析发现，价值观的内容本身中英文都是很简洁的，只是具体含义的解释部分英文较为详细，并且可以看到英文的解释中都采用了第一人称的“we”和“our”，这不仅仅是对阿里巴巴企业价值观的宣传，同时也是对客户负责任的一种承诺。当然，如此翻译跟中英文语言本身的差异不无关系，但从方法上看，更是译者编译思路的体现。值得注意的是，经过多年的商界经营，阿里巴巴的价值观目前也有一些调整（www.alibabagroup.com，2022 年 8 月 1 日），更加细化、朴实、通俗易懂，重视客户利益，知晓变化之道，激励员工奋进，而其翻译也强调准确、忠实于原文，放弃了之前的编译方法。中文网站：

我们的价值观

阿里巴巴集团的六大价值观对于我们如何经营业务、招揽人才、考核员工以及决定员工报酬扮演着重要的角色，六大价值观如下：

客户第一，员工第二，股东第三　这就是我们的选择，是我们的优先级。只有持续为客户创造价值，员工才能成长，股东才能获得长远利益。

因为信任，所以简单　世界上最宝贵的是信任，最脆弱的也是信任。阿里巴巴成长的历史是建立信任、珍惜信任的历史。你复杂，世界便复杂；你简单，世界也简单。阿里人真实不装，互相信任，没那么多顾虑猜忌，问题就简单了，事情也因此高效。

唯一不变的是变化　无论你变不变化，世界在变，客户在变，竞争环境在变。我们要心怀敬畏和谦卑，避免“看不见、看不起、看不懂、追不上”。改变自己，创造变化，都是最好的变化。拥抱变化是我们最独特的 DNA。

今天最好的表现是明天最低的要求　在阿里最困难的时候，正是这样的精神，帮助我们渡过难关，活了下来。逆境时，我们懂得自我激励；顺境时，我们敢于设定具有超越性的目标。面向未来，不进则退，我们仍要敢想敢拼，自我挑战，自我超越。

此时此刻，非我莫属　这是阿里第一个招聘广告，也是阿里第一句土话，是阿里人对使命的相信和“舍我其谁”的担当。

认真生活，快乐工作　工作只是一阵子，生活才是一辈子。工作属于你，而你属于生活，属于家人。像享受生活一样快乐工作，像对待工作一样认真地生活。只有认真对待生活，生活才会公平地对待你。我们每个人都有自己的工作和生活态度，我们尊重每个阿里人的选择。这条价值观的考核，留给生活本身。

英文网站：

OUR VALUES

Our values are fundamental to the way we operate and how we recruit, evaluate and compensate our people. Our six values are:

CUSTOMERS FIRST, EMPLOYEES SECOND, SHAREHOLDERS THIRD This reflects our choice of what's important in the order of priority. Only by creating sustained customer value can employees grow and shareholders achieve long-term benefit.

TRUST MAKES EVERYTHING SIMPLE Trust is both the most precious and fragile thing in the world. The story of Alibaba is a story of building and cherishing trust. Complexity begets complexity, and simplicity breeds simplicity. Aliren are straightforward—what you see is what you get. With trust, there is no second-guessing or suspicion, and the result is simplicity and efficiency.

CHANGE IS THE ONLY CONSTANT Whether you change or not, the world is changing, our customers are changing and the competitive landscape is changing. We must face change with respect and humility. Otherwise, we will fail to see it, fail to respect it, fail to understand it and fail to catch up with it. Whether you change yourself or create change, both are the best kinds of change. Embracing change is the most unique part of our DNA.

TODAY'S BEST PERFORMANCE IS TOMORROW'S BASELINE In Alibaba's most challenging times, this spirit has helped us overcome difficulties and survive. In bad times, we know how to motivate ourselves; in good times, we dare to set "dream targets" (stretch goals). Face the future, or we regress. We must shoot for the moon, challenge ourselves, motivate ourselves and exceed ourselves.

IF NOT NOW, WHEN? IF NOT ME, WHO? This was a tagline in Alibaba's first job advertisement and became our first proverb. It is not a question, but a call of duty. This proverb symbolizes the sense of ownership that each Aliren must possess.

LIVE SERIOUSLY, WORK HAPPILY Work is now, life is forever. What you do in your job is up to you, but you have responsibility to the ones who love you. Enjoy work as you enjoy life; treat life seriously as you do work. If you live with purpose, you will find reward. You make Alibaba different and make your loved ones proud. Everyone has their own view of work and life; we respect each person's choice. Whether you live by this value depends on how you live your life.

PART SIX
企业网站翻译实践

Task I 请将下列网站名称翻译成汉语。

1. www.chinanews.com.cn ____________
2. www.nytsyn.com (nyt 为 New York Times 缩略形式) ____________
3. www.pcpop.com ____________
4. www.youku.com ____________
5. www.51job.com ____________
6. www.aol.com (aol 为 American on Line 的首字母) ____________
7. www.jpwindow.com (jp 为 Japan 的缩略形式) ____________
8. www.cnki.net ____________
9. www.nowpublic.com ____________
10. www.theaustralian.com.au ____________

Task II 试将下面网站宣传标语翻译成英语。

1. 全球最大的采购批发市场。（阿里巴巴）

____

2. 自然之源，重塑你我——用自然的力量来重新塑造一家企业，一个人，甚至一个社会。（中粮集团）

____

3. 我们的发展与创造让所有人受惠。（永大公司）

____

4. 品质优越，彰显高贵。（东莞绿通公司）

____

5. 快乐创造 C 生活。（四川长虹）

____

6. 用心照亮世界。（佛山照明）

____

7. 光明创领未来。（雪莱特光电）

____

8. 创意感动生活。（TCL 集团）

____

9. 共筑美好家园。（广西柳工）

____

10. 站在巨人的肩膀上。（谷歌学术搜索）

____

Task III 请将下列网站栏目名称翻译成英语。

1. 产品系列 ______________________
2. 产品与服务 ______________________
3. 联系我们 ______________________
4. 附件配件 ______________________
5. 企业动态 ______________________
6. 相关链接 ______________________
7. 诚聘英才 ______________________
8. 公司概况 ______________________
9. 投资者关系 ______________________
10. 隐私保护 ______________________

Task IV 分析下面一段企业宣传文字及其原译，看看有何问题，并进行改译。

原文：深圳大光礼品有限公司是一家中外合资的综合性经济实体，为国内首家专业生产、经营各类高中档礼品精品、旅游纪念品、宾馆客房服务系列专用品之企业。

原译：Shenzhen Taikong Gift Co. Ltd. is a jointly ventured comprehensive economic entity, and the first domestic enterprise which specializes in producing and dealing with different kinds of high-grade and intermediate choice gifts and souvenirs, tourist souvenirs and serial appliances for guestrooms in hotel.

改译：____

____

Task V 分析下面一段企业宣传文字的两种翻译，看看哪种更好。

原文：山海关啤酒厂坐落在风景优美的避暑胜地、历史名城——山海关。素有“龙头”之称的万里长城的东部起端，由此伸向大海。该厂始建于 1982 年，后经二次扩建和技术改造，如今已形成了具有年产 8 万吨啤酒和 9 千吨麦芽的生产能力，是我国啤酒行业的重点骨干企业之一。

译文 1：Located in Shanhaiguan, a picturesque summer resort, and the famous historic town, where the east end of the Great Wall called head of dragon extends to the sea, Shanhaiguan Brewery was set in 1982 and has been technically transformed twice and expanded to the present scale with an annual capacity of 80,000 tons of beer and 9,000 tons of malt. The brewery has become one of the key enterprises producing beer in China.

译文 2：Shanhaiguan Brewery is a key enterprise brewing beer in China. It is located in Shanhaiguan, a picturesque summer resort and historical town, where the East End of the Great Wall extends to the sea. Since its founding in 1982, Shanhaiguan Brewery has been technically transformed twice and expanded to the present scale with an annual capacity of 80,000 tons of beer and 9,000 tons of malt.

Task VI 请将下面一段宣传文字翻译成英文，注意编译方法的运用。

杭州市属 3 市 2 县境内，北有超山，西有天目山，溯钱塘江而上，有富阳鹳山、桐庐瑶琳仙境、桐君山和严子陵钓台，建德灵栖三洞，新安江“千岛湖”等名胜，形成一个以西湖为中心的广阔旅游区。

____

____

____

Task VII 请将下面一段宣传文字翻译成英文，注意编译方法的运用。

张家界的山，奇峰叠翠，拔地而起，高耸入云。悬崖峭壁上，生长着茂盛的灌木：舒卷飘逸的云雾缠绕在山腰，时而升腾，时而泻落；山顶上长满了苍劲的松树，参差错落，非常壮观。张家界山的形状千姿百态：有的似猛兽，有的像剑戟，有的像窈窕淑女，有的像关西大汉。

____

____

____

Task VIII 请将下面中国进出口商品交易会网站宣传文字翻译成英文。

中国进出口商品交易会，又称广交会，创办于 1957 年春，每年春秋两季在广州举办。广交会由商务部和广东省人民政府联合主办，中国对外贸易中心承办，是中国目前历史最长、规模最大、商品最全、采购商最多，且来源最广、成交效果最好、信誉最佳的综合性国际贸易盛会，被誉为中国第一展，中国外贸的晴雨表、风向标。

广交会是中国对外开放的窗口、缩影、标志，是国际贸易合作的重要平台。创办以来，广交会历经风雨、从未间断，已成功举办了 134 届，与全球 229 个国家和地区建立了贸易关系，累计出口成交约 1.5 万亿美元，累计到会和线上观展境外采购商超 1 000 万人，有力地促进了中国与世界各国各地区的贸易交流和友好往来。

党中央高度重视广交会，习近平主席于第 120、130 届两次向广交会致重要贺信。在致第 130 届广交会重要贺信中，习近平主席充分肯定了广交会创办 65 年来为服务国际贸易、促进内外联通、推动经济发展作出的重要贡献，赋予广交会崭新的历史使命，为广交会在新时代新征程指明了前进方向。未来，广交会将以习近平新时代中国特色社会主义思想为指导，全面贯彻落实党的二十大精神，深入贯彻落实习近平主席重要贺信精神，认真落实党中央、国务院决策部署，认真落实商务部、广东省工作要求，创新机制，丰富业态，拓展功能，努力打造成为中国全方位对外开放、促进国际贸易高质量发展、联通国内国际双循环的重要平台，更好服务国家战略、服务高水平对外开放、服务外贸创新发展、服务构建新发展格局。

____

____

PART SEVEN
学习参考

1. 万户网站建设网：http://www.wanhu.com.cn
2. 华为网站：https://www.huawei.com
3. 苹果网站：http://www.apple.com
4. 海尔集团网站：http://www.haier.com
5. 宋金亮. 制造业外贸营销网站建设［M］. 沈阳：沈阳出版社，2020.
6. 徐文娟. 企业网站国际传播及影响因素研究［M］. 北京：中国经济出版社，2022.

PART EIGHT
单元预告与实训任务

1. 下一单元我们将讲述广告的翻译，主要讲述广告的语言特点及翻译技巧。
2. 请搜集各种广告至少 10 条，最好是中英文双语广告，并思考其翻译技巧。

第七单元

广告翻译

Unit Seven Translating Advertisements

随着经济全球化和中国经济的腾飞，商务广告在商务活动和人民的经济生活中占据越来越重要的地位。广告对企业而言，是财源的保证；对国家而言，是经济发展的重要手段；对消费者而言，是获得产品信息和服务信息的途径。广告即“广而告之”之意，该词最早出现在 1645 年英国出版的杂志上。英语中的“advertise（广告）”一词来源于拉丁语的“advertere”，表示“唤起大众对某种事物的注意，并诱导一定的方向所使用的一种手段”。广告的作用在于说服顾客购买产品或服务，促进销售。广告无时不有，无处不在，正如英国经济学家布鲁斯·巴顿所说：“Good times, bad times, there will always be advertising. In good times people want advertising; in bad times they have to.（不管是繁荣时期还是萧条时期，广告总会存在。繁荣时，人们想做广告；萧条时，人们不得不做广告。）”但是，由于广告的设计与翻译关系到企业的声誉、企业的形象和企业的利润，无论是广告文案撰写还是广告翻译切不可随意而为，而必须深思熟虑。美国广告经营者戴维克·奥格尔维如是说：“The consumer isn't a moron; she is your wife. You insult her intelligence if you assume that a mere slogan and a few vapid adjectives will persuade her to buy anything.（消费者不是傻瓜；她是你的妻子。如果你认为仅凭几句口号，几个干巴巴的形容词就能诱使她掏腰包购买任何东西的话，那么你就亵渎了她的智慧。）”伴随着中国经济的发展，随着国家层面“中国制造 2025”战略的实施，“中国制造”声名鹊起，中国的产品走向世界，中国的产品广告也走出国门，走向世界。广告翻译势在必行，它成为翻译实践中的一项重大课题，具有重要的理论意义和现实意义。

教学目标

1. 了解广告的含义及其背景知识；
2. 了解广告的语言特点；
3. 掌握广告翻译中直译、意译和创译等翻译技巧；
4. 掌握商务英语中修辞格的翻译技巧。

PART ONE

认识广告与广告翻译

Task I 阅读下列广告并思考：广告是什么？广告由什么构成？广告有哪些种类？

1. 商务部广告

中国制造

Made in China

2. 麦当劳

i'm lovin' it

我 就 喜 欢

3. Gree, master the core technology. (Gree)
4. 滴滴情深自来水，请你拭去我的泪。（节水公益广告）
5. Have you driven a Ford…lately? (Ford Automobile)
6. Huawei—It's Not Only The Top 500 In World. (华为)

Task II 通过分析上述广告及日常生活中的其他广告，讨论广告的语言特征及其功能。

美国营销协会定义委员会（The Committee on Definitions of the American Marketing Association）对广告所做的定义是：Advertising is the non-personal communication of information usually paid for and usually persuasive in nature about products, services or ideas by identified sponsors through various media.（广告是由特定的广告主通常以付费方式，通过各种媒体介绍和推广其产品、服务或观念的具有说服性功能的公众信息交流活动。）《辞海》（李波阳，2005：88）对广告的定义是：广告是通过媒体向公众介绍商品、劳务和企业信息等的一种宣传方式，一般指商业广告。广义而言，凡是向公众传播社会人事动态、文化娱乐、宣传观念的都属于广告范畴。通俗地讲，广告主要是通过广播，电视，报纸以及新媒体等媒介宣传企业、产品、服务和公共事务的具有说服性和鼓动性的商业行为。广告往往由广告词、数字、图片、影像、动画和声音等构成。本单元讲述的广告翻译主要是广告词的翻译。

广告与日常生活息息相关，哪里有人哪里就有广告。它广泛存在于电视、电影、网络、广播之中，商场、马路、电梯、旅游景点等地也处处可见各种广告，可谓无处不在。根据不同的角度和层次，广告的分类也不同。根据宣传目的，可分为商业广告（Commercial Advertising）和公益广告（Public Welfare Advertising）；根据目标顾客群，可分为消费者广告（Consumer Advertising）和企业广告（Business Advertising）；根据覆盖地域，可分为国际广告（International Advertising）、国内广告（National Advertising）、区域广告（Regional Advertising）和地方广告（Local Advertising）；根据广告媒介，可分为印刷广告（Printing Advertising）、电子广告（Electric Advertising）和网络广告（Network Advertising）；根据广告内容，可分为产品广告（Product Advertising）和非产品广告（Non-product Advertising），非产品广告则包括劳务广告（Service Advertising）、招聘广告（Employment Advertising）、旅游广告（Tourism Advertising）和征婚广告（Dating Advertising）等。

人们普遍认为，广告的功能就是说服顾客购买企业的产品或服务。现代广告学将广告的功能归纳为提供信息（Information）、争取顾客（Persuasion）、维持需求（Maintenance of Demand）、扩大市场（Creating Mass Markets）以及确保质量（Quality）等五大功能（刘宓庆，2007：325）。所有这些功能体现了广告为顾客提供服务的同时，主要是为了企业的利益服务，所以人们常常认为广告具有一定的功利性。

为了实现广告的说服性功能，广告设计必须以客户为中心，服从顾客的心理需求和现实需求。从文化语境角度看，广告的社会目的和功能一般遵循 E. S. Lewis 提出的 AIDA 原则：即 Attention（引起注意），Interest（发生兴趣），Desire（产生欲望）和 Action（付诸行动）（孙亮、翟年祥，1997：264）。这四条原则针对顾客而言，具有一定的先后顺序，广告必须首先引起注意才能让受众产生兴趣，继而产生欲望并最终实现付诸行动的目的。

为了实现广告的功能，广告往往具有以下特征：（1）简洁性（Brief）：通常情况下，广告都是三言两语，比如：“Just do it”。因为广告必须利于消费者记忆。在 2010 年南非世界杯赛场上，索尼公司的广告词为“Make •Believe”，它是“Believe that anything you can imagine, you can make real.（创新源于好奇，梦想成就未来）”中的两个关键词，使人过目不忘，记忆深刻。（2）创新性（Innovative）：广告创新的目的是吸引眼球，留住顾客，比如：“今年过节不收礼，收礼还收脑白金”看似有些矛盾，实际上间接标榜自己的产品与众不同，该广告一定为企业赢得了不少利润。（3）审美性（Aesthetic）：广告语言具有时代性和审美性，给人以美的感受，包括语音美、语义美、意境美等，如 Lady Stetson 香水的广告“Her smile could beat up a nation. Her fragrance captured a nation.（迷魂牵魂笑貌，倾国倾城芳香。/笑言迷百姓，香气醉万家。）”，无论是原文还是这两种译文，都让读者产生一种美的享受。（4）说服性（Persuasive）：广告的最终目的就是说服消费者购买该产品或服务，如某刀片的广告“Look sharp! Feel sharp! Be sharp!（好眼光！好锋利！好帅气！）”通过反复强调其产品的“锋利”效果，读了此广告，令人产生不买都想买的感觉。

PART TWO
热身练习

Task I 请搜集中英文双语广告至少 10 条，并分析其翻译技巧。

Task II 请为下列英文选择适当的翻译，并将其编号填入后面的括号中。

1. Take the TOSHIBA, take the world. (TOSHIBA) (　　)
2. Born to shine. (LG Mobile Phone) (　　)
3. Think different. (APPLE) (　　)
4. Focus on life. (Olympus) (　　)
5. A diamond lasts forever. (De Bierres) (　　)
6. Good teeth, good health. (Colgate) (　　)
7. I'm More satisfied. (More) (　　)
8. Fresh-up with Seven-up. (Seven-up) (　　)
9. Take time to indulge. (Nestle Ice-cream) (　　)
10. Good to the last drop. (Maxwell) (　　)

A. 牙齿好，身体就好。（高露洁牙膏）
B. 君饮“七喜”，提神醒脑。（七喜）
C. 尽情享受吧！（雀巢冰激凌）
D. 拥有东芝，拥有世界。（东芝电器）
E. 滴滴香浓，意犹未尽。（麦斯威尔咖啡）
F. 摩尔上口，感觉更优。（摩尔香烟）
G. 钻石恒久远，一颗永流传。（戴比尔斯）
H. 瞄准生活。（奥林巴斯）
I. 我本闪耀！（LG 手机）
J. 苹果电脑，不同凡“想”。（苹果电脑）

Task III 分析上述广告所使用的修辞手法，并具体说明修辞的种类。

PART THREE
广告翻译技巧

Task I 阅读下列广告并归纳广告语言的词汇特征：哪种词类最为常见，是名词还是动词？广告的词汇特征除词类分析外，还可以从哪些方面分析其语言特征？

1. Go well, use Shell. (Shell)
2. Obey your thirst. (Pepsi)

3. We lead. Others copy. (Ricoh)
4. Feast your eyes. (Pond's Cucumber Eye Treatment)
5. Intelligence everywhere. (Motorola)
6. I chocolate you. (LG Mobile Phone)

____

7. 喝孔府宴酒，做天下文章。（孔府宴酒）
8. 坐红旗车，走中国路。（红旗轿车）
9. 喝汇源果汁，走健康之路。（汇源果汁）
10. 好空调，格力造。（格力空调）

____

11. Welcome to the World Wide Wow. (AOL—America Online)
12. We know eggsactly how to sell eggs. (Egg Advertisement)
13. Drinka Pinta Milka Day. (Milk Advertisement)
14. 趁早下“斑”，请勿“痘”留。（化妆品广告）
15. 只要青春不要痘——莎拉娜美容霜。（化妆品广告）
16. 康师傅绿茶，FUN 飞好心情。（康师傅）
17. 快乐起 5，精彩连城。（广州地铁 5 号线）
18. 亚运“城熟”了。（保利公馆房地产）

____

Task II 阅读下列广告，每四条广告为一组，请归纳广告的句法特征。

1. Poetry in motion, dancing close to me. (Toyota)
2. The relentless pursuit of perfection. (Lexus)
3. Intel Inside. (Intel Pentium)
4. 东西南北中，好酒在张弓。（张弓酒）

____

5. Turn it on! (Puma)
6. Obey your thirst. (Sprite)
7. Let's make things better. (Philips)
8. 穿金猴皮鞋，走金光大道。（金猴皮鞋）

____

9. Come to where the flavor is. Marlboro Country. (Marlboro)
10. I never knew you had dandruff. (Head & Shoulders)
11. There is only something you cannot imagine, there is nothing you cannot do. (Li Ning)
12. 人生是一场旅行，不必在乎目的地，在乎的是沿途的风景，以及看风景时的心情，让心灵去旅行！（杭州利群公司）

____

13. Do you love anyone enough to give them your last Rolo? (Rolo Confectionery)

14. Want him to be more of a man? Try being more of a woman! (Coty Perfumes)
15. —What will tomorrow bring?
—Ideas that defy gravity. (Boeing)
16. 手机里的人已坐在对面，你怎么还盯着手机看？（江小白）

____

17. Zoom Zoom Zoom. (Mazda)
18. Ford, safe, quick and with fun, a work of art. (Ford)
19. Snap, Crackle, Pop. (Kellogg's Rice Krispies)
20. You'll enjoy relaxed sunny days. Warm, crystal clear lagoons. Cool, green foliage. Waterfalls. Flowers. Exotic scents. Bright blue skies. Secluded beaches. Graceful palms. Breathtaking sunsets. Soft evening breeze. And food that simply outstanding.（旅游广告）

____

Task III 为了达到说服消费者购买产品或服务的目的，广告语往往采用各种修辞手法，使广告语言形象生动、易于记忆。这些修辞手法包括明喻、暗喻、夸张、对偶、排比等，请列出下列广告语使用了哪些修辞手法。

1. Unlike me, my Rolex never needs a rest. (Rolex) (　　　　)
2. She's the nimblest girl around. Nimble is the way she goes. Nimble is the bread she eats. Light, Delicious, Nimble. (Nimble Bread) (　　　　)
3. A contemporary classic. A timeless timepiece. (Watch Advertisement) (　　　　)
4. Sea, sun, sand, seclusion and Spain! (Spain Tourism Advertisement) (　　　　)
5. East is east and west is west. But Brown's meat is best. (Meat Advertisement) (　　　　)
6. We take no pride in prejudice. (*The Times*) (　　　　)
7. Born in Germany. Bred in Japan. Honored in France. Talk about an international upbringing. (MAZDA Motor Corporation) (　　　　)
8. It keeps going, and going, and going...（Energizer Batteries） (　　　　)
9. Where there is a mountain, there is a road. Where there is a road, there is a Toyota. (Toyota) (　　　　)
10. If people keep telling you to quit smoking cigarettes, don't listen. They're probably trying to trick you into longevity. (Public Welfare Advertisement) (　　　　)
11. We've hidden a garden full of vegetables where you'd never expect. In a pie. (Food Advertisement) (　　　　)

Task IV 翻译下列广告语，归纳翻译技巧：哪些采用直译法，哪些采用意译法？

1. Impossible made possible. (Cannon)

____

2. Give a Timex to all, and to all a good time. (Timex)

____

3. Leave "Managing Money" alone, and money manages to leave you alone. (*Money Weekly*)

______

4. For me, the past is black and white, but the future is always color. (Hennessy)

______

5. Poetry in motion, dancing close to me. (Toyota)

______

6. 只有想不到，没有做不到。（李宁）

______

7. 沟通从心开始。（中国移动）

______

8. 皮张之厚，无以复加；利润之薄，无以复减。（上海鹤鸣皮鞋）

______

9. 药材好，药才好。（仲景六味地黄丸）

______

10. 汰渍到，污渍逃。（汰渍洗衣粉）

______

11. The Who, What, When, Where and Y of Basketball Shoes.（康瓦士篮球鞋）

______

12. Can't beat the real thing. (Coca-Cola）

______

13. For the Road Ahead. (Honda)

______

14. 世界首例，中国一绝，天然椰子汁。（椰树椰汁）

______

15. "美的"家电，美的全面，美的彻底。（美的电器）

______

16. 绿色之光，点亮未来。（飞利浦）

______

Task V　翻译下列广告，从语义增减的角度分析翻译技巧。

1. Intelligence everywhere. (Motorola)

______

2. Every time a good time. (McDonald's)

______

3. A diamond lasts forever. (De Bierres)

______

4. Good to the last drop. (Maxwell)

______

5. Exclusively Fine Champagne Cognac. (Remy Martin XO)

____

6. 你不理财，财不理你。(《理财周刊》)

____

7. 不同的肤色，共同的选择。(青岛啤酒)

____

8. 状元红酒源于唐宋，盛于明清，系中国古老名酒。(状元红)

____

9. 广州是我家，清洁靠大家。(公益广告)

____

Task VI　翻译下列广告，从词类转换角度分析翻译技巧。

1. I Chocolate you. (LG Mobile Phone)

____

2. Poetry in motion, dancing close to me. (Toyota)

____

3. The relentless pursuit of perfection. (Lexus)

____

4. Intel Inside. (Intel Pentium)

____

5. Communication unlimited. (Motorola)

____

6. No business too small, no problem too big. (IBM)

____

Task VII　翻译下列广告，分析翻译技巧。

1. A Mars a day keeps you work, rest and play. (Mars Candy Bars)

____

2. Not all cars are created equal. (Mitsubishi)

____

3. Where there is a way, there is a Toyota. (Toyota)

____

4. 千家万家，不如梦迪一家。(梦迪旅馆)

____

5. 条条道路通罗马，款款百羚进万家。(百羚餐具)

____

6. 绿丹兰——爱您一辈子。(绿丹兰系列化妆品)

____

Task VIII　阅读下列广告及其翻译，你认为译文采用的是直译、意译还是仿译？如果都不是，那么译者采用了什么翻译方法？

1. 原文：A great way to fly! (Singapore Airlines)
   译文：新加坡航空，飞跃万里，超越一切！
2. 原文：It happens at the Hilton! (Hilton)
   译文：希尔顿酒店有求必应！（希尔顿酒店）
3. 原文：It's all within your reach! (AT&T)
   译文：联络世界，触及未来！（美国电讯电报公司）
4. 原文：The best a man can get! (Gillette)
   译文：给你最爽快的早餐！（吉列剃须刀）
5. 原文：Connecting people. (Nokia)
   译文：科技以人为本。（诺基亚）

Task IX　翻译下列广告，讨论使用的翻译技巧。

1. CBD 五千米半径内，最后一个别墅区？（房地产广告）

   ____

2. 所有顾客凭本券享受打折优惠，购买 50 瓶依云矿泉水可享七折优惠。

   ____

3. 夏威夷岛是世界上最美丽的地方之一。这里天气晴朗，气温整年在 60～90 华氏度之间变化。夏天稍暖，冬天稍凉，但对于某些人来说每天都是晒太阳的好日子。（旅游广告）

   ____

PART FOUR

讨论：通过上述翻译任务，你认为广告翻译还可以采用哪些策略？广告翻译需要注意哪些事项？

I. 广告翻译小结

本单元介绍了广告的语言特征并通过不同的翻译任务介绍了广告翻译技巧。广告翻译必须注意语言的简洁性、说服性和可读性。从传统的翻译路径看，可以采用直译法和意译法，对于那些无法采用直译法或者意译法的广告语，可以采用仿译法或者创译法。由于英语中使用名词或者名词短语偏多，而汉语中使用动词或者动词短语偏多，广告翻译中也常常采用词类转换法。从句法的角度看，可以采用分译法或者合译法，比如：

[例 1] 原文：一代“王朝酒”，三次获金牌。（“王朝”牌葡萄酒）
　　　译文：Three gold medals in one Dynasty. (Dynasty Wine)

汉语原文欲给消费者传递的重要信息是王朝酒三次获得了金牌。译文打破原文格局，从全新角度赋予商品内涵，利用“Dynasty”一语双关，不仅指“王朝”酒的品牌，也含有“朝代”的意思。王朝酒获三次金牌的事实，可以彻头彻尾地征服消费者。

需要特别指出的是，广告多种多样，我们重点讨论了广告口号的翻译，实际上还有其他各种广告，同样需要采用直译法、意译法、增译法等技巧进行翻译。

II. 广告翻译中的文化因素

由于生活环境、生活习惯等方面的差异，中国人与西方人在价值观念、思维方式等方面存在较大的差异。广告翻译同样需要关注文化差异及其对广告翻译的影响。

在价值观念上，西方人重个人主义（注意个人主义与自私自利有本质区别），强调个人品位和个性表现，而中国人崇尚集体主义，所以像“大家好才是真的好（广州好迪）”的广告直译就无法收到良好的广告效果。此时，我们可以套用“Give a Timex to all, and to all a good time”，把它翻译成“Give a Houdy to all, and to all a great time.”这样翻译，可以收到事半功倍的效果。

不同文化背景的读者对相同的事物接受程度具有差异性，为了达到广告的促销目的，广告翻译必须迎合读者的期待，引起读者的共鸣。如果遇到难以符合读者已有的文化框架，就有必要更换原文的意象或者信息，以避免引起文化休克现象。例如：

［例 2］原文：衣食住行，有龙则灵。（建设银行龙卡）

译文：Your everyday life is very busy. Our *Long* Card can make it easy.（丁衡祁，2004）

本广告原文仿拟了中国唐朝著名诗人刘禹锡《陋室铭》中的名句：“山不在高，有仙则名；水不在深，有龙则灵。”该广告对中国人而言，耳熟能详，妇孺皆知，饱含中国历史文化信息，一方面让读者产生丰富的互文性联想，可是在译语中难以重现其深刻的内涵；另一方面，“龙”本身具有的象征意义在中西文化中大相径庭。在中国人的心目中，“龙”是神圣的象征，是皇权的象征，也是中华民族凝聚力的标志。但是，在西方“龙”与“dragon”等同；而后者在西方人眼中指张牙舞爪的动物，是“魔鬼和罪恶”的象征。把“龙卡”翻译成“Long Card”，而且将“*Long*”斜体，恰到好处，符合读者的接受心理，可以收到预期的广告效果。

［例 3］原文：团结湖北京烤鸭店为全聚德挂炉烤鸭。为保证宾客品尝精美风味，全部现吃现烤。精选北京白鸭，以果木挂炉烧烤，只需 40 分钟就能品尝到为您特别烤制的色泽枣红、香酥嫩脆、浓香四溢的正宗烤鸭。

译文：Tuanjiehu Beijing Roast Duck Restaurant uses only the finest Beijing Ducks which are only roasted after you place your order. Preparation takes 40 minutes after which we will serve you with a delicious, golden red Beijing Duck with crunchy skin. (陈小慰，2000)

上述北京烤鸭的有关宣传广告中，有些词汇如“挂炉烤鸭”“果木挂炉烧烤”等为专业词汇，即使是中国消费者也未必了解，更何况是外国人，所以翻译时需要考虑到消费者的文化背景及接受程度，采用省译法，把广告中的如“精选北京白鸭”“色泽枣红”“浓香四溢”等吸引消费者的关键信息翻译出来，达到引起消费者兴趣和食欲的目的即可。

［例 4］原文：Give up my Pepsi? Don’t even think about it. BE YOUNG，HAVE FUN，DRINK PEPSI.

译文：新事可乐，旧事可乐，小事可乐，大事可乐，祝您百事可乐。

英文广告体现青春、动感、活力、欢快的情境，这正是西方人追求的境界，让人联想到购买此产品便能体验到产品带来的愉悦心情；原文没有重复，也不啰嗦。但是在中国，“Pepsi”的广告语言反映了中国消费者事事通顺，万事如意的心理需求，尤其是广告的推出选在春节这一传统佳节之际，更加顺应了消费者喜欢讨吉利的心理。汉语采用了增译技巧，利用排比修辞手法，节奏匀称，朗朗上口。

［例 5］原文：酱香突出，幽雅细腻，酒体醇厚，回味悠长，空杯留香持久，历届国家名酒评比之冠，尊为国酒。（茅台酒）

译文：Carefully Brewed

Pure and Mellow

With a Long-Lasting Aroma (*China Pictorial*，Oct. 2002)

中国的酒文化可谓源远流长，自东汉时期始，直到现在，已泱泱绵延两千余年。两千年来，酒，始终在中国文化发展史上扮演着重要的角色，在许多场合都占有着不可替代的地位。人们对酒的研究从未间断，形成了中国独特的酒文化。所以，即使费了九牛二虎之力把原文翻译成英语，恐怕也难以让西方人对中国酒文化有所“品尝”，于是采用归化译法，把关键信息传递给消费者，反而会取得事半功倍的效果。

PART FIVE

译技点津：商务翻译技巧之广告修辞格的翻译

广告语言特点要求广告设计者或者广告撰稿人必须灵活应用多种修辞手法，使广告生动活泼、跃然纸上。因此，广告翻译就必须考虑修辞在翻译中的转换，以期在目的语中产生相近或类似的修辞效果。翻译广告中的修辞可以采用以下译法：

I. 直译法

直译法（Literal Translation）：有些修辞手法在中文和英文中相通或者近似，可以直接移植，采用直译法。

［例 1］原文：像母亲的手一样柔软。（某童鞋）

译文：As soft as mother’s hand.

［例 2］原文：To take BA or not to take BA? What a silly question! (British Airways)

译文：英航，坐还是不坐，那是个愚蠢的问题！（英国航空公司）

［例 3］原文：We are proud of the birthplaces of our children, the grapes of Almaden. (Almaden Wine)

译文：我们为孩子的出生地而自豪，Almaden 葡萄酒。

例 1 中使用了明喻，语言简单朴实，直接翻译即可。例 2 仿拟了莎士比亚名剧《哈姆雷特》中主人公哈姆雷特的个人独白，“To be or not to be, that is the question”。这句经典台词的深刻意义和内涵在广告中同样发挥得淋漓尽致，给人以丰富的互文性联想的同时，也具有强大的鼓动力和经典的文化价值，让人自然而然想到，无须思考，当然要毫不犹豫地选择英国航空公司出行。例 3 采用了比喻修辞格，把葡萄酒比喻成自己的孩子，产生亲情，凝聚感情，甚至共享爱情的结晶，拉近了产品与消费者的距离。

II. 意译法

意译法（Free Translation）：许多广告使用的修辞手法在一种语言中恰如其分，而直译为另一种语言时，需要根据意义进行适当的调整；另外，由于语言的差异，比如押韵等修辞手法难以在目的语中实现。因此，广告修辞格在直译行不通的情况下，就可以采用“取其意，去其形”的意译法。

［例 4］原文：岁月的小皱纹不知不觉地游走了。（美加净化妆品）

译文：Maxam erases years off from your skin. (Maxam Cosmetics)

［例 5］原文：You're better off under the Umbrella.（某保险公司）

试译：拥有保险，倍感安全。

［例 6］原文：Health, Humour & Happiness, gifts we'd love to give.（《星期六晚报》）

试译：健康、幽默和幸福，是我们给您的礼物。

例 4 采用拟人修辞手法，如果直译为“The wrinkles swim away”既不符合英语表达习惯，也缺少了广告的主角“美加净”，根本起不到广告宣传的作用。所以，译文“Maxam erases years off from your skin”直接宣传了该产品的功效，起到促销产品的作用。例 5 采用了暗喻修辞手法，保险公司自喻为“Umbrella”，表示“雨天防湿”的意思，由于是暗喻修辞手法，无法直接翻译成“伞下更好”，所以突出保险作用，当然倍感安全，符合消费者的消费心理。例 6 采用了头韵修辞手法，显然在汉语中无法借用相同的修辞手法，故只能译其“意”，而舍其“形”。

III. 套译法

套译法（Loan Translation）：有些广告本身采用了仿拟修辞手法，译者可以“将计就计”，采用套译法；有些广告直译、意译难度很大或不符合目的语的表达方式，也可以采用套译法。

［例 7］原文：有目共赏——上海牌电视。

译文：Shanghai TV—seeing is believing.

［例 8］原文：百闻不如一尝。（浙江省粮油食品进出口公司）

译文：Tasting is believing.

［例 9］原文：东西南北中，好酒在张弓。（张弓酒）

译文：East or west, Zhanggong is the best.

［例 10］原文：要想体力好，常饮健力宝。（健力宝）

译文：A Jianlibao a day keeps the doctor away.

例 7“有目共赏”本身就仿拟了成语“有目共睹”，引申意义为“眼见为实”，所以干脆直接套用英语谚语“Seeing is believing”。例 8 仿拟汉语成语“百闻不如一见”，由于英语中也有类似的说法，直接套用英语谚语“Seeing is believing”。例 9、例 10 采用了押韵的修辞手法，直译行不通，于是分别翻译成“East or west, Zhanggong is the best”和“A Jianlibao a day keeps the doctor away”，分别套用英语习语“East or west, home is best”和“An apple a day keeps the doctor away”，英语接受者耳熟能详，联想丰富，自然可以收到良好的广告效果。

［例 11］原文：随身携带，有备无患；随身携带，有惊无险。（速效救心丸）

译文：A Friend in need is a friend indeed!

这则广告宣传的是治疗心脏病的一种名叫“速效救心丸”（Quick Results Heart-Save Pill）的药物。该汉语广告运用了反复和排比的修辞手法，不仅突出了药品的优越品质和卓越功效，而且使全文读来抑扬顿挫。如果按字面意义直译会很不好处理，而这里给出的广告英译直接引用了一句英文谚语，看似几乎完全偏离了原文，实际却达到了功能上的等值，“随身携带，有备无患”的药品与“需要他时他就出现的朋友”一样，那真是“患难见真情”，同样拉近了产品与消费者的距离。当然，这里也可以套译为“A medicine in need is a medicine indeed”。

IV. 增译法

增译法（Amplification）：双关是某个词或者短语表示两层意思，有“一石二鸟”之功效，达到诙谐幽默的广告效果。翻译时，多数时候无法将原语的双关通过翻译移植到目的语中，此时，需要采用增译法，表达原文的双重含义。现举例说明如下：

［例 12］原文：The unique spirit of Canada.

　　　　译文：别具风味的加拿大酒，独具一格的加拿大民族精神。

［例 13］原文：A trust will take care of a family. (Trust Company Advertisement)

　　　　译文：家庭需要信任，我们照顾您家。

例 12 中，“spirit”既表示“酒”，也表示“精神”的意思，“unique”与酒搭配时译作“别具风味”，而与精神搭配时，译作“独特”，选择恰当的搭配意义也非常重要，因此把双关含义都翻译出来才能再现原文含义。例 13 为信托公司的广告，“trust”既表示“信任”，也表示“信托行业”，翻译时把两种含义明晰化，更能打动消费者。可见，双关修辞的翻译，不能偏废，必须两种含义同时翻译，才能忠实地传递原文意义。

综上所述，广告中的修辞格翻译需要灵活处理，在忠实或基本忠实于原文意义的情况下，可以采用直译法、意译法、套译法或增译法。

PART SIX

广告翻译实践

Task I　根据下列广告的译文，填写广告原文。

1. The choice is yours, the_______ is ours. (Ford)
   你选择，我荣耀。（福特）
2. Minolta, finest to put you_______. (Minolta)
   第一流的美能达，第一流的你。（美能达）
3. _______on life. (Olympus)
   瞄准生活。（奥林巴斯）
4. The world ________ with *Reader's Digest*. (*Digest*)
   《读者文摘》，为世人带来欢笑。（《读者文摘》）
5. Hand in hand, future in your _______. (Taiping Life Insurance)
   伴您同行，齐握未来。（太平人寿）

6. Take time to________. (Nestle Ice-cream)
   尽情享受吧！（雀巢冰激凌）
7. Any________and size to Europe. (Federal Express)
   不同大小、各种形状，火速直飞欧洲。（联邦快递）
8. Be ________to yourself, fly Emirates. (Emirates Airline)
   珍爱自己，纵横万里。（阿联酋航空公司）

Task II 请在括号中填写下列广告所使用的修辞格，并将下列广告翻译成汉语。

1. Asia Garden Hotel—A Home Away From Home! (Asia Garden Hotel) (　　　)
   ____
2. For the modern Marco Polo. (Cathay Pacific Airlines) (　　　)
   ____
3. Big thrills, small bills. (Budget Car Leasing Center) (　　　)
   ____
4. A day without orange juice is like a day without sunshine. (Florida Citrus Commission) (　　　)
   ____
5. The driver is safer when the road is dry;
   The road is safer when the driver is dry. (Public Welfare Advertisement) (　　　)
   ____
6. It's a matter of pride. Proud tradition. Proud heritage. Proud taste. (L&M cigarette) (　　　)
   ____
7. Pity the pickpockets. (Clothes Advertisement) (　　　)
   ____
8. If it wasn't in VOGUE, it wasn't in vogue. (Vogue Fashion) (　　　)
   ____
9. Wash the big city right out of your hair. (Shampoo Advertisement) (　　　)
   ____

Task III 请为《时代杂志》翻译下列广告。

1. There's never been a better *Time*.
   ____
2. Time Inc. says *Life* is coming back, and if *Life* returns, can *Look* be far behind?
   ____
3. Make Time For *Time*.
   ____

4. The auto industry calls it “Luxury”. ______
The liquor industry calls it “Premium”. ______
The airline industry calls it “First Class”. ______
The hotel industry calls it “Five Star”. ______
The securities industry calls it “Blue Chip”. ______
In the communication industry ______
It is called “TIME”. ______

Task IV　把下列英语广告翻译成汉语。

1. Take TOSHIBA, take the world. (TOSHIBA)

______

2. If you drive, don’t drink; if you drink, don’t drive. (Public Welfare Advertisement)

______

3. Every kid should have an apple after school. (Apple PC)

______

4. The only thing we didn’t improve was the road. (Toyota)

______

5. The most unforgettable women in the world wear Revlon. (Revlon)

______

6. A world of comfort (Japan Airlines)

______

7. M&Ms melt in your mouth, not in your hand. (M&Ms)

______

8. Wherever you are. Whatever you do. The Allianz Group is always on your side. (Allianz Group)

______

9. We are having problems with guests who won’t leave. (Hotel Advertisement)

______

Task V　运用所学的翻译技巧，将下列广告翻译成英文。

1. 蚊子，杀杀杀。（某蚊香广告） ______
2. 谁跑在最后，谁笑得最好。（某轮胎广告） ______
3. 城乡路万千，路路有航天。（航天牌汽车） ______
4. 有了南方，就有了办法。（南方科技咨询公司） ______
5. 要想皮肤好，早晚用“大宝”。（大宝） ______
6. 东奔西走，要喝宋河好酒。（宋河酒） ______
7. 安全驾驶——救人即救己。（公益广告） ______
8. 第一流产品，为足下争光。（上海鞋油） ______

Task VI 阅读下列广告及其翻译，讨论翻译技巧。

1. 原文：Beyond your imagination. (Korean Air)
   译文：意想不到的天空。（大韩航空）
2. 原文：Elegance is an attitude. (Longines)
   译文：优雅态度，真我性格。（浪琴表）
3. 原文：Taking the lead in a Digital World. (Samsung)
   译文：领先数码，超越永恒。（三星）
4. 原文：Your Future is Our Future. (HSBC)
   译文：与您并肩，迈向明天。（汇丰银行）
5. 原文：Prepare to want one. (Hyundai)
   译文：众望所归，翘首以待。（现代汽车）
6. 原文：DHL worldwide express: the Pulse of Business. (DHL)
   译文：商业命脉，随我而动。（敦豪快递）

Task VII 请翻译下列招聘广告。

SIRONA is a global leading dental equipment manufacturer with headquarter in Bensheim, Germany. Sirona Dental Systems (Foshan) Co., Ltd. is now looking for high caliber talents to fill the following positions.

Product Manager: 5 years or above experience in market need research and analysis, product positioning and pricing, competitor analysis and product concept design.

Brand Manager: 4 years or above experience in brand management, good presentation skills.

Sales Controller: 5 years or above experience in finance management/controlling, strong knowledge in finance analysis and reporting. With auditing experience an advantage.

Key Account Manager: 5 years or above sales experience in channel and key account management in dental or related product, with customer base an advantage. (Less experienced candidate would be considered for Sales Representative position.)

QA Supervisor: 8 years or above working experience, in which 3 years or above mechatronic product quality monitoring and analysis experience, good knowledge in testing and QA process improvement.

Candidates are required to speak workable English to apply for the above positions.

PART SEVEN 学习参考

1. 张国才. 图文英语广告文案［M］. 厦门：厦门大学出版社，2023.
2. 彭朝忠. 广告翻译与翻译中的广告视野［M］. 北京：化学工业出版社，2020.
3. 吕和发，李巍. 应用创意翻译研究［M］. 北京：国防工业出版社，2014.
4. 李克兴. 广告翻译理论与实践［M］. 北京：北京大学出版社，2010.
5. 华英，马永堂. 实用英汉广告词汇［M］. 北京：外文出版社，1996.
6. 靳涵身. 诗型广告翻译研究［M］. 成都：四川大学出版社，2005.
7. 石裕晶，陈寅涛. 汉英·英汉广告写作词典［M］. 上海：复旦大学出版社，2000.

PART EIGHT 单元预告与实训任务

1. 下一单元我们将讲述产品介绍的翻译。
2. 请你搜集三种以上产品介绍及其翻译，评价其翻译并思考翻译技巧。

第八单元

产品介绍翻译

Unit Eight　Translating Product Descriptions

据统计，中国有 220 种主要工业产品和 100 多种消费品的产量位居世界第一。中国已成为名副其实的世界“制造大国”，制造业成为中国国民经济的支柱，中国正从“制造大国”向“制造强国”转变。2021 年 3 月 2 日，工信部发布了相关数据。数据显示，2020 年，我国工业增加值达到了 31.31 万亿元，是世界最大的制造国，此前我国已经连续 10 年蝉联全球第一。可以说，世界的每一个角落都有中国制造的产品，许多中国人到国外购买纪念品，回来仔细一看发现“Made in China（中国制造）”。中国的产品已经打入国际市场，参与国际竞争。然而，随着世界经济格局的变化，企业之间的竞争日趋白热化，中国的产品要在世界经济竞争舞台立于不败之地，在提高科技含量和产品质量的同时，还必须关注产品介绍，尤其是产品介绍的翻译。因为产品介绍某种程度上起到广告宣传和促销的作用，对扩大产品的影响和销路起至关重要的作用。粗制滥造的产品介绍翻译会误导消费者，即使是名牌产品也可能被误认为是假冒产品。可见，产品介绍翻译质量的高低同产品销售量的高低不无关系。因此，本单元主要讲述产品介绍的翻译技巧。

教学目标

1. 了解产品介绍的含义及其背景知识；
2. 了解产品介绍的语言特点；
3. 掌握产品介绍的翻译技巧；
4. 掌握商务翻译中的增译法和减译法。

PART ONE
了解产品介绍及产品介绍的翻译

Task I 请将课前收集的三种产品介绍与同学分享，并探讨目前产品介绍及其翻译的现状和你的看法。

Task II 阅读下列产品介绍并思考：什么是产品介绍？产品介绍由什么构成？产品介绍的目的是什么？

1. 英文：Johnson's Baby Soothing Natural Shampoo

Combines the trusted care and gentleness of Johnson's with the healing powers of nature. JOHNSON'S SOOTHING NATURALS™ Nourishing Shampoo is made with a unique blend of Vitamin E, olive leaf extract and skin essential minerals. This unique shampoo gently cleanses baby's hair and helps to soothe and moisturize dry skin on the scalp to leave it feeling healthy and soft from the very first use.

Johnson's Baby Soothing Naturals™ Nourishing Shampoo is specially developed with our unique NO More Tears formula proven to be as mild to the eyes as pure water, so you can trust it for everyday use.

中文：强生婴儿滋养洗发露

萃取天然精华，舒缓头部皮肤

强生婴儿天然舒润™滋养洗发露，蕴含维生素E、天然橄榄叶萃取精华，以及皮肤所必需的多种矿物质，能够温和清洁宝宝的头发，并且能够有效地舒缓和滋润宝宝干燥的头部皮肤，让宝宝拥有健康的头部皮肤和柔软顺滑的头发。

强生婴儿天然舒润™系列特有无泪配方，如清水般温和，即使新生儿也能放心使用。

2. 索尼VAIO Y21系列说明书（摘录）

轻薄外形，上乘质感

如果您正在寻觅一台小型笔记本电脑以便随身携带，但又不想放弃舒适的屏幕尺寸，13.3寸的VAIO Y21系列正是为您度身定做的移动解决方案。VAIO Y21系列在装载了标配电池时仅重约1.79千克，其机身较薄处仅约23.7毫米，同时又不失外形的舒展开阔。这取决于标志性的削边设计和整机的良好材质，为您带来上乘的移动生活。

电力充足，经久耐用

移动性能出色的VAIO Y21系列有着卓越的电池续航能力，标配电池的待机时间长约4小时，外出差旅或者去图书馆、咖啡厅带上VAIO Y21系列，可以让您从容应对。

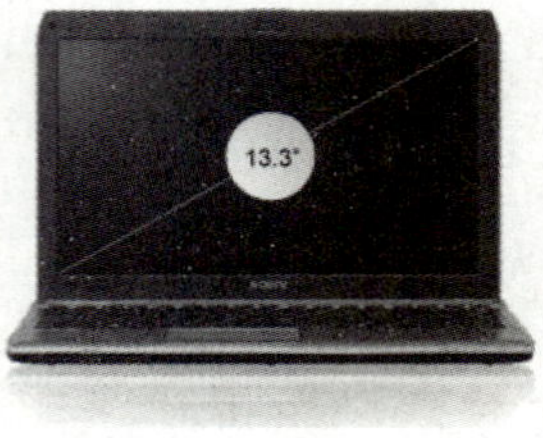

思愈轻 行致远

绿色，感悟新生力量与张扬的个性。

粉色，时尚潮流中绽放耀眼的光芒。

蓝色，彰显大海的气魄与骄傲的灵魂。

黑色，诠释成熟的内敛和不羁的品位。

英特尔新一代处理器

VAIO Y21 系列采用英特尔酷睿 i3-330UM 处理器以及基于 32 纳米技术的英特尔酷睿 2 双核处理器，让您轻松应对各种日常需求。

产品，就传统意义而言，是指具有某种形状并具有某种实际用途的物质产品。当今的产品概念已经有所延伸，从有形的物质产品延伸到无形的服务产品、理财产品等。随着市场竞争日趋激烈，企业不仅重视产品的实用性，也重视产品的非功能性因素，如款式、包装、说明、售后服务等。如今，这些都是吸引消费者的重要因素。产品的层次也从传统意义上的核心产品延伸到形式产品和延伸产品。第一层次为核心产品，是指产品能给顾客提供的基本效用和功能；第二层次为形式产品，是核心产品所展示的外部特征，主要包括款式、质量、品牌、包装等；第三层次为延伸产品，是指顾客因购买产品所得到的全部附加服务与利益，如保证、咨询、送货、安装、调试、维修、清洁等。产品介绍随着产品概念和层次的延伸而拓展。从上述产品介绍可以看出，产品介绍囊括了各种层次产品的介绍。

所谓产品介绍是指企业向消费者简单明了地描述产品，其内容包括产品的性质、特点、优势、材质、加工工艺、使用方法和注意事项等。产品介绍通常由文字、数据、表格和图片等构成。产品介绍往往需要从客户的角度出发，考虑客户的种种需求，洞察消费者的关注点，解决消费者迫切需要解决的问题，比如：“Johnson’s Baby Soothing Naturals Nourishing Shampoo is specially developed with our unique NO More Tears formula proven to be as mild to the eyes as pure water.”无泪配方正好能够满足父母对婴儿洗浴产品的需求，家长不再担心婴儿沐浴产品对婴儿造成过度刺激。许多产品介绍还会做出一定的承诺，包括产品会给消费者带来哪些好处。比如：“移动性能出色的 VAIO Y21 系列有着卓越的电池续航能力，标配电池的待机时间长约 4 小时，外出差旅或者去图书馆、咖啡厅带上 VAIO Y21 系列，可以让您从容应对。”这样，消费者就不用为没有电而发愁了。此外，产品介绍最好能突出利益的支持点，也就是该产品能解决的关键问题，如：“Are you always busy with work and never seem to have the time to vacuum your floors regularly? Then we have the solution for you.”这种产品能够帮助消费者解决定期清洁地板的问题，这是消费者购买该产品的原始动力。

产品介绍的首要目的是向消费者介绍产品的功能、性能、特征、用途、规格、使用方法及注意事项等。产品介绍可以提醒客户重视目前的某些问题及该产品如何解决这些问题；提升消费者购买产品的欲望；最终得到消费者的认同并购买产品。

本单元讲述的产品介绍翻译是广义的产品介绍。根据不同的产品类别和具体使用情况，汉语和英语都有多种表达方式，包括产品介绍（Product Description），产品质量说明（Quality Instructions），产品安装说明（Installation Instructions），产品介绍书（Manual），使用手册（Instruction Manual）、产品申购指示（Instructions for Purchase Order）等。此外，有些说明书使用专门词汇，如药品说明书可以用 Instructions，Directions，Descriptions，Package Insert（或简称 Insert），Leaflets 和 Data Sheets 等。

PART TWO
热身练习

Task I 请翻译服装说明书。

- Material: Soft Polyester, Soft and Comfortable
- Size: Free size (one size fits most)!
- Measurements: Length of the robe 125 cm; Bust 102 cm; Shoulder width 52 cm; Waistline 90 cm; Sleeve length 33 cm
- Multipurpose as it can be worn as a bathrobe, a nightgown or a wrap, etc.
- Machine-washable in general; Dry cleaning is recommended.

____

Task II 请翻译下列有关产品介绍的句子。

1. 服用本品未见有任何毒性或副作用。

____

2. 避免储存于日光下和温度超过 50 度的地方。请勿将本品给小孩玩。

____

3. 取二至三匙（约 40 克）置于杯中，冲入开水（冷或热）或牛奶，充分搅拌至融化即成一杯香甜可口的新鲜饮料。

____

4. 五岁以下儿童每天喝奶至少 500 毫升。

____

Task III 下面是某产品包装说明的翻译，请阅读并改进其英语译文。

1. 原文：将产品放入内包装箱。
   原译：Putting finished goods into inner box.
   改译：______________________________
2. 原文：所有的内包装箱在外包装箱内同一方向放置。
   原译：All the inner boxes are putted in same direction in the outer box.
   改译：______________________________
3. 原文：每个外包装箱只允许有一种设备。
   原译：Each outer box only can contain one type of the Device.
   改译：______________________________
4. 原文：在外包装箱的表面贴上外标签（外标签参见附录 2）。通常情况下，外标签贴在“装运至”字样旁边。
   原译：Attach the out box label on surface of the outer box (label sample refer to the Appendix II). Generally speaking, the outer box label is pasted beside the logo “SHIP TO”.
   改译：______________________________

PART THREE
产品介绍翻译技巧

Task I 请阅读下列产品介绍，并说明产品介绍的语言特征。请思考下列词汇是否与通用英语含义差别较大。

1. Normal skin（中性皮肤） Description（性状）
   Indications （适应证） Dosage and administration（用法与用量）
2. Component（零配件，元件） Heavy duty slide（承重式滑道）
   Electric power tools（电动刀具） Engraving machines（雕刻机）
   Etching machines（蚀刻机） Laser engraving machines（激光雕刻机）
   Finishing machines（修整机）
3. Down wear（羽绒服装） Accessory（辅料）
   Miniskirt（超短裙） Sweetheart neckline/Heart shaped neckline（鸡心领口）
   Pleated skirt（褶裙） Straight skirt（筒裙）
   Tailored skirt（西服裙）
4. Piercing（镂雕，镂空） Burnishing/Polishing（抛光）
   Turning（车削） Forming（成型）
   Repousse（凸纹） Clay processing（瓷土加工）
   Carving（雕刻） Relief（浮雕）
5. Spotlight（聚光灯） Barrier（隔离罩）
   Enclosure（罩壳） Terminal（接线端子）
   Rotary switch（旋转开关） Cord switch（拉线开关）

Task II 请阅读某汽车的产品介绍及其翻译，并讨论产品介绍的语言特点。

Lower fuel consumption and emission	低油耗，低排放
Low running cost (e.g. maintenance)	运行费用（如保养）低
Fun to drive	充分的驾驶乐趣
Low complexity in vehicle assembly and service	整车装配简单，服务便利
Relatively cost efficient automated system	高性价比的自动换挡系统

Task III 请阅读下列 CompactFlash 储存卡的使用说明，并从词类使用方面讨论产品介绍的语言特点。

1. To reduce the risk of fire or electric shock, do not expose this apparatus to rain or moisture.
2. To avoid electric shock, do not open the cabinet. Refer servicing to qualified personnel only.
3. For Customers in Asia Pacific Region, for Sony CompactFlash card only.

4. Limited warranty for Customers in Asia Pacific Region.

____

Task IV 请阅读下列某遥控汽车的遥控系统说明，并从句型方面讨论产品介绍的语言特点。

1. Inspect your model before operation. Make sure all the screws are properly tightened and all the parts are checked after running the car for a long period of time.
2. Always use fresh batteries for your transmitter and for your receiver to avoid losing control of the model.
3. Always test the brakes and the throttle before starting your engine to avoid losing control of the model.
4. Check your radio frequency with the proper operating frequency of the area or country. Always check to see if there are any modelers operating on the same frequency as yours.
5. Do not touch any part of the model that rotates.

____

Task V 阅读下列产品介绍的有关段落，并从时态、语态等方面归纳总结产品介绍的语言特点。

1. Please read this document before you use the ThinkPad R50 Series computer. The ThinkPad 50 Series computer complies with the radio frequency and safety standards of any country or region in which it has been approved for wireless use. You must install and use your ThinkPad computer in strict accordance with the instructions as described hereafter.
2. If this product proves defective in workmanship or materials when used in accordance with the guidelines and conditions presented in the instruction manual, Sony will replace this product with an equivalent product free of charge within 5 years after purchase date. This warranty is subject to the conditions indicated herein. Sony shall not be liable for loss or damage to data stored in the product howsoever caused.

____

Task VI 请翻译婴儿奶粉 Frisomel Advance（金装美素乐）的产品介绍，并讨论使用的翻译技巧。

Directions for use: Follow the instructions carefully for the sake of your baby's health:

____

1. Wash hands and utensils carefully.

____

2. Rinse soap from utensils and boil them for five minutes.

____

3. Boil water for five minutes and allow it to cool to 50℃.

____

4. Pour the indicated amount of water into the bottle or jug.

____

5. Add one leveled scoop of Frisomel Advance to each 30 ml of water.

____

6. Stir or shake until the powder is completely dissolved.

____

7. Test temperature and feed your baby when Frisomel Advance is lukewarm.

____

8. If you do not use the prepared formula immediately, store the feeding in the refrigerator for at maximum 24 hours. Discard unfinished feedings.

____

Storage: Store in a cool and dry place. Close the tin tightly. Use contents within 4 weeks after opening.

____

Task VII　请翻译下列真空吸尘机器人的产品介绍，并讨论你们使用的翻译技巧。

Highlights...

Auto Cleans

Auto Recharges

Effective and powerful

Intelligent Robot Vacuum Cleaner

Cleans both wooden and carpeted floors

Excellent for busy people always on the go

This clever futuristic robotic vacuum cleaner will automatically clean your floors and recharge its power without you ever having to lift a finger. Just program it to sweep and vacuum your floors when you are away so you always come back to a clean home.

The robot vacuum cleaner effectively picks up dirt, debris, pet hair and dust from carpets, wooden floors, marble floors and nylon flooring. The robot vacuum cleaner first sweeps up your floor with the installed counter rotating bristle brushes and beater brush that work together like a dust pan and broom. The sturdy bristle brush digs deep into the carpet fibers to drag dirt, debris, dust and much more out of those hard-to-reach areas. Then the powerful vacuum sucks all that accumulated nasty dirt into the bin leaving your floors and carpets extra clean.

Are you always busy with work and never seem to have the time to vacuum your floors regularly? Then we have the solution for you. With this robot vacuum cleaner you can simply program it to clean at a desired time. This robot vacuum cleaner will not get stuck in corners or fall down the stairs. When faced with obstacles or a surface edge it will simply turn around and continue its primary directive, which is to clean.

Task VIII 请翻译下列产品介绍，并从词义增减角度讨论使用的翻译技巧。

1. Considering the remoteness, wavelengths of X rays that indicate its motion must be shortened to an appropriate cycle.

____

2. Using this detergent, you can get rid of even the most stubborn dirt from your sofa, curtain or linen sheet without hard scratch.

____

3. The newest career pattern from Vogue combines sophisticated coloring and sleek tailoring with the most feminine result.

____

4. All the tinned goods are marked "Produced in accordance with Islamic way of slaughtering animals".

____

5. Combine digital technology with advanced software, smaller and more powerful microprocessors, and exponential growth in fiber and wireless bandwidth, and you get something far more powerful—seamless, universal connectivity.

____

Task IX 阅读下列产品介绍及其原译和改译，比较其区别，并说明原译和改译使用的翻译技巧。

1. 原文：该参茶具有养血复脉，养心安神，补肺定喘，健脾止泻等多种功能。

   原译：It has the functions of nourishing blood circulation, recovering pulse, relieving uneasiness of body and mind, nourishing lungs and calming asthma, invigorating the function of spleen and relieving diarrhea.

   改译：Doing good to your blood circulation, heart, lungs and spleen, it is a multifunctional healthcare tea.

____

2. 原文：本产品是根据中医理论"腰为肾之府""肾为先天之本""脾为后天之本"及"内病外治"的医理，采用高科技方法研制的保健药品。

   原译：This product is a new kind of healthcare medicine developed on the basis of Traditional Chinese Medicine theory to strengthen your kidney and spleen with the state-of-the-art technology.

   改译：This product is a new kind of healthcare medicine developed on the basis of Traditional Chinese Medicine theory for kidney care with the state-of-the-art technology.

____

3. 原文：它保持了酱香浓郁、典雅细致、协调丰满、回味悠长等贵州茅台的特点。

   原译：It possesses the unique style and flavour and is an extensively enjoyable drink.

改译：It is characterized by Moutai's unique style, fragrant flavour and prolonged aftertaste.

____

Task X 请应用前面已经学到的产品介绍翻译技巧，翻译下列曼秀雷敦润唇膏的产品介绍，并讨论你所使用的翻译技巧。

Mentholatum Lip Ice ______________

Moisturizing Color Gloss, protects and softens chapped lips. ______________

Contains the antioxidants of Vitamin C & E. ______________

Helps delay aging and maintain healthy lips. ______________

Gives natural and lovely colors with a glossy shine. ______________

Apply directly on lips or use with other color lip balm. ______________

PART FOUR

讨论：通过上述翻译任务，你认为产品介绍的翻译还可以采用哪些翻译技巧？产品介绍翻译需要注意哪些事项？

I. 产品介绍翻译技巧总结

本单元从产品介绍的含义谈起，讲述了产品介绍的功能、语言特征及翻译技巧。现将产品介绍的语言特征与翻译技巧归纳如下（见表 8-1 和表 8-2）：

表 8-1　　产品介绍的语言特征

产品介绍的语言特征	词汇特征	专业性：产品介绍往往包含各行各业许多专业术语
		评价性：使用评价性且具有褒义的词汇宣传产品
		词类：多用非谓语动词和介词短语
	句式特征	语态：产品介绍被动句使用较多
		时态：通常使用一般现在时
		句型：多用祈使句（说明使用方法或步骤）和复合句（具体说明产品性能和特征）
	总体特征	简洁（Conciseness）：产品介绍一般要求言简意赅，但又必须事无巨细，必须涉及该产品方方面面的信息和用法要求
		清楚（Clearness）：细节介绍必须清楚而不留任何含糊
		准确（Exactness）：术语与用词必须准确无误

表 8-2　　产品介绍的翻译技巧

产品介绍的翻译技巧	直译：多数产品介绍采用直译法，忠实表达原文含义
	意译：产品介绍的宣传性决定了某些部分需要采用意译法
	增译：增加说明性词汇，使表意更加清楚、明确
	减译：基于文化考虑，如中医药和白酒产品介绍中的文化负载词可适当减译

产品介绍是正式文体，翻译时应使用书面语，而忌用口语体。产品介绍的翻译不必字字对译，关键是需要帮助消费者了解产品的重要信息，如产品的材质、功能、使用方法等。

II. 产品介绍翻译的简化原则

产品介绍简洁明了，言简意赅，尽量使用简单句，译文也必须符合产品介绍简洁性特点。

［例 1］原文：此处所指精度标准除另有说明外，均为98%的概率。

原译：The accuracy standards that are specified herein shall be met on a 98 percent probability basis unless those are stated in other places.

改译：The accuracy standards specified herein shall be met on a 98 percent probability basis unless otherwise stated.

［例 2］原文：纱线是由纺织纤维组成的，具有一定力学性质、细度和柔软性的连续长条。

原译：Yarn which is made up of textile fiber is a continuous long sliver with mechanics character, fineness and softness.

改译：With mechanics character, fineness and softness, yarn is a continuous long sliver made up of textile fiber.

例 1 中，原译在不需要使用定语从句的地方用了两个定语从句，使句子啰嗦臃肿，不符合产品介绍的语言特征。例 2 同样采用了定语从句，改译简化了句型，意思清楚明了。

PART FIVE

译技点津：商务翻译技巧之造句法——形合与意合

I. 概念厘定

所谓形合，指句子的词语或者分句之间采用某种语言形式手段（如关联词）连接起来，表达语法语义和逻辑关系。英语造句法为典型的形合法（Hypotaxis）。所谓意合，是指词语分句之间不用某种语言形式或手段连接，句中的语法意义和逻辑关系通过词语或分句表达。汉语造句法为典型的意合法（Parataxis）。

形合和意合的概念有些抽象，王寅教授（1990）有一个非常形象的比喻，他说："有些语言学家形象地将英语句子称为'葡萄型'结构，葡萄主干很短，其上附结着丰硕的果实。而汉语句子则较短，一个短句接一个短句地往下叙述，逐步展开，信息内容像竹竿子一样一节一节地通下去，很少有叠床架屋的结构，因而常被称为'竹竿型'结构。因此英汉互译就犹如'葡萄'与'竹竿'之间的转换，应考虑到从句套从句、句子较长的特征与流畅性节节短句的特征之间的互换。"因此，把英语翻译成汉语时，一方面要准确再现原文意义，另一方面要使用地道的汉语"竹竿"结构表达意义，反之亦然。

需要说明的是，英语和汉语的造句法分别为形合法和意合法，这是普遍现象，但并非绝对现象，也有一些例外情况，在此不一一赘述。

II. 商务翻译中的形合与意合

翻译离不开对语言的把握，精通原语和目的语两种语言的词法和句法是进行语言转换的基础和前提。商务翻译实践中，同样必须注意造句法：形合法与意合法。

［例 1］ 原文：The telephone system can be divided into three networks: the local networks, *which* ties customers to their respective local switching offices; the trunk network, *which* interconnects the switching offices; *and* the long-distance network between cities.

译文：电话系统可分为局域网、干线网和长途网三种。局域网把用户分别和当地的中继局连接起来；干线网把各中继局相互联系起来；而长途网则把各城市连接起来。

［例 2］ 原文：The robot vacuum cleaner first sweeps up your floor with the installed counter rotating bristle brushes and beater brush *that* work together like a dust pan and broom.

译文：真空吸尘机器人的反转毛刷和搅打机刷就像垃圾铲和扫帚一样同时运作，清扫地面。

［例 3］ 原文：Our product warranty is limited only to the CompactFlash card itself, when used normally in accordance with these operating instructions *and with* accessories *that* were included *with* this unit in the specified or recommended system environment.

译文：我们的产品担保仅限于 CompactFlash 储存卡本身，且要遵守这些操作说明，使用本装置附带的附件，在指定或推荐的系统环境下使用。

［例 4］ 原文：Vitamin D, an essential nutrition found in fruits *and* vegetables *and* taken in large doses by many people as a dietary supplement, is a double-edged sword, providing benefits but also inducing the production of compounds associated with cancer.

译文：维生素 D 是水果、蔬菜中的一种重要营养物质，很多人大剂量地服用以作为食品补充。但它也是一把双刃剑，能给身体带来好处，也可能产生致癌化合物。

［例 5］ 原文：When inserting the CompactFlash card into a device, make sure *that* the card is facing the right direction *and* be sure to insert the card all the way into the device's slot.

译文：安装 CompactFlash 储存卡时，请务必按正确的方向完全插入机器的插口。

上述例子可以看出，把英语翻译成汉语时，省去了一些连接句子成分的关系词、连词、介词如“which, that, and, with”等。反之，把汉语翻译成英语时，需要增加表示连接的词汇，如例 6、例 7 和例 8。

［例 6］ 原文：本品为糖衣片，除去糖衣后，显棕褐色；味甘，微苦。（青春宝抗衰老片）

译文：The tablets have sugar coatings. *When* the coatings are removed, they appear brown with light sweet *and* bitter taste.

［例 7］ 原文：妊娠期禁用：本品孕妇或可能怀孕的妇女禁用，因其可能对胚胎带来致命的危险。

译文：Do not use this product during pregnancy. It is contraindicated *in* women *who* are or may become pregnant because the drug may cause fatal result on the fetus.

［例 8］原文：玫瑰女王系列玫瑰酒入口醇厚，余韵绵长，芳香细腻，口感圆润，柔和优雅。（玫瑰女王系列酒）

译文：The Rose Wine is fragrant *and* mild, mellow *and* sweet, leaving you a memorable aftertaste.

分析：原文中五个四字短语，层层叠加而不需任何连词，是典型的意合造句法。翻译成英语时，即使因为文化差异而省略了一些短语，也必须增加一些连词，体现英语形合的语言特征。

上述例子说明产品介绍翻译必须注意形合和意合两种造句法，商务翻译同样如此，下面举例说明：

［例 9］原文：The unprecedented economic and financial transformations worldwide have created new operating environments *that* demand new knowledge *and* skills.

原译：世界经济和财政相互转化，这是史无前例的，由此产生了一种新的操作环境，这种环境要求新知识和新技能。

改译：世界范围内史无前例的经济转型和金融改革形成了新的运营环境，要求人们掌握新知识、新技能。

分析：原译中“史无前例”不需要单独译成分句，而完全可以翻译成“transformation”的定语。原译对“transformation”理解有误，它表示“转型、改革、变革”之意，与不同的词语搭配，需要选择不同的词汇进行翻译，术语“economic and financial transformation”表示“经济转型和金融改革”，“operating environment”用于计算机行业表示“操作环境”，但在经济用语中表示“运营环境”。汉语属于意合语言，改译省略了关系代词“that”和连词“and”，纠正了错误的术语，在“要求新知识、新技术”的基础上增添了“人们掌握”，使译文更准确、自然。

［例 10］原文：We inform you *that* our business, *which* has been carried on most successfully for the last thirty years, will be turned into a limited company on May 1st *and* from that date it will be continued under the name of Square Co., Ltd.

译文：我公司在过去三十年里成就可观。现自 5 月 1 日起改组为股份有限公司，从此日起更名为斯戈尔股份有限公司继续营业。特此公告。

分析：翻译时省略了引导词“that”，关系代词“which”和连词“and”。

［例 11］原文：企业的技术进步应围绕着改进企业的经济效益，大力传播先进、适用的科技成果。

原译：The purpose of making scientific and technological progress is to improve the economic performance of enterprises by disseminating applicable new findings.

改译：The purpose of making scientific *and* technological progress is to improve the economic performance of enterprises by vigorously endeavoring to disseminate advanced *and* applicable findings.

分析：汉语的典型造句法是意合法，如“科技”“先进、适用的”不需要连词，翻译成英语需要增加连词。另外，原译尝试省略部分词汇，如“大力”

"先进"，但此处两个都为实词，不属于冗余信息，所以改译补充了这些词义，以便准确地传递原文含义。

［例 12］原文：人造材料又叫合成材料。许多人造材料正在代替某些天然材料，这或者是由于天然产品的数量不能满足日益增长的需要，或者往往是人们选择了合成材料的一些物理性质并加以突出而造成的。因此合成材料在应用的领域中将具有极大的用途。

译文：Many man-made substances are replacing certain natural materials because either the quantity of the natural product cannot meet the ever-increasing demand, or, more often, *because* the physical property of the synthetic substance, *which* is the common name for man-made materials, has been chosen, and even emphasized, so that it would be of the greatest use in the fields in *which* it is to be applied.

分析：可以看出，译文中增加了连词"because"和关系代词"which"，使译文符合英语语法和表达习惯。英语是典型的形合造句法。

综上所述，商务翻译中应特别注意因造句法即形合和意合为翻译带来的负面影响，积极应对，利用符合目的语表达习惯的句式结构，准确地道地进行翻译。

PART SIX
产品介绍翻译实践

Task I　翻译下列有关产品介绍的词组，了解有关化妆品知识。

1. foundation ________	2. moisturisor ________
3. nail polish ________	4. remover ________
5. sun blocker ________	6. toning lotion ________
7. blusher ________	8. anti-wrinkle ________
9. correct ________	10. essence ________
11. eye mask ________	12. eye shadow ________

Task II　翻译下列有关产品介绍的词组，了解有关服装知识。

1. 运动服 ________	2. 防护服 ________
3. 舞台服 ________	4. 家居服 ________
5. 孕妇装 ________	6. 休闲服 ________
7. 礼服 ________	8. 针织服 ________
9. 机织服 ________	10. 棉类服装 ________
11. 丝绸服装 ________	12. 化纤类服装 ________
13. 中山装 ________	14. 猎装 ________
15. 西服 ________	16. 羽绒服 ________

Task III 请翻译某儿童牙膏的使用说明。

Description:

Clinically Proven Cavity Protection

Do not use if the seal is not intact.

Adults and children 2 years of age and older: brush teeth thoroughly, preferably after each meal or at least twice a day, or as directed by a dentist or physician

Children 2 to 6 years: use only a pea sized amount and supervise child's brushing and rinsing (to minimize swallowing)

Children under 2 years: consult a dentist or physician

____

____

____

Task IV 翻译下列某酒店的服务介绍。

免费接机

____

下午 4:00—6:00 免费下午茶

____

免费西式自助早餐

____

入住套房，送精美果篮一个

____

免费宽带上网

____

免费拨打国内长途电话和本地电话

____

提供免费穿梭巴士往返琶洲馆

____

免费享用健身房、室内外游泳池

____

Task V 翻译下列索尼公司 CompactFlash 储存卡的担保说明，注意应用所学的翻译技巧。

Our product warranty is limited only to the CompactFlash card itself, when used normally in accordance with these operating instructions and with accessories that were included with this unit in the specified or recommended system environment. Services provided by the Company, such as user support, are also subject to these restrictions.

____

____

Sony does not warrant the usage of the product in life support systems or other applications where failure could threaten injury or life.

____

The Company cannot accept liability for damage or loss resulting from the use of this unit, or for any claim from a third party.

____

The Company cannot accept any liability for: problems with your digital still camera or other hardware arising from the use of this product; the suitability of this product for specific hardware, software, or peripherals; operating conflicts with other installed software; data loss; or other accidental or unavoidable damages.

____

____

Task VI　请阅读下列产品介绍的原文和译文，改进其翻译。

1. 原文：本品特点：本豆奶富含多种人体必需的维生素、矿物质及各种氨基酸，有动植物蛋白互补作用，促进成人营养的合理平衡。

   原译：Property of the product: be rich in various vitamin, mineral and amino acid. The animal and plant protein are mutually complementary, so it will promote nutrition absorption reasonable and balance.

   改译：____

   ____

2. 原文：SQ 系列筛选去石组合机主要适用于清除稻谷、麦类、黄豆、菜籽中的大，中，小轻杂质及并肩石等，具有除杂效率高、操作方便、节约能耗等特点。

   原译：The SQ series of Stone Selecting and Removing Machines is mainly used to remove all sizes of impurities in grain, wheat, bean and vegetable seeds. Its operation is convenient and the energy consumption is low.

   改译：____

   ____

3. 原文：我公司现供应的管道燃气是天然气，具有清洁、方便、高效的特点，正常燃烧火焰为蓝色，但有易燃易爆的危害性，使用不当会引起中毒或窒息、火灾、爆炸事故。（广州燃气集团有限公司）

   原译：Present pipe gas we provide is natural gas, which is clean, convenient to use and of high efficiency. Its normal flame is blue or blue with light yellow. It is easy to burn and explode in the fixed range of capacity. And it will lead to be poisoned, fire disaster and explosion when improperly used.

   改译：____

   ____

4. 原文：Choose the right place to operate your remote control (R/C) model. Do not run on

public streets or highways. This could cause serious accidents, personal injuries, and/or property damage. Never run R/C models near people or animals. To avoid injury, do not run in confined spaces. Do not run where loud noises can disturb others, such as hospitals and residential areas. Never run indoors. There is a high risk of fire and/or damage.

原译：请勿于雨天、公众空间、道路、机场附近与其他限制遥控模型活动区域，操控本产品。

改译：____

____

Task VII 储存方法和保质期是产品介绍的两项重要内容，请翻译下列短语或句子。

1. 开盖后请冷藏于 5 摄氏度，并于 3 天内饮用。

____

2. 勿让儿童接触本品。

____

3. 存于 25℃以下，防冻，避光。

____

4. 存于 10℃以上，注意防潮。

____

5. 有效日期

____

Task VIII 应用本单元所讲述的翻译技巧翻译下列产品介绍。

For the details on operations with the compatible device, please refer to the instruction manual itself.

Do not strike, bend, drop or wet the unit.

Do not place the unit in locations that are:

— extremely hot or cold — dusty or dirty
— very humid — vibrating
— exposed to corrosive gasses — exposed to direct sunlight

When inserting the CompactFlash card into a device, make sure that the card is facing the right direction and be sure to insert the card all the way into the device's slot.

Do not attempt to disassemble or modify the CompactFlash card.

Do not attach a label.

We recommend backing up important data.

When writing on the main unit label, use an oil-based pen. Do not use a fountain pen or water-based pen.

Recorded data may be damaged or lost in the following cases:

— removing the CompactFlash card or turning off the device while reading, writing, or formatting of the card is in progress.

— using the CompactFlash card in a location where it may be subjected to static electricity or electrical noise.

If the CompactFlash card is not recognized by the device you are using, remove the CompactFlash card, shut down or restart your device and try inserting the card again.

PART SEVEN
学习参考

1. 赵萱，郑仰成. 科技英语翻译［M］. 北京：外语教学与研究出版社，2006.
2. 中华人民共和国国家标准——服装术语 GBT 15557—2008［M］. 北京：中国标准出版社，2008.
3. 孙昌坤. 实用科技英语翻译（第二版）［M］. 北京：对外经济贸易大学出版社，2021.
4. 潘冀春，刘洁. 科技英语翻译［M］. 北京：北京理工大学出版社，2020.

PART EIGHT
单元预告与实训任务

1. 下一单元我们将讲述商标的翻译。
2. 请你搜集至少 10 种商标及其译文，评价其翻译并思考翻译技巧。

第九单元

商标翻译

Unit Nine　Translating Trademarks

商标在我国俗称“牌子”“品牌”“牌”“货牌”“商牌”等，已经拥有两千多年的历史。商标本身是市场化的产物，随着全球化进程的加快，企业参与全球化竞争趋势愈演愈烈，这不仅是产品质量的竞争，也是产品商标的竞争。创建知名商标与维护知名商标同样重要，商标的命名及其翻译事关产品形象和销路，事关企业的经济利益，正如《论语·子路》中所说：“名不正则言不顺，言不顺则事不成”。全球化要求商家对商标的命名要面向世界，面向未来。商标翻译很重要，有些企业不惜重金面向全球征集商标翻译。本单元主要讲述商标词的翻译技巧。

教学目标

1. 了解商标的含义及其背景知识；
2. 了解商标词的语言特点；
3. 掌握商标翻译中直译、意译和创译等翻译技巧；
4. 掌握文化对商务翻译的影响及其处理策略。

PART ONE

认识商标与商标翻译

Task I 阅读下列商标并思考：商标是什么？商标由什么构成？它有什么特征和功能？

Task II 商标等于品牌或牌子吗？商标和牌子有何区别？

世界知识产权组织（World Intellectual Property Organization）给商标（Trademark or Trade Mark）下的定义是："商标是用来区别某一工业或商业企业或这种企业集团的商品标志。"（崔立红，2003：12）《辞海》对商标的定义是："商标是企业、事业单位和个体工商业者对其生产、制造、加工、拣选或经销的商品所使用的标志。一般用文字、图形或其组合，注明在商品、商品包装、招牌、广告上面。"换言之，商标是指生产者、经营者为使自己的商品或服务区别于他人的商品或服务，而使用在商品及其包装上或服务标记上的由文字、图形、字母、数字、三维标志和颜色组合的一种标志。商标出现在商品包装上时，往往在其右上角或右下角加上®或 TM，分别表示已经注册（Registered）和商标（Trademark）。商标是商品质量和商品信誉的保障，又是商品特征的标志，也是商品广告和商品销售的重要手段。可以说，商标是商品质量的代名词，老百姓选购产品主要依靠商标，也就是商品品牌。商标既是产品的质量象征和形象代表，又是知识产权。因此，商标命名至关重要，在翻译时更要反复推敲。正如严复所言："一名之立，旬月踟躕"。商标翻译的好坏直接影响到其产品形象的好坏和销量的大小。美国学者艾・里斯强调商标译名的优劣时说："在销售成绩上能有千百万美元的差异。"

商标的特征主要包括：（1）依附性。商标不能游离于商品或者服务之外，而必须依附于商品或服务。（2）区别性。商标的区别性表现在它是企业使自己的商品或者服务区别于他人的商品或者服务的标志。（3）专属性。注册商标持有人对其商标具有专用权，受到法律的保护，任何人不得擅自使用与该注册商标相同或相类似的商标。（4）可视性。商标由文字、图案、字母、数字等构成，是一种艺术创造，为已有客户或开发潜在客户提供一种视觉享受。（5）信息性。商标是商品各种信息的载体，是参与市场竞争的工具，商品竞争力与商标知名度成正比。（6）价值性。商标是一种无形资产，具有价值。有些商标价值连城，正如可口可乐前总裁道格拉斯・达夫特所说："如果可口可乐在世界各地的厂房被一把大火烧光，只要可口可乐的品牌还在，一夜之间它会让所有的厂房在废墟上拔地而起。"商标可以有偿转让，经商标所有权人同意，许可他人使用。（7）简洁性。商标必须易读、易写、易记、易辨，才能给消费者留下深刻的印象。（8）创新性。创新是商标的灵魂，是企业制胜的法宝。娃哈哈集团于 1998 年推出了"非常可乐"，面对扬名在先的"可口可乐"和"百事可乐"，该集团创造性地使用了"非常可乐"的商标，并创造性地使用“Future Cola”作为其英文翻译，取得了较大的成功。

商标具有独有的特征，也具有特定的功能。贺川生（1997：18—21）认为，商标具有以下六大功能：（1）刺激消费：对刺激消费者购买欲望起积极作用。（2）识别产品：不同商标代表不同厂家、不同价格和不同售后服务。（3）提供产品信息：即反映该商品属性、特点、用途及功效等。（4）名誉象征：商标是商品质量的保证，是企业信誉的象征。（5）法律保护：商标一经注册即受到法律保护，防止假冒产品。（6）广告宣传：商标是广告的核心，广告宣传首先要突出商标。

通常我们所讲的“牌子”或者“品牌”（Brand），就是产品生产商印制在商品包装上区别于其他产品的标志。品牌经过注册就成为商标，常说注册商标。Brand 并不等于 Trademark。Brand 包括 Brand name（品牌名称，可用语言表达的部分）和 Brand mark（品牌标记，可以识别的非语言部分，如图案、颜色等）。Brand 和 Trademark 是事物的两个方面，前者是商业术语，用以区分同类产品，后者是法律术语，侧重于法律性，受到法律的保护（翁凤翔，2006：191）。本单元所讲述的商标翻译，如无特殊说明，都是指经过注册的商标词的翻译。

PART TWO
热身练习

Task I 请收集 10 种当地产品或服务的商标及其翻译（如果没有翻译，请思考如何翻译），并讨论翻译时使用了哪些翻译技巧？

Task II 请翻译下列商标，并尝试总结翻译技巧。

1. Nike ________	2. Buick ________	3. Belle ________
4. 7-Up ________	5. Dove ________	6. Lexus ________
7. 九阳 ________	8. 传化 ________	9. 老板 ________
10. 九牧王 ________	11. 方正 ________	12. 瑞星 ________

Task III 试分析下列 A、B 两组商标翻译，看看哪组商标翻译较好，为什么？哪组商标的翻译值得改进？如何改进？

A. 1. Coca-Cola（可口可乐） 2. Benz（奔驰） 3. Goldlion（金利来）

B. 4. 三笑牙膏 (Sanxiao) 5. 春兰 (Chunlan) 6. 杜康 (Dukang)

____

____

PART THREE
商标翻译技巧

Task I 商标的语言特征

1. 请朗读下列商标，讨论商标的语音特征。

Kodak（相机）	KitKat（巧克力）	Pifpaf（农药）
蜜蜂（缝纫机）	穗宝（床垫）	娃哈哈（饮料）
U2（衣服）	LUX（香皂）	OIC（眼镜）
Ericsson（手机）	Motorola（手机）	鄂尔多斯（羊毛衫）

2. 阅读下列商标，思考其语义与产品特征的联系。

Triumph（汽车）	Kiss me（化妆品）	Duracell（电池）
快克（药品）	匹克（运动服）	康宝（电器）

3. 阅读下列商标，讨论其词形特征。

P&G（日常用品）	UP2U（化妆品）	HOdo（衬衣）

4. 观察下列商标，说明其语言特征。

360（软件）

益佰 100（药品）

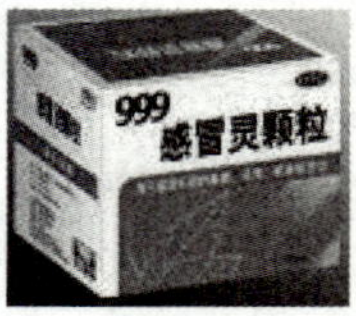

（药品）

361°（鞋类）

5. 分析下列商标在中西文化中的不同含义。
（1）Fortune Duck（皮具）
（2）Opium（香水）
（3）Zephyr（汽车）
（4）白象（方便面）
（5）金龙（汽车）
（6）白猫（洗衣粉）

Task II 商标翻译的原则：请比较下列三组商标的翻译，选择你认为恰当的商标翻译并尝试探讨商标翻译的原则。

第一组

1. Bausch & Lomb（眼镜）	A. 鲍希·龙布	B. 博士伦
2. High Lander（汽车）	A. 海蓝德尔	B. 汉兰达

3. 乌鸡白凤丸　　A. Wuji Baifeng Pills　　B. Black Cock White Phoenix Pills

____

第二组

4. Palid（相机）　　A. 拍立得　　B. 合金

5. Safeguard（香皂）　　A. 保卫者　　B. 舒肤佳

6. Dove（巧克力）　　A. 鸽子　　B. 德芙

7. Avon（化妆品）　　A. 爱雯　　B. 雅芳

____

第三组

8. Poison（香水）　　A. 毒药　　B. 百爱神

9. 帆船（地毯）　　A. Junco　　B. Junk

10. 白象（电池）　　A. Brown Lion　　B. White Elephant

____

Task III　商标翻译技巧：翻译下列商标，并总结商标翻译的技巧。

1. （1）Giant　（2）Porsche　（3）Lincoln　（4）Softto　（5）Aiwa
（6）Nike　（7）Audi　（8）Omega　（9）Boeing　（10）Siemens
（11）立白　（12）春兰　（13）长虹　（14）茅台　（15）娃哈哈

____

2. （1）Apple　（2）Crown　（3）Pioneer　（4）American Standard
（5）Good Companion　（6）光明　（7）熊猫　（8）钻石
（9）雪中飞　（10）大印象

____

3. （1）Unilever　（2）Goldlion　（3）Johnson　（4）Reebok　（5）Puma
（6）西泠　（7）美的　（8）乐百氏　（9）格力　（10）纳爱斯

____

4. （1）Rejoice　（2）Mild Seven　（3）Kleenex　（4）Joy and Peace
（5）Head & Shoulders
（6）新飞　（7）雄山　（8）联想　（9）多喜爱　（10）狗不理

____

5. （1）SK-II　（2）IBM　（3）UP2U　（4）LG　（5）LV

____

PART FOUR

讨论：通过上述翻译任务，你认为商标翻译还可以采用哪些策略？商标翻译需要注意哪些事项？

I. 商标翻译总结

本单元从商标的含义谈起，讲述了商标的语言特征、商标的翻译原则和商标的翻译技巧。现将商标的翻译原则与翻译技巧归纳如下（见表 9-1）：

表 9-1　　商标的翻译原则与翻译技巧

商标的翻译原则	简洁性：商标译文必须简洁、明快、朗朗上口
	关联性：商标译文必须与产品特点紧密相关
	文化适应性：迎合译入语民族的心理特征和审美情趣
商标的翻译技巧	音译法：利用最贴近原语语音的译语进行翻译
	意译法：挖掘原语的意义，体现商品特点和品质
	音意结合法：注重原语和译语读音的协调一致，更强调译文对商品特点的描述
	创译法：根据商品特点另起炉灶进行翻译
	零翻译：主要用于外文缩略语

II. 商标翻译余论

1. 商标起源与商标翻译

商标依附于企业和产品，不能凭空捏造，它是基于企业发展历史并与企业的产品特征、企业文化、经营理念息息相关的。翻译商标必须着眼于商标存在的语境。比如："多喜爱"洋溢着时尚、吉祥、热情的气息，翻译成"Dohia"为音译法。在希腊字母中，Dohia 象征着"超越与完美"，"Do"表示"做"，"hi"与"High（高）"谐音，"a"为英文字母第一个，含义不言自明。整个组合寓意着品牌追求完美，不畏艰辛而勇往直前的开创精神。在寝饰用品界，它代表着"卓越的标志"——时尚设计与精湛工艺之表征。其商标设计中活力四射的太阳（男人）与温情脉脉的月亮（女人），深情相拥，沐浴在美丽的蓝色夜世界，日夜相伴、真诚恒久、共享幸福时光，向家庭、爱情中的男女传达着深深的祝福。（多喜爱官方网站）

又如，SK-II 是知名化妆品品牌。30 多年前，日本科学家发现了天然珍贵的活细胞酵母精华：Pitera®，从而诞生了第一瓶"神仙水"以及 SK-II 这个缔造晶莹剔透肌肤的护肤品牌。SK-II 的全称是"Secret Key to Beautiful Skin"，即"开启美丽的神秘之匙"。如果商标翻译死死扣住原文全部翻译出来，恐怕消费者难以记住，还不如采用商标零翻译，直接使用"SK-II"，简单明了，易记易读。

2. 商标变更与商标翻译

常言道："行不更名，坐不改姓"。但是，由于种种原因可能导致商标改名换姓。2003

年 4 月 28 日，联想集团在北京正式对外宣布启用集团新标识“lenovo 联想”，以“lenovo”代替原有的英文标识“LEGEND”，并在全球范围内注册。中文品牌“联想”则保持不变。联想集团在国内将保持使用“英文+中文”的标识，在海外则单独使用英文标识。“lenovo”是由联想创造的一个单词，其中的“novo”是一个拉丁词根，代表“新意”“创新”，“le”为“legend”一词的继承部分，寓意为“创新的联想”或“联想创新”。显然，联想商标的翻译不是信手拈来，而是译者匠心独运的结果。

Logos, old (top) and new (below)

2004 年 6 月 8 日，为了与 LEXUS 品牌全球形象更匹配，以打造像凯迪拉克这样的国际知名品牌，日本丰田汽车公司把在中国使用了 10 年之久的“凌志”更名为“雷克萨斯”。“凌志”原本在中文中含义深重，为人们带来了丰富的互文性联想，因为人们自然联想到“壮志凌云”，甚至想起毛泽东诗句“久有凌云志，重上井冈山”之壮丽诗篇。丰田公司对更名的解释是“保持品牌的全球一致性”，但是“雷克萨斯”对中国人而言，没有任何具体的含义，也无法产生任何联想，这个音译的名称需要一段时间才能为中国消费者所接受。也许，外国商家了解部分中国人的消费心理，认为外国的品牌质量过硬，倾向于购买外国品牌。这也许才是其改名之秘密。无独有偶，PRADO 原译为霸道，现改译为普拉多；Camry 原译为佳美，现改译为凯美瑞。

3. 商标翻译——“忠”与不“忠”的较量

一百多年前，严复先生就提出了翻译标准的金科玉律，即“信（Faithfulness）、达（Expressiveness）、雅（Elegance）”。“信”也就是“忠”，即翻译需要忠实于原文。商标翻译实践中，多数翻译可以采用音译、意译和音意结合法，比较忠实于原文地进行翻译。但是，基于语言本身、文化、心理、宗教等原因，会出现翻译不忠实于原文的现象：一种情况是译文中缺少了原文本身的含义或者联想意义，比如：“Marlboro（cigarette）”为“Men always remember love because of romance only”的缩写，翻译成“万宝路”，虽有“行万里路，读万卷书”之气概，但失去了原文意义，类似的例子详见表 9-2。

表 9-2　商标翻译“减译”举隅

名称（商品）	原文含义	译名	分析
Pampers（尿片）	纵容、溺爱	帮宝适	原意略带贬义，省略贬义
Canon（电子产品）	标准、准则	佳能	直译不能构成商标专有名词，采用音译，省去原意
Sun Maid（零食）	阳光少女	阳光少女	原文与“Sun made”谐音，表达阳光下天然长成的产品含义，译文略去
Daphne（鞋类）	希腊神话中的美丽女神	达芙妮	译文失去了“美丽”的联想
猴王（鞋类）	猴子之王	Golden Monkey	原文让人联想到《西游记》中的孙悟空，译文无法产生类似联想

另一种情况是译文中增加了一定的含义或者联想意义，比如，著名化妆品品牌“Revlon”。通过公司网站得知，该品牌化妆品于 1932 年由 Charles Revson 和他的兄弟 Joseph 及另一名药剂师 Charles Lachman 共同创立。“Revlon”为“Revson”演绎而来，其中的字母“L”来自“Lachma”，汉译为“露华浓”，原文本是人名，没有特殊意义，而翻译成“露华浓”，让人自然联想到露华浓出自李白《清平调》词三首之一：“云想衣裳花想容，春风拂槛露华浓。若非群玉山头见，会向瑶台月下逢。”相传唐玄宗和杨贵妃在宫中观牡丹花，命李白作诗。李白以花喻人，花即是人，人即是花，杨贵妃美若天仙，集三千宠爱于一身，其花容月貌、倾国倾城之美如若眼前、娇艳欲滴，用“露华浓”来渲染花容，美丽的牡丹花在晶莹的露水中显得更加美丽动人。“露华浓”在中国注定是个成功的翻译，译文中增添了许多原文不曾有的联想意义，类似的例子详见表 9-3。

表 9-3　　商标翻译“增译”举隅

名称（商品）	原文含义	译名	分析
HP（电子产品）	人名	惠普	HP 源于两位创始人 Bill Hewlett 和 Dave Packard 之缩写，无其他意义，译文表示“价格优惠、惠及大众”之意
BMW（汽车）	工厂名	宝马	联想到中国的“汗血宝马”及《西游记》中战功赫赫的白龙马
Ford（汽车）	人名	福特	增加“特别之福气”的意义
Goodyear（轮胎）	人名	固特异	增加产品特点“坚固、牢靠”之意，与其广告词“穿上防弹衣的轮胎”相吻合

商标翻译不能一味追求忠实于原文，而应根据实际情况，尤其是产品特点和销售国文化进行适当处理，为商品确立良好的名声和声誉，促进商品营销。

PART FIVE

译技点津：商务翻译技巧之文化与翻译

I. 文化与商标翻译

1. 文化的含义

《辞海》对文化的定义是：人类社会历史实践过程中所创造的物质财富和精神财富的总和。人类社会进步文明的一切成果均为文化的组成部分，其中包括语言。人们在生活中时时刻刻都在同文化打交道，文化无处不在，翻译活动也受到文化的影响。

商标翻译的文化适应性是指商标翻译必须考虑适应译入语民族的接受心理、避免文化禁忌。民族心理指的是一个民族在漫长的发展进程中，在共同的外部生存条件与内部互相交往的长期磨合中不断形成的性格、气质、情感、价值取向、宗教心态、审美心态等心理模式与特征。在中华文化中，人们喜欢“梅、兰、竹、菊”等植物，俗称“四君子”，分别表示“顽强、高雅、刚毅、勇敢”之含义。古代花鸟绘画多以此为题材，文学作品中也多有描述。但是在日本、西班牙和意大利，人们讨厌菊花，因其有不祥之兆。

2. 商标翻译的文化适应性

不同的生活环境和历史经验导致各民族形成自己独特的心理状况，西方女性热情奔放，开朗大方；东方女性含蓄谨慎，内敛修身。具体到女性化妆品商标翻译时，我们就必须考虑心理因素。比如，前面谈到的“Kiss me”“Poison”香水；另一款女士香水命名为Nency Poppy Flower，中文名“兰西罂粟花”，这与毒品相关联，东方女性恐怕有点望而却步。如果我们搜索化妆品品牌，不难发现，许多品牌翻译与中国女性的命名不无关系，中国女性名字中多有“兰、丽、倩、芳、莲”等，到“天天购物网”上点击“彩妆”一栏，带“兰”字的品牌就有“卡姿兰（Carslan）、兰蔻（Lancome）、兰西（Nency）、娇兰（Guerlain）、娥佩兰（Opera）、玉兰油（Olay）、兰芝（Laneige）、雅诗兰黛（Estee Lauder）、兰瑟（Lansur）”等。“Opium”香水让人们联想到鸦片战争的耻辱经历，翻译时需要慎重处理。全球著名的越野汽车品牌Land Rover，唯一拥有过4个英国皇室荣誉证书的汽车制造商，Land意为“陆地”，Rover则是北欧的一个勇敢善战的海盗民族，无法直译，谁愿意开着“陆路海盗”上路呢？其汉译商标名为“陆虎”，前部分译义，后部分译音。“虎”表示虎虎生威、威猛无敌，该译文迎合了中国顾客的心理。

3. 文化禁忌

商标翻译文化适应性还应避免文化禁忌。常言道：“十里不同风，百里不同俗。”不同国家不同民族的禁忌包括文化禁忌、动物禁忌、数字禁忌等，现分别简述如下：

中国传统文化中，龙凤是吉祥的象征，中华民族是“龙的传人”，“龙”是皇帝的象征，与皇帝有关的东西叫“龙颜、龙体、龙袍、龙椅、龙床”等，不一而足。但是在西方，龙乃是“张牙舞爪的邪恶的东西”。所以，中国服装品牌“龙太子”具有望子成龙之意，如果直译，肯定达不到商标的功能和效果。在西方民族文化中“凤凰（phoenix）”是火鸟，烈火中的再生之鸟，有“冒死”之联想，当然没人愿意“劫后余生、死而复生”了。所以，如果凤凰自行车直译，肯定就无人问津了。

关于数字，各个国家大相径庭。在西方文化中，13是个令人恐惧不安的数字。无论是门牌、楼层及各种编号，还是吃饭，尽量避免13个人坐在一起，上菜不上13道。总之，日常生活中人们都尽量避免13。原因是耶稣和其弟子共进晚餐时，第13个人是犹大，犹大为了30块银币出卖了师傅，致使耶稣在13日（星期五）被钉死在十字架上。但是，中国人对此并不避讳，比如儒家“十三经”、皇陵“十三陵”、商行“十三行”等。

II. 商务翻译中的文化因素

语言与文化息息相关，商务翻译需要译者注意文化因素对翻译带来的影响。现举例说明：红豆衬衫是江苏红豆实业股份有限公司的主打产品，翻译成“HOdo”，虽说其词形有些特别，别无其他含义，即使翻译成“Red Bean”或者“Love Pea”也无法传递红豆的深刻文化内涵。红豆有着极其深厚的文化底蕴。相传，古时有位男子出征，其妻朝夕倚于高山上的大树下祈望。因思念边塞的爱人，哭于树下。泪水流干后，流出来的是粒粒鲜红的血滴。血滴化为红豆，红豆生根发芽，长成大树，结满了一树红豆，人们称之为相思豆。日复一日，春去秋来。大树的果实，伴着姑娘心中的思念，慢慢地变成了地球上最美的红色心形种子——相思豆。红豆让人联想到王维的名诗《相思》，“红豆生南国，春来发几枝？愿君多采撷，此物最相思”。因此，根据红豆的文化含义，建议把“红豆”翻译成“Red Rose”。因为在英文中，“Red Rose”容易让读者联想到 Robert Burns 的名诗“A Red, Red Rose”，同样表达了相思之情。

[例 1] 原文：功课终于做完了，真累啊！如果有一瓶乐百氏奶……（乐百氏饮料广告）

译文：A Robust a day makes me work, rest and play.

广告利用了“An apple a day keeps the doctor away.”和“All work no play makes Jack a dull boy.”两条习语进行套译，充分考虑到西方接受者对西方文化的熟悉程度，这是成功翻译的典范。

[例 2] 原文：The president of the company insisted that he would negotiate with his counterpart of ABC company instead of Tom, Dick and Harry.

译文：该公司总裁坚持要同 ABC 公司总裁进行会谈，而不是张三、李四、王五等普通人员。

在英美国家，Tom，Dick，Harry 都是普通人名，可以泛指任何人，此处不能直译为“汤姆、迪克和哈里”。中西文化具有一定的差异性，这里的差异性不大，尚可以进行移植，可以译成“张三、李四、王五等普通人员”。

PART SIX

商标翻译实践

Task I 请为下列商标选择适当的翻译，并将其代码填入括号中。

1. Colgate	(　　)	A. 爱普生
2. Carrefour	(　　)	B. 克莱斯勒
3. Casio	(　　)	C. 妮维雅
4. Epson	(　　)	D. 百宝利
5. Lego	(　　)	E. 凯蒂猫
6. Nivea	(　　)	F. 博朗
7. Chrysler	(　　)	G. 家乐福
8. Hello Kitty	(　　)	H. 乐高
9. Braun	(　　)	I. 卡西欧
10. Burberry	(　　)	J. 高露洁

Task II　请将下列英文商标翻译成中文。

1. Santana ________　2. Cadillac ________
3. Hummer ________　4. Buick ________
5. Toyota ________　6. Volvo ________
7. Lincoln ________　8. Honda ________
9. Givenchy ________　10. Gucci ________
11. Clinique ________　12. VICHY ________
13. Chanel ________　14. H2O ________
15. Christian Dior (CD) ________

Task III　请将下列中文商标翻译成英文。

1. 海信 ________　2. 美的 ________
3. 荣事达 ________　4. 狗不理 ________
5. 华帝 ________　6. 昂立一号 ________
7. 富绅 ________　8. 科龙 ________
9. 肤美灵 ________　10. 格力 ________
11. 乐百氏 ________　12. 雅戈尔 ________
13. 苏泊尔 ________　14. 非常可乐 ________
15. 志高 ________

Task IV　请判断下列商标翻译，哪一个会更成功？请说明理由。

1. 金星（啤酒）	A. Gold Star	B. King Star	________
2. 黑人（牙膏）	A. Darlie	B. Dark/Negro	________
3. 金纺（纺织品）	A. Gold Textile	B. Comfort	________
4. 美加净（化妆品）	A. Maxam	B. Clean & Beautiful	________
5. 金鸡（闹钟）	A. Golden Cock	B. Golden Rooster	________
6. 鸳鸯（电热毯）	A. Mandarin Duck	B. Love Bird	________

Task V　下列产品商标词相同，但由于产品不同，其翻译也不同。请根据产品特征翻译下列商标词并说明这样翻译的原因。

1. Accord（汽车） ________
2. Accord（手表） ________
3. Triumph（内衣） ________
4. Triumph（汽车） ________
5. Dove（香皂） ________
6. Dove（巧克力） ________

PART SEVEN 学习参考

1. 中国商标网：http://sbj.cnipa.gov.cn/sbj/index.html
2. 商标转让网：http://www.gbicom.cn/
3. 安青虎. 驰名商标和中国的驰名商标保护制度（精）[M]. 北京：商务印书馆，2009.
4. 左旭初. 著名企业家与名牌商标 [M]. 上海：上海社会科学院出版社，2008.
5. 张朝栋. 中国驰名商标攻略——中国驰名商标认定与保护研究 [M]. 北京：中国经济出版社，2010.
6. 白光. 品牌溯源的故事 [M]. 北京：中国经济出版社，2006.
7. 靳埭强. 品牌设计 100+1：100 个品牌商标与 1 个品牌形象设计案例 [M]. 北京：北京大学出版社，2016.
8. 何红华. 农产品商标翻译研究 [M]. 上海：上海交通大学出版社，2016.
9. 胡晓姣. 品牌翻译规范化研究 [M]. 北京：中央民族大学出版社，2017.
10. 刘彦哲. 中外汽车品牌商标命名与翻译研究 [M]. 北京：团结出版社，2024.

PART EIGHT 单元预告与实训任务

1. 下一单元我们将讲述公关文稿的翻译，涉及公共关系各个环节的有关文件翻译。
2. 如果你在中国进出口商品交易会工作，美国贸易代表团来访，请为您的上司准备一份介绍中国进出口商品交易会的文稿（双语），以便在欢迎宴会上发表讲话。

第十单元

公关文稿翻译

Unit Ten　Translating Public Relations Materials

公共关系（Public Relations）是一个组织与其相关公众之间的传播管理，或沟通管理，其目的是对公众舆论产生影响，为某一组织树立良好的形象和声誉。建立良好、有效的公共关系有助于企业与公众之间形成良好的关系，从而尽可能地建立一种与周围环境相适应的发展氛围，并与公众共享利益。而作为信息载体，公关文稿（Public Relations Materials）正是这其中的具体实践之一，是为公共关系的目的而服务的。随着国际贸易规模的扩大，公关领域日趋活跃，公关文稿的翻译也彰显其重要性。通过公关文稿的翻译，可以帮助企业内部或企业与客户、同行等社会各界相互沟通、相互适应，以良好的企业形象赢得广泛的关注和信赖，从而为企业带来显著的社会效益和经济效益。

教学目标

1. 了解公关文稿的基本知识；
2. 了解公关文稿的语言特点；
3. 掌握公关文稿翻译中常用的翻译技巧及注意事项；
4. 学会从语篇视角进行商务翻译。

PART ONE
认识公关文稿

Task I 商务活动中使用到的公关文稿可能包括哪些类型？请举例说明。

Task II 阅读下列两则公关文稿，思考：公关文稿的语言有什么特点？

1.

Mr. Vice President,

Our American friends,

My colleagues,

Ladies and Gentlemen,

On behalf of all the members of our mission, I would like to express our sincere thanks to you for inviting us to such a marvelous Christmas party.

We really enjoyed the delicious food and excellent wine. Also, the music was perfect. I enjoyed meeting and talking to you, and sharing the time together. As we say, well begun is half done. I hope we will be able to maintain this good relationship and make next year another great one together.

Thank you again for the wonderful party, we had a great time.

In closing, I would like to invite you to join me in a toast.

To the health of Mr. Vice President,

To the health of our American friends,

To the health of my colleagues, and

To all the ladies and gentlemen present here,

Cheers!

2.

Notice

A staff meeting about flexible working hours is to be held at 2 p.m., Wednesday, October 18, in the 2nd Conference Hall.

All staff memebers are requested to be present on time.

October 16, 2023

公关文稿广泛应用于企业经营活动的各个过程之中，也是做商务英语翻译最频繁接触到的涉外材料类型。

广义的公关文稿是指在公关活动中通过可能涉及的传播手段所发布的各类文稿，包括公关广告、供销广告、请柬、贺卡、名片、书信、电报、传真、聘书、题赠、对联、演讲稿、公关案例及分析、新闻消息与通信、计划书、总结、会议记录和纪要、通知、备忘录、各种商务报告（调查报告、市场预测报告、可行性报告等，详见第十四单元：商务报告翻译）以及各种合同、意向书等公文文体。总体上，按照用途可以分为内部文稿和对外文稿两大类：

内部文稿：内部文稿指的是企业或组织内部交流常用的各种文函，如议事日程（Agenda）、备忘录（Memorandum）、日程计划（Schedule）、会议记录（Minutes）、通知（Notice）以及各种功能的便条和记录（Note）等。随着国际化进程的加速，内部文稿使用的频率也越来越高。随着信息技术的发展，企业内部上传下达的流程更加电子化、系统化、平台化、便捷化。为了提高企业效率，各个企业都会对其内部各种文稿做相应统一的格式或使用规定。

外部文稿：外部文稿一般指的是企业或组织对外新闻发布使用的新闻通稿（Press/News Release）、新闻发布会（Press Conference）文稿、展览展示会用的公司宣传材料（Commercial Presentation）、商务陈述（Business Presentation）、公益活动用的宣传稿件（Publicity Material）、庆典礼仪活动或会议宴会等场合的各种致辞（Speech）和商务演讲（Business Speech）等。

公共关系的特殊性决定了公关文稿具有以下语言特点：

（1）体现强烈的公关意识

所谓公关意识，实质上是一种以人为根本、以公众利益为出发点的公众导向的观念或意识。公共意识是形象意识、公众意识、沟通意识、信誉意识、服务意识、责任意识、合作意识、创新意识、时效意识、战略意识、审美意识和信息意识的总和。

公关文稿，尤其是外部公关文稿，需要体现强烈的公关意识，如：形象意识——公关文稿须体现在公众中树立企业良好形象，提高企业知名度、名誉度的追求和愿望；沟通意识——对舆论的重要性有充分认识，乐于将企业向公众全方位开放，使企业的信息借助公共媒介广泛传播，与公众沟通；服务意识——乐于为社会服务，为公众服务，为顾客服务；合作意识——谋求互惠合作，共同发展，创造和谐的、有利于企业生存的环境；战略意识——充分认识企业间激烈竞争的必然性，积极参与竞争而不是消极回避，谋求公开、平等的竞争。可以说，每一篇优秀的公关文稿，字里行间都渗透着这种意识。

（2）真实性、准确性

公共关系的主旨在于陈述事实，以便公众根据事实进行公正、准确的评估，引起公众的兴趣，从而对公众产生影响。此外，商业公关文稿经常涉及专业领域或具体的商业信息，因此，公关文稿要求坚持内容真实，信息准确的原则。比如，2014 年，中国百胜餐饮集团在其肉类供应商上海福喜食品公司的“福喜事件”发生之后，发表了一封致全国广大消费者的公开信。为了还原事件真相，避免百胜旗下快餐品牌肯德基、必胜客等遭受更大范围的负面影响，文稿一开始就准确陈述事实，厘清责任方、澄清事实、重塑公司形象：“我们原本以为这样强强联手的合作，上游食品安全的保障会更加令人放心。但事与愿违，在上海福喜先进现代化和合规外表的背后，竟然发生由管理人员带头、有组织实施涉嫌违法违规和不诚信的行为。这对我们是一次刻骨铭心的伤害和教训。”

（3）创造性

作为实施公关方案的一种手段，公关文稿的总体风格是平实的，但好的公关文稿要求平而不淡，实而不死，在准确传达信息的同时需要独具创意，体现策划意识的独创性，使文稿具有引人入胜的可读性、趣味性和感染力。尤其是在社交媒体发达的信息时代，企业可以利用网络和多媒体工具，如在社交网络平台上开展话题标签活动等吸引网民参与，展现正面形象。

（4）语言正式庄重，谦恭得体

公关文稿的语言要求庄重得体、谦恭有礼。这种庄重和礼貌必须出自内心，真挚、诚恳，而不是矫揉造作，表达方式应委婉、积极、措辞得当。以中国百胜为例，在其供应商上海福喜涉嫌将回收食品、超保质期的食品作为原料再生产曝光后，百胜给消费者发出公开信。信件不仅重申了公司的经营理念，还从消费者的角度出发，与广大消费者共情，进行诚恳的道歉和深刻的自我检讨，语气亲切诚恳、谦恭有礼——“近期发生的上海福喜事件震惊了广大消费者和社会大众，引发大家的忧虑和不安。在此，中国百胜致以最深切的歉意。中国百胜从一线员工到集团主席以各种方式公开承诺‘每一口都安心’。但上海福喜事件让这样一个庄严承诺瞬间变得苍白无力。我们完全理解广大消费者对我们的失望和愤怒，实际上中国百胜的每一名员工更加痛心。我们深知社会大众对跨国企业、对我们品牌寄予的厚望和信任，因此我们没有任何借口和托辞。”

PART TWO

热身练习

Task I 试翻译下列公关文稿中常见的词语。

1. call to order ____________	2. adjournment ____________
3. press conference ____________	4. propose a toast ____________
5. distinguished guest ____________	6. 年会 ____________
7. 新闻稿 ____________	8. 就职辞 ____________
9. 开幕式 ____________	10. 道别 ____________

Task II 试翻译下面一则备忘录，体会内部公关文稿的语言特点。

MEMORANDUM

To: Mr. Jones, Manager of Operations

From: Grace Kelly, Supervisor

Subject: Comments on the “punch in” system

Date: October 19

This is further to your memo dated back to September 29, in which you proposed that the employees adopt the “punch in” system.

I fully agree with you that we should take measures to increase the productivity and that we would have a tighter control over the employees if the “punch in” system is adopted.

However, honestly speaking, I don't think that adopting a tighter system will increase productivity. The most effective way to increase productivity, in my opinion, is to give the employees more incentives to work. I think we could further discuss other possibilities of achieving this goal.

Your consideration of this suggestion would be highly appreciated.

Yours sincerely,

Grace Kelly

Task III　请将下列公关文稿分类，把合适选项的代码填入括号中。

A. 欢迎　B. 开幕　C. 祝酒　D. 欢送　E. 祝贺　F. 祝福　G. 道谢

1. We are all thrilled that you won in such a famous contest. (　　)
2. It is my special pleasure to welcome our new staff member, Mr. John Water, who has come here from the United States to assist us in the installation of the new equipment. (　　)
3. May the joy and happiness around you today and always. (　　)
4. First, it is my great honor to be here with all of you and declare open the Conference of International Trade Cooperation. (　　)
5. We are very happy to be here tonight when we can have the opportunity to bid farewell to our Canadian friends. (　　)
6. On behalf of the graduating students of the University, I would like to thank all the parents, families, and friends who encouraged and supported us as we worked towards our graduate degrees. (　　)
7. Now, I'd like to propose a toast to the friendship between our two peoples, to the success of our further cooperation and to the health of all friends here tonight. (　　)

PART THREE

公关文稿翻译技巧

Task I　公关文稿的语言特征

大声朗读以下英文演讲稿，体会演讲稿作为一种正式口头表达方式的语言特征。

Your Honor Mr. Mayor,

My Chinese friends,

Ladies and Gentlemen,

I feel honored to come here on my first visit to your beautiful city. On behalf of all the members of my mission, I would like to take this opportunity to extend our sincere thanks to our host for their earnest invitation and the gracious hospitality we have received since we set foot on this charming land. I am also very happy that this visit has given me an excellent opportunity to convey to you and to the people of Guangzhou warm greetings and the sincere good wishes of the government and the people of my country. Although there is a distance of tens of thousands of miles between us, "Long distances separate no bosom friends", as one of your Tang poets said.

The whole world is watching with great interest the remarkable changes that are taking place in China, particularly in Guangzhou. This is a country with the fastest growing economy in the world. China's rise as one of the strongest economic powers in the Asian-Pacific region has attracted a growing number of the business and financial giants in our country to invest in China, particularly in a number of the long-term projects in the Pearl River Delta. Over the last few years, there has never been a place, other than Huangpu Development Zone, that holds so much attraction for our people in the business community. It is with this awareness that we have come here to seek better ways of promoting our economic and financial cooperation. One of the objectives of my mission is to sign our Investment Protection Agreement. I am also seeking possibilities of establishing, through partnership with our Chinese colleagues, consultancy services for transnational corporations in Guangzhou.

Last but not the least, I would like to extend in person our official invitation to the mayor of Guangzhou. We would like His Honor to visit the city of Frankfurt at his earliest convenience, so as to give us an opportunity to return the warm reception and hospitality we've enjoyed here.

I greatly cherish the close relationship between our two cities. I also greatly value the position we enjoy as one of your most important trading partners. In spite of the worldwide economic recession in recent years, there has been a steady growth in our economic cooperation and trade volume. It is our sincere wish that we continue to work closely together to enhance our friendly relationship and to ensure sustained growth in our economic, financial and trade cooperation.

On the occasion of this reception, I wish Mr. Mayor and all our Chinese friends present here tonight good health.

Thank you all.

____

____

Task II 请翻译下列各题，思考公关文稿的翻译原则。

1.

Employees:	Suzuki, Bank, Randy	**Week:**	The Second Week (June 2-6)
Department:	Logistic Department	**Attention:**	training of new drivers
Week's Objectives		**Week's Accomplishment**	
1. confirm the order for Nanjing Truck Manufacturing Company 2. finish the training of new drivers 3. contact Toyota people for route designing		(to be filled in at the end of the week)	
Remarks:			

2. Thank you for getting in touch during our recent Karicare precautionary product recall. We wanted to take the opportunity to follow up with you to make sure that you and your little one are ok, that your routine is getting back to normal and inform you of some of the additional steps we are taking to avoid the same thing happening again.

During the crisis you were one of over 12,000 concerned parents, grandparents, families and carers who reached out to us. As we hope you'll appreciate, we removed our products from the shelves to ensure that any potential risk, no matter how small, was never given the chance to affect who matters the most, your precious little one.

We experienced firsthand the anguish, distress and inconvenience that this caused parents, families and carers. We know that no one has been more affected by our precautionary product recall decision than you and your baby. For this we are truly sorry and we wanted to personally reassure you that we are committed to going above and beyond in order to regain any lost trust.

____

____

3. 我非常高兴能在此会见来自大洋彼岸的加拿大商业界的朋友。“有朋自远方来，不亦乐乎”——这句话可以表达我此时此刻的心情。中国政府十分重视同加拿大双边经贸关系的发展，并且非常赞赏加中贸易理事会为加强我们这两个伟大的国家商业界的联系而做出的努力和起到的桥梁作用。我感谢理事会所有成员为促进加中贸易做出的努力。加拿大是一个工业发达、资源丰富的国家，中国则是一个劳动力充足、市场巨大的国家。我们希望看到加拿大的企业能够充分利用自己在技术和财力上的优势，赢得中国市场。

____

____

Task III　翻译下列会议记录及演讲节选，并总结公关文稿翻译所采用的翻译技巧。

1.

MINUTES OF THE MARKETING DEPARTMENT MEETING

Venue: Conference Room of the Marketing Department

Date: October 7th, 2022

Presiding: Andrew Brown

Present: Carl Smith, Bill Johnson, James Hart, Caroline Davis

Absent: N/A

The meeting was called to order by the chairman at 9:30 a.m. The minutes of the previous meeting were read and were approved as a true record.

1. Carl Smith reported that the sales figure dropped by 10% in September. Statistics

showed that during the last 6 months, the sales figure dropped consecutively. He proposed some positive strategies be worked out.

2. Bill Johnson proposed that we drop the price to promote the sales as he believed the sales drop was due to the competitors' price strategy.

3. James Hart suggested carrying out a fierce advertising campaign.

4. Andrew Brown pointed out that in either case, our profit would be affected and the shareholders might not be pleased with that.

5. Carl Smith said the market had been sluggish for 6 months, but there were signs of a revival. Dropping the price might affect the profits severely in the long term.

6. It was resolved that an advertising campaign should be started immediately. James Hart was requested to work out a detailed proposal for the next meeting.

It was agreed that the next meeting will be held on October 17, 2022, at 9:30 a.m. in the Conference Room of the Marketing Department.

The meeting adjourned at 11:00 a.m.

Prepared by: Lindy Green

2.

先生们，女士们，下午好！

我是本公司公关部的张小路。今天我在这里要向各位通报一下我们公司和 A 公司进行合并的有关情况。首先要告诉大家的是，两家公司的董事会已正式宣布双方将进行全股合并。新公司将命名为 AZ 公司。我开始会先给大家通报一下合并的初衷并列举一些由此带来的利益；然后再向大家详细介绍新董事会构成情况及合并后对财务方面的影响；最后，我还想给各位简要说明一些合同条款，包括利润分红等有关细节。

本次合并对双方而言都是自然的发展步骤，因为双方享有相同的以科技为本的文化，并对本行业发展持有相同的理念。这一举措带来的收益是很大的。首先，合并后的集团公司将实现强强联合，取得长期的增长，给股东创造更大的价值；此外，通过联合双方在全球范围内的销售和市场营销运作的强势，可以充分挖掘现有及未来产品的潜力。

3. As I look at you graduates, I see you are actually bigger, stronger and smarter than my generation was. You've already done away with so many of the hypocrisies—the dual standards, the cruel prejudices, and environmental insensitivities—that my generation struggled with, and only partially, overcame. You're way ahead of us. Many of you had already recognized the failures of my generation for what they really are—the opportunities of your generation.

The responsibility is awesome. And we parents, while we'll still be there for you, we've come about as far as we can in your future. As the old saying goes, "No matter how tall your father was, you have to do your own growing."

So on this commencement day, I speak to you as a parent. And I join your parents in the best wishes as you go forward: "Please let them fly, but don't let them fall." I also speak as your commencement speaker. And as your speaker, I urge you to go for it—take your chances; follow your bliss.

Good luck. Thank you.

PART FOUR

讨论：通过上述翻译任务，你认为翻译公关文稿还可以采用哪些策略？公关文稿的翻译需要注意哪些事项？

I. 公关文稿翻译总结

本单元从公关文稿的功能和类型谈起，讲述了公关文稿的语言特征、翻译原则和翻译技巧。现将公关文稿的翻译原则与翻译技巧归纳如下（见表 10-1）：

表 10-1　　公关文稿的翻译原则与翻译技巧

公关文稿的翻译原则	简洁性：翻译必须简洁地传达有效信息（尤用于内部文稿）
	准确性：正确理解原文，准确传达原文的信息、语气和态度
	完整性：信息完整；有语篇意识，确保译文是连贯、流畅的完整语篇
	礼貌性：译文必须尽量体现公关文稿的礼貌语气
公关文稿的翻译技巧	直译法：忠实于原文，准确传达原文信息和专业术语，保留原文形式和风格
	意译法：不拘泥于原文，在准确理解原文的基础上进行增、删、补、改，用规范译入语传达原文的内容
	结构调整法（结构拆译与重组）：为了理清逻辑关系，对原文进行结构上的整合或重组，迎合译入语读者的逻辑思维习惯，使得译文在译入语中也是连贯、流畅的完整语篇

II. 公关文稿翻译余论

1. 企业公关新闻稿的翻译

公关文稿中还有相当一部分是企业公关新闻稿。企业公关新闻稿用于对公关事件的媒体发布，既有对事件的总体描述，也要表达对事件的观点，夹叙夹议。对于企业而言，公关新闻是关于企业且有利于塑造企业良好形象、培育良好公共关系的新近事实的报道。翻译新闻稿要站在第三人称即新闻报道员的角度，保持措辞和语气客观、语句简洁、整体风格符合新闻报道。

2. 商务演讲的翻译

在企业举办大型会议、专业研讨会、产品推介会、招待会等公关聚会场合，主办方都会发表商务演讲，其演讲内容决定着整个活动的基调，使参加者了解本次活动的目的所在。在翻译这类商务文稿时要注意以下几点：

（1）了解活动的相关背景知识、活动的级别以及与会者的群体定位；

（2）注意演讲的时限，以此决定相对应的语言组织和措辞；

（3）由于此类活动的功能与目的性较强，加之商贸领域的思想交流与信息传递具有特殊性，所以商务演讲翻译对概念的限定比较严格，这也要求译者掌握语言之外的知识并具备灵活应用的能力。译者不能仅仅满足于对词汇层面的理解，而需要更综合地了解专业领域知识，使得翻译符合有关专业人员的需要。

3. 公关文稿与口译

由于公关文稿大部分内容涉及演讲、致辞、讲解，这往往要求译员有现场口译的能力。

口译就是通过口头表达的方式将一种语言转化成另外一种语言的过程。笔译可以查字典，找参考资料，还可以和同事商讨、琢磨、推敲、斟酌字句。但口译译员要在讲话人说话的同时听清、理解讲话的内容，领会讲话者的意图，记住讲话人的原话、原词，并立即用另一种语言清楚、准确地表达出来。口译译员在工作时，必须保持注意力高度集中，片刻松懈或走神就会导致漏听和漏译。他们还必须在听的同时做笔记，将听到的内容根据笔记和记忆加工成流畅的译文。口译是一项高度紧张的脑力劳动，要求译员不但听力好、理解力强，而且要求记忆力好、反应快。我国著名的口译教学专家梅德明教授把口译的特点归纳为即席性强、压力大、独立性强、综合性强及知识面广。可见口译对译者的语言能力、记忆能力和临场应变能力等方面具有很高的要求。

口译按操作方式可以分为两大类：即席翻译（Consecutive Interpreting）和同声传译（Simultaneous Interpreting）。即席翻译又称为交替传译或连续传译，其方式是讲话人说完一句话、几句话或一段话，停下来让译员进行口头翻译。经常使用即席翻译的场合有：演讲、祝词、授课、谈判、情况介绍会、高级会议、新闻发布会、记者招待会、参观、采访、宴会等。同声传译是指译员在一方讲话的同时不停顿地将其讲话内容传译给另一方的口译方式，译员的口译与一方的讲话几近同步进行。由于节奏紧迫，耳听、脑记、口说同步进行，译员需要注意力高度集中。译员工作强度非常大，一般每工作 20 分钟就要轮换。

笔译和口译有许多共同的特点和要求，也有不少差异，因此，对从事不同翻译工作的人有不同的要求。正因为如此，在联合国系统、欧洲联盟以及在其他一些国家，从事口、笔译的人员是分开的。我国外交翻译的工作人员历来都是多面手，但不管侧重于哪一个方面，每一个人都必须从事笔译，因为笔译是基础。有平时笔译经验的积累，才能练出口译所需要的快速反应和熟练的语言转换能力。

PART FIVE

译技点津：商务翻译的语篇视角

I. 商务英语语篇

从结构方面看，“语篇”（Discourse）是大于句子（Sentence）的语言单位（Discourse is a unit of language above the sentence）。从功能方面看，“语篇”是使用中的语言

（Discourse is language in use）（黄国文，2001：5）。商务英语语篇指在买卖所需商品或服务的商务活动过程中使用的各种正式与非正式文件。商务英语语篇特别注重实用性，具有浓厚的行业特色，并且因涵盖业务范围广、活动类型丰富而拥有各种各样的语篇类型。

从实际运用的角度，商务英语语篇可细分为商务电子邮件（Business Correspondences）、备忘录（Memorandums）、会议纪要（Minutes）、广告（Commercials）、报告（Reports）、通知（Notices）、说明书（Instructions）、协议或合同（Agreements or Contracts）、商务演讲，致辞或讲解（Business Speeches or Presentations）以及各种相关单据与表格（Bills and Forms）等各种语篇类型。

II. 商务翻译中的语篇视角

在实际翻译中，翻译的对象往往是完整的语篇，这就要求其译文也是一个完整通顺的语篇。因此，在翻译过程中，译者不仅要做到正确理解并表达和组织语句，使其与原文对等，还应该考虑到文本作为语篇的语境、文化因素和交际功能，保证译文的衔接和连贯，准确传达出原文中体现的文化特色、语言风格和交际功能。

语篇有三大要素：中心思想、连贯性和一致性。语篇翻译要根据这三大要素，以原文传递的信息为主线，理清脉络，有重点、有取舍地表达原文作者的意图。因此，译文也应该是一篇语义连贯、语法正确、逻辑清晰的完整语篇，而且译文同时还完整、层次分明地传达原文作者的意图。

翻译中的语篇视角有两个重要特征：衔接（Cohesion）和连贯（Coherence）。衔接是通过词汇或语法手段，使语篇获得形式上的联系。一篇译文行文是否清晰流畅，关键在于衔接。在翻译过程中，译者应从整体上把握语篇的意义，透彻理解语篇的信息，根据目的语的要求，采用适当的增减方法对译文进行重构，使译文达到语篇上的衔接。而连贯则是指信息接收者根据语境信息和背景知识，通过逻辑推理来掌握信息发出者的交际意图，即语篇翻译中连贯性的问题是如何保证语篇中语义逻辑的一致性。为了保证译文语义连贯，晓畅明白，适当的增补、语序调整等手段也是保证译文语义逻辑一致的方法。

III. 商务篇章的翻译要点

商务英汉（汉英）翻译的关键在于实现两种语言同一商务语篇在功能上的对等，因此翻译中除了必须再现原文传递的所有内容，还必须再现原文的语气、文体特征和专业特点，使译文和原文发挥类似的功能并实现相同的交际目的。

1. 词汇层面：准确理解原文用词并在译文中精确传达

准确性是商务英语翻译的第一要求。这个要求包括对商务术语、一词多义现象和数字概念等的准确解读和翻译。商务术语是商务英语形成一种相对独立体裁的保障，是商业贸易及谈判的各个专业环节的保障，是保证原文交际者的思想和意图能够得到准确传达的基础。因此，在翻译时必须深刻理解原文术语的含义，并把它们规范准确地体现在译文中。此外，在商务电子邮件，合同和报告等篇章中涉及时间、价格、数量、金额和规格等重要数字概念时，翻译必须慎重处理，不能出错。如：

［例 1］原文：The *financial statements* are the means of conveying to management and to interested outsiders a concise picture of the profitability and financial position of the business.

译文：**财务报表**是向管理层和有关的外部人士展示企业的赢利情况和财务状况的精确图表。

［例 2］原文：Party A shall be unauthorized to accept any orders or to collect any account *on and after* September 20.

译文：**自** 9 月 20 日**起**，甲方已无权接受任何订单或款项。

2. 语法层面：译文必须简洁、严密、庄重

商务英语语句具有简洁、严密的特点，注重表达效果的准确性、时效性和逻辑性。当我们读懂原文的意义时，在准确表达意义的基础上，要尽量用直接易懂、简洁凝练的语言来表达。英汉翻译中还可使用汉语公文体中的客套委婉词语或固定的套语，如“鉴于”“如蒙”“兹”等，使译文简洁规范。例如：

［例 3］原文： Please look into the matter immediately.

译文：恳请速查明此事。

［例 4］原文： Considering the friendly business relationship between our two banks, we decided not to charge the overdue interests.

译文：鉴于贵我两行之间的友好关系，我行决定不收取贵行的过期利息。

3. 语篇层面：注意规范性、整体性及礼貌和功能等方面的对等

就语篇层面而言，译者必须了解商务领域的行业规范和背景知识，熟悉商务运作各个环节所使用的术语和各类商务语篇的表述模式与结构，确保译文的专业性、整体性、礼貌性，并努力使译文的语气与原文一致，传达相同的功能。例 5 是一封商务电子邮件，其译文从整个语篇的角度出发，将其处理成一篇格式、用语均妥当的中文信函，确保了其整体性和礼貌性，实现了信函作为商务语篇的交际功能。例 6 是一份企业对外宣传材料，译者从整体出发，采取了语篇重构的方法，一方面省译了中文的华丽辞藻，另一方面又根据英语读者的思维对语篇内容进行了重新编排。这样做不仅不影响原文信息的传达，反而更有利于实现译文的预期功能。

［例 5］原文：

Dear Sirs,

Our client in Bombay requests us to obtain from you a proforma invoice for color TV sets with the following specifications: Haier brand color TV sets 25-inch and 34-inch (each 500 sets).

Would you please airmail us the soonest possible your proforma invoice for 1,000 color TV sets with prices CIF Bombay, so that we can obtain our client's conformation. There is no question about our getting the necessary import license from our authorities. As soon as the said license is approved, we shall establish an L/C in your favor.

Thank you for your close cooperation.

Yours truly,

John Smith

译文：

> 敬启者：
>
> 我们的一个孟买客户要求我们从贵方取得下列规格的彩色电视机形式发票：海尔牌彩色电视机 25 英寸和 34 英寸各 500 台。
>
> 请尽速航邮注有孟买到岸价格的 1 000 台彩色电视机的形式发票，以便我们取得客户确认。从当局取得必要的进口许可证当无问题。
>
> 一旦取得许可证即开立以贵方为受益人的信用证。
>
> 感谢贵方的密切合作。
>
> 此致
>
> 敬礼

［例 6］原文：在中国经济高速发展的伟大进程中，它容纳百川，汇成大海的壮阔。在一片创造神话，抒写千年梦想的热土上，它上下求索，承载着历史的重托。1986 年 8 月 16 日，联塑集团的诞生，宣告了一个童话与奇迹的诞生，从此它以横空跃世的雄姿，它以锐不可当的气势，致力于改善给水排水管道的环保卫生、致力于保障人民身体健康和提高人民的生活品质。

译文：Along with the fast development of China's economy, Liansu Group has made great achievements by drawing strength from this process. China's development has been a miracle and the country is reshaping in every aspect. Liansu is also well advanced in its own miracle-achieving mission. On August 16th, 1986, the establishment of Liansu proclaims the birth of both a tale and a miracle. From then on, it has displayed to the world its superior ambition and majestic strength.

PART SIX

公关文稿翻译实践

Task I 请翻译下列句子或段落。

1. I would also ask you, Mr. Chairman, to help increase the awareness of Wales among Chinese companies, particularly among Chinese companies that are considering their first move into Europe. For many years, Wales has been one of the most popular destinations for foreign investment in Europe. Investors in Wales have brought over 12 billion pounds into the country and continue to reinvest once established.

____

____

2. This is to introduce to you the bearer of this letter, Dr. Li Shaolin, vice director of our

Economic Research Center and his assistant Zhao Chong, who are going to your city to do some survey on the development of economic bodies in towns, which will last for seven days. We should greatly appreciate any assistance you may be able to give them, which will be considered as a personal favor to us.

____

____

3. 我很高兴今天能有机会与各位朋友共聚一堂，共商经贸合作。我愿向各位朋友介绍广东的经济发展情况以及未来经济发展的战略和规划，希望有助于增进各位朋友对广东的了解。广东是中国大陆最南端的省份，拥有 17.98 万平方千米的土地和 7 700 多万人口。我们广东人才汇集，对外交往便利，对外贸易历史悠久。

____

____

4.

通　　知

兹定于 10 月 24 日（星期一）上午 9 时在教学楼 401 室，由 Henry Smith 博士给经管系 2021 级 7 班上英语公开课。全体英语老师务必出席。欢迎其他系科任教师参加。

系主任办公室

2022年10月20日

____

____

Task II　请翻译下列文稿。

1.

女士们，先生们：

上午好！各位贵客不远万里从美国来访，我们深感荣幸。首先，我代表 NOVO 公司，对在座的各位朋友和同行表示我们最热烈的欢迎和最衷心的感谢。下面我简单介绍一下我公司的基本情况。

NOVO 公司成立于 1990 年，总部设在中国深圳。业务主要是电信设备的研发、制造和销售。现在 NOVO 已成为中国电信市场的佼佼者，与此同时，我们也在积极开拓国际市场。

今天，NOVO 的产品已经销售到德国、法国、英国、西班牙、日本、巴西、俄罗斯、埃及、泰国、新加坡等 40 个国家和地区。目前，员工总数达到 22 000 人，有 3 500 名工程师在中国深圳、上海、北京，以及瑞典、美国、印度等世界各地的 NOVO 研究机构从事新产品研发工作。

根据我们的计划安排，今天要邀请各位参观我们新建的工厂和研究中心。我公司全体员工会竭尽全力，确保各位参观愉快、不虚此行。如果大家有什么问题，别客气，请尽管提问。

再次向各位表达最诚挚的欢迎。谢谢！

2.

Mr. Zhang, Ladies and Gentlemen,

On behalf of the foreign guests attending this workshop, let me say a most sincere "thank you" for your warm and gracious welcome. From the little I've seen in the short time when I've been here, I'd have to say China is a very beautiful country and your people are very friendly. I know that I can speak for everyone when I say that, from the moment when we arrived at the airport, there have been many helpful and considerate people to take care of all the little things that make the difference between a hectic and a relaxing trip. The accommodations you have provided are very comfortable and the setting for this workshop is relaxed, yet business like.

We are all glad to be here to participate in this workshop on computer technology. We've all read about phenomenal success with computers in China and we've all seen the numbers on how healthy the industry is here, and now we get the opportunity for a closer look. I know we have a lot to learn from your experience here in China, and hope our experience will be helpful to you here also.

I think we share the sentiments expressed by Mr. Zhang in his welcome address that as a worldwide industry, we can learn to cooperate more, to share new ideas and developments, to coordinate research efforts between countries, and to make computers more accessible and understandable to the average person. Working together, we can all move forward quickly.

This is an exciting time for the computer industry worldwide, and we are excited to have the opportunity to participate in this workshop. Thank you for the invitation and the warm reception.

PART SEVEN 学习参考

1. 刘洪泉，韩静芸. 英语应用文写作［M］. 上海：上海外语教育出版社，2018.
2. 林静. 商务英语应用文写作与翻译（第二版）［M］. 北京：北京大学出版社，2022.
3. 利嘉敏. 互联网+：企业公关案例与策略［M］. 北京：北京时代华文书局，2017.
4. Stephen E. Lucas, Paul Stob. 演讲的艺术（第 13 版）（中国版）［M］. 北京：外语教学与研究出版社，2021.

PART EIGHT 单元预告与实训任务

1. 下一单元我们将讲述商务电子邮件翻译，涉及商务交往各个过程中往来电子邮件的有关翻译。
2. 请思考商务电子邮件的翻译需要注意什么问题？

第十一单元

商务电子邮件翻译

Unit Eleven　Translating Business E-mails

党的十八大以来，我国对外贸易取得了历史性成就，贸易大国地位进一步巩固，未来贸易仍将是我国经济高质量发展的重要动力。在加快建设贸易强国的进程中，国际商务活动会更加频繁，随着经济贸易与合作的领域不断扩大，跨国商务电子邮件作为合作商家之间，厂家与客户之间联系业务、沟通商情、咨询答复的主要途径和工具将受到更多重视。商务电子邮件是国际贸易与国际交往过程中必不可少的沟通与交流方式，得体、规范的商务电子邮件能与外商建立并保持良好的业务关系，甚至能避免因纠纷而产生的种种不良后果。本单元首先介绍商务电子邮件的格式，然后通过翻译实践让读者了解其文体特点，再总结商务电子邮件翻译的基本原则和注意事项。

教学目标

1. 了解商务电子邮件格式；
2. 了解商务电子邮件篇章结构；
3. 掌握商务电子邮件的文体特点及翻译技巧；
4. 掌握商务电子邮件翻译中正反交替翻译技巧。

PART ONE

商务电子邮件的分类、功能及篇章结构

Task I　阅读以下商务电子邮件并思考：写此邮件的目的是什么？

Dear Mr. Li,

Our order No. 3979: 50 Electric Drills

As it is now more than two months since we opened a letter of credit in your favor, we should like to know exactly when you could arrange shipment of the goods. Your prompt response will be highly appreciated.

Sincerely,

Marco Fillmore
Managing Director

Task II 请讨论商务电子邮件与一般信函的异同。

商务信函是涉外商务沟通过程中所使用的各种函件的总称，是“人们互相联系，彼此交往、交流思想、沟通信息、洽谈事务所使用的一种应用文”（黎运汉，2005：365）。虽然电话和社交媒体通信等方式已被广泛使用在商务领域，但以电子邮件呈现的商务信函包括电子邮件和传真作为一种有效的法律依据，而且不限时间、地点和篇幅，可充分陈述理由和分析问题，使双方能够更有效地进行沟通交流，因此至今仍然是商务交际中最主要的工具。商务电子邮件具有一般书信的特点，同时又属于一般公务信函，它们涉及商务和贸易过程中的各个环节如询盘、报盘、还盘等。从信函的文体正式程度来看，可以分为便函和正式函两大类。便函一般用于商务应酬中双方联络感情、促进贸易关系的信函，可以细分为商务活动中的感谢信、祝贺信、慰问信、邀请信等。正式函一般格式较严谨、篇幅较长、内容完整，用于处理具有实质内容的商业事务，可归纳为建立业务关系类、产品推销类、资信查询类、询盘类、发盘还盘类、订购类、支付类、索赔类、保险类等，贯穿进出口外贸业务的全过程。

当下，商务信函最重要的形式就是电子邮件。电子邮件的格式与信件基本类似，但整体更短小精悍。下面我们以英文商务电子邮件中最通用的格式——齐头式为例。这种格式的主要特征就是每行均从左边顶格写，信中各段落之间均空一行。

From: powerbitz@netexucutive.com
To: sales@pinganchorage.com.my
Subject: Travel Inquiry

Dear Sir or Madam,

We are going to make a week’s tour in Malaysia. Would you give us some advice about the trip and arrange two twin beds rooms from Oct. 1 to Oct. 7 for us?

Look forward to your reply. Many thanks.

Sincerely,
×××
××× Ltd.

中文的商务电子邮件一般使用缩进式。下面来看一篇中文例子：

××先生：

贵方 10 月 1 日有关保险事宜的来邮知悉，特函告如下：

一、综合险。在没有得到我们顾客明确指示的情况下，我们一般投保水渍险和偷窃提货不着险。如贵方愿投保综合险，我方可以稍高的保费代保此险。

二、破碎险。破碎险是一种特别保险，需收取额外保费。该险现行保险费率为 2%，损失只赔超过 5%的部分。

三、保险金额。我方注意到贵方欲为装运给贵方的货物按发票金额另加 10%投保，我方当照此办理。

我方希望上述答复将满足贵方的要求，并等候贵方的答复。

此致

敬礼！

××公司

翻译商务电子邮件时，应当保留原文的篇章结构。需要注意的是，中文邮件的署名即写信人签名，通常写在结尾后另起一行（或空一、二行）的偏右下方位置。以单位名义发出的商业信函，署名时可写单位名称或单位内具体部门名称，也可同时署写信人的姓名。

PART TWO
热身练习

Task I　请翻译以下商务函电中常用的英语词汇。

1. standing orders ________________	2. competitive price ________________
3. deal on credit ________________	4. packing list ________________
5. ETA ________________	6. ETD ________________
7. cargo capacity ________________	8. direct steamer ________________
9. freight prepaid ________________	10. B/L ________________

Task II　请翻译下列选自商务电子邮件的句子，并指出这些句子的语言特点和翻译难点。

1. We have heard from China Council for the Promotion of International Trade that you are in the market for electric appliance.

____

2. Thank you for your e-mail of 1st September suggesting that we grant you a sole agency for our household linen.

____

3. 现欲扩展业务范围，盼能惠赐商品目录和报价表。

____

4. 兹通知，标题所述货物已于昨日由“胜利”号货轮运出。

____

5. 我们希望此批订货质量与以前供应的完全一样。

____

PART THREE
商务电子邮件翻译技巧

Task I 商务电子邮件的词汇特点。

1. 对比以下几组句子，判断每组里哪一句更符合商务电子邮件的用词规范，并说明原因。

第一组：

(1) We are happy to tell you that your order No. 57 has been sent according to your instruction.

(2) We are pleased to advice you that your order No. 57 has been dispatched in accordance with your instruction.

第二组：

(1) We will meet you half way by offering a discount of 5% thinking of our long pleasant relations.

(2) We will meet you half way by offering a discount of 5% in view of our long pleasant relations.

第三组：

(1) In attachment please find the quotation sheet. All offers and sales are subject to the terms and conditions printed on the reverse side hereof.

(2) In attachment please find the quotation sheet. All offers and sales are subject to the terms and conditions printed on the reverse side of this sheet.

2. 翻译以下商务电子邮件中常用贸易术语及缩略语。

(1) sole agency	________	(2) close price	________
(3) offer	________	(4) counter offer	________
(5) acceptance	________	(6) licensor	________
(7) freight forwarder	________	(8) commercial invoice	________
(9) payment currency	________	(10) payment in advance	________
(11) point of delivery	________	(12) CIF	________
(13) CFR	________	(14) FOB	________
(15) D/P	________	(16) D/A	________
(17) G.W.	________	(18) N.W.	________

(19) S/C ____________　　(20) L/C ____________

(21) P/L ____________　　(22) T/T ____________

3. 翻译以下句子，注意斜体词在句中的意思与其常用词义的区别。

(1) Average is of two kinds: General *Average* and Particular *Average*.

____

(2) Chinese silk is very popular in Europe. We would like to work with you to *market* it in the US and South America.

____

(3) We shall write and ask for their *ceiling* for the advertising project and then we can budget accordingly.

____

(4) We wonder whether you are satisfied with our *quotations*.

____

4. 判断下列句子翻译的正误，正确的在括号内画“√”，错误的画“×”并将其改正。

（1）原文：Your claim should be supported by sufficient evidence.
译文：你方索赔须有充分的证据。（　　）

____

（2）原文：We shall take out insurance at this end under our Open Policy.
译文：我们将在开放政策下在此办理保险。（　　）

____

（3）原文：卖方须于 9 月 10 日前（不含 9 月 10 日）将货物交给买方。
译文：The vendor shall deliver the goods to the vendee by September 10.（　　）

____

（4）原文：该产品在本地的销售看好，我方出价可达每吨 150 美元或以上。
译文：The market here for this product is active, and the best price we can offer is over US$ 150 per ton.（　　）

____

Task II　翻译以下几组商务电子邮件句子，讨论每一组的句式特点。

第一组：

1. We have been doing business with you for many years and hope that you will quote us your rock-bottom price against our enquiries; otherwise we'll have no choice but to place our order elsewhere.

____

2. To meet this important client's request for moving up the time of delivery, a special arrangement has been made and we are now pleased to inform you that the full quantity of your order will be shipped in the beginning of May.

____

3. 在我方同各国商人的贸易中，一贯坚持平等互利的原则，希望通过双方努力，促进对彼此互利的业务和友谊。

____

第二组：

4. Please be informed that, on account of the fluctuations of foreign exchanges the quotation is subject to change without previous notice.

____

5. We should be grateful if you would give us further details of Chinese leather shoes.

____

6. 现附上商品小册子和价格表各一份，以便贵公司能对我们出口棉布的情况有一个大概的了解。

____

7. 兹确认我方今天发出电子装运通知，并通知贵方，本公司已装运贵方订购的 5 000 吨铁屑，经由“太平洋号”货轮于 5 月 20 日载离此处。

____

Task III 完成以下练习，注意把握商务电子邮件的语气特点。

1. 对比以下每组内的两个句子，判断哪些句子更符合商务电子邮件的语气要求。

第一组：

(1) We have not received your payment of the balance of US$ 5,000.

(2) We regret having to remind you that we have not received your payment of the balance of US$ 5,000.

第二组：

(1) You have to replace the damaged goods.

(2) We will appreciate it if you replace the damaged goods.

第三组：

(1) We cannot fill your order because you failed to send your check.

(2) We shall be glad to fill your order as soon as we receive your check.

2. 翻译以下句子，注意保持原文的语气。

（1）感谢贵方 6 月 6 日来邮，现附上第 2245 号女鞋订单。

____

（2）根据贵方 5 月 6 日来邮，我方乐意订购下列货物。

____

（3）If you can accept US$ 275 and send us a proforma invoice, we will open a letter of credit for 1,000 sets.

____

（4）In reply to your enquiry of May 12, we regret to tell you that our cotton sweaters do not come in any size larger than 18.

____

PART FOUR

讨论：通过上述翻译任务，你认为翻译商务电子邮件需要注意哪些事项？同时可以采取哪些翻译策略？

I. 商务电子邮件翻译总结

本单元从商务电子邮件的定义和格式谈起，讲述了商务电子邮件的词汇、句式和语气特点。现将商务电子邮件的语言特点与翻译技巧归纳如下（见表 11－1）：

表 11－1 商务电子邮件的语言特点与翻译技巧

商务电子邮件的语言特点	用词恰当：尽量使用客气、礼貌、正式、严谨、专业的词汇
	句式规范：注意长句或分词短语、不定式短语、独立主格、插入语等的使用，尽量使译文句子符合句式规范
	语气贴切：措辞委婉、礼貌得体
	选词准确：选用庄重规范的词语
商务电子邮件的翻译技巧	拆句法：翻译复杂句时可先拆句，然后根据逻辑关系进行组合
	套译法：找到目的语相应的套语
	语气移植：采用情态动词、被动语态、虚拟语气、please、疑问句等来表达礼貌和委婉的语气

II. 商务电子邮件翻译余论

1. 商务电子邮件翻译技巧

商务电子邮件翻译过程中，可能采用各种翻译技巧，使其译文忠实、通顺、准确、清楚。比如：

［例 1］原文：Enclosed please find the price list and catalogue of this season. Would you be kind enough to study them and inform us your requirements for the coming season?

译文：随函附上我方本季产品目录及价格单。阅后请告诉我方，贵方对下一季节产品的要求好吗？

本句中原文使用非常委婉客气的结构“Would you be kind enough to”，翻译成汉语时尽量维持原文语气，使用了“贵方”，以示尊重。商务电子邮件翻译还可以灵活应用拆译法、增词法等翻译方法，比如：

［例 2］原文：We look forward to your quotations for the arts and crafts which we are interested in.

译文：我方对贵公司工艺品很感兴趣，期待报价。

［例 3］原文：We are pleased to advise you that your order No. 1245 dated October 1, 2022 has now been put on the No. 888 Guangzhou-Bangkok express. Enclosed is consignment note No. 20221001 which should be presented on collection. Thank you for your order.

译文：我方很高兴通知贵方，你方 2022 年 10 月 1 日 1245 号订单所订货物已由 888 号广州至曼谷快车装运，随函附上 20221001 号发货通知书，提货时请出示。感谢贵方订购。

［例 4］原文：We want to notice you that prices of copier parts and components have gone up steadily since the second half of the year. Though we have tried hard to keep our quotations down, we are afraid the margin for keeping on going like this will not last long. Therefore, we suggest that you will let us have your order before further rises in costs, which will lead to a raise in prices very soon unavoidably.

译文：我方想通知贵方，自下半年以来，复印机的零部件价格一直不断上涨。尽管我方尽量压低报价，但恐怕这种情况不会维持太久。因此，建议贵方在零部件再次涨价，并不可避免地引起成品涨价之前便向我方订货。

例 2 是带定语从句的复合句，如果按照常规译法，把定语从句翻译成定语，则译文为“我方期待贵方对我方感兴趣的工艺品报价”，这样就不够清楚，而采用拆译法就清楚多了。例 3 中“Enclosed is consignment note No. 20221001 which should be presented on collection”同样采用了拆译法，翻译成“随函附上 20221001 号发货通知书，提货时请出示”，而不是“随函附上提货时须出示的 20221001 号发货通知书”。另外，“order No. 1245”此处增加了“所订货物”，因为不可能把订单交列车装运，而是“订单所订货物”。例 4 中“will let us have your order before further rises in costs, which will lead to a raise in prices very soon unavoidably”，“cost”指“零部件成本”，“prices”指“复印机价格或成品价格”，这都需要根据语境在翻译中补充完整，才能使译文表意清楚。

2. 商务电子邮件称呼的翻译及注意事项

商务电子邮件最常见的称呼有：Dear Sirs/Madam, My dear Sir, Dear Mr., My dear Ms. ×××, Gentlemen 等。在商务英语信函翻译中应注意以下几点：

（1）对女性的称呼，无论是已婚还是未婚，都统称：Dear Madam，切忌使用 Dear Miss。

（2）英国人偏爱使用 Dear Sirs；而美国人偏爱使用 Dear Gentlemen。

（3）Gentlemen 仅用复数形式，不用单数形式 Gentleman，也不用 Dear Gentleman。

（4）My dear Mrs. Hartley 并不意味着比 Dear Mrs. Hartley 更亲密，相反前者是更为正式的称呼。

英文商务电子邮件里的称呼往往是和结束语紧密相关的。最常见的结束语有：Yours truly, Yours sincerely, Yours faithfully。如何把这些称呼和结束语译成汉语，是至关重要的问题。最糟糕的莫过于错将“Dear Madam”译成“亲爱的夫人”，而将“Yours sincerely”译成“您的忠诚的”。英文商务电子邮件中的“Dear”，是一种对收信人的尊称，只不过是一种礼节、俗套而已；而在汉语的书信称呼中，“亲爱的”却是一种昵称，仅用于私人关系非常亲密的人，如家人或情侣之间。因此，“Dear”和“亲爱的”在书信里的称呼并不等值。英语商务电子邮件的结束语“Yours sincerely”等，也只是程式上的要求，同样不能按字面直译。

那么该如何翻译英语商务电子邮件中的称呼和结束语呢？从大量的信函翻译实践中来看，其译法不尽相同。如果称呼是泛称“Gentlemen”或“Dear Sirs”，或“My dear Sirs”，可简单地译作“先生”，略过“Dear”或“My dear”，或加上“尊敬的”。如果有具体收信人名字的，按现代书信的格式，可译成：

“某某先生 / 某某女士/ 某某同志：

　您好！”

汉译英的情况也值得注意。在汉语的书信称呼里，如果是寄给个人的，人们往往习惯于在收信人的姓名后加上头衔或职业名称，如：“李教授”“王老师”“张局长”“肖经理”等。但在英语信件中，只有少数几个显要的头衔才可用于称呼，如“Professor（教授）”“Doctor（博士）”“President（总统）”“Mayor（市长）”。因此，“史密斯教授”，在称呼里就可英译为“Dear Professor Smith”，但“史密斯老师”“史密斯局长”“史密斯经理”等，按照英语的表达习惯，统称为“Dear Mr. Smith”。如果收信人是已婚女性，则译为“Dear Mrs. Smith”。

至于英文商务电子邮件的结束语，事实上只不过是一种谦称，不必照字面直译成“您的忠诚的”或“您的忠实的”，这不符合汉语的表达习惯。我国公函中有相当的礼辞，如“谨启”“谨上”“敬上”，在此不妨套用。在特定的场合，也可译为“顺致敬意！”，或写成两行：

　此致

敬礼！

　或：

　此致

×××谨上 / 上

如果是回信也可译成“×××谨复”。如果是汉译英，解决的办法就更为简单，对于“谨启”“谨上”“敬上”之类则可根据信头的称呼，统统还原为“Yours sincerely”或“Yours truly”等。汉语信尾的那些结束语是可有可无的，可在英文信件中则是不可缺少的组成部分。因此，汉语原文信尾即使没有使用像“谨启”“谨上”“敬上”之类，也应相应地增译“Yours sincerely”或“Yours truly”等。

此外，英语商务电子邮件的结尾常常使用一些套语，见表 11－2。

表 11－2

序号	原文	原译	改译
1	Your favorable information will be appreciated.	我们期望得到你们的好消息。	恭候佳音！
2	Your early reply will be highly appreciated.	我们将会十分感激你们的早日答复。	如蒙早复，不胜感激！
3	Awaiting your immediate reply.	等候你们的早日回信。	请即复！

原译虽说没有曲解原文的意思，但却行文啰嗦，有失汉语的语言风格。实际上，汉语也有类似的客套话，言简意赅，译者可充分发挥译入语的语言优势。

PART FIVE

译技点津：商务翻译技巧之正反转换翻译

每一种语言都有肯定和否定的表达方式。英语的否定表达按语言学家们的划分大致有4类：完全否定（带no的词语，如nothing，none等）、半否定（hardly，scarcely等）、部分否定（not all，not every等）及带否定意义的词语（fail, without等）。一般情况下肯定和否定可以对号入座，但是英汉翻译过程中经常遇到这样的情况：英语词、句在字面上是肯定形式，但若照着直译，往往语句不通；倘若译为汉语的否定词或其他否定形式，反倒文从字顺。因此有时需要采用正反交替的方法，正说反译、反说正译，这样才能准确地传达出原文的语言内涵。

I. 英语为肯定式，汉语译作否定式

由于思维习惯和语言习惯的问题，翻译过程中如果采用直译会造成文句不通的现象，因此需要正说反译。譬如“Please keep the fire burning.”，我们一般不说“请保持火燃烧”，而是译作“别让火灭了”。这种方法可广泛用于各种词类、短语，甚至整个句子的翻译，比如：

［例1］原文：Such a chance was denied (to) me.
译文：我**没有得到**这样一个机会。

［例2］原文：The pair of shoes is past repair.
译文：这双鞋子**无法**修补了。

［例3］原文：This is more than we could bear.
译文：这是我们所**不能**忍受的。

［例4］原文：It was beyond his power to sign such a contract.
译文：他**无权**签订这种合同。

［例5］原文：His anger is out of hand.
译文：他怒**不**可遏。

［例6］原文：They feel great anxiety about his sickness.
译文：他的病情让他们感到**焦虑不安**。

［例7］原文：If it worked once, it can work twice.
译文：一次得手，再次**不愁**。

［例8］原文：His refusal is final.
译文：他的拒绝是**不可**更改的。

II. 英语为否定式，汉语译作肯定式

英语中有大量含有否定意义的肯定句。许多含有not, no, none, never, hardly, scarcely, little等否定意义的动词、形容词、副词、介词短语，以及有些包含了否定词的句子，可以运用“负负得正”的反译法来处理否定式，一方面可以准确传达原义，另一方面可以顺应汉语的表达习惯。

［例 9］原文：He is no idiot.
译文：他**精明**得很。

［例 10］原文：We can't wait to meet you.
译文：我们要**立刻**见到你。（我们**迫不及待**地想见到你。）

［例 11］原文：Don't forget to tell me about it.
译文：一定**记着**告诉我。

［例 12］原文：We must never stop taking an optimistic view of life.
译文：对生活，我们要**永远保持**乐观的态度。

［例 13］原文：Students, with no exception, are to hand in your exercises this afternoon.
译文：今天下午学生**统一**交作业。

III. 英语中的双重否定结构

在同一个句子中，两次运用否定手段就称为双重否定，通常由否定词 no，not，never 等表示否定意义的词连用构成，如“not... without...”为否定结构，翻译中有时译成肯定句更好，有时则译成双重否定比较妥当。例如：

［例 14］原文：In a small company such things cannot be done without remark.
译文 1：在一家小公司里，这类事情**不可能不**受到关注。
译文 2：在一家小公司里，这类事情**注定会**引起别人的注意。

英语中的双重否定结构往往可以翻译成肯定句，比如：

［例 15］原文：They never meet without a quarrel but they still have not resolved the dispute of the contract.
译文：他们总是一见面**就**吵架，但还是没有解决合同纠纷。

［例 16］原文：Mexico City is in an earthquake zone and earth tremors are not unusual.
译文：墨西哥城位于地震带，**时常有**小震。

［例 17］原文：It's a rare book on reengineering that doesn't include an insurance example.
译文：几乎**所有**讨论组合的书**都**会以保险行业为例。

英语中应用双重否定形式，一般是用来加强或减弱语气，有时为了语气委婉，可以译为汉语的双重否定句，保留原文的修辞色彩。例如：

［例 18］原文：The offer is not unacceptable.
译文：此报价**并不是不可**接受的。

［例 19］原文：There is no smoke without fire.
译文：**无**风**不**起浪。

［例 20］原文：Few persons dissented from this suggestion.
译文：几乎**没有人不同**意这个建议。

［例 21］原文：As we all know, no life can exist without water.
译文：正如我们所知，**没有**水，任何生命都将**不复存在**。

［例 22］原文：Japan cannot be economically independent without trade with foreign countries.
译文：日本**不与**外国通商，经济上**不可能**独立。

PART SIX
商务电子邮件翻译实践

Task I 请翻译下列商务电子邮件常用语句。

1. We should be glad to hear at your earliest convenience the terms and conditions on which you are prepared to supply.

____

2. We have seen your advertisement in the *Business World* and would be pleased to have your catalogue and price lists of your KV-180 printers.

____

3. Please find the attachment a full specification of our products.

____

4. With an eye to our future business, we'll agree to change the terms of payment from L/C at sight to D/P at sight.

____

5. We are sorry to inform you that the listed terms of payment do not correspond to our customary business practice.

____

6. Please ship the first lot under Contract No. 45379 by s.s. "WUXI" scheduled to sail on or about July 5.

____

7. We really must apologize for the great inconvenience caused to you.

____

8. But for our good relations, we would not have quoted the price.

____

9. Your price is out of the line with the market level at our end. Please adjust it according to the conditions of the international market.

____

10. According to the terms of the contract the shipment is to be effected by the 20th June and we must have the B/L by the 25th at the latest.

____

11. 贵方所提供的包装方式与质量必须完全符合我们的要求。

____

12. 为拓展我公司在贵国的出口业务，我方希望能同贵方建立直接的业务联系。

____

13. 我方盼望收到贵方的订单，同时附寄一份我们认为贵方可能感兴趣的一些产品的目录。

____

14. 贵方 7 月 5 日关于标题所列商品的询盘收悉，谢谢。

____

15. 为安排装船，信用证不得迟于 9 月 1 日到达我方。

____

16. 贵方 3 月 4 日来邮收悉，得知我方发错货物，深表遗憾，我方会尽力做一些补偿。

____

17. 鉴于供货数量有限，若我方报价能满足贵公司要求，则请早日订购。

____

18. 谢谢贵方 10 月 11 日寄给我方样品，现我方乐意订货，详情请见所附订单。

____

19. 请将货款汇往中国银行广州分行我方账户，账号为 14236538，收款人为广州 XYZ 公司。

____

20. 货物将由“东风号”轮 183 航次装运，该轮预定于 10 月 31 日抵达哥本哈根港，请速订舱。请确认货物将按时备妥。

____

Task II 请翻译以下电子邮件。

1.

Sub: Bluetooth Speakers

Dear Sir/Madam,

We are the manufacturers of BM cars and coaches. Our company is a subsidiary of BM Inc. of Houston, Texas. We are seeking an alternative supplier of bluetooth speakers to equip our cars and coaches. As far as we are aware you do not have a local distributor of your products in this country.

A full specification of our requirements is given on the attached sheet.

Quantity required: 2,500 sets
Delivery: by 20 April, 2023

Please quote us your best CIF Laredo price, giving a full specification of your products.
We would need to have samples of the speakers to test in our laboratories before placing an order.

We usually deal with new suppliers on the basis of payment in US dollar by confirmed irrevocable sight letter of credit.

If your laboratory tests are satisfactory and you can provide us with a good price and service, we will be happy to place more substantial orders on a regular basis.

We look forward to receiving an early reply to this enquiry.

Yours truly,
John P. Rogers
Purchasing Manager

2.
Dear Sirs,

We are in receipt of your e-mail of May 6, from which we understand that you have booked our order for 2,000 dozens of shirts.

In reply, we have the pleasure of informing you that the confirmed, irrevocable Letter of Credit No. 7634, amounting to US$ 17,000, has been opened this morning through the Commercial Bank, Tokyo. Upon receipt of the same, please arrange shipment of the goods booked by us with the least possible delay. We are informed that Vessel "WUXI" is scheduled to sail from your city to our port on May 28. We wish that the shipment will be carried by that freighter.

Should this trial order prove satisfactory to our customers, we can assure you that repeat orders in increased quantities will be placed.

Your close cooperation in this respect will be highly appreciated. In the meantime we look forward to your shipping advice.

Yours sincerely,
Peter Johnson
Trade Department

3.

先生：

贵方9月10日询价邮件已收悉，首先对贵方有兴趣购买我方皮鞋和手提包表示感谢。

附件是我司插图版产品目录。我方所提供的产品均用优质皮革制成。鲜艳的色泽、优雅的设计，加之精湛的制作工艺，使这些产品必能满足贵方市场主流的需求。

我公司有一位代表目前正在香港。他下星期将去贵处拜访，并随带我们手工制作的全套样品。他已被授权与贵方商讨订货条款或谈判签订合同。如蒙贵方给予他建议和协助，我们将不胜感激。

敬上

4.

回复：男士皮包

琼斯先生：

我们接受贵方3月8日的还盘，现非常高兴地与贵方确认我们双方已就上述货物买卖达成交易。从我方厂家获悉，目前他们每周可生产皮包3万只。因此，贵方需下月装运的5万只皮包的订单可如约履行，敬请放心。

同时，我们想要强调的是，贵方信用证必须在本月底前开到我处，否则，装运将会延迟。

附件是一式两份我方第03M15号销售确认书。请会签后寄回我方一份存档。感谢贵方的合作，相信我们的产品会令你们满意。

销售经理

×××谨上

PART SEVEN 学习参考

1. 网易外贸通：https://waimao.163.com/
2. 环球资源网：www.supplier-globalsources.com
3. 应用翻译研究网：http://www.practicaltrans.com
4. 景志华，张云勤. 商务英语翻译［M］. 北京：对外经济贸易大学出版社，2015.

5. 徐珺. 国际贸易翻译实务［M］. 北京：清华大学出版社，2018.
6. 刘杰英. 世纪商务英语函电与单证（第六版）［M］. 大连：大连理工大学出版社，2021.
7. 黎运汉. 商务语言教程［M］. 广州：暨南大学出版社，2005.

PART EIGHT
单元预告与实训任务

1. 下一单元我们将讲述国际商务合同翻译。
2. 请同学们搜集 2 份中英文对照的合同。

第十二单元

国际商务合同翻译

Unit Twelve Translating International Business Contracts

《中华人民共和国合同法》第二条规定“合同是平等主体的自然人、法人、其他组织之间设立、变更、终止民事权利义务关系的协议。(Contracts referred to in this Law are agreements between equal natural persons, legal persons and other organizations for the purpose of establishing, altering and terminating mutual civil rights and obligations.)”因为合同是当事人按照法律规范的要求达成的协议，产生当事人所预期的法律后果，具有法律强制作用，所以合法有效的合同原则上内容必须明确，而且具备一定的形式。正式合同一般采用书面形式订立。古语有云：白纸黑字、立字为据、签字画押等。由于书面合同中通常明确地记载了合同双方当事人的权利义务、解决争议的方法等具体内容，发生争议时可以按照合同的规定进行处理，比较容易解决纠纷，摆脱了“口说无凭”的状况。

合同属于法律性公文，合同的书面语言有别于一般书面语言、技术书面语言和文学书面语言。合同和合同语言具体有哪些特点？合同翻译时应采用何种翻译技巧？这是本章要探讨的问题。

教学目标

1. 了解国际商务合同的法律特征和结构；
2. 掌握国际商务合同的语言特征及常见翻译技巧；
3. 熟悉国际商务合同的句型特征及常见翻译技巧。

PART ONE

认识国际商务合同与国际商务合同翻译

Task I 请结合自己的生活经历，谈谈你对合同形式多样性和合同合法性的理解。

Task II 阅读你收集的国际商务合同并思考：国际商务合同由哪几部分构成？

商务合同是自然人或法人为实现一定的商务目的，按照法律程序达成的旨在规定相互权利和义务的契约，对签约双方都具有法律约束力。由于此类合同具有涉外交易性质，因此通常采用中英文书面形式。商务合同的书面形式有多种，最通常的是当事人双方对合同有关内容进行协商订立的并由双方签字（或者同时盖章）的合同文本，也称作合同书或者书面合同。合同书的种类很多，有行业协会等制定的示范性合同文本，国际上也有通行的某种行业的标准文本，也有营业者提供的由营业者制订的格式合同文本，还有双方当事人自己签订的合同文本，这种情况更为普遍。合同也可以信件订立，也就是平时我们所说的书信。书信有平信、邮政快件、挂号信以及特快专递等多种形式。电报、电传、传真也属于书面形式。国际贸易或者国际商务活动中，大量的合同通过这三种形式订立。无论采用何种书面形式，由于合同具有法律效力，合同双方必须严格按照合同的约定，全面履行合同义务，这就需要对合同的文字斟词酌句，力求准确无误。

根据我国《民法典》的相关规定以及国际贸易惯例，商务合同必须具备以下要件才能视为具有法律效力的有效合同：（1）当事人具备法定行为能力；（2）买卖双方意思表示一致；（3）合同内容合法；（4）具备法定形式。

I. 国际商务合同的当事人

在国际贸易中，国际商务合同的当事人可以是个人、法人、国际组织或国家。对于我国来说，为了遵守加入世贸组织的承诺，进一步放宽外贸经营权的范围，在 2004 年 7 月 1 日起实施的新《对外贸易法》中，允许自然人从事外贸经营活动。但从事货物进出口或者技术进出口的对外贸易经营者，应当向国务院对外贸易主管部门或者其委托的机构办理备案登记，如果未按照规定办理备案登记的，海关不予办理进出口货物的报关验放手续。

II. 双方意思表示一致

实践中，通常做法是，买卖双方就合同条款举行面对面的谈判，或由一方提出标准合同文本，双方进行磋商讨论，最后达成一致意见，签订书面协议，这时意味着双方意思表示一致。

III. 合同的内容

根据《民法典》规定，买卖合同标的物必须是属于出让人所有或出卖人有权处分的物品，而且不得违反国家法律和行政法规禁止和限制转让的有关规定，否则买卖合同无效。《对外贸易法》第十六条对限制和禁止进出口的产品进一步做出了明确的规定，具体包括：

1. 为维护国家安全、社会公共利益或者公共道德，需要限制或者禁止进口或者出口的；

2. 为保护人的健康或者安全，保护动物、植物的生命或者健康，保护环境，需要限制或者禁止进口或者出口的；

3. 为实施与黄金或者白银进出口有关的措施，需要限制或者禁止进口或者出口的；

4. 国内供应短缺或者为有效保护可能用竭的自然资源，需要限制或者禁止出口的；

5. 输往国家或者地区的市场容量有限，需要限制出口的；

6. 出口经营秩序出现严重混乱，需要限制出口的；

7. 为建立或者加快建立国内特定产业，需要限制进口的；

8. 对任何形式的农业、牧业、渔业产品有必要限制进口的；

9. 为保障国家国际金融地位和国际收支平衡，需要限制进口的；

10. 依照法律、行政法规的规定，其他需要限制或者禁止进口或者出口的；

11. 根据我国缔结或者参加的国际条约、协定的规定，其他需要限制或者禁止进口或者出口的。

IV. 合同的形式

《联合国国际货物买卖合同公约》第 11 条、第 12 条规定，买卖合同，包括其更改或终止、要约或承诺，或者其他意思表示，无须以书面订立或书面证明。在形式上也不受其他条件的限制，可以用包括证人在内的任何方式证明。《中华人民共和国民法典》第 469 条规定，当事人订立合同，可以采用书面形式、口头形式或者其他形式。

一份完整的商务合同通常可以分为标题（Title）、前言（Preamble）、正文（Habendum），以及结尾条款（Witness Clause）四大部分。

1. 合同标题

英文合同和中文合同都一样，标题并不是一定要有的，因为当事人之间的法律关系由合同内容来判断，标题基本不产生任何影响。但是为了方便辨识，合同起草者通常会依照合同的性质，在合同首页上方起草一个合适的标题。

2. 合同前言

该部分内容言简意赅，一般包括订约日期和地点（Signing Date/Place）、合同当事人及其国籍、主要营业场所或住所（Signing Parties and Their Nationalities, Principal Place of Business or Residence Address）、当事人合法依据（Each Party's Authority）、订约缘由/说明条款（Recitals/Whereas Clause）。

3. 合同正文

正文（Habendum）部分也称为 Operative Part/Clauses 或 Body，具体约定当事人的权利和义务，是合同最核心的部分，也是篇幅最大的部分。具体细则包括：合同的种类与合同的范围（Type of Contract and Scope of the Object in the Contract）、合同价格、支付金额、支付方式和各种附带的费用（The Contract Price, Amount, Method of Payment, Other Various Incidental Charges）、合同的转让条件（The Conditions for the Assignment of Contract）、违反合同的赔偿及责任（Liability to Pay Compensation and Other Liabilities for Breach of Contract）、合同发生争议时的解决办法（The Ways for Setting Contract Disputes）、保险条款（Insurance Clause）、不可抗力条款（Force Majeure）、合同的有效期限（A Period of Validity for the Contract）。

4. 结尾条款

它一般包括合同的份数（Copies of the Contract）、使用的文字和效力（Language and Their Effectiveness）、签名（Signature）和盖章（Seal）等。

PART TWO

热身练习

Task I 阅读下列合同，找出其标题、前言、正文和结尾条款，并翻译成汉语。

Sales Contract ________________

No.: ________________

Date : ________________

Signed at: ________________

Sellers: ________________

Address: ________________ Postal Code: ________________

Tel: ________________ Fax: ________________

Buyers: ________________

Address: ________________ Postal Code: ________________

Tel: ________________ Fax: ________________

The Seller agrees to sell and the Buyer agrees to buy the undermentioned goods on the terms and conditions stated below:

1. Article No.: ________________
2. Description & Specification: ________________
3. Quantity: ________________
4. Unit Price: ________________
5. Total Amount: ________________
6. Country of Origin and Manufacturer: ________________
7. Packing: ________________
8. Shipping Marks: ________________
9. Time of Shipment: ________________
10. Port of Loading: ________________
11. Port of Destination: ________________
12. Insurance: ________________
13. Payment: ________________
14. Documents: ________________
15. Terms of Shipment: ________________
16. Quality/Quantity Discrepancy and Claim: ________________

17. Force Majeure: ________________
18. Arbitration: ________________
19. Remark: ________________

Sellers: ________________ Buyers: ________________
Signature: ________________ Signature: ________________

Task II 请将下列短语翻译成汉语。

1. acceptor ____________________
2. document against payment ____________________
3. terms and conditions ____________________
4. hereinafter referred to as ____________________
5. international trade contract ____________________
6. in witness whereof ____________________
7. in accordance with ____________________
8. principal place of business ____________________
9. the above-mentioned ____________________
10. to execute/fulfill a contract ____________________

Task III 翻译下列句子。

1. The contract is made out in English and Chinese languages in quadruplicate, both texts being equally authentic, and each Party shall hold two copies of each text.

   ____

2. In no event shall the Seller be liable for lost profits, delay, injury to goodwill or any special or consequential damages howsoever any of the same are caused.

   ____

3. The Buyer hereby orders from the Seller the undermentioned goods subject to the following conditions.

   ____

4. For purpose of this, Capital Account shall be adjusted hypothetically as provided for in Section 4.6 herein.

   ____

5. Party B shall ship the goods within one month of the date of signing this Contract, i.e. not later than December 15.

   ____

PART THREE

国际商务合同的语言特点与翻译技巧

Task I 请阅读并翻译下列英文合同条款，并说明商务合同的语言特征。

1. This Contract is made and concluded on __________ (date), __________ (year), by and between ___________ (hereinafter called Party A) on the one hand and __________ (hereinafter called Party B) on the other hand.
2. This contract, made and entered into in ___________ (place of signature) the (this/on), __________ (date), __________ (year), by and between ___________ (name of one party), a corporation duly organize and existing under the laws of _________ (name of country) with its domicile at __________ (address) (hereinafter called Party A), and _________ (name of the other party), a company incorporated and existing under the laws of _________ (name of country) with its domicile at __________ (address) (hereinafter called Party B).

Task II 请阅读以下英文合同条款，分析划线的词语，讨论商务合同的语言特征。

1. Party A and Party B have entered into this contract through amicable consultation. Both parties should try to abide by and carry out the contract in accordance with the regulations relating to the tourism administration of China.
2. An allowance on the basis of 2% of the sales price for each unit shall be calculated and deducted from the purchase price pro rata.
3. Where a wholly foreign-owned enterprise is a limited liability company, the foreign investor shall be liable to the enterprise within the limit of the capital subscribed by it.

Task III 请阅读下列英文合同条款，并比较两种译文，讨论商务合同的语言特征。

1. 原文：In case of quality discrepancy, claim should be filed by the Buyer within 30 days after the arrival of the goods at the port of destination.

   译文 1：如果质量不符，买方应在货物到达目的港之后 30 天内提出。

   译文 2：买方提出索赔，凡属品质异议，应于货物到达目的港之日起 30 日内提出。

2. 原文：Shipment will be made within the last ten-day period of April, 2023, subject to acceptable L/C reaches the Seller before the last ten-day period of January, 2023, and partial shipment is not allowed.

   译文 1：2023 年 4 月最后 10 天装运。但要以卖方 2023 年 1 月最后 10 天以前收到可接受信用证为条件，不允许分批装运。

   译文 2：2023 年 4 月下旬装运。但要以卖方 2023 年 1 月下旬以前收到可接受信用证为条件，不允许分批装运。

Task IV　请比较以下合同条款的两种译文，分析商务合同的语言特征。

1. 原文：每年可就租赁费用作 5%～10%的调整。

   译文 1：The rental fee will be increased by five percent to ten percent annually.

   译文 2：The rental fee will be adjusted 5%～10% each year.

2. 原文：Total value: US$ 5,400,000.00 (Say: US Dollars FIVE MILLION FOUR HUNDRED THOUSAND ONLY)

   译文 1：总价：5 400 000.00 美元。

   译文 2：总价：5 400 000.00 美元（大写：伍佰肆拾万美元整）。

Task V　请阅读以下规定的中英文，试分析划线部分译文是否存在问题。

原文：保税区的减免税货物、保税货物的监管手续费，应当按照《中华人民共和国海关对进口减税、免税和保税货物征收海关监管手续费的办法》办理。

译文：The Customs supervising fees on the import goods granted with duty reduction and exemption and that on the goods in bond shall be collected in accordance with the *Customs Regulations of the People's Republic of China Governing the Collection of Customs Supervising Fees on Import Goods Granted with Duty Reduction or Exemption and Bonded Goods*.（李克兴，2006：209）

Task VI　请翻译下列国际商务合同条款，注意斜体部分语态的转换。

An agreement must *be reached* between the two parties on solving the dispute through arbitration. Without this agreement, no arbitrator shall accept an application for arbitration. The agreement may *be reached* before or after the occurrence of a dispute, that is, by signing a written arbitration agreement between the interested parties. When applying for arbitration, the parties concerned must submit the contract which includes a clause for arbitration or a temporary agreement on arbitration, otherwise their application will *be rejected*.

PART FOUR

讨论：通过上述分析和讨论，你认为商务合同都具有哪些语言特点？商务合同翻译需要掌握哪些翻译技巧？

商务合同属于庄重文体，与日常英语和文学等体裁不同，合同语言以用词准确、结构严谨为首要特点，在用词、句法结构和行文程式上都有严格要求，避免使用浮华或带有感情色彩的词语，不追求文采、韵味和修辞等。具体来说，商务合同有如下语言特点（刘季春，2007：183—222）：

1. 格式化

商务合同文本大都有沿用已久并相对统一的格式，具有格式化、条款化等特点。同业见之，循例办理。商务合同翻译不同于文学翻译，符合惯例，忠于原文才是合同翻译的目标。为了使商务合同译文的篇章规范、格式统一，译文从整体上应符合译入语合同的编排格式。因此，熟悉各种商务合同的格式是进行商务合同翻译的基本要求。翻译者如果善于积累，学会套用，将会收到事半功倍的效果。

2. 准确性

商务合同是具有法律效力的正式文件。因此，在商务合同中，用词确切是第一要旨。准确、严谨的合同语言既可以避免产生误解和歧义，又可以明确和保证合同各方的权利和义务。在翻译过程中，要达到措辞精确的效果，可采取下列几种翻译技巧：

（1）使用专门术语

合同语言是法律语言，它和口头语言有明显区别。比如：accept 在通常情况下可译为“接受”，但在商务合同中，该词常译为“承兑”。又比如：“At the request of Party B, Party A agrees to send an engineer to assist Party B to maintain the equipment”，在这句话中，显然“assist”一词比“help”更准确、正式。

（2）使用古（旧）体词汇

合同中经常出现由 here/there/where + 各种介词所构成的古（旧）体词汇，其中 here 相当于 this，there 相当于 that，where 相当于 which 或 what。例如：herein 的意思等于 in this，hereafter 等于 after this，thereof 等于 of that，whereby 等于 by which。使用这些词语能够使合同的行文显得正式、准确、简洁。请看例句：

［例 1］原文：Party B should bear all the losses herefrom.

译文：乙方须承担由此产生的一切损失。

［例 2］原文：Party B shall inspect the raw materials supplied by Party A immediately upon receipt thereof.

译文：乙方一俟收到甲方提供的原材料应立即进行检验。

商务英语中常见的古体词还包括：hereafter（本文以下），therefore（因此），whereas（而），hereby（因此，据此），hereinafter/hereinbelow（在下文），thereinbefore（在上文中，在上一部分中），thereinafter（在下文中，在下一部分中），hereof（……中的），herewith（与……一道），thereafter（从那以后……），thereon/ thereupon（在其上），thereunder（在其下），hereto（对于这个），hereinabove/hereinbefore（在上文）等。

（3）同义词叠用

为了克服由于许多英语词汇一词多义的特点而导致对合同的不同解释，在合同中对于一些关键性的词常使用同义词叠用法，通过双联词组或三联词组的使用，确保合同在内容上表意精确。例如：made and entered into（签订协议），by and between（强调合同是由“双方”签订），complaints and claims（索赔），fulfill or perform（履行），power and authority（权利），bind and obligate（约束），sole and exclusive（唯一的），final and conclusive（最终的）等。请见例句：

［例 3］原文：This Agreement, and all rights vested in the Second Party, shall forthwith become *null and void*, if the Second Party shall violate, or omit to perform, any of the following *terms, provisions and conditions.*

译文：如乙方违反或忘记执行以下**条款及条件**，本协议及赋予乙方之所有权利将立即**失效**。

3. 严谨性

合同中经常使用大量的数字，这些数字涉及时间、金额、数量等。这些数字不仅用在计算时间上，也用在量化所售货物或所提供服务的数或量上。几乎每一份合同都会涉及时间、金额和数量的规定。因此翻译合同必须准确严谨，避免造成不必要的损失。在翻译时，可从以下几方面着手：

（1）注意时间的表示法

在合同中，与时间有关的表述方式常引起歧义，例如："Seller may exercise its right between August 1, 2023 and August 29, 2023." 在这句话中，"between" 是否包括 "August 1" 和 "August 29" 不清楚。为了避免产生歧义，英语中可以使用两个介词，或采用其他增词手段。如该例句可根据合同意思改为："Seller may exercise its right <u>after</u> August 1，2023 and <u>before</u> August 29, 2023." 或 "Seller's right <u>begins on</u> August 1, 2023 and <u>ends on</u> August 29, 2023."

（2）注意金额、数字的表示法

合同标的最重要方面是有关支付款项的规定。为避免合同漏洞，规避法律风险，在翻译合同金额和数字时，跟英语使用方法相一致，应该坚持大、小写并用，即在小写之后，再在括号内用大写重复一次。在英语中，大写金额后习惯上分别加上："SAY" 和 "ONLY"，相当于汉语的 "大写" 和 "整"。另外，在翻译合同金额时要特别注意金额中是小数点（.）还是分节号（，）。一旦在这两个符号上出现翻译失误，所产生的法律后果将不堪设想。

［例 4］原文：The registered capital of the Joint Venture Company shall be __________ (SAY: __________ U.S. Dollars Only) of which Party A and Party B shall each invest fifty percent (50%), that is __________ (SAY: __________ U.S. Dollars Only). The Parties shall share the profits, losses and risks in proportion to their investment contributed.

译文：合资公司的注册资本__________（大写：__________美元整），甲方和乙方各出资百分之五十（50%），计__________（大写：__________美元整），双方将按上述投资比例分享利润、承担亏损和风险。

例 4 中 "百分之五十" 和括号中的 "50%" 具有双重作用：一是出于严谨，二是为了突出数字。

4. 同一性和一致性

在文学作品、新闻报道以及其他日常信函的写作和翻译中，作者或译者为了丰富作品的语言，增强作品的可读性，经常使用同义词和近义词来表达相同的概念或思想。而在商务合同中，自始至终使用同一词汇表达同一概念或思想是合同起草的黄金法则。在合同翻译中保持这种统一性和一致性能够使合同中的概念或思想保持前后一致、上下一致，避免出现曲解合同本意的合同解释。在例 5 和例 6 汉英对照《中华人民共和国外资企业法》中的第九条、第十四条在英译两处“吊销营业执照”时使用“cancel”和“revoke”两个不同的动词，这种译法就违反了同一性和一致性这一黄金法则。

［例 5］原文：第九条　外资企业应当在审查批准机关核准的期限内在中国境内投资；逾期不投资的，工商行政管理机关有权吊销营业执照。

译文：Article 9　An enterprise with foreign capital shall make investments in China within the period approved by the authorities in charge of examination and approval. If it fails to do so, the industry and commerce administration authorities may cancel its business licence.

［例 6］原文：第十四条　外资企业拒绝在中国境内设置会计账簿的，财政税务机关可以处以罚款，工商行政管理机关可以责令停止营业或者吊销营业执照。

译文：If an enterprise with foreign capital refuses to maintain account books in China, the financial and tax authorities may impose a fine on it, and the industry and commerce administration authorities may order it to suspend operations or may revoke its business licence.

5. 庄重性

商务合同属于法律文体，合同英语是各种英语文体中规范程度最高的一种，即“庄重文体”（frozen style），其用语通常较为正式。合同用词通常选择意义明确，不含歧义的词语，以免引起不必要的误解或纠纷。如多用于正式文体的特殊动词 submit，abide by，endorse，effect，confirm，present，implement，bear the expense 以及抽象名词 presentation，implementation, shipment，commencement，settlement，postponement, execution 等在经贸合同中出现的频率非常高。一方面是因为这些词比较正式、庄重；另一方面也是因为这些词在其他文体中较少使用，没有什么联想意义，词义明确，符合合同这一文体对于语言严谨性的要求。合同中应尽量避免使用口语词汇，注意用词的规范性，尽量使用书面语，以传达出原文庄重严谨的语言风格。例如：

［例 7］原文：The Seller should present the following documents to the negotiation bank for payment.

译文：卖方应向议付行提供下列文件。

［例 8］原文：At the request of Party B, Party A agrees to assist Party B to install the equipment.

译文：应乙方要求，甲方同意派遣技术人员协助乙方安装设备。

［例 9］原文：Arbitration fees shall be borne by the losing party, unless otherwise awarded.

译文：仲裁费用由败诉方负担，仲裁裁定中另有规定者除外。

在上述例句中，“present, assist, to bear the expense”分别要比“give，help，to pay”等词语规范，尽管意义相近，但在合同中，常见使用前者，而鲜见后者。在经贸合同中没有普通文体中的一词多义现象，词义是单一的、确定的，只有所指意义，没有联想意义，如法律词语 Party A 仅指“甲方”，Party B 仅指“乙方”。而合同中把某些关键词的首字母大写，使这些词具有了专有名词的特征，即单一性、确定性，如 the Seller, the Buyer, Contractor 等分别仅指合同中约定的“买方”“卖方”和“承包商”。首字母的大写使得词义更加明确，也使得合同语言的表述更加严谨。

文体的庄重感也体现在句型的选择上。例如，在英语的商务合同中随处可见以 where 引导的条件句（与日常英语中引导地点状语的用法不同）。这种用法比使用 if 或者 when 引导条件句显得更为庄重和正式。如例 10：

［例 10］原文：Where a dispatched worker is under any of the circumstances as mentioned in Article 39 and Subparagraphs (1) and (2) of Article 40, the accepting entity may return the worker back to the labor dispatch service provider, the labor dispatch service provider may discharge the labor contract therebetween as prescribed in this Law.

译文：被派遣劳动者有本法第三十九条和第四十条第一项、第二项规定情形的，用工单位可以将劳动者退回劳务派遣单位，劳务派遣单位依照本法有关规定，可以与劳动者解除劳动合同。

PART FIVE

译技点津：商务翻译技巧之长句翻译

为了确保国际商务合同每一条款逻辑紧密、无懈可击，把所有可能产生的误解及歧义都排除在外，国际商务合同的英语语句多以庞杂的从句和（或）短语并列的复合长句为主，而很少使用简单句。在合同中运用长句有两种优势：第一，长句可以使合同更正式、严密，更具有逻辑性；第二，长句可以界定在何种情况下、以何种方式、在何时何地合同双方行使权利或履行义务，这样可以避免出现瑕疵和纰漏，从而在出现争议时，也就更能保护双方的法律利益。

在国际商务合同中经常使用的长句的典型结构有如下几种，现分别介绍其译法：

I. 简单长句及其翻译

英汉两种语言的句子在措辞、语序、结构上各有特点。大致说来，英语句子长，动词较少，词序灵活，讲究平衡；而汉语句子短，动词多，语序较固定，讲究对称。在翻译国际商务合同中的简单长句时，首先要正确理解各种相关成分的逻辑关系；然后再适当切分，理出句子的主干成分，翻译时以句子的主干为主导；最后再按汉语表达习惯，变动语序，重新组合，这样才能连贯、准确、清晰地予以表达。

［例 1］原文：A bank utilizing the services of another bank for the purpose of giving effect to the instructions of the Applicant does so for the account of and at risk of such Applicant.

译文：为执行申请人的指示，银行利用其他银行的服务，其费用和风险应由该申请人承担。

例 1 的主干是“A bank... does so...”。主语 A bank 后面跟着一个由“utilizing”开头的较长后置定语，“for the purpose of...”是用来修饰分词短语的状语。这句话的谓语是“does”，而“for the account of...”则是修饰谓语动词的状语。本句的翻译采用了拆分的方法，将一个简单长句拆分成三个分句，不仅使翻译更加顺达，意思更加明晰，而且体现了原句中并不明显的因果关系。

［例 2］原文：The Buyers may, within 15 days after arrival of the goods at the destination, lodge a claim against the sellers for short weight being supported by Inspection Certificate issued by a reputable public surveyor.

译文：货物抵达目的港 15 天内，买方可以凭有信誉的公共检验员出示的检验证明向卖方提出短重索赔。

例 2 的主干为“The Buyers may...lodge a claim...”，修饰谓语动词的状语有三个，分别为时间状语“within 15 days after arrival of the goods at the destination”，方式状语“being supported by Inspection Certificate issued by a reputable public surveyor”和原因状语“for short weight”，而且状语中还嵌有状语，作定语的过去分词“issued”还有自己的状语“by a reputable public surveyor”。在英语中，状语的位置可以十分灵活，然而按照汉语的行文规范，方式状语一般应位于动词之前；而有些状语在译文中可以灵活处理，例如本句中的时间状语，可以提前至句首。

II. 复合长句及其翻译

为了保持合同条款表述的严谨性和准确性，英文商务合同中经常使用含有多个从句的复合长句，以致句子结构长、语法关系复杂。这种长句看似盘根错节，但却脉络清晰，长而不乱。在翻译这种类型的长句时，必须弄清原句结构关系，分清主次，翻译时以主句为主导，从句做说明，用规范的中文准确地传达出原文的意义。例如：

［例 3］原文：Proof to the contrary by the multimodal transport operator shall not be admissible if the multimodal transport document is issued in negotiable form and has been transferred to a third party, including a consignee, who has acted in good faith in reliance on the description of the goods therein.

译文：如果多式联运单据是以可转让方式签发的，而且已转让给正当信赖该单据所载明的货物状况的、包括收货人在内的第三方时，多式联运经营人提出的反证不予接受。

分析：这句话是一个主从复合句。翻译时应首先从纷杂的结构中把主要线索梳理出来（例句中下划线部分），确定各个内容成分之间的关系，把握语义，调整语序，然后才能译出表述妥帖，语义通顺的译文。这句话的表意顺序是：

（1）多式联运经营人提出的反证不予接受；

（2）如果多式联运单据是以可转让方式签发的，而且已转让给第三方；

（3）包括收货人在内的第三方；

（4）正当信赖该单据所载明的货物状况的第三方。

根据中文的条件句在前，定语前置的习惯，这句可采用倒译的方法进行翻译，所以译文的顺序应调整为：（2）、（4）、（3）、（1）（卢秋帆，2013：150—151）。

III. 并列长句及其翻译

由于撰写合同时不能遗漏任何可能情况，所以国际商务合同中常常有大量并列成分。这些并列成分包括并列的词、短语以及从句。在翻译由两个或两个以上的并列单句构成的复杂长句时可以采用分译法。并列长句的分句之间的语义关系往往比较松散，因此翻译时可以断开，分解成单句。例如：

［例 4］原文：The Buyer shall have the right to claim against the Seller for compensation of losses within 60 days after arrival of the goods at the port of destination, should the quality of the goods be found not in conformity with the specifications stipulated in the Contract after reinspection by the China Commodity Inspection Bureau (CCIB) and the Buyer shall have the right to claim against the Sellers for compensation of shortweight within 60 days after arrival of the goods at the port of destination, should the weight be found not in conformity with that stipulated in the Bill of Lading after reinspection by the CCIB.

译文：若货物经中国商品检验局复检后发现质量与本合同之规定不符，买方有权于货物抵达目的港后的 60 天内向卖方提出索赔。若经中国商品检验局复检发现货物质量与提单所示重量不符，买方有权于货物抵达目的港后的 60 天内向卖方提出短重索赔。

分析：这句话由两个结构相同的并列分句组成，均为主句在前，条件状语在后，两个条件状语中都含有时间状语。此外，两个并列分句中也都含有时间状语，均为“within 60 days after arrival of the goods at the port of destination”，在译成中文时，条件状语应分别置于主句之前，而所有的时间状语均放在各自修饰的动词的前面。同时，为了符合汉语句式较短的特点，可以将两个并列分句断开，采用拆译法分解成两个单句。

PART SIX

国际商务合同翻译实践

Task I　请翻译以下合同标题，体会合同在格式上的规范性和完整性。

出 口 合 同

合同编号：SZ0207426

签约日期：2023 年 10 月 10 日

签约地点：中国广州白天鹅宾馆

卖方：健力集团	买方：美国 AFG 贸易有限公司
地址：中国广州天沙路 38 号	地址：美国纽约州纽约市 126 号
电话：	电话：
传真：	传真：
电传：	电传：

双方同意按照下列条款由卖方出售、买方购进下列货物。

____

____

Task II 请翻译以下合同条款，注意国际商务合同的准确性。

1. Insurance should be covered by the buyer against All Risks.
2. The date of receipt issued by the transportation department concerned shall be regarded as the delivery of goods.
3. The contract is concluded in case of acceptance of the offer.
4. Damages for breach of contract by one Party consist of a sum equal to the loss, including loss of profit, suffered by the other Party as a consequence of the breach.
5. Such consequences would normally be that the contract is declared null and void.
6. Any modification or alternation of the contract should be based on the agreement of both parties.
7. This contract is made and entered into (in) Beijing on January 10, 2022 by and between 3A (hereinafter referred to as the "Seller") and 3B (hereinafter referred to as the "Buyer").
8. This contract shall be written in English and Chinese languages, with two originals and one copy for each side. This contract shall come into effect from the date it is signed by the representatives of both sides. After the signing of the Contract, all the letters or telex shall become null and void.

Task III 请将以下英文合同条款翻译成中文，特别注意数字、时间的严谨性和准确性。

1. Party A shall deliver the goods to Party B on July 28, 2022.
2. Party A shall deliver the goods to Party B by July 28, 2022.
3. Party A shall deliver the goods to Party B before July 28, 2022.
4. Shipment: To be shipped on or before February 28, 2022.
5. The balance shall be settled upon the arrival of the goods at the port of destination.
6. Total value: US$ 5,200,000.00 (Say: US Dollars FIVE MILLION TWO HUNDRED THOUSAND ONLY)

7. The registered capital of the Joint Venture Company shall be ________ (SAY:______ US Dollars) of which Party A and Party B shall each invent fifty percent (50%), that is ________ (SAY:______ US Dollars). The Parties shall share the profits, losses and risks in proportion to their investment contributed.

____

8. The increase of investment was one and a half times or from one million USD to one and a half million USD.

____

Task IV 请将合同条款中"通知"一词的英译填在空格内，注意遵循合同词汇的同一性特征。

原文：卖方必须在合同规定的交货期限 30 天前，将合同号码、货物名称、数量、装运口岸及预计货物运达装运口岸日期，以电传通知买方以便买方安排舱位并同时通知买方在装运港的船代理。倘在规定期限内买方未接到前述通知，即作为卖方同意在合同规定期限内任何日期交货，并由买方主动租订舱位。

译文：The Sellers shall ________ the Buyers by telex, and simultaneously ________ the buyers' shipping agent at the loading port, 30 days before the contracted time of shipment, of the Contract No., name of commodity, quantity, loading port and expected date of arrival of the goods at the loading port, enabling the buyers to arrange for shipping space. Absence of such ________ within the time specified above shall be considered as sellers' readiness to deliver the goods during the time of shipment contracted and the Buyers shall arrange for shipping space accordingly.

Task V 请将下列合同长句翻译成中文。

1. If the period for late delivery of the Technical Documentation and Software exceeds 6 (six) months， the Licensee shall be entitled to terminate the Contract. In such case， the Licensor shall return to the Licensee the total amounts which the Licensee has already paid plus interest at the rate of 12% per annual thereon.

____

2. The contract will be awarded to the lowest responsive bidder complying with the conditions and specifications of the invitation for bids provided his bid is reasonable and it is to the interest of the United Nations Fund for Population Activities (UNFPA) to accept it.

____

3. If any record subject to inspection pursuant to this chapter is not maintained in written form, a request for inspection is not complied with unless and until the corporation at its expense makes such record available in written form.

____

4. The seller shall not be responsible for the delay of shipment or non-delivery of the goods due to Force Majeure, which might occur during the process of manufacturing or in the

course of loading or transit.

____

5. The Credit could cover 85% of the local expenses if they are made under the responsibility of the British Contractor and within the limit of the down payments paid on the Contract, i.e., 15% as a maximum.

____

6. The seller must deliver goods which are of the quantity, quality and descriptions required by the contract and which are contained or packed in the manner required by the contract.

____

7. In accordance with the *Law of the People's Republic of China on Chinese-Foreign Cooperative Joint Ventures* and other relevant Chinese laws and regulations, A Company (China) and B Company (the UK), in accordance with the principle of equality and mutual benefit and through friendly consultations, agree to jointly set up a cooperative venture in Guangzhou, Guangdong, the People's Republic of China.

____

8. In the event the Buyer does not furnish the Seller with shipping instructions on or before August 1, 2023, the Seller may at his option cancel this contract and demand the Buyer to pay any damages he has sustained on account of such failure of the Buyer to give such instructions.

____

PART SEVEN
学习参考

1. 世贸人才网：http:class.wtojob.com
2. 法律英语学习网：http://www.for68.com/faluyingyu/
3. 应用翻译研究网：http://www.practicaltrans.com
4. 张林玲. 商务英语合同翻译与写作［M］. 北京：机械工业出版社，2009.
5. 兰天. 国际商务翻译教程（第四版）［M］. 大连：东北财经大学出版社，2019.
6. 卢秋帆. 国际贸易法律文本特点及其变迁研究［M］. 北京：中国政法大学出版社，2013.
7. 彭萍. 非文学语篇翻译［M］. 北京：中译出版社，2024.

PART EIGHT
单元预告与实训任务

1. 下一单元我们将讲述商务英语中技术术语的翻译。
2. 请搜集英文技术术语的有关材料。

第十三单元

技术术语翻译

Unit Thirteen Translating Technical Terms

自 20 世纪 70 年代以来，国际上对技术翻译给予了极大的关注，不少学者对它进行了专门研究。21 世纪，随着我国科学工作者外语水平的提高，科技工作者、理工院校师生以及技术翻译工作者加入翻译行列的比例越来越大，技术翻译已经逐渐成为我国翻译事业的重要组成部分。

技术术语及技术文献在技术引进、专利引进等方面起着重要作用，其翻译也是商务翻译的组成部分。技术文章的特点主要是要求概念准确清楚、结构严谨、逻辑性强、重点突出，且使用较多专业词汇和被动句式以及较为复杂的句子结构。凡此种种，都使译者在翻译时需要遵循一定的原则，考虑其独特的文体特点与行文规律。

技术翻译首先要求译者必须读懂原文，然后再用目的语加以表达。因此，译者应具备一定的英语水平和较高的汉语修养，还应对本专业的知识有较深入的了解和掌握，具有较宽广的技术知识面。翻译界常闻“译事三难”，具体到技术翻译也是三句话：原文理解难，译文表达难，专业知识水平要求高。本章将根据英汉两种语言文化的特点及其差异，从技术翻译的文体特征出发，结合翻译实例，阐述技术翻译常用的技巧与方法。

党的二十大报告强调，要“加快建设教育强国、科技强国、人才强国”“加快实施创新驱动发展战略”。技术翻译作为科技创新和对外交流的重要桥梁，将在这一伟大进程中发挥不可替代的作用。通过加强技术翻译人才培养、完善技术翻译标准和规范，我们可以进一步提升我国技术翻译水平，为科技强国建设和中华民族伟大复兴贡献力量。

教学目标

1. 了解技术翻译的含义及其行业要求；
2. 了解技术术语的语言特点；
3. 掌握技术翻译的音译、意译、形译和创译；
4. 掌握技术翻译能力培养的策略。

PART ONE

认识技术翻译及其文体范围和语言特征

Task I 阅读下列技术术语及其翻译并思考：术语是什么？术语由什么构成？它有什么特征和功能？

1. All-in-one Printing Machines（印刷一体机）
2. Overhead Projector（投影仪）
3. Ink Cartredge（墨盒）
4. Time Reverse（逆时空胶原重组疗程）
5. Cellular Energy Revital Mask（活力更新膜）
6. Platinum Cellular Silky Cream（铂金尊宠面霜）
7. Vita-Mineral Revitalization Therapy（鲜活新生套组）
8. Female Hormones Function Conditioning Therapy（女性荷尔蒙机能调理疗程）

Task II 技术翻译等于科技翻译吗？技术翻译和普通翻译有何区别？

技术文体大致可以分成两大系列：一类是科技论文，另一类是科技应用文。前者包括研究、综合论述、提出假说、批驳谬论等文体；后者包括研究应用文（如研究报告、科技成果报告、调查报告、实验室实验报告等）、事务应用文（如协议与合同、技术鉴定书、产品目录和说明书、发明专利申报书与自然科学奖申请书、技术信函与会议纪要等）、情报应用文（如文摘、综述、简报、新闻等）、科普应用文（如知识性科普作品、技术性科普读物等）。从事技术翻译的第一步，是必须辩明技术文体属于哪一系列、哪一类别，才能准确地把握其文体结构特征。

技术翻译涉及的内容十分广泛，现就几个重要方面简介如下：

1. 程式化

某些正式化程度很高的技术文献，其语言程式、体例大致相同。这就要求译者要遵循约定俗成的规矩，按定型或基本定型的程式或语句模式来进行翻译，否则难免有不伦不类、不够正规或是“外行”的感觉。当然程式化仅仅是科技文体特征的一个方面，不能因此就认为科技翻译是刻板的、简单的。对初涉翻译者来说，要掌握不同文献的体例程式，熟悉专门用语，并非一朝一夕的事。

2. 复杂化

技术翻译往往要接触具有不同语言特点的多种多样的文献资料，其体系庞大，形成技术翻译错综复杂的情况。（1）文献品种：技术文献资料品种繁多，包括文摘、论文、标准、专利、会议记录、实验报告、政府研究报告、技术合同、意向书、产品样本等多种形式。不同的文献品种，具有不同的语言特点、体例和检索方法。（2）文献来源：文献来源十分广泛，不仅来自讲英语的国家，也可能来自非英语国家，其中还不乏所谓的“German English”和“Italian English”，因此可能存在语法上、拼写上、印刷上，甚至其他一些误差。对此，译者在落笔之前，经常要下一番功夫纠错。（3）翻译方式：翻译方式除了口笔译之分外，根据需要笔译又分全译、摘译或编译。由于文献来源特点，译者必须尊重事实，尽量核实资料，在存有疑问的地方，可用译注形式加以说明，切不可为了“盲目忠实于原文”而以讹传讹。

3. 跨度大

文体跨度指的是文体正式程度的差别，它既有涉及正式程度很高的、十分严谨的专利文献和标准文献，又有知识性、趣味性、形象性融为一体的正式程度较低的科普读物。技术文献多样化的特点决定了其文体复杂性，译者必须能够适应不同的体裁风格。不能把绘声绘色的科幻小说风格带到科技论文、专利、标准等文献中，不能把科普文章译得晦涩难懂、高深莫测，也不能用产品广告口吻来翻译正式文章。从文体学的角度来讲，就是要求在适当的场合使用适当的词语或句式，如“Many of these fine products are in stock, ready for your order”就可以翻译为“上述多种优质产品，备有现货，欢迎订购”。把“ready for your order”译为“欢迎订购”，是按广告语惯例，对原意作了引申。但同样是“ready for”，在有关术语的句子中，就不能这样引申，如把“The program ready for the computer to ‘read’ is prepared in a specially designed language”译为“准备给计算机‘读’的程序用专门设计的语言编制”。本句中的“ready for”按意思直译。由此可见，同一短语，使用场合不同，译法就不一样，这在很大程度上反映了文体与翻译的内在关系。

在技术文体中，除了在句法上大量使用名词化结构、广泛使用被动语句、非限定动词后置定语、定语从句、长句等之外，还大量使用复合词与缩略词，常常采用假借构词法。现具体分析如下：（1）复合词与缩略词：大量使用复合词与缩略词是技术文章的特点之一，复合词从过去的双词组合发展到多词组合；缩略词趋向于任意构词，这给翻译工作带来一定的困难。例如：full-enclosed 全封闭的（双词合成词），on-and-off-the-road 路面越野两用的（多词合成词），radiophotography 无线电传真（无连字符复合词），cpd（compound）化合物，P. S. I.（pounds per square inch）每平方英寸磅数，SCR（silicon controlled rectifier）可控硅整流器。（2）假借构词法：即根据普通词汇所表示的事物与某一技术事物间的相似性，借用普通词表示技术概念。“finish”在“look at the finish”中出现时，它表示“光洁度”，而不是普通意义的“终点”；而“commissioning，mounting，maintenance”几个词出现在技术文件中时，就不是通常意义的“发委任状，骑马和坚持”，而分别表示“试投产、安装和合同期内的维修”的意思。还有一些生活词汇如“ball，banana，butterfly，sandwich”等都翻译为其相应的“滚珠”“香蕉型物”“蝶型物”“夹层板”等。

PART TWO
热身练习

Task I 请搜集三份有关当地产品或服务的产品说明书（如果没有翻译，请思考如何翻译？）讨论翻译当地的产品或服务时使用了哪些翻译技巧？请注意有关术语的翻译。

Task II 请翻译下列技术术语并尝试总结翻译技巧。

1. terminal ______	2. detect ______
3. Haro Galaxy ______	4. Gregory ______
5. South Island ______	6. child-resistant packaging ______
7. 丁字板 ______	8. 三角皮带 ______
9. X 射线 ______	10. 自动控制 ______
11. 半金属 ______	12. 调频 ______

Task III 试分析下列 A、B 两组技术翻译，看看哪组技术翻译较好，为什么？哪组技术翻译值得改进？如何改进？

A. 1.Vitamin（维他命） 2. Cartoon（卡通） 3. Penicillin（盘尼西林）

B. 4. Microphone（话筒） 5. Engine（发动机） 6. Motor（电动机）

PART THREE
技术术语翻译技巧

Task I 技术术语的语言特征：请阅读下列三组术语及其翻译，讨论技术术语的语音特征和翻译技巧。

第一组 beer（啤酒） card（卡片） jeep（吉普车） carbine（卡宾枪）

第二组 neon sign（霓虹灯） motor-cycle（摩托车）

第三组 servo（伺服系统） typhoon（台风） bandage（绷带）

Task II 技术术语翻译的词义选择：请比较下列两组技术术语翻译的句子，选择你认为恰当的翻译并尝试探讨技术术语翻译中词义选择的原则。

第一组：A. 能力 B. 电力 C. 方 D. 功率

1. Power can be transmitted over a long distance. (　　)
2. Energy is the power to do work. (　　)
3. Friction causes a loss of power in every machine. (　　)
4. The fourth power of three is eighty-one. (　　)

第二组：A. 设施 B. 建设 C. 安装 D. 装置

5. Installations of rubble dams are increasing throughout the world. (　　)
6. Hydroelectric installation is extremely simple and usually a single anchor is required on the upstream edge. (　　)
7. The 10 MW（Mega Watts）installation provides the additional power needed in the region with its annual generation of approximately 70 GWh (gigawatt-hour). (　　)
8. The original installation of the north shore fish way facility consisted of a conventional fish ladder, a vertical fish lock, a holding pond and the auxiliary water supply. (　　)

Task III　技术术语翻译技巧：请翻译下列技术名称，并总结技术术语翻译的技巧。

1. (1) semi-metal ________　(2) diode ________
   (3) digital computer ________　(4) air compressor ________
   (5) input ________　(6) output ________
   (7) holography ________　(8) semiconductor ________
   (9) 单极 ________　(10) 多路调制器 ________
   (11) 频带宽度 ________　(12) 放射性 ________
   (13) 蓝图 ________　(14) 齿轮箱 ________
   (15) 工件 ________
2. (1) Newton ________　(2) Watt ________
   (3) mol ________　(4) Hertz ________
   (5) Volt ________　(6) clone ________
   (7) gene ________　(8) nanotechnology ________
   (9) nylon ________　(10) calorie ________
3. (1) beer ________　(2) Doppler effect ________
   (3) Morse code ________　(4) Rockwell hardness ________
   (5) bandage ________　(6) Para ________
4. (1) I-bar ________　(2) U-iron ________
   (3) H-beam ________　(4) cross bit ________
   (5) O-ring ________　(6) 三角皮带 ________
   (7) 丁字尺 ________　(8) 麻花钻 ________
   (9) X 射线 ________　(10) 十字路口 ________
5. (1) carbon ________　(2) uranium ________
   (3) benzene ________　(4) ether ________
   (5) radon ________

PART FOUR

讨论：通过上述翻译任务，你认为技术术语翻译还可以采用哪些策略？技术术语翻译需要注意哪些事项？

I. 技术术语翻译总结

本单元从技术的含义谈起，讲述了技术文体的语言特征、技术翻译的原则和技术翻译技巧。现将技术术语的翻译原则与翻译技巧归纳如下（见表 13－1）：

表 13－1　　技术术语的翻译原则与翻译技巧

技术术语的翻译原则	科学性：表达含义要科学合理，如公路中的 catwalk 曾称“猫道”，现在翻译为“施工步道”更加具有科学性
	统一性：一个术语只能表达一个概念，反过来，一个概念也只能有一个术语与之相对应。如大气科学中的 Nowcasting 曾有“现时预报”“现场预报”“即日预报”“短时预报”“临近预报”等 5 个译名，现在统一翻译为“临近预报”
	简明性：文字简洁概要。如 radio detecting and ranging 意思是“无线电探测与定位”，按英文词首 radar 音译定名为“雷达”
	习惯性：遵循人们用语的习惯。如英文 robot 定名为“机器人”不够准确，其本质不是“人”而是“机器”，称其为“拟人机”或“智能机”更确切。但是考虑到社会上已普遍接受“机器人”这个约定俗成的称呼，就不再改称，以免引起新的混乱
	系统性：相关联术语的翻译要形成体系。如 highway、expressway、freeway 过去都译为“高速公路”，现在分别译为“公路”“快速路”“高速公路”
	协调性：同一术语的翻译在不同学科中要做到统一。如 probability 这一概念，在数学中定名为“概率”，而在物理学及其他学科中，过去多翻译为“几率”或“或然率”。其实“概率”“几率”“或然率”说的都是一回事。现在统一按其主学科数学定名为“概率”
	国际性：从意思和发音上便于国际交流。如采用原文“音+义”的方法进行翻译，把 AIDS 翻译成“艾滋病”
技术术语的翻译技巧	音译法：根据原文的发音译成读音与原词大致相同的译文
	意译法：译出原词所表达的具体事物和概念的科学含义
	音意结合法：根据原文的含义，部分采用音译，部分采用意译
	形译法：用原文常用文字的形象为形状相似的物体定名
	创造新词译法：主要用于化学元素、化学名称、核物理名词

II. 技术术语翻译余论

1. 技术翻译的行业要求

一般情况下，世界各大城市都有翻译公司。这些翻译公司承担翻译多种文字的科技文献和法律文件的任务，通称为技术翻译。它们对技术翻译的行业要求如下：

（1）接受任务

如有客户，翻译公司即通知领取文件。文件首页为“翻译简况”，要求用英语填写。

内容包括译者姓名、作者姓名、英译标题、原文标题（中文用罗马字母填写）、文章来源（期刊名、卷号、期号、页码、出版日期）、作者单位及职称/职务、有关原件发表情况（论文提交日期、系列标题、会议情况等）、原件语言。封页上注明翻译文件代号、何时完成、是否急件等。

（2）一般要求

① 全文翻译

译出每一个数字、句子和段落。不增添内容使文字流畅。翻译的职责是译出原文一切内容，由编辑（专业人员）进行审改，需要注意以下几点：

第一，勿压缩原文段落。原文有段，译文也要有段。逐段翻译，便于客户理解。如原文用6段描述一个过程，尽管译者能用2段表达出来，而且文字简洁，但仍应设法译成相应的6段。

第二，同样原则，勿扩展原文段落。不要把一个原文段扩展成两个以上译文段。不管原文段如何复杂，分解成数段后表达有多清楚，也不要这样做。

第三，可将原文一个长句译成几个句子，但一定要把这些句子放在与原文相应的段落中。

第四，不省略任何文字内容。比如，“flange(s)”一词原文出现三次，译文中也要出现三次。这是为了帮助编辑标注出原文文理不通之处。

② 专利翻译

要将每项权利主张译成一个不完整句，不要译成一个完整句，也不要译成若干单句。对于专利文件末的修正案，要加进译文中。专利文件中的表格、数字，始终要插在与原件相应处。

③ 论文翻译

译文中的数字、表格，要插在第一次提及的段落之后，或插在提到这些数字或表格的文字之后。先写数字，再列表格。

④ 对于译文中无把握的词语和术语要在其前后用双斜线（//）注明以便编辑核实。

（3）打印体例

要求译文以电子文稿形式送交。值得注意的体例是：

① 标题句向左边缘排齐，仅第一词首字母大写。主标题下划横线，副标题下不划线。

② 提及某一插图时，要将 Figure 一词大写：

如“As shown in Figure 1-3 and in Figure 7, this invention provides an improved device.”不写“Fig. 1”“FIG. 1”“figure 1”或“drawing 1”。

③ 逗号后留一个空格，句号后留两个空格，分号前不留空格。每段第一个词前留五个空格。行间留两行空白，便于编辑修改。

总之，美国翻译公司对技术翻译的要求有三个特点：第一，翻译要对客户负责；第二，译件要便于编辑技术上把关；第三，要准确、忠实，尤其是数字、表格和插图。

2. 技术术语中译英的翻译方法

中译英看似简单，要译出地道的英文来却很难，以下比较详细地介绍了专业术语中译英的技巧，供大家参考。

（1）从英文参考文献中学习：参考文献的摘要中往往会包括大部分专业词汇。当然，最好选择英美人撰写的英文文献。

（2）从专业教科书中学习：找英文教科书最好，可参阅相关章节以及中文教科书后面的索引。

（3）从中文参考文献的英文摘要学习：为了防止译文不地道，最好找国内的权威性杂志，至少关键词应当正确。

（4）找一本专业词典，或一个在线翻译网站。

（5）在 Google 中文、百度里搜寻：选中文术语或与这个术语相关的英文词，再从结果中筛选。Google 中文搜出的结果中, PowerDict 的结果较可信赖。Wikipedia 中文版如果有英语注释也是很规范的。百度能够搜出很多 Google 搜不到的中文文章的英文摘要。

（6）如果搜 Google 时使用英文作为界面语言的话（使用偏爱——界面语言——英文），在结果页的右上角会出现类似 Results 1-100 of about 466,000 for ×××［definition］.（0.11 seconds）的文字，其中的［definition］是一个链接。点击该链接就会进入 http://www.answers.com 网站对于某词的解释。此网站将众多高质量在线词典、百科全书的结果汇集到一页，包括 wikipedia, Stedman, American Heritage 等，解释较为全面、权威，更有众多同义词、近义词、相关词，方便快捷。

技术术语的翻译，同样要遵循“信、达、雅”的原则。对于技术英语的翻译，不仅要求译者对本行业有扎实的专业知识，也要求具备良好的中、英文功底。要提高翻译水平，最便捷的途径就是多做练习，多看国外规范文本的原文，这样才能尽快了解专业用语和习惯表达。

3. 技术术语的翻译工具

作为全球专业翻译领域的标准工具，塔多思（TRADOS）系列工具已经成为业界的标准，其核心技术——翻译记忆（Translation Memory）是目前世界上领先的专业翻译领域的计算机辅助翻译技术。实践证明，应用塔多思解决方案后，用户的翻译工作效率提高了 30%～80%，翻译成本降低了 30%～60%。

塔多思的产品特点如下：

（1）基于翻译记忆的原理，是目前世界上最好的专业翻译软件，已经成为专业翻译领域的标准。

（2）支持 57 种语言之间的双向互译。

（3）大大提高工作效率、降低成本、提高质量。

（4）后台是一个非常强大的神经网络数据库，保证系统及信息安全。

（5）支持所有流行文档格式，用户无须排版。

（6）完善的辅助功能，如时间、度量、表格、固定格式的自动替换等能够帮助客户大大提高工作效率。

（7）目前已经垄断了翻译和本地化公司，是国内所有的外企、国内大型公司和专业翻译人员的首选。

（8）专业的技术支持及开发中心。

（9）15 年的成长历史使塔多思不断完善和丰富，满足客户的需求。

塔多思为专业翻译提供完整的解决方案。该软件包内有以下模块：

Translator's Workbench：与 MS Word 97/2000 无缝集成，用户在熟悉的 Word 环境中进行交互翻译。Workbench 利用后台强大的神经网络数据库，为用户储存并管理原文和译文，实现对译文的部分自动翻译，动态提示相关译文语句，自动保留原文格式。此外，一整套翻译项目管理功能，帮助用户有效管理项目。

WinAlign：帮助用户回收已有的翻译资料，通过对原文和译文的比较和匹配，建立起翻译记忆库（Translation Memory），直接供 Workbench 使用，实现对知识的管理和再利用。

TagEditor：完美的网页翻译解决方案。与 Workbench 协同工作，应用翻译记忆库直接实现网页的翻译。通过对网页（HTML/SGML/XML/ASP/JSP）文件的格式保护，大大减轻了网页翻译过程中的再制作工作。

S-Tagger：用于转换 Adobe FrameMaker 和 Interleaf 文件格式，使用可在熟悉的 Word 环境中处理这两种特殊格式文档。支持文件格式：DOC、RTF、HTML、SGML、XML、ASP、JSP、FrameMaker、Interleaf、RC、Quake Express、AutoCAD（DXF）。

此外，基于人工智能的兴起，像 ChatGPT 这样的机器人程序也开始涉猎翻译领域。ChatGPT 仍处于开发阶段，其翻译输出可能并不完美无缺。在使用翻译之前，始终建议进行人工审查和编辑，并灵活使用以下策略。

1. 明确您的目标：确定您需要翻译的文本类型、所需的语言，以及翻译的预期用途。

2. 提供上下文：向 ChatGPT 提供有关文本的任何相关背景信息，例如主题、目标受众和语调。

3. 使用清晰的语言：以清晰简洁的方式表述您的翻译请求，避免使用模棱两可或含糊不清的语言。

4. 指定语言：明确指出您要翻译成的目标语言。

5. 检查输出：在使用 ChatGPT 生成的翻译之前，请仔细检查其准确性和流畅性。必要时进行编辑和修改。

6. 利用提示工程：使用提示工程技术来微调 ChatGPT 的输出。例如，您可以提供示例翻译，或要求特定风格或语调。

7. 提供反馈：如果您对 ChatGPT 生成的翻译不满意，请提供反馈以帮助改进。

8. 结合其他工具：将 ChatGPT 与其他翻译工具或资源结合使用，例如机器翻译引擎或术语库，以提高准确性和一致性。

PART FIVE

译技点津：商务翻译技巧之术语翻译

I. 被动语态与技术翻译

由于技术英语的主要目的是表述科学发现、科学事实、实验报告和各种说明等，以体现客观陈述为主，因而技术英语大量使用被动语态，有时需要根据汉语习惯转换成主动语态进行翻译。如果是带有定语从句的主从复合句，主句是一个主谓结构的被动语态句式时，可将主语作中心词，谓语作中心词的动词性修饰语。如：

［例 1］原文：Various criteria have been suggested in the past to predict the yielding of metals under complex stresses.

译文：过去已经提出的各种各样的屈服准则用来预测金属在复杂应力状态下的屈服。

分析：在译文中“have been suggested”译成“criteria”的动词性修饰语。

［例 2］原文：If, on the contrary, a structure is endowed with more than three external constraints, such a structure can usually be considered both as externally or internally indeterminate.

译文：反之，假如一个结构被赋予多余三个的外部约束，这种结构通常都可以考虑为外部超静定或内部超静定。

分析：此句原语为被动语态，为准确表达原语含义，翻译时仍使用被动语态。

II. 关系词与技术翻译

1. 英汉关系词使用的区别

英语中关系词和关系手段较多，各种短语、并列成分、附加成分、从句常用关系词连接，构成很长的句子，但汉语没有关系代词和关系副词，连词的数量也比较少，句子通常比较简短。虽然在科技文体中汉语句子也稍长一点，但比起技术英语来，却要逊色很多。请对比下面句子中英汉语言的差异：

［例 3］原文：(Not every patient does so well.) In fact, a nation wide trial, open to melanoma patients at high risk for recurrence, showed that vaccination boosted the five-year survival rate by a modest 15 percent.

译文：（此种疗法并不是对每一个病人都有效。）黑色素瘤病复发率高。实际上，对全国的黑色素瘤患者所做的一项试验表明，疫苗疗法只使百分之十五的患者生存率提高了五年。

［例 4］原文：This information is assembled on maps and cross sections, and fitted together in the mind of the petroleum geologist, where it is interpreted and translated into the best place to drill a well that will penetrate a trap below the surface of the ground and thereby enable the well to test the trap's content.

译文：石油地质学家将这些资料绘制在地质图或剖面图上，经过综合分析，确定最佳井位，这样就可以钻穿地下圈闭，从而测试出圈闭中油气的储量。

分析：本句中“translated”和“interpreted”直译是“翻译、口译、解释”的意思，而在这里更确切的意思是“综合分析”。

王力在《中国语法论》中说，英国人写文章常化零为整，而中国人往往化整为零。所以，我们在翻译英语长句时，一定要遵循这一原则，把英语长句中的从句、短语、并列成分和附加成分一一拆开，然后按照汉语习惯重新加以组织。这样就能避免生搬硬套英语结构，造成译文冗长啰嗦，甚至出现误译，如例 5：

［例 5］原文：When you flip the power switch on your computer system, you set into motion a series of steps that must occur before you can see the DOS prompt, which signals that your computer is ready to use.

原译：一开机，你要采取一系列的步骤后才能看到标志着计算机已经准备好了的 DOS 提示符。

改译：打开计算机电源，就会启动一系列的程序，这些程序完成之后，就会看到 DOS 提示符，它表示计算机已准备就绪，可以使用了。

［例 6］原文：The breakthrough by a team from the New York University Medical Center means that nearly all the scientific work necessary to create genetically identical copies of humans is complete.

原译：来自纽约大学医学中心的一个小组所取得的这个突破意味着制造从遗传上说相同的人类复制品所需的科学工作差不多全部完成了。（《大学英语》1998 年 3 月刊，郭辉译注。）

分析：英语原文中的主语部分含有 by 引导的介词短语作定语，我们可以把这一部分单独译成一个句子，这样，既突出了 breakthrough，又很好地承接了上文，更符合文章主题。

改译：这一突破是纽约大学医学中心的一个小组取得的，它意味着复制基因相同的人所需要的科学工作几乎全部完成了。

［例 7］原文：Analog computing systems are frequently used to control processes such as those found in an oil refinery where flow and temperature measurements are important.

原译：模拟计算机系统常常用于炼油厂中控制诸如流量和温度测量等重要过程。

分析：英语原文中短语 such as those found in an oil refinery 和 where 引导的定语从句都是修饰 processes 的，翻译时，可拆开译成两句。原译文歪曲了英语原文的意思。

改译：模拟计算机经常用于控制诸如炼油厂中所见到的那样一些工艺过程，在这些工艺过程中，测定流量和温度很重要。

2. 技术翻译中连词的处理

英语句子借助各种关系词，各成分间的隶属关系十分清楚；汉语不用或少用关系词，句子的起、承、转、合通常由意思本身连接。英译汉时，必须先分析句子的结构、形式，结合上下文对原文有一个全面、正确的理解，然后按照时间和逻辑顺序，准确地表达原文的意思。请看例句：

［例 8］原文：Throughout our lives, we're told that creativity is rare and mysterious, that only artists are creative, that it's a "right brain" function, whatever that means.

原译：在我们的一生中，有人告诉我们创造力是稀有的而且很神秘，只有艺术家才有创造力，那是“右脑”的功能，不管这是什么意思。（本例摘自《大学英语》1998 年 5 月刊，张晓东译注。）

分析：英语原文借助 throughout 引导的介词短语、that 和 whatever 引导的从句以及被动结构，条理清楚、意思明白，整个句子构成了一个有机的整体。而原译文忽视了汉语的行文特点，盲目模仿英语原文，使读者不知所云。英语原文中 whatever that means 修饰 we are told，意思是“不管这种观点作何种解释，我们一生都接受着这种观点。”

改译：我们一生都灌输着一种莫名其妙的思想，即创造力是罕见的并且很神秘，只有艺术家才有创造力，它是“右脑”的功能。

［例 9］原文：The geologist must do his best to work out the geology of an area from what is visible or what can be mapped at the surface, and from all available well and geophysical data for depth ranging up to three miles or more below the surface.

原译：地质学家必须通过综合分析地表上可以看到的和可以测绘到的地质现象，以及从全部可以利用的钻井及三英里多深的地下地球物理数据中努力解决地质学问题。

分析：原文中，for 引导的介词短语作定语，修饰 data；ranging up…below the surface 是现在分词短语作定语，修饰 depth；below the surface 是介词短语作状语，修饰 ranging up to three miles or more。因此，将 from all available…below the surface 译成“从全部可以利用的钻井及三英里多深的地下地球物理数据中”是不正确的。

改译：地质学家必须依据地表上可以看到的或可以测绘到的地质现象，以及全部可以获得的从地表至地下三英里，甚至更深处的钻井和地球物理数据，尽力弄清某一区域的地质状况。

PART SIX

技术术语翻译实践

Task I 请为下列技术术语选择适当的翻译，并将其编号填入括号中。

1. suitable skin	(　　)	A. 注意事项
2. attention	(　　)	B. 激光
3. laser	(　　)	C. 三角形槽
4. V-slot	(　　)	D. 适用肤质
5. Silky Toner	(　　)	E. 排毒因子
6. Detox Factor	(　　)	F. 滋润液
7. radar-man	(　　)	G. 阀导
8. valve-guide	(　　)	H. 雷达手
9. A-frame	(　　)	I. 双重活性因子
10. dual active factors	(　　)	J. A 形架

Task II 请将下列英文术语翻译成中文。

1. firewall ____________ 2. collagen fiber ____________
3. skin tone ____________ 4. firming skin therapy ____________
5. firming gel ____________ 6. regeneration serum ____________
7. vaseline ____________ 8. regeneration activator ____________
9. functional moisturizing cream ____________
10. D-valve ____________ 11. NMF ____________
12. decibel ____________ 13. skin softening ____________
14. revital mask ____________ 15. logic ____________

Task III 请将下列中文术语翻译成英文。

1. 镀层 ____________ 2. 激活醒肤粉 ____________
3. 弹性 ____________ 4. 胶原蛋白 ____________
5. 成分 ____________ 6. 抗衰老成分 ____________
7. 表皮层 ____________ 8. 真皮层 ____________
9. 试管 ____________ 10. 函数 ____________
11. 温柔洁净 ____________ 12. 活肤 ____________
13. 颈轮廓 ____________ 14. 亮肤 ____________
15. 皮肤微循环 ____________

Task IV 请判断下列技术翻译，哪一个会更成功？请说明理由。

1. nose ( ) A. 鼻 B. 喷嘴
2. fox ( ) A. 绳索 B. 狐狸
3. disk ( ) A. 唱片 B. 硬磨盘
4. shoe ( ) A. 履带片 B. 鞋
5. cock ( ) A. 吊车 B. 公鸡
6. hand ( ) A. 指针 B. 手

Task V 请翻译下列技术术语句子。

1. BCT-4D firming skin care aims to restore the natural inborn self-healing ability of the skin and to generate a large amount of dermal collagen through improving the cell function.

____

2. Today except in China and some other areas, virtually everyone in society is affected by the availability and price of oil and gas: directly in terms of domestic use and family transportation; indirectly in relation to jobs and to many other aspects of national economies, whether they are buoyant or in difficulty.

____

3. Ultraviolet rays, radiation, air pollution and other factors are damaging our skin every day. As we grow older, the sebum membrane is becoming thinner and it is not as healthy as it is before, which can easily lead to some toxic and sensitive substances to invade the skin.

____

4. Repair the epidermis, reconstruct the sebum membrane, and restore the natural protective barrier for the skin.

____

5. No makeup exceeds makeup.

____

6. 即刻而持久地紧致肌肤，有效改善松弛和纹路。

____

7. 眼见奇迹，仿佛从未被岁月刻划。

____

8. 设计师必须备有所使用材料的储备表。

____

9. 融汇珍贵铂金液与瑞士顶级干细胞科技，为您重新打造年轻肌肤。

____

10. 生成式对抗网络（GAN）是一种人工智能技术。它可以生成逼真的图像、文本和音乐。

____

PART SEVEN
学习参考

1. 术语在线：https://www.proz.com/termonline/
2. Translators without Borders: https://translatorswithoutborders.org/training/
3. 何家弘. 术语翻译：理论与实践［M］. 北京：外语教学与研究出版社，2022.
4. 马思. 术语管理：术语翻译的理论与实践［M］. 北京：外语教学与研究出版社，2021.

PART EIGHT
单元预告与实训任务

1. 下一单元我们将讲述商务报告的翻译，涉及商务报告及相关文件翻译。
2. 如果你在一家翻译公司工作，一家外贸公司提供了中文版本的企业年报要求翻译，而你在这方面并没有太多的经验。为了能够更有效地完成翻译工作，你应该从哪些方面去做准备？

第十四单元

商务报告翻译

Unit Fourteen　Translating Business Reports

威廉·迪兰尼在其著作《小型企业失败的原因》中谈到报告时如是说："如果我们知道做什么，我们就做。如果我们不知道做什么好，我们就谈论一番。如果连讨论什么也不知道，我们就写一份报告。"这一点在商务领域尤为凸显。无论是在计划的制定、项目的执行，还是在工作的总结与分析中，书面报告都是必不可少的。商务报告覆盖了从个人工作计划到企业年报，再到政府工作报告或联合国工作报告等众多方面。它们不仅帮助决策者清晰理解当前状况、做出明智的决策，同时在国际化和全球化的背景下，也成为分析竞争对手和了解国际市场的重要工具。

在全球化的今天，商务报告的翻译不仅是语言的转换，更是文化的交流和传递。这要求翻译者不仅要精通语言，还需要具备对不同文化背景的深刻理解和尊重，确保报告能够在不同文化语境中准确传达，从而促进国际间的理解和合作。因此，商务报告的翻译至关重要。本单元将探讨商务报告翻译的关键技巧，以确保报告不只准确传递信息，还能促进跨文化交流和国际合作。

教学目标

1. 了解商务报告的含义及其背景知识；
2. 了解商务报告的语言特点；
3. 掌握商务报告的翻译技巧；
4. 掌握商务翻译中数字的翻译。

PART ONE

认识商务报告与商务报告翻译

Task I 请将课前收集的两份商务报告与同学交换阅读，探讨你对商务报告及其翻译的看法。

Task II 阅读下列商务报告并思考：什么是商务报告？商务报告的功能是什么？商务报告由哪些部分组成？商务报告有哪些种类？

To: Mr. John Andrew, General Manager

Drilling Conditions in the Gulf of Mexico

The first two or three feet were fairly easy to drill through, but after passing through a layer of chalk, we ran into our first layer of hard basalt. At this stage we had to change the drilling bit, and as a result, the drilling became slower. As we went through this hard layer, we had to stop often to make sure that the bit was not getting too hot.

The third stage of the drilling was varied. Sometimes there were hard rocks or pebbles, and sometimes soft chalk. Although the ground was generally softer than the second layer, we could not go much faster because it was never soft for long, and changing the bits took a lot of time.

During the last stage we had to pass through even harder rock and many times the drilling bit did overheat. However, through patience and some skillful work by the mechanics, we finally reached the oil deposits.

Zhang Fei

Manager of Engineering Department

商务报告是日常商务活动中常见的一种公文文体。商务报告是指针对某种特殊的、有意义的商务目的，就某一重大事件或重大问题向一个人或多个人提供的公正、客观和系统的事实陈述。报告中所陈述的事实必须与事件、条件、质量、进展、结果、问题或提议的解决方案有关，帮助当事人了解复杂的商业情况和计划进程，解决问题，提供建议，使上级领导就一系列事件做出决策。

商务报告应用极其广泛，在财务、金融、投资、管理、营销、生产、外贸等方面更为常用，如营销人员需要对产品情况、销售对象、广告方式、销售手段、销售状况、竞争对手等方面进行分析调查，从而制定策略以提升销售量。从商务报告的定义可以看出，商务报告提供的信息包括调研过程、结果和建议等，可以帮助决策者制定决策。商务报告还可以就某事进行解释、说服或鼓动管理人员做出某项决策，商务报告也可以就某事提供启发性的建议或者意见，供领导参考。因此，商务报告具有如下功能：信息功能（Informative Function）、解释功能（Explanatory Function）、说服功能（Persuasive Function）、鼓动功能（Inciting Function）以及启发功能（Suggestive Function）。

从上述商务报告可以看出，商务报告包括呈送对象、标题、正文和结尾等部分。通常情况下，一份完整、正式的商务报告包括题目（Title）、呈送对象（Transmittal）、目录（Table of Contents）、摘要/提要（Abstract）、前言/引言/导言/序言（Introduction）、正文（Body）、结论（Conclusion）、建议（Recommendations）、参考文献/参考资料（Bibliography/References）、附录/附件（Appendices）等。其中，题目、前言、正文和结论是商务报告中必不可少的重要组成部分。

商务报告使用范围很广，种类众多，根据不同的分类标准有多种分类方法。根据报告的语体，可分为正式报告（Formal Reports）和非正式报告（Informal Reports）；根据报告频率，可分为周报（Weekly Reports）、月报（Monthly Reports）、季报（Quarterly Reports）、年报（Annual Reports）、例行报告（Routine Reports）和定期报告（Periodical Reports）；根据报告的内容，可分为事件调查报告（Investigation Reports）、意见调查报告（Survey Reports）、工作进展报告（Progress Reports）、市场调查报告（Market Research Reports）、商务旅行报告（Business Trip Reports）、可行性报告（Feasibility Reports）、促销报告（Promotion Reports）、效益报告（Business Results Reports）等；根据报告的写作手法，可分为信息式报告（Informational Reports）和分析式报告（Analytical Reports）。可见，不同种类的商务报告既具有报告的基本特点，又各有自身特点，但因其复杂性，分类互有重叠，不能穷尽。本单元讲述商务报告的翻译主要是指正式的商务报告的翻译。

PART TWO
热身练习

Task I 请将下列商务报告翻译成汉语。

1. Presently, there are about 6,000 fruit juice producers in China, more than 1,000 of which have certain production capacity. And the fruit juice market of China is divided into three forces, one by famous Chinese mainland-based enterprises like Huiyuan and Wahaha; one of which is led by Taiwan-based enterprises like President Enterprise and Master Kang; and another one by large transnational producers like Coca Cola and Pepsi Cola.

2. According to the National Bureau of Statistics of China, most of the fruit juice manufacturers are located in East and South China. In detail, the South China area produces about 359,799 tons, taking up 22% of the total, while the East China area produces 476,562 tons, occupying 29%.

Task II 请将下列商务报告的摘要翻译成汉语。

This report ranks 50 appliance manufacturers selected according to their volume of sales.

The total turnover of the analyzed companies is worth around EUR 587 billion, including EUR 125 billion of the major appliances considered in this report: refrigerators and freezers, washers and driers, dishwashers, hoods, cooking appliances, microwave ovens, air conditioners, vacuum cleaners.

Considering the country of the headquarters, 11 companies are Chinese, 6 American, 6 Italian, 14 of other European countries, 13 among Japan, the Republic of Korea, New Zealand and India.

Company profiles are available for each of the 50 appliance manufacturers, with information on company background, historical and recent facts, basic data (including total turnover of the last two years, white appliances turnover and white appliances share on total production, number of employees and turnover per employee, as well as number of household appliances sold, when available), sales breakdown by business, by product and by geographical area, production sites, brands, divisions, controlled companies and subsidiaries with office addresses and contacts. (*Profiles of 50 Major Appliance Manufacturers Worldwide*)

PART THREE

商务报告翻译技巧

Task I 请阅读下列商务报告，并讨论商务报告的语言特征。

1. In the fiscal year of 2009, the company has experienced a remarkable recovery in demand for most of its products. In general the demand for home appliances has shown the biggest increase for many reasons. Especially there has been a sharp increase in our sales in rural areas in the west regions.
2. China's total import and export from Jan. to Dec. in 2009 amounted to US$ 2.207,27 trillion，down by 13.9% on a year-on-year basis. Of which export was US$ 1.201,66 trillion and import US$ 1.005,6 trillion, down by 16% and 11.2% respectively. In Dec., total import and export in the nation reached US$ 243.02 billion, up by 32.7% year on year. Of which export was US$ 130.72 billion, up by 17.7%, and import was US$ 112.29 billion, up by 55.9%. (*A Brief on China's Import & Export 2009*, Ministry of Commerce of People's Republic of China)
3. In 2007, for the fifth consecutive year, the expansion of the world economy is expected to

maintain its momentum with an estimated overall output growth of 3.4 percent. Thus developing countries, including many of the poorest, should continue to benefit from strong demand for primary commodities. In many developing countries, including in Africa, positive trends in terms of trade since 2003 have contributed to improved external and fiscal balances. These have paved the way for more expansionary policies, and for a widespread recovery in investment rates. Africa is set to continue growing at around 6 percent in 2007, while growth rate in Latin America and West Asia is expected to slow down slightly to close to 5 percent. Indeed, over the past five years, per capita GDP in Africa, West Asia and Latin America has increased by more than 15 percent, a rate not seen in these regions since the early 1980s. This certainly raises hopes for greater progress towards meeting the United Nations Millennium Development Goals. However, it has to be noted that not all developing countries have experienced improvements in their terms of trade, because they have to contend with higher oil import bills while the prices of the products they export have not increased at similar rates. (*Trade and Development Report*, 2007)

Task II　翻译下列商务报告，讨论商务报告的翻译技巧。

1. Grow our leading, global brands. Our portfolio includes 23 brands that generate over $1 billion in annual sales and 20 brands that generate approximately US$ 500 million or more in annual sales. Combined, these 43 brands account for 85% or more of our sales and profits. These brands are platforms for future innovations that will drive sales growth. (*P&G 2009 Annual Report*)

2. In China, juice beverages contain fruit & vegetable juice. The fruit & vegetable juice is made directly from fresh or chilled fruits and vegetables. Fruit & vegetable beverages are made into ready-for-drink beverages by adding water, sugar liquor and sour agent etc. into the juice. In China, the juice content for fruit & vegetable beverages should be no less than 10%, otherwise they belong to other categories of beverages. (*Research Report on Chinese Juice Beverage Industry, 2010—2011*)

3. Based on the previous comparison and analysis, we put forward the following recommendations on the adjustment of Siemens' business strategy in terms of its price level and after-sales services. We should cut down the current quotation by 3%～5% in order to make Siemens'

price the same as or a little lower than the average level in China's home appliances market. Only in this way can Siemens' offer become more competitive. We should prolong the period of free guarantee from 1 year to 2 years or even longer, so as to present to customers our sincerity of emphasizing after-sales services and enhance customers' confidence in our company.

____

____

____

4. HKSAR's post-quake reconstruction work in Sichuan has been proceeding smoothly; and project funds are being released in accordance with the progress of work. We will next focus on our efforts on the management of projects funds, as well as the management, monitoring and auditing of projects etc., so as to ensure proper, effective and efficient use of the HKSAR's support funds. (*Progress Report on HKSAR's Work in Support of Reconstruction in the Sichuan Earthquake Stricken Areas*)

____

____

____

5. The Sichuan Government attaches great importance to the monitoring of reconstruction projects and has issued a series of regulatory documents and to clearly specify the mode of work, the accountability and responsibilities. The Sichuan side has also enhanced the internal accountability and supervisory structure. Coordination mechanisms at provincial, city (prefecture) and county levels have been established to clearly define the management of project implementation and supervisory responsibilities. (*Progress Report on HKSAR's Work in Support of Reconstruction in the Sichuan Earthquake Stricken Areas*)

____

____

____

Task III 翻译下列商务报告，注意斜体部分，讨论翻译中使用的技巧。

1. *Low* interest rates, *higher* profits and the *recovery* of asset prices, principally in developed countries, contributed to an *upturn* in merger and acquisition (M&A), including cross-border M&As; their value shot up by 28% to US$ 381 billion. These transactions played an important part in the continued restructuring and consolidation process of many industries, especially in the developed world. (*World Investment Report 2005*)

____

____

____

2. By helping employees change their behavior patterns and choose more healthy lifestyles, Corporate Fitness Club will lower companies' health care expenditures, while raising worker

productivity. Health care expenditures will decrease due to *reduced* medical insurance premiums, *reduced* absenteeism, *reduced* turnover rates, *reduced* worker's compensation claims, *reduced* tardiness, *shorter* hospital stays, etc.

____

____

____

3. *The Trade and Development Report 2007*, subtitled *Regional Cooperation for Development*, recommends that developing countries should strengthen regional cooperation with other developing countries, but proceed carefully with regard to North-South bilateral or regional preferential trade agreements. Such agreements may offer gains in terms of market access and *higher* foreign direct investment, but they can also limit national policy space, which can play an important role in the medium and long-term *growth* of competitive industries. By contrast, *strengthened* regional cooperation among developing countries can help accelerate *industrialization* and structural *change* and ease *integration* into the global economy. However, to achieve this, trade *liberalization* is not enough; active regional cooperation should also extend to areas of policy that strengthen the potential for growth and structural change, including monetary and financial arrangements, large infrastructure and knowledge-generation projects, and industrial policies.

____

____

____

Task IV 翻译下列商务报告，讨论斜体部分的翻译技巧。

1. Comfortable, hygienic and well-designed underwear will secure good sales while *inferior items* will be forced out of the market.

____

2. Despite the gigantic population, Chinese consumption of juice beverages is quite low. The annual juice beverage consumption per capita was *below 10 litres* in 2009.

____

3. *No company in the world has invested more in consumer and market research than P&G.* We interact with more than 5 million consumers each year in nearly 60 countries. We invest more than US$ 350 million a year in consumer understanding. This results in insights that tell us where the innovation opportunities are and how to serve and communicate with consumers. (*P&G 2009 Annual Report*)

____

____

____

4. Qingdao Haier Co., the air-conditioner and refrigerator unit of China's biggest appliance maker, reported 2009 profit rose 50 percent as sales of more expensive, energy-saving

products grew. The company benefited as China last year expanded a rural subsidy program nationwide to boost *purchases* of products including televisions, refrigerators, washing machines, mobile phones and computers. The government has paid out about 6.3 billion yuan of subsidies as of Dec. 15, and the money budgeted for this year may more than double to 15.2 billion yuan, the Ministry of Finance data showed.

____

____

____

5. Moreover, research and development is taken to be *the least "fragmentable" of economic activities* because it involves knowledge that is strategic to firms, and because it often requires dense knowledge exchange (much of it tacit) between users and producers within localized clusters.

____

____

____

Task V 翻译下列商务报告，总结使用的翻译技巧。

Eight Major Trends in China's Clothing Market

According to China's clothing industry, the following eight trends will dominate the domestic garment market for some time to come.

Traditional western suits will see steady growth as people go after new suits that are attractive, comfortable and can reflect their personal taste. Products of fine fabrics, modern designs and superb workmanship will capture a significant share of the market.

Company uniforms are becoming more popular. Since 1998, many companies have made uniforms part of their corporate image. Demand is on the increase, especially for designs that are unique and innovative.

The market for mature consumers continues to expand. With 300 million people over the age of 45, the potential of this market is huge. To tap this growing market, refined taste is the buzzword.

Demand for underwear of better quality is on the rise. With the improvement in living standard, people now attach more importance to their undergarments. Comfortable, hygienic and well-designed underwear will secure good sales while inferior items will be forced out of the market.

The consumption pattern and design of childrenswear will undergo a complete change. In the past, little attention was paid to the design and health factor of children's clothing. Today, as people focus more on the physical, mental and psychological development of the young generation, demand for childrenswear (including primary and secondary school uniforms) that is simple, practical and attractive is strong.

With China's entry into the WTO, womenswear will be the first to bear the brunt in the clothing market. Since domestically-made womenswear lags far behind world standards in fabrics, accessories, designs and workmanship, action must be taken soon to make new breakthroughs.

Sportswear will continue to be a hit. Driven by growing health consciousness and the fitness wave across the country, sportswear has become an indispensable item in people's wardrobe. Today's sportswear stresses comfort and practicality. Low-end products will not have a market.

The tailor-made clothing market will grow further. As people increasingly go after outfits that can best express their taste and individuality, mass-produced ready-to-wear garments can no longer satisfy their needs. It can be expected that upmarket boutiques and specialty stores offering custom-made formal attires will mushroom. (Hong Kong Trade and Development Commission Website)

PART FOUR

讨论：通过上述翻译任务，你认为商务报告翻译还可以采用哪些翻译策略或技巧？商务报告翻译需要注意哪些事项？

I. 商务报告翻译小结

本单元讲述了商务报告的定义、功能、语言特征和翻译技巧。商务报告翻译主要采用直译法，视翻译过程中的具体情况而言，需要特别关注视角转换法的使用，包括词类转换法、语态转换法、肯定与否定转换法等。商务报告中往往有一些句式结构复杂的长句，可以根据实际情况采用顺译法或者拆译法，以符合目的语的语言表达习惯。另外，商务报告翻译中必须注意数字的翻译，这点将在译技点津一节中详细讲述。

II. 商务报告翻译：翻译技巧的综合应用

绝大多数情况下，商务报告是独立的完整篇章，翻译过程中需要处理篇章翻译的普遍性和商务翻译的特殊性，需要综合应用各种翻译技巧，除了已经讲述的翻译技巧外，现举例说明如下：

［例 1］ 原文：Finally, the ownership model of the farms *as well as* financial subsidies, investors *and* funding sources would give an idea of linkages within the production *and* consumption network.

译文：最后，农场的所有制模式、财政补贴、投资者、资金来源会告诉我们生产和消费网络内部之间的关系。

分析：译文采用了省译法。英语连词众多，属于形合语言；汉语属于意合语言，翻译时省略了“as well as, and”这些连接词。

［例 2］原文：Adherence with government regulations is a basic benchmark for evaluating farmers as often the regulation in practice is *below* what should be enforced and implemented.

译文：评估农民的基本标准是执行政府规定，这些规定在实践中往往**没有很好地**贯彻落实。

分析：译文采用了结构调整法和视角转换法。如果按原文结构翻译成“执行政府规定是评估农民的基本标准，这些规定在实践中往往没有很好贯彻落实”，显得前后不够连贯，把“政府规定”后移，可以使译文更连贯。另外，“below”表示“低于”的意思，此处无法直译，必须转换角度，“低于”不是“没有执行”，而是“没有很好地执行或没有完全执行”，所以，这里翻译成“没有很好贯彻落实政府规定”。

［例 3］原文：In all developing regions, except Latin America, the Caribbean and South-East Asia, girls are *less likely than boys to remain in school. The gap between girls and boys* is greatest in the 22 countries where fewer than 60 percent of children complete their primary education.

译文：所有的发展中地区，除拉美、加勒比海和东南亚地区外，**女孩比男孩失学的可能性更大**。在完成小学教育人数不到 60%的 22 个国家中，女孩和男孩的**入学情况**差距最大。

分析：译文采用了增词法和视角转换法。原文“girls are less likely than boys to remain in school”如果译成“女孩不大可能跟男孩一样上学”就显得不清楚，译者需要转换视角，把“男孩”和“女孩”对调，把“上学”改为“失学”，译成“女孩比男孩失学的可能性更大”就清楚了。此外，“The gap between girls and boys”如果只是翻译成“男孩和女孩的差距”就不清楚，加上“入学情况”就非常清楚了。

［例 4］原文：In dishwashers, where Panasonic has led the market since it produced Japan's first model 46 years ago, the Company's aggregate production reached 5 million units in May 2006.

译文：在洗碗机方面，自从 46 年前制造出第一台洗碗机以来，松下一直领先市场。2006 年 5 月，松下公司洗碗机总产量达 500 万台。

分析：译文采用长句顺译法。原文是带有非限制性定语从句的长句，此处采用顺译法。

［例 5］原文：Extreme poverty remains a daily reality for more than 1 billion people who subsist on less than US$ 1 a day.

译文：超过 10 亿人口每天都处于极度贫困状态，他们的生活费用不到 1 美元。

分析：译文采用拆译法。原文是定语从句，如果直接译成定语，不够清晰，因此，把定语从句拆译成两个分句，意思清楚明了。

PART FIVE

译技点津：商务翻译技巧之数字翻译

I. 数字的应用范畴

数词是日常生产、生活、工作、研究等活动中必不可少的一种词类。数字大量应用于文学作品和实用文体中。文学作品中的数字往往具有一定的修辞含义，如例 1 和例 2；实用文体中的数字往往表示实指，如例 3：

[例 1] 原文：I will love you three score and ten.

译文：我会爱你一辈子。/我会爱你一生一世。

[例 2] 原文：There were 60 million Americans at home working to turn out the thousand and one things required to wage war.

译文：美国国内有六千万人在生产成千上万的军需品。

[例 3] 原文：Malnutrition in children contributes to over half of children deaths. It is caused not only by food deprivation, but also by the debilitating effects of infectious diseases and lack of care. Progress in reducing child malnutrition has been slow. Over 150 million children under age 5 in the developing world are underweight, including almost half the children in Southern Asia. In sub-Saharan Africa, the number of underweight children increased from 29 million to 37 million between 1990 and 2003. Progress was made in Eastern Asia where the number of malnourished children declined from 24 million to 10 million. (*The Millennium Development Goals Report*, 2005)

译文：儿童死亡人数中一半以上是由于营养不良造成的，这不仅是由于缺少食物，而且是由于传染病导致身体虚弱且缺少照顾造成的。减少儿童营养不良现象一直进展缓慢。发展中国家超过 1.5 亿 5 岁以下儿童体重不达标，其中差不多一半在南亚。撒哈拉沙漠以南的非洲，体重不达标的儿童在 1990 年至 2003 年期间从 2 900 万增至 3 700 万。东亚取得了一些进展，营养不良儿童从 2 400 万降低到了 1 000 万（《千年发展目标报告》，2005）。

例 1 和例 2 中的数字“three score and ten”和“the thousand and one”都不是实指，而具有一定的夸张含义。“three score and ten”在《旧约》中表示人的寿命大约为 70 岁，此处不能按实际时间翻译，而表示“一生一世、天长地久”的意思；而“the thousand and one”表示数量很大，不计其数。本单元讨论的数字翻译并不包括文学作品中的数字的翻译，也不包括具有深刻文化内涵的数字的翻译，而仅仅讨论商务英语中有关数字准确翻译，如例 3 中的数字翻译。

II. 商务翻译中数字的翻译

商务活动中，任何时候都离不开数字。数字可以准确地表达事物的状况，可以翔实地记录事物的发展状态，也可以科学地证明某些观点。在商务报告中，可以说数字的应用比比皆是。本单元重点阐述数字翻译以及与数字紧密相关的表达法如“上升、下降”等词汇的翻译。我们知道，“失之毫厘，差之千里”，数字及有关数字翻译的重要原则就是“准确性”。

1. 英汉数字翻译

英语和汉语数字的读法和记录方式差别很大，汉语按“个十百千万”记录，而英语按数字分节号记录，每三位数字为一节。要进行数字翻译，必须掌握基本的英汉数字对应，现归纳表示如下：

例如：1，	0	0	0，	0	0	0，	0	0	0
英文：billion			million			thousand			
中文：十亿，	亿	千万	百万，	十万	万	千，	百	十	个

2.“数量增加”的翻译

英语中，表示数量增加的词语或者短语包括“increase, rise, grow, up, reach”，增长了多少可以用“up, by”表示，增长到多少用“increase to, arrive at”表示。另外，表示迅速增长或者急剧上升可以用“rocket, skyrocket, jump, leap, soar, shoot up, increase dramatically, increase sharply”等表示。

［例 4］原文：This report provides information about the growth rates in the ownership of mobile phones in Europe, USA and Asia in the years between 1997 and 2002. During the five years, there was a general increase in the mobile phone ownership in all three parts of the world. In Europe, the number of mobile phone owners accounted for about 4% of the total number of telephone users in 1997. The percentage rose to 14% or so in 2002. In USA, the percentage was about 8% in 1997, the highest among the three groups. It increased to about 18% in 2002. The increase in Asia reached three times in these years, from only 2% to about 8% in 2002. So we can expect that the mobile phone market in Asia would be developing much faster than in the other two areas.

译文：本报告提供了 1997 年至 2002 年欧洲、美国和亚洲手机增长率的有关信息。在这五年期间，这些地方的手机拥有量普遍增长了。1997 年，欧洲手机用户人数约占电话用户总人数的 4%，2002 年上升到约 14%。1997 年，美国手机用户约占电话用户总人数的 8%，为欧洲、美国和亚洲三者之最，2002 年上升到约 18%。期间，亚洲手机用户占电话用户的比例增长了 3 倍，从 2%增长到 2002 年的 8%左右。我们可以预测，亚洲手机市场将比欧洲和美国手机市场发展得更快。

［例 5］原文：This report illustrates the changes of the total production cost of ABC company between 2000 and 2010. The production cost went down gradually from US$ 55 million in 2000 to US$ 40 million in 2003. However, it suddenly started to increase dramatically in the following 2 years and reached a new high of US$ 60 million in 2005. At this turning point, the Company successfully controlled such a rocketing cost of production and made great efforts to cut it and in 2008, it reached a new low. Unfortunately, starting from 2009, the production cost began to go up again and in 2010 it reached the same level as high as that in the year 2005.

译文：本报告阐明了 2000 年到 2010 年 ABC 公司生产成本的变化。生产成本从 2000 年的 5 500 万美元逐步下降到 2003 年的 4 000 万美元。然而，接下来 2 年内，生产成本猛增，2005 年达到新高，成本高达 6 000 万美元。这是个转折点，公司成功控制急剧上扬的生产成本，努力削减成本，2008 年降到最低。不幸的是，2009 年开始，生产成本开始上升，2010 年生产成本与 2005 年持平。

［例 6］原文：China's actual foreign direct investment (FDI) rose by 24% to US$ 4.58 billion in the first two months of this year while contracted FDI shot up by 37.8% in the same period.

译文：中国今年头两个月实际外商直接投资增长了 24%，达 45.8 亿美元，而同期合同外商直接投资猛增 37.8%。

［例 7］原文：Through optimizing the economic structure and improving economic returns while reducing consumption of resources and protecting the environment, China will have quadrupled its GDP per capita of the year 2000 by 2020.

译文：通过优化结构、提高效益、降低消耗、保护环境，2020 年中国将实现人均国内生产总值比 2000 年翻两番。

3.“数量减少”的翻译

英语中可以用“decrease, fall, reduce, down, drop, slide, slip, shrink, dip, diminish, lessen, descend, come down”等表示减少、下降或下降百分之多少，用“plunge, plummet, fall dramatically”表示迅速降低、大幅下跌、暴跌的意思，也可以通过比较级如“less than”表示减少的意思。例如：

［例 8］原文：It is expected that the cost of superconducting cable might plummet soon with the rapid advancement of technology in the near future.

译文：可以预见，随着技术的快速发展，超导电缆的成本不久就会大幅下降。

［例 9］原文：Through rounds of WTO negotiations, the average tariff rate has been reduced dramatically from nearly 40% right after the Second World War to about 4% of the developed nations and 13% of the developing countries in recent years.

译文：经过几轮 WTO 谈判，近年来平均关税已从“二战”后的 40%大幅下调到发达国家的 4%和发展中国家的 13%。

［例 10］原文：Due to the influence of the global financial crisis, the average salary of the company this year is US$ 1,200 less than that of last year.

译文：由于全球金融危机的影响，该公司今年平均工资比去年少了 1 200 美元。

［例 11］原文：前三季度，消费价格与去年同期相比下跌 0.8%，城乡分别下跌 1%和 0.4%。在商品类别方面，服务项目价格上涨 2%，而消费品价格下跌 1.6%。头 9 个月，商品零售价格比上年同期下跌 1.4%。工业产品出厂价下跌了 2%。其中，生产资料和生活资料分别下跌 3.1%和 2.2%。原材料、燃料和电力采购价下降了 3.2%。从发展趋势看，第三季度各种商品的市场价比前两个季度下降幅度放缓，多数商品价格环比由降转稳，一些商品价格甚至略有上升。

译文：In the first three quarters, the consumer price dropped by 0.8% from last year's same period, with that in urban and rural areas decreasing by 1% and 0.4% respectively. In terms of commodity categories, the price of service items rose by 2%, while that of consumer goods dropped by 1.6%. In the first nine months, the retail price of commodities dropped by 1.4% from last year's same periods. The ex-factory price of industrial goods dropped by 2%. Of this, the price of the means of production and the means of livelihood decreased by 3.1% and 2.2% respectively. The purchasing price of raw materials, fuel and power came down by 3.2%. In development trend, the decline of the market price of various kinds of commodities in the third quarter was lower than that in the first two quarters, with the chain index of most commodities reversing from decline to stability and that of some even going up slightly.

4. "数量保持不变"的翻译

英语中"stand at, remain at"表示保持在某种特定的水平或程度上；而"hover around, fluctuate"则表示保持在某种水平或程度上下，比如：

［例 12］原文：China's GDP growth rate in the first half of this year was 7%—among the highest in the world—and is forecast to remain at 7% for the whole year.

译文：中国上半年 GDP 增长率为 7%，是世界上增长最快的国家之一，据预测，今年全年增长率为 7%。

［例 13］原文：Due to the changeable weather, the prices of vegetables fluctuate between 6 yuan and 12 yuan per kilo.

译文：由于天气变幻无常，蔬菜价格波动很大，每公斤价格在 6～12 元之间。

5. "约数"的翻译

我们在前面讲过，商务英语中一般不用约数，但实际应用中也难免会出现一些约数或者故意使用一些约数作为谈判技巧，翻译时也需要准确翻译原文约数的"不确定性"。英语往往用"about, around, nearly, some, approximately, roughly, more or less, or so"表示约数。

［例 14］原文：This year's floods, which affect 250 million people or so and 2.25 million hectares of farmlands, have caused more than 200 billion yuan of direct losses.

译文：今年的洪灾受灾人口大约为 2.5 亿人，农田受灾面积为 225 万公顷，造成的直接经济损失超过 2 000 亿元人民币。

需要特别说明的是，由于英语是"形合"语言，往往只能有一个动词作谓语。把汉语翻译成英语时，需要特别注意，很多时候需要把增幅译成非谓语动词，如"up, increasing by, representing an increase of"等，如：

［例 15］原文：今年 1—8 月，广东与加拿大进出口贸易总值达 25 亿美元，增长 20.9%。其中，广东对加拿大出口 17.38 亿美元，增长 38.2%。

译文：From January to August this year, total import and export trade volume between Guangdong Province and Canada reached US$ 2.5 billion, representing an increase of (increasing by) 20.9%. Export from Guangdong Province to Canada amounted to US$ 1.738 billion, an increase of 38.2%.

PART SIX
商务报告翻译实践

Task I　翻译下列句子，注意商务报告翻译的准确性。

1. At the suggestion of the Equipment Division of the plant, the survey panel conducted on-the-spot observations in the workshop on July 15, 2023.

____

2. China's export to the United States, Japan and the members of the European Union accounts for 53.6% of its total export, but most China's enterprises are not familiar with international standards.

____

3. China-India trade increased fast in recent years and the trade volume kept growing at a high speed. Bilateral trade increased from US$ 2.914 billion in 2000 to US$ 18.703 billion in 2005, with an annual increase of 45% on the average.

____

____

4. Education gives people choices regarding the kind of lives they wish to lead. It enables them to express themselves with confidence in their personal relationships, in the community and at work. But for more than 115 million children of primary school age who are out of school, this human right is being denied. These are mostly children from poor households, whose mothers often have no formal education either. (*The Millennium Development Goals Report*, 2005)

____

____

5. Real exports of developing economies more than doubled between 1998 and 2006, whereas those of the G-7 rose by less than 50 percent. Among the developing regions, East and South Asia were clearly the most successful in increasing exports (by volume), at rate of about 160 percent, despite a deterioration in their terms of trade. In other developing regions, export volumes grew at a more moderate pace, close to that of the G-7, but gains from the terms of trade boosted the purchasing power, and consequently their imports. Overall, the share of

developing countries in global trade rose from 29 percent in 1996 to 37 percent in 2006. (*Trade and Development Report 2007*)

____

____

____

Task II 翻译下列商务报告，注意使用学过的翻译技巧。

China is abundant in fruit resources. In 2009, the Chinese fruit yield reached about 120 million tons (excluding melons), ranking at the top of the world rankings. Despite the gigantic population, Chinese consumption of juice beverages is quite low. The annual juice beverage consumption per capita was below 10 litres in 2009. According to a market investigation, in 2009, Chinese juice beverage production amounted to 13.47 million tons, a 14.2% increase over 2008; the market scale reached approximately RMB 57.5 billion, rising by 15% year on year (YOY).

The market investigation showed that, in the Chinese juice beverage market, the market share for 100% concentration juice is only 5%～6%, while the most shares are held by low-concentration juice beverages (with a juice content of no more than 25%). This is mainly due to the purchase capacity and consumption behaviour of consumers.

By the end of 2009, there were already over 1,000 juice processing enterprises in China, but few of them are large-scale ones. Apart from the products of several enterprises such as Huiyuan, Coca-Cola and Pepsi that sell well all over China, most other enterprises can only sell their products in regional markets. Restricted by the financial capacity and marketing channels etc., those regional enterprises are unable to operate in the national market. In the long run, these regional enterprises are likely to become acquisition objects of the giants in the juice beverage market, who can improve their regional market shares and set up localized production bases through the acquisition.

The outbreak of the international financial crisis in 2008 resulted in a big blow to Chinese juice beverage exports. In 2008, China's total export volume of juice beverage decreased to 794,000 tons and the export value reached US$ 1.26 billion, dropping by 30.4% YOY and 7% YOY separately. The international financial crisis impacted the Chinese juice beverage export market greatly. In 2009, China's export volume of juice beverages rose to 897,000 tons. However, due to the declining export price, the export value dropped by 39.4% YOY to US$ 762.40 million. In the first quarter of 2010, Chinese juice beverage exports continued to decrease.

A large part of the Chinese juice beverage market is occupied by cheap low-concentration juice beverages, with only a small percentage of high-priced, high-concentration juice beverages. Generally, consumers did not cut down their expenditure on juice beverages. Therefore, the domestic juice beverage market did not suffer great losses in the global financial crisis.

According to an investigation into the development of the world beverage markets, when the GDP per capita reaches US$ 3,000, residents will pay more attention to vitamin supplement beverages. In 2009, Chinese GDP per capita exceeded US$ 3,000. It is forecast that the Chinese juice beverage market will sustain rapid growth in 2010–2014 and the juice beverage consumption per capita will also rise fast in China. In the following years, the Chinese juice beverage market is expected to become the competition focus of domestic and foreign enterprises.

____

____

____

____

____

Task III 翻译下列商务报告，注意使用各种翻译技巧。

In theory, the internationalization of research and development (R&D) into developing countries is both expected and unexpected. It is expected for two reasons. First, as transnational corporations (TNCs) increase their production in developing countries, some R&D (of adaptive kind) can be expected to follow. Second, R&D is a form of service activity and like other services, it is "fragmenting", with certain segments being located where they can be performed most efficiently. Indeed, according to a survey of Europe's largest firms conducted in 2004 by United Nations Conference on Trade and Development and Roland Berger Consultancy Company, all service functions—including R&D—are now candidates for offshoring. It is unexpected in that R&D is a service activity with very demanding skills, knowledge and support needs, traditionally only in developed countries with strong national innovation systems. Moreover, R&D is taken to be the least "fragmentable" of economic activities because it involves knowledge that is strategic to firms, and because it often requires dense knowledge exchange (much of it tacit) between users and producers within localized clusters.

It is clear that, to date, only a small number of developing countries and economies in transition are participating in the process of R&D internationalization. However, the fact that some are now perceived as attractive locations for highly complex R&D indicates that it is possible for countries to develop the capabilities that are needed to connect with the global R&D systems of TNCs. From a host-country perspective, R&D internationalization opens the door not only for the transfer of technology created elsewhere, but also for the technology creation process itself. This may enable some host countries to strengthen their technological and innovation capabilities. But it may also widen the gap with those that fail to connect with the global innovation network. (*World Investment Report 2005*)

____

____

____

____

____

PART SEVEN

学习参考

1. 市场调研网：http://market-research.alltop.com/
2. 研究与市场网：http://www.researchandmarkets.com/
3. 原版英语阅读网：http://www.en8848.com.cn/yingyu/97/category-catid-397.html
4. 杨伶俐．商务英语写作教程（第三版）［M］．北京：中国人民大学出版社，2022.
5. 赵兴民，蔡力坚．商务翻译 译·注·评［M］．北京：清华大学出版社，2020.
6. 李冬梅，郑志明．新时代商务英语翻译教程［M］．大连：大连理工大学出版社，2024.

PART EIGHT

单元预告与实训任务

1. 下一单元我们将讲述商务报刊文摘的翻译。
2. 请你搜集两篇以上原版英语文摘并阅读，体验商务报刊文摘的语言特点。

第十五单元

商务文摘翻译

Unit Fifteen　Translating Business Excerpts

在全球经济一体化的背景下，商务英语在国际经济交流中发挥着越来越重要的作用。在“互联网+商务”的背景下，掌握国际经济与商务活动的有关信息成为企业经营的重要部分。阅读经济商务类的读物文摘也变成人们日常生活中不可缺少的一部分。人们不仅关注国内的商业读物，对国际上一些知名的报纸杂志也相当关注，特别是欧美地区的一些经济读物，例如《商业周刊》（*Business Week*）、《金融时报》（*Financial Times*）、《财富》（*Fortune*）、《华尔街日报》（*The Wall Street Journal*）、《纽约时报》（*New York Times*）、《时代》（*The Time*）等。商务类报刊有别于普通类报刊文摘，具有其独特的语言特点和写作风格。在翻译商务文摘之前，有必要进一步了解商务报刊文章的语言特点，掌握相关的专业知识，以便在翻译过程中更好地理解和把握原文的风格，做到用词专业，表达准确。本单元主要讲述商务文摘的语言特征和翻译技巧。

教学目标

1. 了解商务文摘的语言特点；
2. 掌握商务文摘的翻译技巧；
3. 掌握商务英语中被动语态的翻译方法。

PART ONE
认识商务文摘及商务文摘翻译

Task 阅读下文，体会并讨论商务文摘的语言特点。

1. During the past few years a major objective of the Chinese authorities has been to reduce the proportion of agricultural exports, while increasing that of industrial and mineral products. A wide variety of industrial goods are now exported and Chinese capital equipment has been used by a number of developing countries to establish projects in areas such as agriculture, forestry, light industry, food processing, water conservation, transport and communications.

2. Asia definitely has the most potential of any region in the memorabilia market. Precise figures for the size of the global market for memorabilia—a rough term that includes autographs and artifacts from historical figures to modern celebrities, and whose buyers range from serious fans to even more serious investors—are tough to come by. Insiders estimate around US$ 50 million changes hands annually, depending on what comes to market, with so-called blue chip pieces—items connected to global icons like Madonna or Charlie Chaplin, or historically important figures like Winston Churchill—boosting sales in any given year.

3. In Asia, the market for memorabilia lags far behind that of the West, according to most in the industry. While in recent months wealthy Asian buyers have bid record sums to capture rare wines, prized art, sought-after stamps and more, the region's memorabilia market has yet to make the same sort of impact. The Asian outposts of major auction houses Sotheby's, Christies and Bonham's have no specialists on memorabilia in the region and refer questions on the market to their London, New York or Los Angeles offices.

商务人士阅读报刊的目的是寻求信息，寻找商机。商务文摘具有信息性，即为读者提供一定的商务信息，可能包括投资信息、理财信息、行业动态信息等方面。这些信息必须与时俱进，贴近现实，往往包含一定的专业知识。如上例中“Asia definitely has the most potential of any region in the memorabilia market”告诉人们亚洲纪念品市场大有可为，潜力巨大，商机无限，某些从事纪念品行业的商人可能见机行事，捕捉商机。

PART TWO
热身练习

Task　请翻译下列商务文摘。

1. China has the largest number of internet users and is the world's top e-commerce and mobile payment market by transaction volume.

____

2. It is estimated that over 3,000 companies (including non-technology companies) have received venture capital at some point in their development over the past two decades.

____

3. On January 1, 2002, twelve countries in Europe woke up to a brand new currency and over the following two months would see their national currencies phased out forever. In the most ambitious currency change the world has ever seen, more than 14.5 billion notes and 56 billion coins were distributed around the 12 participating countries and major public awareness campaigns were undertaken to ensure that the transition runs as smoothly as possible.

____

4. China's gross domestic product (GDP) will grow about 9 percent next year, but the economy will be challenged by rising labor costs, liquidity problems and difficulty in sustaining rapid growth in the long run, a senior researcher at the country's top think-tank said Saturday.

____

5. A well-known Chinese entrepreneur and philanthropist has pledged to donate his entire fortune to charity after his death, becoming the first in China to respond to the campaign launched in the US by Bill Gates and Warren Buffett, who will soon visit China to advocate philanthropy.

____

PART THREE
商务文摘翻译技巧

Task I　阅读下列报刊文摘并讨论其语言特点。

1. 阅读下列句子，讨论斜体词汇的特点。

(1) Fast food still represents a US$ 102 billion a year industry, but growth has turned sluggish recently amid tough competition from *retail food stores* and a more affluent population willing to try new things and spend more, analysts say.

(2) China's venture capital industry is also focused on the digital world. The majority of investments are in digital technologies such as big data, *AI* and financial technology

companies. In particular, China enters the top three in the world for venture capital investments in *VR*, autonomous vehicles, robotics and drones, according to the report.

(3) Many auto dealers in China are suffering from financing problems and some might be in danger of bankruptcy this year, according to a recent survey of dealers across the country. A majority of dealers were unprofitable in 2008 with about 60 percent *in the red*, said the survey by Lianxin, an independent research company. It *polled* 1,252 dealers of 21 domestic and foreign brands.

---

2. 阅读下列句子，讨论斜体词汇的特点。

(1) *It is reported* that the unemployment rate in this country has reached 7 percent.

(2) Of course, global sales do not mean global brands, as many enterprise leaders *point out*.

(3) "I believe that as this century unfolds and people look back on this day, they will conclude that in admitting China to the WTO we took a decisive step in strengthening the global economic trading system," U.S. Trade Representative Robert Zoellick *told* the meeting.

(4) The survey also *showed* only 17.3 percent of dealers were "satisfied" or "relatively satisfied" with their fiscal capability. Over 70 percent *said* they had used private financing with a higher interest rate.

(5) Scientists *think* it will be possible to record people's dreams and then interpret them, *according to* a new report. They claim to have developed a system which allows them to record higher level brain activity.

(6) The US recession has driven bosses and their employees closer together and only 30 percent of employees want their bosses' stressful job, recruitment firm Adecco Staffing US *found in a poll* tied to National Boss Day in mid-October. But the survey found that some people are willing to go to greater lengths to keep their jobs in a tough market.

---

3. 阅读下列句子，分析斜体单词的词汇特征。

(1) "*Funemployment*" describes the enjoyment had while on an unforeseen break from work and "*PIIGS*" is an acronym for Portugal, Italy, Ireland, Greece and Spain, the countries most at risk from the European sovereign debt crisis.

(2) "*Broken society*" or "*social recession*" describes the perceived erosion of moral values while "*ghost estate*", an unfinished housing development abandoned due to the downturn, is now in the dictionary.

(3) One of the highlights of the proposed changes to *Chinese Advertisement Law* includes making celebrity spokespersons more responsible for the endorsement deals they take on. These changes were made to strengthen controls over *celebrity endorsements* and advertising.

---

4. 阅读下列句子，注意从时态、语态分析其特点，注意对斜体部分进行用法分析。

(1) In the Special Economic Zones, which are being built almost from scratch, foreigners can invest in anything which the state deems useful for the country, *for example*, production of goods for export or construction of private-housing estates.

(2) Although the weakness in demand in the United States led to a sharp decline in short-term dollar interest rates—*a positive development for many developing countries*—it also contributed to a drop of over 6 percent in commodity prices and to a slackening，to 3 percent, in the growth of world trade.

(3) With average annual growth in America being some 7.5 percentage points lower during the 2000s, then assuming that this will continue and that the real exchange rate of the yuan will appreciate by 3 percent per year on the average (quite reasonable)，then it will only take 11 years before the Chinese economy becomes bigger, *meaning that by 2020*, China's economy will be the biggest in the world.

(4) More goods *were needed to be produced* so more jobs and profits *were created*.

____

Task II 阅读下列商务报刊文章的标题并翻译，讨论其翻译技巧。

1. The Curtain Goes Up
   — Peking permits foreign investment all along its coastline ____________
2. Recession Drives Bosses and Workers Closer (*China Daily*, October 13, 2010)
   ____
3. Hong Kong is Tops at Cracking U.S. Shell Eggs ____________
4. The Comeback of International Barter ____________
5. Economic Troubles Cloud New Market's Future ____________
6. NEET Generation (*The Guardian*, Nov. 2, 2004) ____________
7. West Point Makes a Comeback (*Time*, April 18, 2005) ____________
8. Gearing up for Milan (*China Daily*, October 29, 2010) ____________
9. The Logic of Empire (*The Guardian*, August 6, 2002) ____________
10. Women are Better Managers in Most Areas (*Reuters*, May 5, 2008)
    ____

Task III 试译下列商务文摘的句子，注意斜体词汇在不同语篇中的不同含义。

1. There are no official statistics covering the invisible *account* of the balance of payments, but the size of the visible trade surplus during 2005—2010 and a pronounced increase in earnings from tourism suggest that the current *account* has been in surplus over the past few years.

   ____

2. When the debt is cleared—as it must be by the time the customer retires—and the *account*

goes into credit, it will attract interest at about 5 percent.

____

3. Analysts said that the tight monetary policy put in place at the end of last year has brought about great difficulties for many *firm*s, especially private ones. Thousands of small and medium enterprises have gone bankrupt in the coastal areas as they could hardly get loans from banks, reports said. Fast appreciating yuan value, rising cost of labor and raw materials are also key reasons for the situation.

____

4. Advertising serves directly to assist a rapid distribution of goods at reasonable price, thereby establishing a *firm* home market so making it possible to provide for export at competitive prices.

____

Task IV 商务文摘翻译技巧：翻译下列段落，并注意斜体句子，总结商务文摘翻译技巧。

Trade Barriers

A third unique problem is trade barriers. For one reason or another, all countries impose trade barriers on certain goods crossing their borders. Some trade barriers are directly related to exports. *For example, the United States permits strategic military material to be shipped abroad only after government permission has been obtained.* Most trade barriers, however, are designed to restrict imports. Two of the most common import barriers are quotas and tariffs.

Quotas

A quota is a quantitative restriction that is expressed in terms of either physical quantity or value. For example, a quota states that no more than 50, 000 Class A widgets that may be imported from Europe each year is a restriction stated in terms of physical quantity. Meanwhile, a quota that restricts the importation of a certain type of Japanese glassware to no more than US$ 1 million worth a year is stated in terms of value.

Tariffs

A tariff is a duty or fee levied on goods being imported into the country. These tariffs can be of two types: revenue and protective. *A revenue tariff is designed to raise money for the government.* These tariffs are usually low, often amounting to less than twenty-five cents per item or pound. A protective tariff is designed to discourage foreign businesses from shipping certain goods into the country. The basic reason for a protective tariff is to keep out goods that will undersell products made in the home country. For this reason, protective tariffs are often very high, thereby forcing the foreign business to raise its prices to cover the tariff.

Task V　请翻译下列报刊文摘，注意斜体句子的翻译技巧。

Asia, You Cost Too Much

The International Monetary Fund just predicted that Asia's economic boom will continue for the next several years. Sony just announced that it will no longer export TV sets from Japan because it's impossible to price the sets competitively. Which of the two should Asian business pay attention to?

Listen to Sony. Because even in a growing market, costs count. And for many businesses, Asia is beginning to cost too much.

The Asian economic miracle can be best summed up as the biggest price undercut in history. Asian grew because it was the cheapest source for the low-tech consumer goods that the West craves. Korea didn't invent new or more efficient manufacturing techniques. They simply bought market share with low wages.

PART FOUR

讨论：通过上述翻译任务，你认为商务文摘翻译的要点是什么？商务文摘翻译需要注意哪些事项？

考虑到商务文摘独特的语言特点和性质，在翻译该类文体的时候，译者应该注意以下事项：

I. 标题翻译要概括简练，醒目生动

标题是一篇文章的眼睛，好的标题翻译能够吸引读者的注意力。商务报刊文章的标题很讲究简洁性、清晰性。译者在翻译文章标题的时候，为了更好地把握主旨，可以在阅读完全篇文章，掌握了大意之后，再确定如何翻译。有时候，由于英汉两种语言的差异，不能直接把标题翻译成汉语，而需要灵活地采用意译的办法，更好地凸现文章的要旨。

［例 1］原文：Here comes Korea, Inc.

译文：韩国企业的兴起

如果将该标题直译成“韩国企业到来”，那么并不能很好地概括该篇文章的主旨，而用“兴起”一词，直截了当地告诉读者文章的大意，既简练又清晰。

II. 在词汇层面上必须做到准确无误

翻译的最基本标准是“功能对等”，即译文必须实现与原文相通的交际功能和实现与原文相同的交际目的（潘红，2004：30）。准确性是实现翻译功能对等的必然要求。商务文摘中存在大量的商务英语词汇，专业性非常强，一词多义现象也十分普遍。在翻译时要做到准确无误，不仅要看其一般含义，还要分析其所在语境，从专业的角度去审查它的特殊含义。

［例 2］原文：Last year the BeiBei Company in Zhangjiagang *cleared* US$ 14 million on exports of 10 million pairs of shoes to U.S. department stores.

译文：去年，张家港的贝贝公司向美国百货商场出口 1 000 万双鞋子，净赚 1 400 万美元。

分析：“Clear”作为动词的基本含义是“清除，使明亮”，但是在这个句子中，它却是“净赚”的意思。

商务文摘中经常大量使用缩略语，主要是一些国际机构的名称或商务术语的首字母缩略。在翻译的时候，我们应该特别注意，因为有时一个缩略语可能指代多个名称，例如 WTO，可以指 World Tourism Organization（世界旅游组织），也可以指 World Trade Organization（世界贸易组织），因此，在翻译时一定要结合具体的语境，准确把握其含义。

III. 在句法层面上要做到严密，措辞符合新闻体的风格

商务文摘与一般的语篇不同，具有较多的行业套语，译者在翻译前可参考相应的汉语新闻报刊文章，以熟悉新闻体的风格，在翻译时更好地把握正确的措辞。商务文摘中有大量的插入语，信息量较大，翻译时应先理清句子中各成分的内在关系，将原文的信息分解成小块，再用符合中文习惯的表达将信息重新组织起来，做到达意又通顺。新闻英语中常用“It is asserted that…（有人断言）、It is considered that…（人们认为）、It is well known that…（众所周知）”等，如例 3：

［例 3］原文：It is well-known that the industrial structure is an important part of economic structure. The market and government are two kinds of basic means of industrial structure adjustment.

译文：众所周知，产业结构是经济结构的重要组成部分，市场和政府是产业结构调整的两种基本方式。

PART FIVE

译技点津：商务翻译技巧之语态翻译

I. 英汉语篇中的语态比较

英语和汉语都有被动语态，但两者的使用范围很不一样。在英语中，被动语态的使用非常广泛，而汉语虽然也有被动语态的表达法，但是其使用的频率却明显低于英语。

这是由于英语和汉语各自独特的语言特点所决定的。英语是以形合为特点的语言，即主要依靠句法手段和词汇手段来连接句子、词语等，表达一定的语法意义和逻辑意义。因此，凡是在不必或不愿意说出动作发出者，无法说出动作发出者，或是为了便于连贯上下文等场合，往往都会使用被动语态。而汉语则重意合，其表意功能主要通过上下文的联系和每个词的不同含义来表达。汉语被动句中的“被”常可以省略。此外，汉语中主语常常是能执行动作或有生命的物体，所以汉语多用主动句。

利用被动语态叙述事件能够使语气显得客观、委婉，而英语商务文摘由于以叙述客观事实为主，因而广泛使用被动语态。由于英汉表达习惯的不同，翻译时应该选择符合汉语表达习惯的译文。

II. 商务文摘中被动语态的翻译方法

英语被动结构的句子可以译成汉语主动句或者被动句，现分析如下：

1. 以原文主语作为译文的主语：有时可以翻译成“……的……”结构，如例 1；一些特殊结构如“I'm convinced”可直接翻译为“我相信”，如例 2。

[例 1] 原文： As its name implies, the World Bank is formed to provide sound long-term loans for reconstruction and development.

译文：顾名思义，世界银行的成立是为了各国的复兴和发展提供可靠的长期贷款。

[例 2] 原文： I am convinced that, in the future as in the past, problems can be overcome.

译文：我相信，将来会与过去一样，问题是可以克服的。

[例 3] 原文： The World Trade Organization was founded in 1993.

译文：世界贸易组织创建于 1993 年。

[例 4] 原文： Foreign makers of telecom equipment are also expected to prosper from WTO.

译文：外国电信设备制造商预计也将得益于世界贸易组织。

2. 以原文主语作为译文的宾语

[例 5] 原文： In addition, over one-half billion dollars have been invested by US corporations in offshore oil exploration.

译文：此外，美国公司对近海石油勘探投资 5 亿多美元。

[例 6] 原文： Only cash would be supplanted by electronic money. The use of checks, drafts, money orders, traveler's checks, cashier's checks, as well as letters of credit, acceptances and other financial instruments would remain in regular use.

译文：电子货币只取代现金。支票、汇票、邮政汇票、旅游支票、银行支票以及信用证、承兑和其他金融证券仍照常使用。

[例 7] 原文： Throughout history taxes have been levied on many unusual things such as hats, beds, baths, marriages, and funerals.

译文：在整个历史中，曾经对许多稀罕的东西如帽子、床、澡堂、婚姻和葬礼征税。

3. 译成汉语无主句

英语中的许多被动句无法说出或不必说出动作的发出者，翻译时可以采用无主句的形式来表达。

［例 8］原文：New sources of energy must be found to avoid causing energy shortages in the world.

译文：必须找到新的能源，以避免造成世界上能源的短缺。

［例 9］原文：The practical bottlenecks in the economy must be tackled so that more foreign technology can be introduced.

译文：必须先解决经济中的实际瓶颈问题，才能引进更多的国外技术。

［例 10］原文：Seven *multilateral tariff negotiations have been held* since 1948, the results of which have been to extend the 1948 agreement.

译文：自 1948 年以来，共举行了 7 次多边关税谈判，其结果是 1948 协定一直被延续下来。

4. 译成汉语被动句

英语中的被动语态译成汉语被动句时，除了“被”字外，还有许多不同的表达，例如“遭”“受”“给”“使”“让”“为……所”“予以”等。

［例 11］原文：The future of economic cooperation between China and its industrialized country trading partners should be viewed with a combination of enthusiasm and realism.

译文：中国同工业化国家贸易伙伴间的经济合作的前途应被视为是热情与现实主义的结合。

［例 12］原文：The growth of foreign trade was disrupted again when agricultural and industrial production fell sharply and transportation constraints became more serious.

译文：农业和工业生产急剧下降，运输管制变得更糟糕，外贸增长又一次被打断了。

［例 13］原文：The energy problem will be discussed at the meeting tomorrow.

译文：能源问题将在明天的会上予以讨论。

5. 特殊句型翻译

英语被动语态中，有一些以形式主语“it”开头的句型，例如“It is said...”“It is reported...”。我们翻译这些句子时，可以不加主语，也可以加上表示不确定的主语，如“我们”“人们”“大家”“有人”等。

［例 14］原文：Marketing is seen as the task of finding and stimulating buyers for the firm's output.

译文：人们认为营销就是为公司的产品寻找买主，并鼓励其购买。

下面列举的是常见的以 it 作形式主语的被动句型译法：

It is reported that... 据报道

It is estimated that.... 据推测

It is hoped that.... 希望

It must be admitted that... 必须承认

It is believed that... 有人认为

PART SIX
商务文摘翻译实践

Task I 请阅读下列商务文摘的原文和译文，分析其中的问题并改进译文。

原文：A market is simply the sum of contacts between buyers and sellers of a product or service. A market may, or may not, be formally organized and geographically centered, as are the New York Stock Exchange, the Fulton Fish Market, or the Chicago Board of Trade. Neither the market for shoes nor the market for structural steel is formally organized, and neither of them can be located at some particular place on a map. Markets are simply the process through which buyers and sellers interact and by which prices and quantities are determined.

原译：市场只不过是某一种产品或劳务的买卖双方彼此进行接触的总和。一个市场可以是，也可以不是像纽约证券交易所、福尔敦鱼市场或芝加哥商会那样正式组织起来并集中在某一具体地点找到它们的位置。市场仅仅是一种买卖过程，通过这一过程买卖双方互相影响，并通过它来确定成交的价格与数量。

改译：____

____

Task II 请将下列商务文摘翻译成中文。

1. He said the different generations of employees do not have the same expectations of work and values of employment, which is a difficult gap to bridge.

____

____

2. How does trade take place? If an American buys oranges from Florida, he /she naturally wants to pay in dollars, also, the grower expects to be paid in dollars for, after all, their expenses and living costs are settled in dollars. Within a country, economic transactions seem simple.

____

____

3. Goods are produced according to a sample provided by the customer, while strong encouragement is given to compensation trade whereby a foreign seller supplies raw materials and equipment and receives manufactured goods, produced by the equipment provided, in return. Compensation trade differs from barter or counter-trade insofar as there is a direct link between the equipment supplied from abroad and the manufactured product.

____

____

4. Major suppliers to the Hong Kong egg market are making greater efforts to increase the competitiveness of their products in order to maintain or expand market shares. To promote sales of Chinese eggs, the Chinese Eggs and Products Company recently held a "lucky draw"—a popular promotional activity in Hong Kong—with prizes in solid gold for winning retailers. Attractive posters are designed to promote both fresh eggs and preserved Chinese eggs.

____

____

5. The crucial Christmas trading season can be make or break for retailers. As the festive season got under way, companies faced intense competition to win sales as cash-strapped consumers constrained by falling real pay sought out the best deals. It was tough for the whole retail market but, with most of the major retailers having now reported, more winners have emerged than losers.

____

____

Task III　请将下列中文文摘翻译成英文。

1. 自 1851 年英国首开世界博览会至 1999 年，在近一个半世纪的风雨岁月中，人类经历了两次世界大战的灾难。残酷的现实和血的教训，唤起了人们对和平的期盼。伴随着人类对美好生活的追求，三次科技革命蓬勃兴起，迎来了前所未有的科技进步和经济增长，有力地促进了各国生产力的发展和经济社会的长足进步。

____

____

2. 根据国际货币基金组织的统计，截至 2000 年底，全球约有 64.8%的外汇储备是美元，欧元外汇储备占 12.7%。但是，各中央银行持有美元外汇还有更加实际的原因，例如一个国家的外汇汇率体制便是原因之一。1997—1998 年亚洲金融危机之后，大部分政府采取了浮动汇率制度。但许多中央银行继续以美元来确定自己的核心汇率，持有美元对于调整货币流动是绝对必要的。

____

____

PART SEVEN

学习参考

1. 中国日报网站：http://www.chinadaily.com.cn/language_tips/news/news_bilingual.html
2. 《时代》：http://www.time.com/time/
3. 《商业周刊》：http://www.businessweek.com/
4. 周建萍. 经贸英语报刊阅读教程［M］. 南京：南京大学出版社，2014.

5. 张健. 英语报刊阅读教程［M］. 北京：外语教学与研究出版社，2020.
6. 张剑，李京廉. 英语报刊阅读教程（第二版）［M］. 北京：中国人民大学出版社，2021.

PART EIGHT 实训任务

1. 请总结本单元讲述的商务文摘翻译技巧。
2. 请回顾本课程讲述的商务翻译技巧。

参 考 答 案

第一单元　商务翻译概论

PART ONE
认识商务英语及商务翻译

Task

【解析】商务英语与通用英语的本质区别在于其专门性，体现在词汇的专业性、语言的严谨性和简洁性，商务英语专门用于解决商务活动中出现的各种问题。本部分参考译文如下：

1. 数字化是公司增长的支柱，未来五年，公司收入将会翻倍。

2. 麦当劳上周宣布重新推出四川辣酱，并称将在美国的指定门店“限量发放，数量极其有限”。

3. 世界各国从事的贸易千差万别，错综复杂，有形贸易和无形贸易并存。大多数国家对出口的依赖，都大于对其他活动的依赖。出口所赚取的外汇用来支付进口货物需要的费用。一个国家的收支平衡就是这些错综复杂的交易记录。通过用货币形式来反映所有这些交易，一个国家能够把比如出口、外国游客的花费和移民汇款的收入汇总在一起。这些收入汇总起来，便可以支付诸如购买其他国家的制成品、本国居民到其他国家旅游和雇用建筑工程师的费用等。

PART TWO
商务翻译热身练习

Task I

1. Cash Before Delivery 付款后交货/ Central Business District 中央商务区

2. PPP（Public-Private Partnership），又叫 PPP 模式，即政府和社会资本合作（它是公共基础设施中的一种项目运作模式。在该模式下，鼓励私营企业、民营资本与政府进行合作，参与公共基础设施的建设。杭绍台铁路 PPP 项目是中国第一条 PPP 模式进行建设的高铁。）

3. Cost, Insurance and Freight 成本、保险加运费价

4. Free on Board 船上交货价

5. Foreign Direct Investment 外商直接投资

6. Bill of Lading 海运提单

7. Consumer Price Index 消费者价格指数

8. Gross Domestic Product 国内生产总值

9. Quality Specification 质量标准

10. Wholly Foreign-Owned Enterprises 外资独资企业

Task II

1. 我们很遗憾地通知贵方，你方价格无竞争力。若贵方能将价格降至国际市场价格，我们仍对交易感兴趣。

2. 经过对货物损害的全面调查，我方发现货运提单显示船公司收到货物时，外表良好。因此，该损害我方并无责任。

3. 当发盘针对一个或几个特定的收盘人，明示或者暗示发盘人在明确、完整和最终的条件下订立合同的明确意图时，该盘为实盘。

4. 随着市场的真正全球化以及距离、时间、语言和法规等方面的障碍变得越来越小，市场参与者之间的竞争达到前所未有的激烈程度。

PART THREE
商务英语语言特点

Task I

【解析】从这些短语不难看出，商务英语具有专业术语丰富的特点。

Task II

【解析】商务英语的语言具有规范化特征，语言统一、客观，准确传递作者意图。规范性还体现在语言的正式性和合理性上。

Task III

【解析】程式化或公式化是商务英语的另一特征。商务活动中，很多活动或者行为都具有一定的规律性，故其语言也具有一定的规定性，逐渐形成了程式化的商务用语。

Task IV

【解析】从事商务活动讲究效率，商务英语必须做到简单明了。简洁性是商务英语的一大特征，具体体现在缩略语的广泛使用方面。缩略语可以让人一目了然，缩短阅读时间。参考译文及解释如下：

1. 电汇（国际贸易常用术语）
2. 货到付款（国际贸易常用术语。POD 的全称还可以是 print on demand，表示“按需打印/出版”的意思）
3. 贸易差额
4. 装货单（国际贸易常用术语）
5. 增值税（税收的一种）
6. 金砖四国
7. “一带一路”倡议
8. 亚洲基础设施投资银行（简称亚投行）

Task V

【解析】在商务活动中，语言应当具有准确性。上述句子中，“on or before Sept. 10”“SAY FIVE THOUSAND US DOLLARS ONLY”等都表明其准确性。

Task VI

【解析】商务英语尤其是书面语言往往使用在正式场合，其特点为正式性，体现在语言庄重、得体、严谨。参考译文如下：

1. 一般而言，进出口双方发生争议时，可以通过友好协商、诉讼或仲裁解决。友好协商或调解是最好的办法，对双方都有益。大多数争议通过友好协商解决，进出口双方的良好业务关系得以维持。如果友好协商或者调解无法解决争议，仲裁是第二个最佳选择，因为诉讼往往费时费钱。

2. 我们特此证明本发票真实无误，与我方账目相符；同时，所装运的货物产于中国广州，并符合中华人民共和国原产地规则。

PART FOUR 商务英语翻译标准

Task I

【解析】商务翻译属于应用翻译范畴，准确传递原文含义是其主要目标，忠实性仍然是商务翻译的首要标准。参考译文如下：

1. 每天在伦敦港卸下的货物超过5万吨。
2. 由于我方顾客急需此货，请尽快空运。
3. 英格兰出售的鱼很多是从苏格兰以陆路运输方式运来的。
4. 为减轻重量，现在许多机器零件不用金属而用塑料制造。

Task II

【解析】在忠实性基础之上，统一性和连贯性（流畅性）也是商务翻译的重要标准。统一性体现在术语、表达、图表等方面的一致性；连贯性体现在连词、关系词等具有衔接功能的词语的使用，以实现语言的连贯性。参考译文如下：

1. 一个重要的社会影响是广告为大众媒体提供财政支持：报纸收入的2/3、广播收入几乎全部来自广告。媒体运营商不把公众当成他们的基本受众，而当成吸引广告商的诱饵。总而言之，媒体内容的设计是为了吸引消费能力巨大的老百姓。

2. 工业和信息化部称，近年来，我国数字经济蓬勃发展，产业规模持续快速增长。据统计，从2012年至2021年，我国数字经济规模从11万亿元增长到超45万亿元，数字经济占GDP比重由21.6%提升至39.8%。

PART SIX 商务翻译实践

Task I

1. 支付条款	2. 付款通知	3. 流动资本
4. 固定资本	5. 数字经济	6. 货币政策
7. 商业发票	8. 营业时间	9. 商品库存
10. 营业状况	11. 批发商	12. 质量控制

Task II

【解析】商务英语紧跟时代的脉搏，随时出现许多新词新语，要求译者必须与时俱进，掌握符合时代要求的翻译。参考译文如下：

1. 中国政府本周三强调了努力推进发展战略性*新兴产业*的重要性。

2. 在2010全球城市信息化论坛上，科技部部长万钢在演讲中称将优先为农村地区提供信息科技服务。他说："中国需要进一步消除城乡间的'*数字鸿沟*'。"

3. 当地政府周日表示，新政策允许前往浙江省的外国旅游团取得*落地签证*，此举将极大地推动当地旅游业的发展。

4. 中国和印度的*包容性增长*使两国在全球经济中扮演了重要角色。中印两国在劳动法规、农业技术及基础设施等方面促进包容性增长，引起了世界关注。包容性增长还包括计划通过实施积极政策帮助本国落后地区、赋权贫困人口，以便他们能够平等地参与市场。

Task III

【解析】商务翻译必须综合应用各种翻译技巧，现具体分析如下：

1. 增译法，即为了使译文清楚明白，增加适当词语。如把"the cost and time benefits of online transactions"翻译成"网上交易在节约成本和时间方面的好处"，增加了"节约"，如果只翻译成"网上交易在成本和时间方面的好处"就不够清楚。

参考译文：电子商务的发展与因特网的发展紧密联系是因为供应商和客户意识到网上交易在节约成本和时间方面的好处。整个公司的供应链都使用在线系统，业务效率就更高了。电子商务的真正挑战在于通过各种销售渠道为客户提供最新数据。

2. 参考译文：在数字经济时代，你必须为不断变化的未来做好准备。改变你对未来的看法，与你的员工、供应商和合作伙伴精诚合作、努力革新，学会像你的顾客那样看待你的公司。电子商务必须以顾客为中心，你不得不利用你的市场知识来考虑将来顾客期望会如何变化。

3. 参考译文：电子商务的黄金准则是顾客是上帝。你的顾客在大街上购物或者通过电话或电邮购物时，他们直接比较产品价格的机会是有限的。因特网使得个人客户或者企业客户更容易对产品价格做出比较，在家或者在办公室完成购物。许多网站存在的目的是让顾客比较购物。你应当明白，权力在你的顾客手中，你必须把他们的需求作为你的业务的中心。

第二单元　名片翻译

参考译文与解析：

PART TWO

热身练习

Task II

1. D　　2. B　　3. A　　4. B　　5. C

Task III

1—4 KAGF　　5—8 CDEI　　9—12 HJBL

PART THREE 名片翻译技巧

Task I

【解析】姓名的翻译可以采用音译法和定译法。

1. Ma Longxiang
2. Li Yunfei
3. Sima Xiangru
4. Wang Hongxiang
5. Wen Shu'an
6. Ang Lee
7. Kevin Michael Rudd
8. Tony Leung
9. Confucius
10. Bruce Lee

Task II

【解析】政府行政人员职务名称的翻译是一项复杂的任务。一是因为中国与英语国家的行政划分大为不同。中国的行政级别繁多，名目也较英语国家更丰富。二是中英行政职务有诸多不对等之处，许多在中国街知巷闻的职务在英语国家难觅踪迹。

第一组

1. Minister
2. Director General
3. Bureau Director
4. Governor
5. Chief Executive/County Government
6. Chief Executive/Township Government
7. Secretary-General
8. Director/General Office
9. Division Chief/Director
10. Section Chief
11. Clerk/Officer
12. Spokesperson
13. Adviser/Consultant
14. Inspector/Monitor
15. Commissioner
16. Consul General
17. Chief Judge
18. Supervisor
19. Legal Medical Expert
20. Consul

第二组

1. President
2. Chair/Chairperson
3. Honorary Adviser
4. Trustee/Council Member
5. Director-General
6. Director
7. Chairman
8. President
9. General Manager/CEO
10. Finance Controller
11. PR Manager
12. Business Manager
13. Sales Manager
14. Cashier
15. Workshop Manager
16. Purchaser/Buyer
17. Technician
18. Captain
19. Storekeeper
20. Auditing Clerk

第三组

1. Senior Engineer
2. Professor
3. Architect
4. Designer
5. Mechanic
6. Chemical Analyst

7. Quality Inspector
8. Agricultural Technician
9. Surgeon-in-charge
10. Doctor-in-charge
11. Editor-in-chief
12. Reporter
13. Assistant Translator/Interpreter
14. Sound Engineer
15. Choreographer
16. Art Director
17. Make-up Artist
18. Stage Manager
19. Cameraman
20. TV Presenter

Task III

1. Midea Group
2. Hang Seng Bank
3. China Construction Bank
4. Ningbo Aux Air Conditioner Co., Ltd.
5. Tsingtao Brewery Co., Ltd.
6. Sinotrans Limited
7. Guangzhou Railway Group
8. China Southern Power Grid
9. Huawei Technologies Co., Ltd.
10. Shenzhen Shining Ocean International Logistics Co., Ltd.

Task IV

1. International Wushu Federation
2. International Organization for Migration
3. Greenpeace
4. China Calligraphers Association
5. China Wildlife Conservation Association
6. China Volunteers Association on Protection for Tibetan Antelope
7. Translators Association of China
8. Zhongshan Furniture Trade Association
9. China Society for Sustainable Development
10. Beijing Association of New Energy and Renewable Energy

Task V

1. Head Office
2. Branch Office
3. General Affairs Department
4. Personnel Department
5. Financial Department
6. Sales Department
7. International Department
8. Export Department
9. Import Department
10. Public Relations Department
11. Advertising Department
12. Planning Department
13. Training Department
14. Quality Control Department
15. Board of Directors
16. Marketing Department
17. Logistics Department
18. Engineering Department
19. Research and Development Department（R&D)
20. Customer Service Department/Aftersales Service Department

Task VI

【解析】地名翻译主要遵循汉语从大到小而英语从小到大的原则即可。

1. No. 12, Urumqizhong Road, Shanghai
2. 1st fl., Jingdong Hotel Conference Centre, No. 1, Haiyuncang Alley, Dongcheng District, Beijing
3. 4th fl., No. 3 of Zhushikou Street (East), Xicheng District, Beijing
4. No. 23rd Art Museum Backstreet, Dongcheng District, Beijing
5. No. 380, Yuejiangzhong Road, Haizhu District, Guangzhou
6. Room 7201—7202, Citic Plaza, No. 233, Tianhe Road (N), Guangzhou
7. No. 66, Huangpudadao (W), Guangzhou
8. 4—5th fl., Changsheng Building, No. 126, Pedestrian Sreet, Wuhan
9. Room 1102, Yunhe Building, Yuemachang, Wuge Road, Wuchang District, Wuhan
10. 1st fl., Building A of Fuhua Mansion, No. 8, Chaoyangmen Street (N), Dongcheng District, Beijing

PART SIX
名片翻译实践

Task I

第一组

1. Technical Director
2. IT Manager
3. IT Supervisor
4. IT Specialist
5. Project Supervisor
6. Information Security Engineer
7. Software QA Engineer
8. Hardware QA Engineer
9. Test Engineer
10. Web Operations Manager
11. Customer Service Manager
12. Customer Service Supervisor

第二组

1. Sales Director
2. Sales Manager
3. Regional Sales Manager
4. Account Manager
5. Channel/Distribution Manager
6. Channel Supervisor
7. Sales Engineer
8. Sales Assistant
9. Sales Administration Manager
10. Sales Administration Supervisor
11. Acting Manager
12. Chairman of the Board of Directors and General Manager

Task II

1. 工厂经理/厂长
2. 总工程师
3. 项目经理
4. 项目工程师
5. 运营经理
6. 营运主管

7. 生产经理
8. 车间主任
9. 生产计划协调员
10. 生产主管
11. 技术/工业设计经理
12. 技术/工业设计工程师
13. 实验室负责人/工程师
14. 设备经理
15. 工程/设备主管
16. 设备工程师
17. 电气工程师
18. 机械工程师
19. 维修工程师
20. 安全经理/主管

Task III

1.

Ausnow
International

Liu Genwang
Sales Supervisor

Marketing Centre, Ausnow International (China)
Zhongshan Jiadanting Daily Products, Co., Ltd.
Add: Third Industrial Building, Shenyong, Xiaolan East District, Zhongshan, Guangdong, China
Tel: +86-752-588888
Fax: +86-752-588886
Mobile: 19888888888
Website: www.ausnow.cn

2.

Tesda Trading Co., Ltd.

Liu Yueru
Sales Manager
19342255555

Add: Rm. 1308, Times International Building, No. 187, Dongfeng Road (W), Guangzhou
Tel: 020-96668888 96668889
Fax: 020-96668885
E-mail: tessteps_trading@126.com

3.

TOYATA
FINANCIAL SERVICES

Toyota Motor Finance (China) Co., Ltd.

Liu Genbao
Market Dept. Manager

Add: Rm 818, 8th fl, No. 1, Jianguomenwai Street, Beijing, China
Postcode: 100004 Tel: (010) 65055557 Ext.: 500
Fax: (010) 65058765
Mobile: 19999893123 E-mail: abcd@tischina.com.cn
Website: http://www.tischina.com.cn

4.

LEXUS
FINANCIAL SERVICES

Toyota Motor Finance (China) Co., Ltd.

Project Manager
Dept. of Business Development
Bai Hongxing

Add: Rm 818, 8th fl, No. 1, Jianguomenwai Street, Beijing, China
Postcode:100004 Tel: (010) 65055557 Ext.: 123
Fax: (010) 65058765
Mobile:19999893188 E-mail: abcd@tischina.com.cn
Website: http://www.tischina.com.cn

5.

China National Pharmaceutical Industry
Corporation Limited
Ministry of Commerce

China National
Pharmaceutical Group Corporation

Wang Zhenwei

Yinxing Mansion,

Add: 19th floor, Yinxing Mansion, No. 9, Beisihuanxi Road, Haidian District, Beijing
Tel: 010-82008500-8302
Cell: 19998888888
Fax: 010-88880000 88880001
E-mail: wangzhenwei@cnpic.com.cn
Postcode: 100080

第三单元　公示语翻译

参考译文与解析：

PART TWO

热身练习

Task I

1. B　　2. F　　3. H　　4. E　　5. G　　6. D　　7. C　　8. A

Task II

1. 正在检修，请绕行。
2. 正在检修，请您稍候。
3. 电梯维修，暂停使用
4. 禁止鸣笛
5. 服务区
6. 服务监督电话
7. 检票处
8. 售票处

Task III

【解析】总体而言，许多公示语的问题出在死译和硬译两个方面。第 1、2、3 小题尽管汉语有所差别，充满文学色彩，但根本目的只有一个，那就是“请勿践踏草坪”。很多地方为了使标语生动形象，采用了一些文学性的语言或者修辞手法，又如“小草在休息，请您别打扰”“青青的草，怕你的脚”，在英语中，所有这些公示语都可以用“PLEASE KEEP OFF THE GRASS”进行翻译。第 4 小题，“宾客止步”可以翻译成“Staff Only”即可。第 5 小题纯粹字字对译，这种属于低级错误，根据意义和语境，可以修改为“No Littering”，如果确实需要翻译得更为忠实，也可以翻译为“Please Do Not Throw Waste Out of the Window”，这样完全可以表述原文含义。第六小题的原翻译“Keep Your Valuables in View”强调将贵重物品保持在可见范围内。然而，这样的翻译没有明确指出需要采取措施来保护这些物品。改进后的翻译“Safeguard Your Valuables”更准确地传达了原文的意图，即提醒人们要积极保护自己的财物。

PART THREE

公示语翻译技巧

Task I

【解析】通读所有公示语，不难发现，公示语广泛使用名词、动词、动名词、词组、短语、缩略语等；就时态而言，常用现在时态；就句型而言，公示语常用祈使句，语言简洁，措辞精确，用词规范。第 1 题中，公示语大量使用表示“静态”的名词、动名词或者名词性短语，用于为公众提供必要的说明性或者指示性信息。公示语还会使用动词短语和缩略语，缩略语用最简词汇向公众传递必要的信息。第 2 题使用了祈使句，对公众的各种行为提出明确的要求，应该怎样做和不应该怎样做，公众一目了然。第 3 题的公示语使用一般现在时，公示语是对在特定区域范围的公众行为的指示、提示、限制、强制，所以英语中仅限于一般现在时，而汉语公示语一般不需要考虑时态问题。

Task II

1.

（1）注意：此时请勿游泳。

（2）法律规定：请系安全带。

（3）前方弯道

（4）勿用水浇灭

（5）本告示牌边缘锋利，请勿用手触摸。

2.

(1) Priority Seats/Courtesy Seats

(2) Caution: No Climbing

(3) No Littering

(4) Please Don't Get Lipstick Stain on the Dress

(5) Night Bell

3.

(1) Tsinghua University　Qinghua South Rd.（请特别注意道路的缩写形式"Rd."）

(2) Sun Yat-sen University　Zhongshan Zhuang Franchised Store　Zhongshan 2nd Rd.

Task III

根据公示语翻译忠实性原则，本项翻译任务采用直译法。

1. 买一赠一　　2. 请勿投喂山羊

3. 禁止掉头　　4. 前方修路

5. 礼品包装　　6. 除危险情况，禁止鸣笛

7. 注意行人　　8. 严禁穿行

9. 收费处　　10. 失物招领处

11. One World, One Dream

12. No Waste Water Discharge/Do Not Discharge Waste Water

13. Don't Burn Incense in the Hall

14. Children Under 1 Meter Must Be Accompanied by an Adult

15. No Refund. No Exchange.

Task IV

1. Staff Parking

2. Slimming Tea

3. Inter-city Bus Station/Coach Station

4. Happy Time Dating Agency

5. Everyone is responsible for protecting the greenery!/ Let's Protect the Environment!

Task V

1. Please Be Seated When the Bus Is in Motion

2. Keep Away for Safety
3. Consumption of MacDonald Foods Only
4. Staff Only
5. Flood Control Channel. Keep Clear!
6. Motor Vehicles Only
7. Please Keep Hands Off/Hands Off
8. Keep Arms Inside the Carriage

Task VI

1. Automatic Flush
2. Three Guarantees for Products: Repair, Replacement and Refund
3. No Littering
4. Please Return Books on Time
5. Do Not Waste Toilet Paper
6. Tickets Available

PART SIX 公示语翻译实践

Task I

1. E　2. D　3. I　4. G　5. A　6. H　7. F　8. B　9. J　10. C

Task II

1. 禁止吸烟　　2. 严禁烟火　　3. 行人勿近
4. 勿用水浇灭　　5. 不可饮用　　6. 未经许可，不能入内

Task III

1. 访客停车　　2. 擅自停车，一律拖走，费用自负
3. 军事设施，严禁闯入　　4. 横穿马路，按下按钮，等候通行信号
5. 请勿大声喧哗　　6. 注意行人
7. 戴好安全帽　　8. 停车限时 3 分钟，司机不得离车
9. 灭火专用　　10. 危险：高速列车，切勿进入

Task IV

1. Cigarette Sales to Adults Only
2. Authorized Cars Only
3. Wet Paint
4. Keep Away from Fire
5. Do Not Leave Your Belongings Behind
6. Adults Only
7. Keep Windows Closed/Don’t Open Windows
8. Machine Room. Staff Only.

9. Keep Upright
10. Beyond This Point
11. Staff Only
12. Please Don't Leave Valuables Unattended
13. Passengers Only
14. No Freight Allowed
15. Performance in progress, please keep your voices down and stay in your seat.

Task V

1. Slow Down, Look Around and Cross
2. Do Not Disturb
3. Detour, Maintenance in Progress
4. Automatic Tap
5. Don't Exceed Weight Limit/Do Not Overload
6. Please Don't Leave Your Children Unattended
7. Please Protect Public Facilities
8. Clearance Sale
9. Lower Window for Ventilation
10. Shark Sighted
11. No Overnight Parking
12. No Bills
13. Keep in Shade
14. Keep in Dark Place
15. Guard Against Damp
16. Complaint Box
17. Do Not Take the Overtaking Lane for Long
18. Inflammables & Explosives Strictly Prohibited/Dangerous Articles Prohibited
19. Fewer/No Plastic Bags for Environmental Protection
20. Children Must Be Accompanied on Escalator

Task VI

【解析】本部分公示语翻译既有理解错误，也有译文错误，具体分析如下：

1. "欢迎到某地"在英语中直接翻译成"Welcome to…"。许多地方都有公示语"欢迎您再来"，翻译成"Welcome you to come again!"的错误在于字字对译，不符合语法规范。我们可以按照英美人的表达习惯翻译成：Please come again!

2. 原译文语法错误，没有"take care to"的说法，而且"not to take water please"表示"请勿取水"，与原文相去甚远。原文表达警示意义，故可以翻译为：Caution: Deep Water, No Swimming

3. 原文的语用意义为不要践踏草坪，所以翻译成：Please Keep Off the Grass

4. 原文语用意义同上句，根据英语表达习惯，故译为：Please Keep Off the Grass

5.“垃圾在此投放”翻译成“The garbage throws in here”完全不符合语法规范。原文意义是告诉公众垃圾桶在此处，可以投放垃圾，翻译成“Dust Bin”就足够了。

6. 原译“Please take good personal luggage”表示“看好好的行李”，显然属于误译，建议译为：Please Do Not Leave Your Belongings Unattended

7. 原译错误在于万绿湖不应直接按拼音翻译为“Wanlühu”，从其官方网站，很容易就可以看到其译文为“Lake Wanlühu”，原译表示“万绿湖买票、游览”，属于误译。另外，翻译必须考虑语境，游客已经到达万绿湖，此处可以省略；该公示语的意图在于告诉游客购票处在此，至于买完票游览之事，译出来也是多此一举。根据以上分析，建议翻译为：Ticket Office/Box

8. 此处字字照译，错误非常明显，如果把“Fall Down Carefully”回译，就成了“小心地倒下”，违背了原意。建议译为：Slippery/Wet Floor

9. 受汉语影响，英文字字对译，原译“consciously”属于多余。“自觉”对应的英文单词是“conscientiously”而非“consciously（有意识的）”；另外，英文中没有这种表达法。建议改译为：Please Buy Tickets，或者直接借用英语中现成的表达法：Tickets Only

10. 这里亦步亦趋，按照字面翻译，汉语多用动词，而英语多用名词表示“静态”，所以建议译为：Under Construction/Repair, Sorry for the Inconvenience

11. 购物凭证就是“proof of purchase”，而不应当包括保修，因为在中国“保修”必须出示正规发票，而小票绝不能作为维修凭证，所以“guarantee”为过度翻译，建议译为：Please Keep the Receipt as Proof of Your Purchase

12.“Pure Land”表示纯洁的土地，“preservation”表示“保持”之意，原文的目的是请游客保持景区环境卫生，建议译为：Please Help Us to Protect the Environment/Keep it Clean and Tidy

13. 原译“Carrying Flammable, Explosive Materials Prohibited”属于对原文的字字对译，“prohibit”一般用法为“doing sth. is prohibited”，“carrying”一词属于多余，可以表示携带，也可以表示“背、抱、拿”等，显然，无论以哪种方式携带，这些物品都禁带。建议简化，译为：No Flammables or Explosives

14. 把白云山当成“我家”，还有“爱护她”，都是指爱护环境，所以建议意译为：Keep Baiyun Mountain Clean/ Do Not Litter/ No Littering

15. 原译采用直译法，显得非常啰嗦、累赘，不符合公示语短小精悍的使用原则。可以采用视角转换法，原文意思是此处只能进食本餐厅食品，如果这样说，可能有些人不自觉，还是进食外带食品，所以汉语原文采用了双重否定，加强了语气。建议译为：Omic Food Only

16. 原译“circumstance”表示“与某事件或某人有关的情况或事实”，保护环境中的环境应是“environment”，指具体的自然和人居环境，所以，建议译为：Keep Our City Clean

Task VII

1. 原文：讲究文明　保护环境　爱护绿化　注意安全

原译：Please respect the tranquility of the environment. Protect the environment. Protect Nature. Take precautions for your safety.

建议译为：Please Protect the Environment and Watch Out for Your Safety

2. 原文：1974 年，当地农民打井，在此发现了一堆破碎的陶俑残片。

原译：It was in 1974, when local farmers were drilling a well in search of water, some pottery fragments were discovered.

建议译为：In 1974, local farmers discovered some pottery fragments when drilling a well in search of water.

3. 原文：温馨提示 小心跌滑 注意安全

原译：Warm Prompt Falls carefully slides, Safety-conscious

建议译为：Caution: Wet and Slippery

4. 原文：安全提示 此处坡陡路滑 请勿擅自攀爬

原译：Safe prompt: Here slope steep road slides, please arbitrarily do not climb up.

建议译为：Steep Slope and Wet Road, No Climbing

Task VIII

1. 因包装不当导致损失，本公司**有权**向卖方提出索赔。
2. 尽管他忠心耿耿地为公司**工作**了十多年，不幸的是，他还是被炒掉了。
3. **拯救**国家经济的最好办法就是节约。
4. 专家们说，这项新研究更**证明**了体育锻炼有助于保持身体健康。
5. 对医生这样的专业人员而言，电脑的作用可能比我们想象的更大。电脑能比人**检查得更细心、更勤快**。
6. 中国地大物博，近年来经济**发展**速度惊人，已经成为当代国际经济中一支日益重要的力量。
7. **考虑**到双方在此提出的契约和协议，同意订立如下条款。
8. 中国如果**缺少**钢铁，其工业**发展**就会遇到很大困难。
9. 我们刚签订了一份**有利于**我们公司的合同。
10. 我们坚信已经向前**迈进**了一步。

第四单元　组织机构翻译

参考译文与译例分析：

PART ONE

认识组织机构与组织机构翻译

Task

1. 这是联合国（United Nations）的标志，联合国是一个世界性、综合性的政府间国际组织，现有 193 个会员。

2. “bp” 是 “British Petroleum” 的缩写，它是世界上最大的能源公司之一，向顾客提供运输燃料、光热能源、油品零售服务以及与人们日常生活密切相关的各种石化产品。

3. 世界自然基金会（World Wide Fund for Nature or World Wildlife Fund）是在全球享有盛誉的、最大的独立性非政府环境保护组织之一。自 1961 年成立以来，WWF 一直致力于环保事业，是在全世界拥有超过 500 万支持者和超过 100 个国家参与的项目网络。

4.“APEC”是 Asia-Pacific Economic Cooperation（亚太经济合作组织）的缩写，它是亚太地区最具影响的经济合作官方论坛，成立于 1989 年。

PART TWO

热身练习

Task I

【解析】组织机构，因其本身内涵的确定性及严肃性，所以在英译时更要注重查核权威依据。

1. 世界银行集团
2. 国际能源组织
3. 国际标准化组织
4. 世界卫生组织
5. State Administration of Taxation
6. Ministry of Foreign Affairs of the People's Republic of China
7. General Administration of Customs
8. The People's Bank of China

Task II

【解析】组织机构名称一般可缩略，而且通常采用的是首字母缩略法。在缩略过程中，虚词通常都略去。

1. North Atlantic Treaty Organization
2. World Trade Organization
3. International Monetary Fund
4. Central Intelligence Agency
5. International Atomic Energy Agency
6. Group of 20
7. European Union
8. Federation of International Football Association

Task III

【解析】题目给出的都是世界知名企业，这些企业的本名和译名都很有特色。

1. 2006 年，美国《财富》杂志评出的世界 500 强公司之首是埃克森美孚（Exxon Mobil）。早在多年前，美国这家石油公司为了设计出既适应世界各地风俗，又符合各个国家法律的名字和图案，邀请了多方面专家和机构，历时 6 年，耗资 1 亿美元调查了 55 个国家和地区，最后才确定了埃克森（EXXON）的命名，并且从设计出来的一万多个商标中筛选出一个。如今这个品牌通行全球，品牌价值已达上百亿美元。

2. 中国石油化工集团有限公司。公司名称 Sinopec 由两部分组成，Sino 表示其地域，pec 是 Petroleum and Chemical Corporation 的缩写，表示其所主营的产品，简洁易记。

3. 汇丰控股起源于汇丰银行。汇丰银行是为了向从事对华贸易的公司提供融资和结算服务而于 1864 年在香港成立的。它的名称体现了传统的起名方法，使用吉祥色彩的词“丰”“顺”“兴”“福”“仁”“和”等。英文全名 Hong Kong and Shanghai Banking Corporation，简称 HSBC。

4. 标致，法国标致雪铁龙集团（PSA）旗下著名的汽车和自行车品牌。其译名“标致”，含义为外表、风度等接近完美或理想境界，唤起美感上的享受，符合其高品质的内涵和要求。

5. 有时缩略MS，作为全球最著名的软件商，美国软件巨头微软公司的名字，Microsoft由两个英语单词组成：Micro意为“微小”，Soft意为“软的”，此处应为“Software（软件）”。顾名思义，微软（Microsoft）是专门生产软件的公司。

6. 作为一家物流运输企业，Fedex这个名字的构造很巧妙，Fed指联邦，ex指“迅速的，快捷的”。这个新造词在发音上也很干脆利落，很符合企业的特质。

7. 成功的企业推广和成功的产品是分不开的。百事作为一个中文译名与其产品——可乐很好地搭配，符合中国人讨喜的心理。

8. Boeing翻译成波音，是典型的音译法。

参考译文如下：

1. 埃克森美孚	2. 中国石化	3. 汇丰控股	4. 标致
5. Microsoft	6. Fedex	7. Pepsi	8. Boeing

PART THREE
组织机构翻译技巧

Task I

1. 单位部门名称由于在英语中属于专有名词范畴，要求做到专词专用，所以一个单位只能使用一种译名，包括词序，缩写形式都应该是唯一的。按此原则，在翻译单位名称时，应首先查阅有关资料，确定是否有普遍接受的定译，尤其是政府机构的译名，更应采用中央有关部门对外正式名称，绝不能按字面随意翻译。

2. WHO　NYSE　OPEC　ILO　ICBC　CCPIT

3.【解析】企业名称词读音最好能朗朗上口，易于记忆。第一行三个词读起来给人的感觉是富有特色，简短明快，如Fedex，其中的ex能令人联想到“迅捷的”，Fedex的整个发音也给人一种干脆利落的感觉。第二行名称的谐音与产品特征相互吻合，如美的（电器）可以“美化生活，令生活更简便，生活原来可以更美的”，“贝亲”原为“pigeon”，作为婴幼儿用品和孕妇用品的生产企业，这样的名字令人联想到“加倍亲近”“亲爱的宝贝”“可爱的宝贝”“令人爱不释手”之意。娃哈哈（饮料）中“哈哈”表达欢快愉悦之意。由此可见，企业或者商标命名必须考虑其读音或者谐音是否跟产品或者产品特征紧密相连。

4.【解析】企业名称要富于吉祥色彩，彰显传统文化底蕴，令人产生美好的联想。如Haier与“Higher（更高）”谐音。Triumph有“胜利，欢呼”之意，作为一个生产女性内衣品牌的公司，能令人联想到塑造完美的女性曲线与形象，令人惊喜的意思。“lenovo”是由联想创造的一个单词，其中的“novo”是一个拉丁词根，代表“新意”“创新”，“le”为“legend”一词的继承部分，寓意为“创新的联想”或“联想创新”。“Goodyear”令人联想到好年景，而好日子也有异曲同工之妙。“强生”（药品与婴儿用品）与“强壮新生/生命”。“周大福”作为一个大型加工销售珠宝的连锁，它的命名中带有“福”字是回归传统的做法，同时，带有姓氏的店名总是给人一种有一定历史的感觉，有一种手艺代代流传的信誉保证。所以，无论是加工珠宝的工艺或是销售珠宝的品质，都令人觉得可信。“喜多”（婴儿用品品牌）寓意宝贝的降临总是带给人“诸多的惊喜”。

Task II

1.【解析】机构名称通常依顺序由地域、所属领域、（功能）组织名称几部分组成。有时组织名会前置，如此题中的 Ministry of Foreign Affairs of the People's Republic of China，这种情况下，Ministry 前置就表示庄重和正式。

2.（1）欧洲人工智能协会，for 表示“关于”。
（2）国际商会，of 表示“属于，关于”。
（3）国际法院，of 表示“属于，关于”。
（4）联合国贸易和发展会议，on 表示对象，“对，对于”。
（5）美国教育委员会，on 表示对象，“对，对于”。

3.（1）音译法：耐克　路易威登　索尼　Luk-fook　Dabao　Wahaha
（2）意译法：联邦快递　电子湾　英国石油　Panda　Bright　Diamond
（3）音意结合法：联合利华　金利来　星巴克　Midea　Robust　Gree

PART SIX
组织机构翻译实践

Task I

1. B　2. E　3. A　4. G　5. D　6. C　7. H　8. F

Task II

1. Ministry of Natural Resources
2. Chinese Academy of Sciences
3. Ministry of Ecological Environment
4. National Audit Office
5. National Health Commission
6. 国家外汇管理局
7. 科学技术部
8. 国家发展和改革委员会
9. 交通运输部
10. 国家邮政局

Task III

1. 麻省理工学院
2. 宾夕法尼亚大学
3. 西北大学
4. 加州大学洛杉矶分校
5. 伦敦政治经济学院
6. National University of Singapore
7. The University of Hong Kong
8. South China Normal University
9. Sun Yat-Sen University
10. Guangdong University of Foreign Studies

Task IV

1. World Wide Web
2. Date of Birth
3. For Your Information
4. Artificial Intelligence
5. Business to Business
6. Federation of Football Association
7. Very Important Person
8. Small Office Home Office
9. Express Mail Service
10. Office Automation

Task V

1. administrative
2. part-time
3. location
4. background
5. business
6. mechanic
7. position
8. division
9. references
10. full time

Task VI

1. abbreviation
2. actual weight
3. approve
4. balance sheet
5. before
6. bill of lading
7. cash on delivery
8. deep water port
9. export declaration
10. fully paid
11. government
12. group
13. gross weight
14. hour
15. in bulk
16. in due course
17. meantime
18. on board
19. package
20. payment in advance

第五单元　企业简介翻译

参考译文与译例分析：

PART TWO 热身练习

Task I

1. 资产总额
2. 合资企业
3. 营业收入
4. 国有企业
5. 制造业
6. business portfolio
7. stockholder
8. partnership
9. management level
10. business philosophy

Task II

1. Our corporation will provide thorough services.

2. Sichuan Real Estate Development Corporation was set up with the approval of Sichuan provincial government.

3. The company's annual output of shoes ranges from 1.5 million to 1.8 million pairs which have been exported to more than 40 countries and regions such as America, Russia, Canada, European countries, Central and South America, the Middle East, and the Southeast Asia.

4. 本公司自 1950 年起从事制造业，1952 年命名为 GUMOTEX。

5. 瑞士邮政巴士旅游局的理念是可靠、安全、亲近顾客。

Task III 略

PART THREE
企业简介翻译技巧

Task I

【解析】英语和汉语两种语言及中西方文化的区别，决定了汉语和英语企业简介在语言方面也各有其特征，比如英文重逻辑、汉语重描述，英文重平实、中文重渲染等。

1. 华丽（Rhetorical）与平实（Plain）：A 段是四联美发美容中心的企业简介。短短几句话，使用了“先进”“高超”“细腻”“时尚”“朴实”“庄重”“美而不艳”“秀丽清新”等形容词来描述该企业的特点，传达美感的同时也起到了渲染和宣传的作用。而从 B 段的企业简介文字可以看出，英文的企业简介在叙述时往往不会过多地使用溢美之词，反而多用比较简单平实的词汇，浅显易懂，照顾到各个层次的读者。

2. 程式化（Stylized）与专业化（Specialized）：很多汉语的企业简介都会有这样的相似结构：“×××公司是……（性质）公司”“公司成立于……”“注册资本为……”“公司位于……，占地……”“现有员工……人”“公司是集……和……业务为一体的……（规模）集团”“公司以……为宗旨”等。英语的企业简介虽然没有那么明显的程式化用语，但是也不乏行业术语，如 B 段中出现的照明行业术语 electronic control gear (ECG), optical semiconductors, display-optic lamp 等。这就要求译者在翻译时对某一领域有所了解，或者参考词典、专业书籍等。

3. 务虚口号（Sloganized）与务实介绍（Pragmatic）：A 段是内蒙古小肥羊餐饮连锁有限公司的企业简介。通读后不难发现，除了使用多个形容词来进行描述之外，文中更明显的特征是各种奖项和荣誉的罗列。对比 B 段的英文企业简介，便会发现英语企业简介注重突出公司形象及产品，注重事实和客观陈述，语言中更多强调的是公司对社会的实际贡献和对消费者的有效承诺。

4. 繁复（Complex）与简洁（Brief）：中文的企业宣传材料善用修辞，因为使用修辞能够使语言更加生动和形象，为读者带来美的感受。B 段是宝洁公司企业简介中的一段话，从平实简单的语句中，却可以感受到该企业“顾客至上”的优良态度和对其合作伙伴的关注和尊重，以及对社会的爱护之心。这种语言上的区别决定了汉语企业简介的翻译绝不可能是逐字逐句直译，而需要考虑如何处理汉语中传达美感的华丽辞藻。

Task II

1. Xianyang Textiles Group Co., Ltd., established in 2012 and covering an area of 43.5 hectares, stands as a large state-owned enterprise with the registered capital of RMB 400 million.

2. The Hubao Group has a high standard of quality and is well-equipped with the world's most advanced technology. It is taking the lead in designing new fashions and maintaining high quality products.

3. 本公司是全球移动通信业的领头羊，现已成为全球最大的移动电话生产商。凭借丰富的经验、创新的科技、简便的操作及安全可靠的解决方案，公司在移动电话、固定宽频及 IP 网络方面均遥遥领先。

4. Dongpeng, a household name among consumers and decoration industry insiders, has been dazzling in more than ten thousand key projects of the country such as Tian'anmen Rostrum, the State Council Administration Building, and the National Grand Theater.

5. As a result of over ten years' development, ABC Company has evolved into a leader of China's painting industry.

Task III

【解析】我们可以对企业简介翻译技巧作如下归纳：

翻译第 1 题时采用了省译法。中国企业的外宣材料通常会使用一些华丽的辞藻，在文化层面上对英语读者来说是冗余的信息。而西方的企业简介通常是简单明了，表述事实。因此，在翻译时，译者应该根据西方人的表达习惯和思维方式，将此类语言化繁为简，采取省译法来简化语句和结构，以达到突出文章事实和重点的目的。

翻译第 2 题时采用了增译法。增译法指的是为了使译文的表达形式更加完整、内容更容易被读者所接受、语气传达更准确，适当地增加隐含的或者没有的词语或信息。由于英文企业简介的语言风格倾向于简单易懂，而中文的企业简介更强调语言的渲染，在将英文企业简介翻译成中文时，译者就应该照顾到中文读者的思维方式和审美标准，在保持原文信息不变的情况下，找一些较为优美或能增强语气和宣传效果的汉语表达，增加其美感。

翻译第 3 题时采用的是结构整合与重组的翻译方法。受汉语思维的影响，汉语企业简介材料篇章布局倾向于先进行一系列的渲染、铺垫、引用等，然后才进入主题；而西方文体倾向于开门见山，直入主题。因此，在处理两种语言文化的翻译转换时，有必要对原文的结构进行整合或重组，以便更好地迎合译文读者的思维习惯和审美心理。

PART SIX
企业简介翻译实践

Task I

1. 顺丰于 1993 年诞生于广东顺德，现已成为国内最大的快递物流综合服务商、全球第四大快递公司。

2. 我们的宗旨是通过有意义的创新来造福人们的健康福祉。我们的创新信念一如既往：总有办法创造更美好的生活。

3. 皇家飞利浦电子集团在《财富》杂志电子行业排行榜中名列第十。公司经营 60 多种业务，涵盖范围从商品电子元件到家用小电器，从安全系统到半导体等多个领域。

4. 一个多世纪以来，我们一直是汽车照明领域的领头羊，也是当今 100 多家汽车制造商的首选供应商。我们致力于为整个汽车零部件市场提供同类最优产品和最佳服务。我们成熟的创新能力为汽车照明领域带来最新的技术进步，为所有车辆用户带来极致的驾驶安全和舒适体验。

Task II

1. Established in 2012, our company is a well-known global technology consumer electronics company integrating R&D, design, production and sales.

2. Version 1: The factory has been registered/certified to ISO9002 and QS9000.

Version 2: The factory is ISO9002 and QS9000 registered/certified.

3. Under the principle of "Promptness, Quality and Credit", we will offer you our products and services to your every satisfaction.

4. NiuTrans Cloud Platform, founded in 2017, provides machine translation solutions for enterprise users. Aiming at providing high-quality machine translation, with its profound independent research and development background, it is committed to solving cross-language communication barriers for users at home and abroad.

Task III 略

第六单元　企业网站翻译

参考译文与译例分析：

PART TWO

热身练习

Task I

【解析】网站名称的构成大致有以下几种方式：

第一，首字母式。如 www.icbc.com.icbc 是中国工商银行全称 Industrial and Commercial Bank of China 的首字母缩略。

第二，词汇或词汇组合式。如 www.netease.com 等。

第三，字母词汇组合式。如 www.ebay.com, www.etang.com 等。

第四，数字式。如 www.163.com 等。

第五，拼缀式。如 www.51dh.com.cn, www.sinosky.com 等。

本部分具体分析如下：

1. 谷歌。google 并非正确的英文单词，其创立者本来使用的应该是 googol 一词，意为“10 的 100 次方”，之所以使用这个词，是为了反映其整合全球海量(并且似乎是无穷无尽的)信息的使命，使人人皆可访问并从中受益，后来由于误传才形成了现在的 google。利用谐音翻译成“谷歌”是比较妥当的，因为“谷歌”即“丰收之歌”，寓意丰富多彩的搜索体验。

2. 搜房网。利用谐音，其中 sou 对应中文“搜”，fun 对应中文“房”，表明是跟房产有关的网站，同时，fun 在英文中意为“乐趣，娱乐”，暗示在搜房网上找房子乐趣多多。

3. 阿里妈妈。这是一个全新的交易平台，它首次引入“广告是商品”的概念，让广告第一次作为商品呈现在交易市场里，让买家和卖家都能清清楚楚地看到。阿里妈妈能够让买家（广告主）和卖家（网站主）轻松找到对方。阿里妈妈与阿里巴巴相对应，因为巴巴（爸爸）对应妈妈，容易让人记住。

4. 顺德城市网。直接利用 shunde 和 city 对应的中文翻译，表达了网站的真实内容。

5. 中华网。China 对应“中华”，让人觉得该网络信息的可靠性和权威性。

6. 广州购书中心。利用 Guangzhou 的首字母以及 book center 所对应的中文来翻译，译出了网站的功能。

7. 网易。利用互联网技术，人与人之间更易于进行信息的交流和共享，实现公司口号“网聚人的力量”。

8. 京东。利用“京东”拼音首字母，简洁易记，又较好地宣传京东的品牌。

9. 爱去网。利用 2797 的谐音“爱去就去”，翻译成“爱去网”，名字表达了该票务网站的主要功能。

10. 中国制造网。直接将英文翻译成中文对应词，这一翻译较为简洁，也较好地体现了网站的功能。

Task II

1. Keep moving.
2. Together for a shared future.
3. Speed, Responsibility, Pioneer.

Task III

1. About Us
2. Contact Us
3. Site Map
4. Disclaimer
5. Employment/Jobs
6. FAQs
7. Links/Quick Links
8. Forum
9. Stock Quote/Share Prices
10. Register
11. Login
12. Search

Task IV

【解析】译文 2 非常简洁，而译文 1 中的某些内容需要删除。为了达到简洁的目的，网络语言也普遍使用缩略语。如同仁堂的英文翻译中就使用“TRT”来代替“Tongrentang”。本例译文 2 中也采用“GWF”来代替“Guangzhou Watch Factory”。当然，在强调简洁的同时，也要注意准确性，要重点突出，不能主次不分。特别是企业的翻译，需要强调其规范性，同时要了解访问者的需求，把访问者最想知道的信息放在最醒目的位置。

PART THREE
企业网站翻译技巧

Task I

【解析】英语网站名称的翻译方法一般有四种，即音译法、意译法、音意结合法和谐音取义法。

第一，音译法。如 www.yahoo.com 翻译成“雅虎网”。

第二，意译法。如 www.china.com 翻译成“中华网”，www.shundecity.com 翻译成“顺德城市网”。

第三，音意结合法。如 www.netease.com 翻译成“网易网”。

第四，谐音取义法。如 www.segate.com 翻译成“希捷网”。

参考译文及分析如下：

1. 亚马逊。利用谐音，翻译时将其译成“亚马逊”。

2. 博鳌亚洲论坛。将地名拼音 boao 翻译成“博鳌”，forum 翻译成“论坛”，同时增加“亚洲”两字，清晰易懂。

3. 宝钢集团。将“宝”直接对应其拼音“bao”，突出其品牌与价值，钢对应其英文“steel”，容易理解，整个网站构成属于中文拼音与英文单词的混用。

4. 东方网。将 eastday 翻译成“东方网”，比较简洁。

5. 一带一路网。根据汉语拼音翻译。

6. 利多网。如果意译，则是“不动产商网”，显得不够简练，故采用音译法，即“利多网”。

7. 太平洋电脑网。pc 本是 personal computer 的缩写，此处翻译把 pc 理解成 pacific，即太平洋，表现出生意人的一种大气。

8. 新华网。中国人比较熟悉“新华”二字，如新华社，新华字典等，此处翻成“新华网”，国人足知其权威性。

9. 人民网。People 直接翻译成汉语对应词“人民”，表达出一种为人民服务的宗旨。

10. 返利网。事实上，这是一个购物网站，根据谐音翻译成“返利网”，表达出网站购物“返还利润，物有所值”之意，以吸引顾客。

Task II

1. Your happiness, our devotion.

2. It's your idea.

3. Here for good.

Task III

【解析】网站栏目翻译时要考虑以下四点：

第一，不重要的栏目要舍弃。

第二，栏目翻译要准确。

第三，栏目翻译要简洁。

第四，栏目翻译要符合企业文化和网站风格。

参考译文如下：

A：北京同仁堂

1. 首页（Home）：根据英文网站的习惯，首页一般用 Home 或者 Home Page 表达即可，但是有不少英文网站为了节省空间甚至把这一栏目省略掉，如美国广播公司（http://abc.go.com）和苹果公司（http://www.apple.com）。

2. 走进同仁堂（About TRT）：这部分其实是企业介绍，由于 Tongrentang 比较长，所以网站用了缩略形式 TRT，对于访问者来说也不会造成理解上的困难。所以，为了节省空间，这样翻译是恰当的。

3. 新闻中心（News）：国内很多网站比较习惯用“新闻中心”，如海尔集团（http://www.haier.cn），国外一般直接用 News 表达，简洁明了。当然，有的时候为了更好地吸引访问者的眼球，也可以用 Hot News 或 Latest News 等。

4. 同仁堂旗下（Subsidiary）：同仁堂旗下其实就是旗下的子公司介绍，因此，直接用 Subsidiary 来翻译。

5. 全球分布（Global distribution）：这种翻译属于直译，是较为妥当的翻译。但是缺乏了一点“劝说性”，有的时候为了有更强的劝说性，可以用更人性化的表达，如苹果公司网站（http://www.apple.com/choose-your-country）就用 Choose your country or region 来表达。

B：华帝燃具

1. 认识华帝（Recognition of Vatti）：其实此栏目的目的是介绍华帝，所以用 recognition 并不恰当，可以用 Company Information（Information 一般简写为 Info），About Vatti 等译法。

2. 品牌中心（Brand Center）：此处翻译是可以接受的，但是为了简洁，节省空间，可以直接翻译为 Brands。

3. 厨卫精品（Products）：此翻译是根据网站的功能来翻译的，厨卫精品包括燃气灶、抽油烟机、热水器等众多产品，若全部翻译出来就显得啰嗦，不够简练，所以此处用 Products 来概括各种产品是比较恰当的。

4. 服务专区（Special Service Area）：此翻译其实不大符合英文的习惯，并且占用较多空间，可以直接用 Services 来翻译。

5. 公益华帝（Public-welfare Vatti）：此栏目事实上对于外国访问者来说，并不是必需的栏目，他们也不会关心，所以可以不用翻译。如果确实需要翻译，可以与国际接轨，翻译成 Corporate Social Responsibilities（CSR，企业社会责任）。

Task IV

改译：In the new century, Tsingtao Brewery Co., Ltd. will try to develop into an internationalized and learning-type enterprise through innovation and improvement of core competitiveness.

Task V

Founded in 1987, Huawei is a leading global provider of information and communications technology (ICT) infrastructure and smart devices. We have approximately 195,000 employees and we operate in over 170 countries and regions, serving more than three billion people around the world.

Huawei's mission is to bring digital to every person, home and organization for a fully connected, intelligent world. To this end, we will drive ubiquitous connectivity and promote equal access to networks to lay the foundation for the intelligent world; provide diversified computing power to deliver ubiquitous cloud and intelligence; build powerful digital platforms to help all industries and organizations become more agile, efficient, and dynamic; redefine user experience with AI, offering consumers a more personalized and intelligent experience across all scenarios, including home, travel, office, entertainment, and fitness & health.

PART SIX

企业网站翻译实践

Task I

1. 中国新闻网	2. 纽约时报
3. 泡泡网	4. 优酷网
5. 前程无忧	6. 美国在线
7. 日本之窗	8. 中国知网
9. 公民新闻网	10. 澳洲人报

Task II

1. Global trade starts here.
2. Nature shapes us: Nature shapes an enterprise, an individual and even a community.
3. Everyone benefits from our creation and development.
4. Superior quality sheds dignity.
5. Clever, Comfort, Cool.
6. Light up the world.
7. Light the future.
8. The creative life.
9. Shaping the future together.
10. Stand on the shoulders of giants.

Task III

1. Products	2. Products & Services
3. Contact Us	4. Accessories
5. What's New	6. Links/Quick Links
7. Jobs	8. Company Profile
9. Investor Relations	10. Privacy

Task IV

【解析】不当之处有四点：第一，economic entity 与 enterprise 语义重复，哪个企业不是一个经济实体？第二，producing，dealing with，specializes in 三者语义重复。第三，礼品包括了精品，故 choice gifts 用 gifts 一词即可。第四，纪念品就包括了旅游纪念品，故 souvenirs 与 tourist souvenirs 保留后者即可。

改译：Shenzhen Taikong Gift Co., Ltd. is a joint venture，the first domestic enterprise which specializes in high-grade and intermediate gifts，tourist souvenirs and serial appliances for guestrooms in hotel.

Task V

【解析】译文 2 更好。中国人的思维方式以直觉和具体为特征，因此汉语语篇组成往往采用“旁敲侧击”“含而不漏”的归纳推理法。而西方文化注重线形的因果思维，因而他们偏爱开门见山、直入主题的演绎推理法。此宣传资料原文属归纳式的行文方式，最后才提到中心信息“重点骨干企业之一”。译文 1 采用以原语语言文化为取向的策略，逐字逐句进行对等翻译，显然违反了西方广告先突出重要信息，然后用实例或细节加以详尽叙述或论证的特点。译文 2 通过调整句序，将重点信息置于句首，使广告贴近英文的行文习惯，并且译文还删除了可能引起不良联想的信息“head of dragon”等，因而突出了信息功能，增强了移情功能和呼唤功能。

Task VI

译文：The scenic spots in the vicinity of Hangzhou form a vast area for tourists, with the West Lake as its center. To the north of Hangzhou stands Chaoshan Hill, and to the west Mount Tianmu. Going up the Qiantang River one finds oneself at Stork Hill near the Terrace where Yan Ziling, a hermit of the Eastern Han Dynasty (25AD—220AD) , loved to go angling by the Fuchun River in Fuyang City. Nearby are the Yaolin Wonderland in Tonglu County, Tongjun Hill and the three Lingqi Caves in Jiande County, and finally the Thousand Islet Lake which is at the source of the Xin’anjiang River.

Task VII

译文：Zhangjiajie is best known for its towering peaks, cloaked in cloud and mist, and covered in different shades of green. Thick shrubs cover the cliff surface, and pines flourish on the mountain tops. Various shapes can be discerned in its peaks of animals, swords and humans.

Task VIII

译文：China Import and Export Fair, also known as the Canton Fair, was established in the spring of 1957. Co-hosted by the Ministry of Commerce of PRC and the People’s Government of Guangdong Province and organized by China Foreign Trade Centre, it is held every spring and autumn in Guangzhou, China. As a comprehensive international trading event with the longest history, the largest scale, the most complete exhibit variety, the largest buyer attendance, the most diverse buyer origin and the greatest business turnover in China, Canton Fair is hailed as China’s No. 1 Fair and the barometer of China’s foreign trade.

As the window, epitome and symbol of China's opening up and an important platform for international trade cooperation, Canton Fair has withstood various challenges and never been interrupted in the past 65 years. It has been successfully held for 134 sessions and established trade relations with more than 229 countries and regions around the world. The accumulated export volume has amounted to about USD 1.5 trillion and the total number of overseas buyers attending the Canton Fair onsite and online has exceeded 10 million. The Fair has effectively promoted trade connections and friendly exchanges between China and the world.

The Central Committee of the CPC attaches great importance to the Canton Fair. President Xi Jinping sent important congratulatory letters to the 120th and 130th Canton Fair. In his letter to the 130th Canton Fair, he noted that it made significant contribution to facilitating international trade, connection between domestic and international markets, and economic development over the past 65 years. The letter endowed Canton Fair with a new historic mission, pointing a way for the Fair in the new journey of the new era. In the future, under the guidance of Xi Jinping Thought on Socialism with Chinese Characteristics for a New Era, the Canton Fair will fully implement the spirit of the 20th National Congress of the CPC and President Xi's congratulatory letter, follow through the decisions of the CPC Central Committee and the State Council, as well as the requirements of the Ministry of Commerce and Guangdong Province. All-round efforts will be made to innovate mechanism, create more business models and expand the Fair's role to become a vital platform for China's opening-up on all fronts, the high-quality development of global trade and the dual circulation of domestic and overseas markets, so as to better serve national strategies, high-quality opening up, the innovative development of foreign trade, and the building of a new development paradigm.

第七单元 广 告 翻 译

参考译文与参考答案：

PART TWO

热身练习

Task I 略

Task II

1. D 2. I 3. J 4. H 5. G 6. A 7. F 8. B 9. C 10. E

Task III

Take the TOSHIBA, take the world.（对偶）

I'm More satisfied. （双关，More 既表示品牌，又表示更加的意思）

Born to shine. （拟人）

Think different. （拟人，把电脑比拟成人，具有“思考”的能力）

PART THREE 广告翻译技巧

Task I

广告口号的词汇具有动态性、简洁性和创新性等特点。

创新是广告的灵魂，广告创新要么采用创词法，要么采用创句法，要么采用创意法。例 11 中，America Online（美国在线）的广告故意将"World Wide Web"写成"World Wide Wow"，用"Wow"表示该网站会给读者带来惊喜的感觉。例 12 是销售鸡蛋的广告，故意把"exactly"写成"eggsactly"，重复使用"egg"，使消费者对这种鸡蛋印象深刻。例 13 故意把"Drink a pint of milk a day"写成了"Drinka Pinta Milka Day"，吸引消费者，体现广告的创新性。例 14 至 18 都是各种文字游戏，新颖的搭配起到了吸引消费者或广告受众的作用。

Task II 略

Task III

1. 拟人（Personification）
2. 双关（Pun）
3. 对比或对照（Antithesis）
4. 头韵（Alliteration）
5. 押韵（Rhyme）
6. 典故（Allusion）
7. 排比（Parallelism）
8. 重复（Repetition）
9. 仿拟（Parody）
10. 反语（Irony）
11. 夸张（Hyperbole）

Task IV

1. 使不可能成为可能。（佳能）
2. 拥有一块天美时表，拥有一段美好时光。（天美时）
3. 你不理财，财不理你。（《理财周刊》）
4. 对我而言，过去平淡无奇；而未来，却是绚烂缤纷。(轩尼诗酒)
5. 动态的诗，向我舞近。（丰田汽车）
6. There is only something you cannot imagine, there is nothing you cannot do. (Li Ning)
7. Reaching out from the heart. (China Mobile)
8. Version 1: The leather we use is quite thick; the profit we make is fairly thin.

   Version 2: The leather shoes made are thick enough; the profit obtained is slight enough. (Heming Shoes)

9. Only fine medicinal herbs make fine herbal medicines. (Liuwei Dihuangwan (Zhongjing))

10. Tide's in, dirt's out. (Tides)

【解析】从以上广告翻译可以看出，由于中西思维方式和认知能力具有一定的相似性，多数广告翻译可以采用直译法。

11. 本广告中套用了叙事的五要素，即 Who, What, When, Where 和 Why，而且创造性地把“Why”改成谐音大写的字母“Y”，含义是康瓦士篮球想到了方方面面，都能做到想你所想，所以翻译成“康瓦士篮球鞋——想你所想”。

12. 本广告如果直译成“无法打败真事情”，实在有些勉强和晦涩难懂，其原意为其他东西都无法战胜可乐带来的感觉，所以翻译成“挡不住的诱惑”。

13. 本句如果直译成“前面的道路”或者“路在前方”都过于平实，不符合广告必须具备吸引力的特点。既然是汽车广告，消费者肯定希望未来之路宽阔平坦、四通八达，故译作“康庄大道”，其近义词为“阳关大道”，暗示“前程似锦”。西汉司马迁《史记·孟子荀卿列传》：“皆命曰列大夫，为开第康庄之衢，高门大屋，尊宠之。”这对中国读者而言具有特殊的联想意义。

14. 本广告中“世界首例，中国一绝”采用了夸张的手法，如果直译为“World's pioneer, China's top juice”难以让西方人信服本广告夸下的如此海口，所以意译为“Natural Coco Juice: a world special. You enjoy beyond all your words.”这一译法抓住了广告产品的核心特点“天然，特别”，故能够吸引消费者购买。

15. 本广告采用双关和重复修辞手法，直译有一定的难度，采用意译法翻译成“Midea household appliances are beautiful—beautiful from head to toe, beautiful inside out.（Midea household appliances）”。这样不仅保留了原文的重复修辞手法，还添加了拟人修辞，与原文有异曲同工之妙。

16. 当今时代倡导低碳生活、绿色生活，飞利浦提出“探求节能照明新技术，打造人性化绿色空间，力求可持续性发展”的照明理念，意译为“Deliver Meaningful Sustainability”把握住原文的“可持续”精髓。

Task V

1. 本广告直译为“智慧，无处不在”，但是，由于汉语讲究对称与平稳，所以增加词语“演绎”，使广告更具有诗情画意与文学色彩，提高了吸引力，故翻译为“智慧演绎，无处不在”。

2. 翻译本广告时增加了动词“聚”，使其更加形象生动。“分分秒秒欢聚欢笑”语言平实、对称，表达了“欢声笑语”汇聚麦当劳的意义。

3. 本广告如果按照意思进行翻译，只需要翻译出“钻石恒久远”即可，为了使语言朗朗上口，增加表现力，翻译时增加了“一颗永流传”。于是“钻石恒久远，一颗永流传”表达了浓浓爱意，象征爱情天长地久，岂不美哉。

4. 本广告表达了“每滴咖啡都味道香醇”的意思，但翻译成“滴滴香浓，意犹未尽”，增加了“意犹未尽”，表示“喝了还想喝”，恰到好处。

5. 本广告翻译过程中增加了“好事自然来”，译文中采用对偶和押韵修辞手法，语言生动、朗朗上口，表达喜庆的氛围，于是翻译为“人头马一开，好事自然来”。

6. 根据英语重形合、汉语重意合的语言特点，增加了使句子符合语法的连接词。译文：Leave “Managing Money” alone, and money manages to leave you alone. 或 If you leave “Managing Money” alone, money will manage to leave you alone.

7. 为了使译文对偶和押韵，增加了“far and near”，使译文语言流畅，朗朗上口。译文：People’s skin colors are different far and near, but their choice can be the same for Tsingtao Beer.

8. 本广告既是对状元红的介绍，也是一种广告形式。文中涉及中国的朝代，中国历史悠久，经历了不同的时代和朝代，即使是中国人都可能对各朝代的时间也不太清楚，更何况是外国读者。所以，根据读者友好的原则，降低读者的阅读成本，增加了各朝代的具体时间。译文：Zhuangyuan Hong, the Number One Scholar Red, is one of China’s best-known wines, first produced in Tang (618—907) and Song (960—1279), and became nation-wide popular in Ming (1368—1644) and Qing (1616—1911) dynasties.

9. 本广告如果直译为“Guangzhou is my home; its cleanness depends on all of us.”就显得有些啰嗦含糊。该公益口号的含义就是让大家保持城市卫生，所以删繁就简，翻译成“Keep our city clean!”简单明了，也达到了原文的宣传目的。

Task VI

1. 爱巧克力哟！（LG 手机）
2. 动态的诗，向我舞近。（丰田汽车）
3. 不懈追求完美。（雷克萨斯轿车）
4. 给你一颗奔腾的“芯”。（英特尔奔腾）
5. 沟通无极限。（摩托罗拉）
6. 没有不做的小生意，没有解决不了的大问题。（IBM）

Task VII

1. 每天吃一块 Mars 巧克力，保您工作、休息、娱乐随心意。
2. 并非所有的汽车都有相同的品质。
3. 车到山前必有路，有路必有丰田车。
4. East or west, Meng Di is best !
5. All roads lead to Rome. All “Bailing” leads to home.
6. Lvdanlan cosmetics—Love me tender, love me true.

Task VIII

【解析】

1. 把“A great way to fly!”翻译成“新加坡航空，飞跃万里，超越一切！”突出了汉语气势磅礴的语势。

2. 本广告中“happen”原本是中性词，这里显然是表达在本酒店什么事情都有可能，于是选取褒义，即一切好事皆有可能。翻译时与服务业紧密联系，于是翻译成“有求必应”，凸显了该酒店满足顾客需求的特色。

3. 本广告译文“联络世界”是原意的表达，增加了“触及未来”，使广告词朗朗上口，对仗工整。

4. 本广告原意为“男人得到的最好的东西”，显然难以起到促销作用。而剃须是男人早上起床的第一件事。当今商业社会，生活节奏加快，人们希望迅速修面，所以创造性地利用比喻，翻译成“给你最爽快的早餐”，变换了人称，拉近了产品与消费者的距离。

5. 诺基亚作为移动电话生产商，一直信奉创新原则，视研发与科技创新为企业的生命，故创造性地把企业文化融入广告翻译之中，合情合理。

Task IX

1. Just 5 kilometers away from the central business districts, is it your dream life living in the last villa of the city?

2. All customers must present this coupon to receive a discount of 30% off when purchasing fifty bottles of Evian Mineral Water.

3. The Hawaiian Islands are one of the most beautiful places on earth. The weather is friendly. The temperature ranges from 60～90 degrees Fahrenheit all year long. It's a little warmer in summer, and a little cooler in winter, but every day is a beach day for somebody.

PART SIX

广告翻译实践

Task I

1. honor	2. finest	3. Focus	4. smiles
5. hand	6. indulge	7. shape	8. good

Task II

1. 亚洲花园酒店——您在远方的家。本广告采用暗喻（Metaphor）修辞手法，把亚洲花园酒店比喻成顾客的家，说明酒店给顾客带来宾至如归的感觉。

2. 现代的马可·波罗。本广告采用典故（Allusion）修辞手法。马可·波罗是意大利著名的商人、旅行家和探险家，曾在中国游历17载。他是英勇无畏探险精神的杰出代表，暗示了航空公司的企业精神。

3. 大刺激，小花费。本广告采用对照（Contrast）修辞手法，“大”与“小”相对，简洁明了。

4. 一天没有橙汁就像一天没有阳光。本广告采用明喻（Simile）修辞手法，直截了当地表达了橙汁在人们的生活中像阳光一样必不可少。

5. 道路不沾水，司机更安全；
司机不沾酒，道路更安全。

这则交通宣传广告语重点突出了“road，driver，safer，dry”这四个词，两个句子整齐对称，是典型的对偶（Antithesis）修辞手法。

6. 这是引以为豪之事。自豪的传统，自豪的传承，自豪的味道。

本广告采用了重复（Repetition）和排比（Parallelism）的修辞手法，一气呵成，让消费者觉得该产品真的具有挡不住的诱惑。

7. 可怜那些三只手吧。本广告是某种衣服的广告，由于其口袋设计与众不同，可以防盗，采用反语（Irony）修辞手法，达到嘲笑小偷、宣传自身产品的目的。

8. 不穿“时尚”，就不时尚。本广告采用了双关（Pun）修辞手法。“Vogue”一语双关，既是品牌，又表“时尚”之意。

9. 洗净城市的灰尘。本广告使用了转喻（Metonymy）修辞手法，即用一种事物代替另一种相关的事物并与后者相搭配的词配合使用的一种修辞手法。本广告中用“city”代替了“dirt”，也夸张地说明了该品牌洗发水的强大功效。

Task III

1. 从未有过的好时代。（《时代周刊》）
2. 《时代》杂志公司说，《生活》即将返回人间，如果《生活》回到人间，《展望》岂会遥远？
3. 阅读《时代》能为您赢得时间。
4. 汽车行业把它称之为豪华轿车。
   制酒工业把它称之为高档酒。
   航空工业把它称之为头等舱。
   酒店行业把它称之为五星级。
   证券行业把它称之为绩优股。
   信息行业把它称之为《时代杂志》。

Task IV

1. 拥有东芝，拥有世界。（东芝）
2. 严禁酒后驾车。（公益广告）
3. 每个孩子放学回家都该有个“苹果”。（苹果电脑）
4. 万事俱备，只看路况。（丰田）
5. 世上最令人难以忘怀的女人都用露华浓。（露华浓）
6. 充满舒适与温馨的世界（日本航空公司）
7. 只溶在口，不溶在手。（玛氏巧克力豆）
8. 安联集团，永远站在你身边。（安联集团）
9. 我们的烦恼是：顾客待在酒店流连忘返。（某酒店）

Task V

1. Mosquito Bye Bye Bye.（Bye bye bye，显然比用 kill, kill, kill 委婉，汉语中使用三个“杀”，显示了产品灭蚊的功能，但英语中如果直接使用“kill”，给人以血腥和暴力的联想。）
2. He who lasts last laughs best.（采用仿译）
3. East or west, Hangtian is best.（仿译法，也可翻译成 Where there is road, there is a Hangtian.）
4. Where there is South, there is a way.（仿译法）
5. Applying Dabao morning and night, makes your skincare a real delight.（原文采用押韵修辞手法，译文也尽量做到押韵。它又可译为，A fair skin now? Dabao knows how.）
6. East or west, Songhe is in my chest.（仿译法，借用 East or west, home is best.）

7. Drive carefully—the life you save may be your own.（直译法）

8. Our shoe polish is surely of the first rate; it shines your shoes and you look great.（把双关语“足下”分解成“您”和“鞋子”进行翻译。）

Task VI

【解析】本部分翻译全部采用了增译法，增添译文的美感、说服性和可读性。

Task VII

西诺德总部位于德国苯茨海姆，是世界主要的牙科设备生产商。西诺德（佛山）牙科设备有限公司诚聘英才，岗位如下：

产品经理：五年或五年以上市场调研分析、产品定位、产品定价、竞争对手分析和产品概念设计经验

品牌经理：四年或者四年以上品牌管理经验，具备良好的讲解技能

销售主管：五年或者五年以上财务管理经验，具备丰富的财务分析和财务报告知识，有审计经验者优先

大客户经理：五年或五年以上牙科产品或相关产品的渠道管理或者客户管理经验，有客户基础优先（经验不够者可考虑销售代表职位）

质量主管：八年或八年以上工作经验，其中三年或者三年以上机电产品质量监控与分析经验，熟悉产品测试和质量提升

上述职位申请者要求在工作中能用英语流利表达。

第八单元　产品介绍翻译

解析与参考答案：

PART TWO

热身练习

Task I 略

Task II

1. Neither toxic nor side effect has been observed after taking this medicine.

2. Do not expose to sunshine or temperature over 50 degrees centigrade. Do not let your children play with it.

3. Put two or three teaspoonfuls (about 40 g) of it in a cup. Pour in boiled water (hot or cold) or milk and stir well to dissolve, and then a very delicious and refreshing drink will be ready for you.

4. Children under five years old are recommended to drink at least 500 ml of milk daily.

Task III

【解析】

1. 此类句子最好用祈使句。建议改为：Put the finished goods in the inner box.

2. 本句中“putted”属于误用。建议改为：All the inner boxes are placed in the same direction in master packing.

3. 本句中“only can”语序不对。建议改为：Only one type of the device can be contained in master packing.

4.“Attach”后面一般接“to”，所以可以直接用“put on”；括号中“label sample refer to the Appendix II”不符合语法规范，应当是某人或某些人参考附录而不是“label sample”；“generally speaking”多用于口语，表示总结陈词，此处可改为“generally/usually”。建议改为：Put the master packing label on the surface of the master packing (Please refer to Appendix II for label sample). Generally, the master packing label is pasted beside the mark “SHIP TO”.

PART THREE

产品介绍翻译技巧

Task I 略

Task II

【解析】既然是产品介绍，就必须介绍、宣传产品的优势，所以产品介绍中一定有许多形容词或形容词短语等具有褒义的评价性词语，如“low, lower, fun”等词用于突出产品的卓越特点。

Task III

1. 为减少火灾或触电的危险，请勿将本装置暴露在雨中或潮湿环境中。
2. 为防止触电，请勿打开机盒。只能由有资质的人员进行维修。
3. 仅适用于亚太地区客户，仅用于 CompactFlash 储存卡。
4. 亚太地区客户有限保修。

Task IV

1. 操作前，请检查遥控模型车。检查所有零件，确保使用一段时间后所有螺丝锁紧。
2. 请为发射器和接收器安装新电池，以免发生失控事件。
3. 启动引擎前，检查刹车和油门，以免发生失控事件。
4. 请确认你所在国家或地区的射频规定，选择适当的射频。操作模型前，检查附近是否有其他人员使用相同频率的操作模型。
5. 请勿触摸任何旋转的装置。

Task V

1. 在使用 ThinkPad R50 系列计算机之前请先阅读本文档。ThinkPad R50 系列计算机符合任何批准无线使用的国家或地区的射频和安全标准。您必须严格按照以下描述的说明来安装和使用 ThinkPad 计算机。

2. 在说明手册各项指引和条件下使用，本产品工艺或材质若有瑕疵，自购买之日起 5 年内，索尼将免费为客户更换相当产品。本项保修仅适用于此处所述的保修条款。本产品内所储存的资料由于任何原因导致的损毁，索尼恕不承担任何责任。

Task VI

食用方法：为了宝宝的健康，请遵照以下说明：

1. 仔细清洗双手及所有器具。
2. 将器具冲洗干净，并放入沸水中煮 5 分钟。
3. 煮沸清水，之后放凉至 50 度。
4. 将适量的温开水注入奶瓶或杯子。
5. 每 30 毫升温开水加入一平匙金装美素乐。
6. 搅拌或摇晃奶瓶至奶粉完全溶解。
7. 测试牛奶的温度，待温度适中后，方可喂给宝宝。
8. 冲调好的牛奶最多可在冰箱存储 24 小时。请将没有喂完的倒掉。

储藏方法：存放在阴凉、干燥处，务必盖紧罐盖。开罐后请在 4 周内食用完毕。

Task VII

突出优势：

自动清洁

自动充电

效率高，功能强

智能型真空吸尘机器人

清洁木地板和地毯

大忙人的好帮手

这种面向未来的真空吸尘机器人聪明灵巧，能自动清洁地板，自动充电，而您无须动用一根手指头。离家时，只需要设定好清扫和吸尘的程序，回来时，家里干干净净。

真空吸尘机器人能有效清除地毯、木地板、大理石地板和尼龙地面的泥土，碎片和宠物毛发。吸尘机器人的反转毛刷和搅打机刷就像是垃圾铲和扫帚一样同时运作，可以清扫地面。结实的鬃毛刷可以深入到地毯纤维等卫生死角，扫除泥土、碎片、灰尘及其他垃圾。它能有力地把所有脏东西吸入其集尘箱，使地板和地毯干干净净。

您是否太忙而无法定期吸尘呢？我们为您准备了解决办法。使用真空吸尘机器人，您想什么时候清扫，就可以设定它什么时候清扫。它不会被卡在角落或掉下楼梯。遇到障碍或者曲面边界时，它会掉头，继续执行原来的指令，继续清扫。

Task VIII

1. 考虑到**被观测物距离**遥远，标示其运动的 X 射线波长应缩短到适当的范围。

2. 用这种清洗剂**清洗**沙发套、窗帘或者床套，不用大力搓洗，就能洗净顽固的污渍。

3. 来自 Vogue 的最新职业款式把精致的色彩与雅致的剪裁融为一体，**产生了**最为女性化的效果。

4. 所有**肉禽**罐头上标明“按伊斯兰教规宰杀制成”。

5. 把数字技术与先进的软件，**体积**更小、**功能**更强大的微型处理器以及快速增长的光纤和无限频带宽度（带宽）发展相结合，你就会获得功能更强大的无缝隙全方位的连接。

Task IX

【解析】

第 1 题是参茶功能的说明。中文更像是药品说明书，如果按照原译，该参茶的作用肯定有所夸大，可能误导消费者，聪明的消费者也认为宣传有些夸夸其谈，而不会购买该产品。另外，如“养心安神”之类的说法务虚不务实，国外的消费者难以接受或者无法理解。因此，需要对原文进行减译，删除某些不必要的词汇并对原意进行概括。

第 2 题中的中医理论描述“腰为肾之府”“肾为先天之本”“脾为后天之本”及“内病外治”即使是中国的普通人也难以理解，对中医一窍不通的西方人如读天书，这点原译巧妙省去这些繁琐的理论，但略微谈到强肾和健脾。其实，西方更多称为“kidney care”，如英国专门有“National Health Service Kidney Care Center”，这就符合西方的表达习惯。

第 3 题原文中“酱香浓郁、典雅细致、协调丰满、回味悠长”是对中国白酒口感的描述。中国的普通饮者都难以表达和体会，更何况是很少喝白酒的西方人，因此肯定无法直译而需要删除部分具有中国白酒特色的描述性词汇。原译中“possess”表示“占有，拥有，持有，摆布，支配”等，本文中表示酒具有的特点，英语习惯使用句型“be characterized by”。另外，改译中并未删除“回味悠长”，因为西方人经常用来形容咖啡或者红酒，其对应译法为“prolonged aftertaste”，此处也可借用来描述白酒的特点。

Task X

曼秀雷敦淡彩润唇啫喱（润唇膏）

时尚淡彩啫喱配方，保湿滋润，全面修护。

蕴涵**丰富**维生素 C、维生素 E。有效保护双唇健康，抗衡氧化，延缓老化。

增添双唇**如珍珠般的**淡淡色彩，自然亮丽。

可单独使用或与不同口红搭配，**创出喜爱色调**。

PART SIX

产品介绍翻译实践

Task I

1. 粉底　2. 润肤霜　3. 指甲油　4. 卸妆水　5. 防晒乳
6. 化妆水　7. 腮红　8. 抗老防皱　9. 遮瑕膏　10. 精华液
11. 眼膜　12. 眼影

Task II

1. sportswear　2. protective work wear　3. stage costume　4. dressing gown
5. maternity wear　6. casual wear　7. formal wear　8. knitted garments
9. woven garments　10. cotton garments　11. silk garments
12. synthetic-made garments　13. Zhongshan Zhuang
14. safari jacket　15. tailored suit　16. down wear

Task III

使用说明：

临床证明有效防止蛀牙

如无密封铝箔，请勿使用。

成人或 2 岁以上儿童：彻底清洁牙齿，最好每次饭后或至少每天 2 次刷牙，或遵医嘱。

2—6 岁儿童：只要挤豌豆大小体积的牙膏并监督孩子刷牙漱口（尽量不要吞咽）。

2 岁以下儿童：请咨询牙科医生或内科医生。

Task IV

Complimentary airport pick-up

Complimentary high tea from 4 p.m. to 6 p.m.

Complimentary western buffet breakfast

Complimentary exquisite fruit basket for suite guests

Complimentary high speed Internet access in guest rooms

Free domestic call & local call

Complimentary shuttle bus service to and from the Pazhou Complex on a fixed schedule

Complimentary entry for gym, indoor and outdoor swimming pools

Task V

我们的产品担保仅限于 CompactFlash 储存卡本身，且要遵守这些操作说明，使用本装置附带的附件，在指定或推荐的系统环境下使用。

在生命保障系统或其他一些应用中，过失可能导致伤害或生命危险，索尼不保证该产品在此类情况下的使用。

本公司对因使用本机导致的损害或损失，或任何第三方的索赔不承担责任。

本公司对下列情况不承担任何责任：由于使用本产品导致您的数码相机或其他硬件出现的问题；本产品对特定硬件、软件或外围设备的适应性；同已安装的其他软件产生的冲突；数据损失；或其他意外或不可避免的损害。

Task VI

1. 建议改译为：Properties of the product: rich in various vitamins, minerals and amino acids. With mutually complementary animal and plant proteins, it promotes absorption of balanced nutrition.

2. 建议改译为：The SQ series of Stone Selecting and Removing Machines are mainly used to remove all sizes of impurities in grain, wheat, bean and vegetable seeds. They are characterized by high efficiency, easy operation and low energy consumption.

3. 建议改译为：The natural gas offered by our company is clean, convenient and efficient with blue flame. As it is inflammable and explosive, improper use of it may result in poison, choking, fire and explosion.

4. 建议改译为：选择适当的地方操作遥控模型。不得在街道或马路上操作，这可能引起严重事故，造成人身伤害和（或）财产损失。不要在靠近人畜的地方操作。为避免伤害，不要在限制区域操作。不要在医院和住宅区操作，其噪声可能影响他人。不要在室内操作，造成火灾或损失的风险很高。

Task VII

1. Please refrigerate at 5℃ after opening and consume within 3 days.
2. Keep away from children. /Keep out of reach of children.
3. Store below 25℃ and protect from freezing and light.
4. Store above 10℃ and guard against damp.
5. Validity. 关于产品的有效期，表达方法因具体产品而不同。表达方法较多，比如 Validity（有效期），Expiry（Exp.）Date（失效日期），Expiration Date（失效日期），也可以用 Shelf Life, Storage Life（储存期），也有产品使用 Best Before（此前最佳）等。

Task VIII

有关兼容设备操作的详细内容，请参阅设备的使用说明书。

请勿敲击、弯曲、摔落或弄湿本品。

不要将本品放在以下场所：

—非常冷或非常热的地方

—非常潮湿的地方

—有腐蚀性气体的地方

—灰尘多或者肮脏的地方

—震动大的地方

—阳光直射的地方

安装时，请将 CompactFlash 储存卡以正确的方式完全插入机器的插口。

请勿拆开或改造本产品。

请勿在本品上贴标签。

重要的资料务必备份。

在主机标签上书写时，请使用圆珠笔，请勿使用钢笔或水笔。

在以下情况下，记录的资料会被破坏（消除）：

—在读取、记录或格式化的过程中将 CompactFlash 储存卡取出，或关闭机器的电源

—在受静电或电气噪声影响的场所使用

如您所使用的设备无法识别 CompactFlash 储存卡，请拔出，关闭或重启设备，并再次尝试将卡插入。

第九单元　商 标 翻 译

PART TWO

热身练习

Task I 略

Task II

1. 耐克	2. 别克	3. 百丽
4. 七喜	5. 多芬	6. 凌志（现名雷克萨斯）
7. Joyoung	8. Transfar（生化集团）	9. Robam
10. JOE ONE	11. Founder	12. Rising

Task III

【解析】A 组的商标翻译相对 B 组而言更为成功，主要从商标原语和译语的音、形、义三方面进行分析。

1. Coca-Cola 最初翻译成“蝌蝌啃蜡”，让人想到味同嚼蜡，效果可想而知。20 世纪 20 年代，蒋彝教授把它翻译成“可口可乐”取得了巨大成功。该译文一直像其产品一样让人津津乐道，被称为神来之笔。当时的奖金为 350 英镑，但“可口可乐”这一翻译为企业创造了巨大的财富。该译文不但保持了英文的发音，而且把产品特征与客户紧密联系，刺激了消费者的消费欲望。“可口可乐”四个字生动再现了产品特征及其为消费者带来的感受——好喝与快乐——既可口又可乐。

2. 德国人 Carl Benz（卡尔·本茨）是汽车的发明者之一，世界第一辆汽车的制造者。他创立的奔驰汽车公司于 1886 年 1 月 29 日获得汽车制造专利权，这一天被公认为世界上首辆汽车的诞生日。Benz 曾被翻译成本茨，但对中国人而言，只是一个外国人名的音译，别无他意。在中国香港，Benz 被翻译成“平治”，不禁让人想起《孟子》一书中“修身、齐家、治国、平天下”的名言，既突出了汽车本身的稳重、高贵，也突出车主的显赫身份和高贵地位。在中国内地，采用音译法，“Benz”被翻译成“奔驰”，语音与语义巧妙搭配。“奔”腾飞跃，“驰”骋千里，风驰电掣，充满活力动感，这正是 Benz 的最佳写照。

3. 金利来有限公司总部位于香港，其创始人曾宪梓先生开始把“Goldlion”直译成“金狮”，但“金狮”与普通话的“金失”“尽失”和广东话的“尽输”谐音，这种译法自然难以让人接受。把“Goldlion”翻译成“金利来”，由于它主要生产男人服饰，男人又往往是家里的顶梁柱，所以男人都渴望“财源滚滚来”，金利来因此成为成功男人的标志。

4. 把“三笑”翻译成“Sanxiao”对外国人而言没有任何意义。“三笑”原意为使用了该品牌的牙膏后，牙齿亮白，笑容满面。所以，我们建议把“三笑”翻译成“Sunshine”，喻意使用该品牌的牙膏，让人总是春风得意，笑容如阳光般灿烂。无独有偶，该集团的“睡的香”蚊香，直接用拼音（Shuidexiang）翻译，而“娇爽”卫生巾则翻译成了“Smilefree”，“free”表示没有，如 dutyfree 表示免税，carefree 表示无忧无虑。此处“Smilefree”意思是“没有笑容”。使用该产品让人没有笑容，谁还会用呢？

5. 把“春兰”直接音译成“Chunlan”，虽然比较简洁，但无法传递原文中春天的感觉，建议直译为“Spring Orchid”。

6. 杜康，一个传说不断、富有传奇色彩的名字。相传杜康为一个牧羊人，把装于竹筒的米饭置于树下，数日返回，发现有奇味，饮而醉人，因而他是中国造酒第一人。杜康酒素有“开坛香十里，隔壁醉三家”的美誉。商标“杜康”不仅让人联想到杜康造酒的传说，还联想到唐代诗圣杜甫“杜酒频劳劝，张梨不外求”以及曹操《短歌行》中的诗句“慨当以慷，忧思难忘。何以解忧？唯有杜康。”杜康的名字在中国妇孺皆知，家喻户晓，具有很高的商业价值，这也是河南和陕西两家企业 20 多年来一直争夺“杜康”商标的原因所在。如果仅把“杜康”翻译成“Dukang”则失去了许多联想意义。根据西方人善用古希腊神话人物命名商标的习惯，建议使用古希腊神话中的酒神 Dionysos（狄俄尼索斯）或者古罗马神话中的酒神 Bacchus（巴克斯）。西方接受者对此可以产生中国人听到杜康类似的联想，这种译文对中国读者而言一无所知，而对于外国读者则是耳熟能详的名字，其效可嘉。

PART THREE

商标翻译技巧

Task I

【解析】

1. 商标词读音必须朗朗上口，易于记忆。第一组三个词都是拟声词，Kodak 缘于照相是按下快门“咔嚓”一声，形象生动，记忆永恒。KitKat 描述了享用巧克力时“香脆可口”的声音，与其广告词“Have a break. Have a KitKat（轻松一刻，奇巧时刻）”是绝佳搭配。Pitpaf 是农药品牌，是喷洒农药的拟声词，翻译成“必扑”，取“必定扑杀”之意，恰好与农药的功效紧密相连。第二组、第三组商标的谐音与产品特征相互吻合，如蜜蜂（缝纫机）与密缝，穗宝（床垫）与睡宝，娃哈哈（饮料）与“哇，哈哈”。第三组商标 U2，LUX，OIC 的谐音分别是 You too（你也想穿），Lucks（幸运）和 Oh, I See（哦，看见了），都与其相应产品衣服、香皂和眼镜的特征或功能密不可分。由此可见，商标命名必须考虑其读音或者谐音是否跟产品或者产品特征紧密相连。

2. 俗语云：“名副其实”，商标名称必须与商品特征保持高度一致。Triumph 作为汽车商标，其含义为“胜利、喜悦”，中文名为“凯旋”，取“驾车凯旋”之意。Kiss me 则彰显西方女性对待感情直白外露，表现了她们豪放自由、风情万种的迷人风采。Duracell 中“dura”取自“durable”，表示电池经久耐用之意。后面的快克、匹克和康宝分别表示“迅速攻克病毒”“克敌制胜”和“健康之宝”的意思。

3. 商标必须创新，体现在词形的多种多样，从 P&G，UP2U，HOdo（红豆衬衫）等商标中可以看出词形的创意。

4. 数字在日常生活中必不可少，中外商标中也常见用数字作为商标，比如：999 感冒灵、361° 运动鞋等。

5. 语言植根于文化之中，是民族文化的历史积淀，是文化的结晶。有些商标词本身就是文化负载词（Culture-loaded words），比如中文的梅兰竹菊就是典型的文化负载词，商标翻译必须考虑文化因素。

Fortune Duck 中的鸭子在中国文化中并非好事，如果翻译成“幸运鸭”是不成功的，因为在汉语中，“鸭”指“吃软饭的人”，也指“男性性工作者”。Opium 香水以其辛辣、神秘的芬芳香味风靡西方世界，但是如果不考虑中国特定的历史文化而直接翻译成“鸦片”香水，那就会无人问津，因为鸦片让中国人想到充满奇耻大辱的鸦片战争。英国汽车商标 Zephyr 原意为“西风”，因为英国是岛国，从其西面大西洋吹来的海风往往是和煦的暖风，难怪雪莱在《西风颂》中热情讴歌西风。而在中国，西风表示寒冷刺骨的冷风，或者表示没有食物的意思，比如“吹西北风、喝西北风”。在中国，白象、金龙、白猫分别表示“干净”“高贵”和“洁净”，如果直接翻译成英语就是“White Elephant, Gold Dragon, White Cat”，由于中西文化差异，英文含义分别为“大而累赘的东西，张牙舞爪而邪恶的东西，恶毒的女人”，这些都是没有考虑文化差异的翻译。

Task II

1. B　2. B　3. A　4. A　5. B　6. B　7. B　8. B　9. A　10. A

Task III

1. （1）捷安特　（2）保时捷　（3）林肯　（4）索芙特　（5）爱华
（6）耐克　（7）奥迪　（8）欧米茄　（9）波音　（10）西门子
（11）Liby　（12）Chunlan　（13）Chang Hong　（14）Moutai　（15）Wahaha

2. （1）苹果　（2）皇冠　（3）先锋　（4）美标　（5）良友
（6）Bright　（7）Panda　（8）Diamond　（9）Snow Flying
（10）Great Impression

3. （1）联合利华　（2）金利来　（3）强生　（4）锐步　（5）彪马
（6）Serene　（7）Midea　（8）Robust　（9）Gree　（10）Nice

4. （1）飘柔　（2）万事发　（3）舒洁　（4）真美诗　（5）海飞丝
（6）Freshtech　（7）Hillo　（8）Lenovo　（9）Dohia
（10）Go Believe

5. （1）SK-II　（2）IBM　（3）UP2U　（4）LG　（5）LV

（本题采用零翻译。）

PART SIX

商标翻译实践

Task I

1. J　2. G　3. I　4. A　5. H　6. C　7. B　8. E　9. F　10. D

Task II

1. 桑塔纳　2. 凯迪拉克　3. 悍马　4. 别克
5. 丰田　6. 沃尔沃　7. 林肯　8. 本田
9. 纪梵希　10. 古驰　11. 倩碧　12. 薇姿
13. 香奈儿　14. 水之澳　15. 迪奥

Task III

1. “Hisense”表示“High sense”，即“感觉很好”的意思。
2. “Midea”与“My dear”谐音，表示产品非常惹人喜欢。
3. “Royal Star”表示尊贵之意。
4. “Go Believe”表达了“眼见为实”的意思，促使消费者尝试它，欣赏它。
5. “Vatti”，采用音译法。
6. “Only One”表示“只此一家”之意。
7. “Virtue”表示“品德”的意思。
8. “Kelon”，采用音译法进行翻译。
9. “Skinice”是“Skin nice”结合创造而来。

10. “Gree”既与格力谐音，又具有“优越、杰出、胜利”的意思。

11. “Robust”表示“强壮”的意思。

12. “Youngor”与“雅戈尔”谐音，又与“younger”谐音，其表示“越穿越年轻”的含义。

13. “Supor”与“苏泊尔”谐音，而且表示“超越”的含义。

14. 面对扬名在先的可口可乐和百事可乐，非常可乐必须出奇制胜，所以翻译成“Future Cola”，永远面向未来，走在前面，是非常恰当的翻译。

15. “Chigo”与“志高”谐音。

Task IV

1. B. Gold Star 在美国表示阵亡将士的代名词，不符合有关语言和风俗习惯。

2. A. 将黑人直接翻译成 Negro 是行不通的，Negro 具有贬义，即使是翻译成表示中性含义的 Black 仍不妥帖。但是翻译成 Darlie，与 Darling 谐音，听起来舒适上口，效果非同一般。

3. B. Gold Textile 容易误解成“金纺织品”或者“含金的纺织品”，而翻译成“Comfort”表达了该纺织品给人“舒适”的感觉，其发音也与汉语的“金纺”非常接近。

4. A. “MAXAM”在发音上接近于原商标名，而且其发音效果与“maximum”接近，有“最高、极致”的意思。同时，译名拼写简短，首尾都是“M”，在形态上也产生平衡美感，是一个很成功的商标名，具备商标名内容美和形式美的统一，只是它的内容美和形式美换了一种方式。

5. B. Cock 在英文中指男性性器官，是不雅之词，不能用于商标，只能译成 Rooster.

6. B. 汉语中的“鸳鸯”经常出现在中国古代文学作品和神话传说中。鸳指雄鸟，鸯指雌鸟，一旦结为配偶，便陪伴终生，甚为忠诚。中国人常用鸳鸯喻指恩爱的夫妻。但其英语译名“Mandarin Duck”却没有相关的联想意义，所以“鸳鸯”牌翻译时可以采用意译法，译为“Love Bird”才能传递它在原语文化中的特殊内涵。

Task V

1. 雅阁。雅指“优雅”之意，阁有“房间、阁楼”之意。汽车如自己的房子般舒服，谁不想拥有它呢？

2. 雅确。手表必须精确无误。

3. 黛安芬。由于是内衣品牌，它需要顾及女性朋友的审美心理，故得此译名。

4. 凯旋。“Triumph”原指“胜利”之意。车主驾车胜利归来，当然叫“凯旋”了。

5. 多芬。它取香皂芬芳的意思。

6. 德芙。它取富贵之意。

第十单元 公关文稿翻译

参考译文与译例分析：

PART ONE 认识公关文稿

Task I

广义的公关文稿指在公关活动中通过可能涉及的传播手段所发布的各类文稿，包括公关广告、供销广告、请柬、贺卡、名片、书信、电报、传真、聘书、题赠、对联、演讲稿、公关案例及分析、新闻消息与通讯、计划书、总结、会议记录和纪要、备忘录、各种商务报告以及各种合同、意向书等公文文体。

Task II

1. 副主席先生，美国朋友们，同事们，女士们，先生们：

我谨代表我们代表团的所有成员，为邀请我们参加这个盛大的圣诞晚会表示衷心的感谢！

我们享受了美酒佳肴，聆听了美妙的音乐。我很高兴能有机会和大家共聚一堂，共同度过这美好的夜晚。俗话说，“良好的开端是成功的一半”。我希望我们能够保持这种良好的关系，在新的一年里取得更大的成就。

再次感谢盛情邀请，感谢你们使我们度过了欢乐的时光。

最后，请各位与我一起举杯

为副主席先生的健康，

为美国朋友们的健康，

为我的同事们的健康，

为在座所有的女士们、先生们，

干杯！

2.

通　知
兹定于本周三（10月18日）下午两点（14:00）在第二会议厅召开关于弹性工作时间的会议，请所有员工按时到会。
2023 年 10 月 15 日

PART TWO

热身练习

Task I

1. 宣布会议正式开始（用于会议开始前，由会议主持人宣布会议开始，提醒与会者遵守会议秩序）
2. 散会、休会
3. 记者招待会、新闻发布会
4. 提议（向……）敬酒
5. （尊敬的）来宾/贵宾/嘉宾
6. annual conference
7. press release/news release
8. inaugural speech
9. opening ceremony
10. to bid farewell to…/to say goodbye to…

Task II

【解析】由于内部文稿多是企业内部交流使用的文函形式，其格式一般比较固定，但在不同的公司，对于格式的规定也不同。以备忘录为例，在商业办公、法律文件或外交谈判中，一些非正式或半正式的文件通常都会被称为备忘录，是用来简单说明主题与相关事件的书面资料。它可以是简单的字条、文件，或是通讯记录。备忘录可以有各种形式，也不一定有固定格式，随着呈送或接收对象不同，其行文的语气和表达也会发生变化。翻译时应该注意目的、结构及行文习惯，文字尽量浅显确切，提供实质性信息，强调简洁、紧凑、客观。此外，还存在一些固定的程式化用语，如上文中的“预知如下情况”和“呈报”等。

备忘录

收件人：运营部经理 琼斯先生
发件人：主管 格蕾丝·凯莉
事由/主题：关于打卡考勤制度的意见
发件日期：10 月 19 日

兹回复你 9 月 29 日建议全体员工采用打卡考勤制度的备忘录。

你提到公司应采取措施提高工作效率，采用打卡考勤制度则可以更严格地管控员工，对此我毫无异议。然而，我实则不认为实行打卡制度就能提高工作效率。我认为，提高工作效率最好的方法就是给予员工更多的激励措施。当然，我们可以继续探讨其他可行的方法。

请认真考虑我的建议。谢谢！

Task III

1. E　2. A　3. F　4. B　5. D　6. G　7. C

PART THREE
公关文稿翻译技巧

Task I

【解析】公关文稿的语言特征

翻译致辞、演讲等公关文稿时要注意其语言特点。根据场合的不同，致辞、演讲也可以分为正式讲稿和非正式讲稿。若是用于政府、公司会谈，一般都比较正式，语言上除了颂扬彼此的交往友谊，还会就重大的问题发表自己的看法，形式严谨，语言规范。除了语言上特别注重礼仪之外，还会出现各个领域的专业词汇，如经济、政治等领域内的专业词汇。而一般性的相互来访或交流活动，则多属于非正式的范畴，语言比较随和，基调也较轻松。译者在翻译时不仅要注意根据场合和致辞内容进行语气上的准确传达，还要多了解常用的外交辞令、客套语等，从中英文对应的角度去寻找两者之间的契合点。

此外，因为致辞和演讲归根结底都是口头表达，它们还具有以下特征：

1. 语言清楚易懂，句子简短明了，稿件口语化；
2. 语言生动贴切，亲切热诚；
3. 稿件中常会出现引用典故、成语、格言或新词新语，要在理解的基础上进行意译，不能死译。很多常用词语已有现成的译法，比如演讲中常用到的“海内存知己，天涯若比邻”译为“A bosom friend afar brings a distant land near”或“Long distances separates no bosom friends”。如果翻译时在另外一种语言中找不到相应的表达方式，不要被原文捆住手脚，根据上下文理解意义和色彩，把意思翻译出来，如有的人喜欢用“王小二过年，一年不如一年”来形容经济不景气，翻译时按照意思就可以译成“Things are said to be going from bad to worse for the company with each passing year”等。

Task II

【解析】前文中提到，公关文稿按使用范围可分为外部文稿和内部文稿，在处理这两种文稿的时候，译者需要注意理解它们各自的适用范围和语言特点，如除了注重完整性和正确性的原则之外，还要注意语言的语气和效果是否得到有效传达。

题目 1 以表格的方式呈现，属于内部公关文稿，主要用于组织或企业内部交流。为了提高工作效率，各个组织或企业都对内部的各种文稿作了统一规定，主要是以各种类似表格的形式体现出来。本题属于周工作计划表，这种内部文函的格式比较灵活，可以根据不同的事务来选择不同的格式，一般包括以下几个必要的元素：时间跨度（如本题中的 Week）、施事主体（本题中的 Employees 和 Department）、具体事件（本题中的 Week’s Objectives）。除了以上的必要元素之外，有些日程安排还会标注每件事情的重要程度或特别提醒（如本题中的 Attention 一栏），为工作中的决策提供参考；或在某些特别注意的事件后面加上备注（Remarks），以便引起施事主体的注意。而在翻译此类文稿的时候，要注意语言的简练明确——语言应该简单明了，基本不用修饰性语言，如副词、形容词等；同时，句子的主语在施事主体明确的前提下都可以省略，多使用分词短语或短句等语法上不完整的英文句子。翻译中应该紧扣此类文稿的特点，做到译文和原文都一样简洁、准确、有效。

题目 2 和 3 都属于外部文稿，内容偏重商务性。此类文稿大部分篇幅长、句子复杂、行业术语多，有时候甚至涉及数据、对重大问题的态度等精确信息，形式严谨，语言规范，译者翻译时要注意遵循准确、完整和礼貌的原则。

准确（Accuracy）：公关文稿的翻译要力求准确。内容上、措辞上尽量忠实于原文，译者在将原文语言转换到译文语言的过程中应该准确选词，切忌自由发挥，以臆测代替原文的意思。尤其是遇到行业术语的时候，必须认真查证后才能翻译。译者在接到行业相关的翻译任务时，首先必须要对该行业涉及的基本信息、行业规范和背景知识有所了解，参考相关资料，熟悉行业术语，不说外行话，确保翻译的准确性。

完整（Completeness）：即译文须正确传递原文信息，要求译文读者获得的信息与原文读者获得的信息能够等值。原文中所要传达的信息都在翻译中体现出来，不要遗漏任何一点，有时候甚至语气上的细微差别，也会传递出不同的态度。如题目 3 中原文使用了不少表达强烈语气的副词“非常高兴”“十分重视”“非常赞赏”。在汉语的外部文稿中，尤其是外交或商务相关的演讲稿中，经常出现这种强调性的词语，目的是强调说话人的诚意及对这种友好合作关系的尊重和珍惜。英语译文中，要表达出说话人的语气和态度，也不能把这些副词遗漏。本题中的译文就使用了“I'm very pleased…”“attach great importance to…”以及“commend”这个正式的表示“赞扬”的词汇，把说话人的语气完整地传达出来了。当然，完整性原则同时也可理解为确保译文篇章的整体性。大部分公关文稿都会以篇章的形式出现，译者在翻译时不能断章取义，要照顾到上下文，注意语言的衔接与连贯，确保翻译出来的语篇不仅仅是句子或段落的堆叠，而是一个通顺、符合语法和逻辑的完整语篇，层次分明地传达原文作者的意图。

礼貌（Courtesy）：很多公关文稿都有相应的读者群或听众群，也有很多公关文稿用于不同层次的商务场合、外交场合等，有的文稿语言正式精准，有的生动风趣，有的亲切热忱，但无论是哪种风格的文稿，都起着交际和沟通的作用。因此，在翻译时不可不强调的原则就是礼貌性。题目 3 中在演讲一开始就引用了一句中国的古语“有朋自远方来，不亦乐乎”，表达了中国对加拿大商业界朋友的热忱欢迎，翻译中将其处理为感叹句“How delightful I am to have friends coming from afar!”，简明易懂，亲切热情。题目 2 是 2013 年新西兰婴儿奶粉 Karicare 的供应商恒天然（Fonterra）被曝光原料问题后，立即召回潜在问题产品，并向消费者发布的一封感谢信，全文大篇幅使用第一人称 we 和第二人称 you，企业与客户的即时交流感十足，如“We wanted to take the opportunity to follow up with you to make sure that you and your little one are ok, that your routine is getting back to normal and inform you of some of the additional steps we are taking at...”等。第二人称的使用能够拉近说话人和听众的距离，非常亲切和友好，让读者“身临其境”，起到良好的“近距离”沟通作用。翻译的时候也要注意传达文中体贴、恳切的语气。

本部分参考译文如下：

1.

员工：	铃木，班克，兰迪	周数	第二周（6 月 2 日—6 月 6 日）
部门：	物流部	工作重点：	新司机培训
本周目标		本周成果	
1. 确认南京卡车制造公司的订单 2. 完成新司机培训 3. 联系丰田人员，规划路线		（周末填写）	
备注：			

2. 感谢您在最近的 Karicare 预防性召回期间与我们取得联系。我们也希望借此机会与您跟进，确保您和您的宝宝目前一切安好、确认您的日常生活恢复正常，并同时希望您知道，为了避免同样的事情再次发生，目前我们正采取一系列额外措施。

在本次事件期间，有超过 12 000 名忧心忡忡的家长、看护人向我们伸出了援手，您也是其中之一。希望您能理解我们目前的做法：我们已下架了该产品。是的，即便是再小的潜在风险，我们也要确保它无法影响到您生命中最重要的人——您珍贵的小宝宝。

本次事件给千万信任 Karicare 的父母、家庭带来的困扰和不便，我们感同身受。我们知道，这次预防性召回对您和您的宝宝造成极大影响。对此，我们深表歉意，并向您保证：请相信我们将不遗余力地处理本次事件。

3. I'm very pleased to meet here with my friends from the Canadian business community, who've come all the way from the other side of the Pacific. My current feeling can best be expressed by an ancient Chinese greeting: "How delightful I am to have friends coming from afar." The Chinese government attaches great importance to the development of bilateral economic and trade relations with Canada and appreciates the efforts made by the Canadian-Chinese Trade Council serving as a bridge linking the business communities of our two great nations. I commend all the members of the Council for their efforts in promoting trade with China. Canada is a country with well-developed industries and abundant resources, while China has a plentiful supply of labor and a potentially huge market. We hope to see Canadian enterprises make full use of their technical and financial advantages and compete well in the Chinese market.

Task III

【解析】由于公关文稿根据使用范围可分为外部文稿和内部文稿，翻译时也会相应地根据其不同特征采取不同的方法和技巧。通过上面的翻译实践，我们可以大概对公关文稿翻译技巧作如下归纳：

题目 1 是一个会议记录，属于公关文稿中典型的内部文稿。根据不同公司或机构的工作惯例，会议记录会有不同的格式，但基本上都会采取简洁明了的格式和语言，让读者一目了然。英文会议记录（或纪要）通常包含三部分：开头，主要介绍会议的召开时间、地点、出席人、缺席人、会议类型等；主体，即会议的主要报告、议题、讨论、决策等；结尾部分通常是记录人的签名。

会议记录不仅是存档的需要，也能帮助与会人员甚至非与会人员了解会议的议题，为下一步工作计划提供依据。因此，无论是撰写还是翻译会议记录，都必须遵循准确和简洁的原则，使用准确、精练的语言。此外，作为使用频率极高的内部文稿，会议记录有一些固定的格式模板或语言套话，这不仅给文秘人员也为译者带来便利。在翻译此类文本的时候，采用最多的翻译方法是直译法，即在形式和语言上都遵循忠实于原文，保留原文中会议记录的格式，准确传达会议记录中的议题和决策内容。

题目 2 和 3 作为从演讲中截取出来的语篇，翻译要努力传达出说话人语言中传达的信息和态度。作为语篇来说，此类文稿翻译时需要使用的翻译技巧比较综合，不仅涉及最基本的直译法（如题目 2 基本上都使用直译的方法），还需要根据实际情况使用到其他翻译技巧，如在译文中进行适当的增、删、补、改等。此外，作为语篇的翻译来说，还需注意到语言的连贯和流畅，即在翻译时要注意到翻译的不仅仅是单独的词语和句子，还必须站在语篇的高度上来检视译文，考虑到语篇本身的语境、交际功能甚至文化因素，从而对译文进行调整和修改。题目 3 选自美国福特公司前董事长 Donald E. Petersen 于 1996 年在密西西比州米尔萨普斯（Millsaps）学院毕业典礼上的讲话，他以过来人和父辈的身份给予毕业生们谆谆劝导和热情祝福，语言简洁轻松，循循善诱，充满热情。译文也在语言上尽量保持这种亲切热情的口气，并且根据中文的语言习惯对原文第一段中使用了两个破折号的“You've already done away with so many of the hypocrisies—the dual standards, the cruel prejudices, and environmental insensitivities—that my generation struggled with, and only partially, overcame.”一句进行了拆分，将其分成了两个句子。这样的处理不失连贯性和流畅性，使得中文读者读起译文来会更轻松自然，也更易于理解。

1.

市场营销部会议记录

地点：市场营销部会议室

日期：2022 年 10 月 7 日

主持人：安德鲁 • 布朗

出席：卡尔 • 史密斯、比尔 • 约翰逊、詹姆斯 • 哈特、卡罗琳 • 戴维斯

缺席：无

上午 9:30，主持人/主席宣布会议开始。宣读上次会议记录，确定会议内容真实有效、一致通过。

1. 卡尔 • 史密斯报告：9 月销售额下降 10%。统计显示销售额已连续下降 6 个月。建议采取积极的应对措施。

2. 比尔 • 约翰逊提议：降低价格以提高销售额；认为销售额下降是因为竞争者的价格策略。

3. 詹姆斯 • 哈特建议：大力开展广告宣传活动。

4. 安德鲁 • 布朗指出：不论采取两者中任何一种办法，都会影响公司利润，并可能引起股东不满。

5. 卡尔·史密斯表示：市场已经低迷了6个月，但有迹象表明复苏。从长远来看，降价可能会严重影响利润。

6. 会议决定立即开展广告宣传活动。委派詹姆斯·哈特做出详细计划书，并于下次会议提交。

全体一致同意下次会议将于2022年10月17日上午9:30在市场营销部会议室召开。

会议于上午11:00结束。

下次会议定于10月27日在会议室召开。

2. Good afternoon, Ladies and Gentlemen,

I'm Zhang Xiaolu from the Public Affairs Department of the company. I'm here today to tell you a little bit more about the merger between us and A Company. So first of all, the boards of two companies have announced that there is to be an all-share merger of the two companies. The new company will be called AZ. I'll begin by going through the rationale for the merger and listing some of its benefits. Then I'll go on to give some details about the new board and talk about the financial effects of the merger. And finally, I'll give a brief summary of the terms, including details about dividends and so on.

The merger is a natural step for both partners as they both share the same science-based culture as well as a common vision concerning the future of the industry. The benefits of this move are many. To begin with, the merged group will have an enhanced ability to create long-term growth and increased value for its shareholders. Furthermore, it will be able to deliver the full potential of its existing and future products through the joint strength and worldwide presence of its global sales and marketing operations.

3. 当我看着你们这些毕业生，我发现你们其实比我们这代人更高大、更强壮，也比我们更聪明。你们已经抛开了许多虚伪的东西，比如各种双重标准、残酷的偏见和对环境保护的轻视等。我们这代人与这些虚伪的东西斗争过，而且要说取得胜利，也只是部分的。你们比我们强，你们中有些人已经意识到了我们这代人的失败之处——这本身就是你们的机遇。

你们责任重大。我们做父母的虽然会一直在你们身边，但对你们的未来，我们已经尽力了。古人云：“不管你们的父母有多高大，成长还是得靠自己。”

因此，在你们的毕业典礼上，我以一个家长的身份跟你们说这番话。而且我会和你们的父母一起在你们前进时为你们祝福：“请让他们展翅高飞吧，但不要让他们摔下来。”我也以毕业典礼致辞者的身份讲这番话，以这个身份，我鼓励你们能有这样的追求：抓住机遇，追随天赐之福。

祝大家好运！谢谢。

PART SIX
公关文稿翻译实践

Task I

1. 我也想请您，主席先生，为在中国公司中提高对威尔士的认识助我们一臂之力，尤其是那些正在考虑打入欧洲的中国公司。多年来，威尔士一直是外国在欧洲投资最受欢迎的去处/地方之一。投资者给威尔士带来了 120 亿英镑收入，而且，投资者们一旦立足，就会继续追加投资。

2. 兹有执信人李少林博士与助手赵崇前往贵市调查经济体发展情况。李少林博士与其助手系我经济研究中心成员，二人将在贵市停留 7 日。如贵市政府能提供必要之协助，则不胜感激。

3. I'm delighted to have the opportunity today to be here with you and to talk about economic and trade relations. I'd like to introduce to you the economic development in Guangdong, as well as our strategies and plans. I hope this will help you understand Guangdong better. Guangdong is at the southern end of China, covering an area of 179,800 square kilometers, with a population of over 77 million. We have an abundant supply of talents, excellent external communications and a long history in foreign trade.

4.

October 20th, 2022

Notice

An open English class will be given by Dr. Henry Smith to Class 7, Grade 2021 of the Department of Economic Management in Room 401 at 9:00 a.m. on October 24th (Monday). All English teachers are required to attend. Teachers of other departments are welcome.

Dean's Office

Task II

1.

Ladies and Gentlemen,

Good morning! It is our great honor to have you, my distinguished guests, who have come all the way from America to visit our company. First, on behalf of NOVO, I'd like to extend our warmest welcome and heartfelt thanks to all the friends and colleagues present. Please allow me to take this opportunity to make a brief introduction to our company.

Established in 1990 and headquartered in Shenzhen, NOVO specializes in the R&D, production and marketing of telecom equipment. NOVO is now a key player in China's telecom market and has been making great efforts in exploring the global market.

To date, NOVO's products have been sold to over 40 countries and regions including Germany, France, UK, Spain, Japan, Brazil, Russia, Egypt, Thailand and Singapore. There are 22,000 employees working at NOVO currently, among whom over 3,500 engineers are engaged in new product development in our R&D institutes located in Shenzhen, Shanghai and Beijing in China, as well as Sweden, India and the United States.

According to our schedule, we will visit NOVO's new factory and research center today. Our staff will do their best to make your visit comfortable and worthwhile. Please do not hesitate to ask if you have any questions.

Once again, I want to extend my warmest welcome to all of you. Thank you!

2.

张先生、女士们、先生们：

本人谨代表所有参与此次研讨会的外国友人，向各位表达最诚挚的谢意，感谢你们温暖热情的欢迎。从我抵此的短暂时间所见到的点滴来看，我必须说，中国是一个很美丽的国家，中国人民也非常友善。我知道我可以代表每一个人来说这番话，因为从我们到达机场那一刻开始，就有许多能干且考虑周到的人来处理我们的各种琐碎事情，使得整个紧张的旅程变得轻松愉快。你们提供的住宿条件非常舒适，会议场所也布置得轻松合宜，井然有序。

我们全都很高兴来此参加这次电脑技术研讨会。我们都阅读过有关中国电脑非凡成就的报道，我们也都看到足以证明这一产业在中国健全发展的各项数据，现在我们有了更缜密观察的机会，我知道我们可以从你们的经验中学到很多，也希望我们的经验对你们能有所帮助。

我认为我们对张先生在其欢迎词中所表达的想法都抱有同感，作为一项世界性的产业，我们可以学会加强合作、分享新观念和各项发展、协调各国之间的研究工作，使电脑对普通人来说变得更容易使用和了解。通力合作，我们就能够快速进步。

对全世界电脑业界而言，这是令人兴奋的时刻，我们很高兴能有这个机会来参加研讨会，谢谢你们的热诚相邀和盛情款待。

第十一单元　商务电子邮件翻译

参考译文与解析：

PART TWO

热身练习

Task I

1. 长期订单
2. 有竞争力的价格
3. 信用交易/赊账买卖
4. 装箱单
5. 估计到达时间（Estimated Time of Arrival）

6. 估计离开时间（Estimated Time of Departure） 7. 载货能力
8. 直达船 9. 运费已付 10. 提单（Bill of Lading）

Task II

1. 我们从中国贸易促进会得知贵方正在寻找电器产品的供应商。

2. 您9月1日有关建议担任家用亚麻制品独家代理的来信收悉，谨致衷心谢意。

3. At present, we are interested in extending our range and would appreciate your catalogues and quotations.

4. We are pleased to advise you that the captioned goods were shipped yesterday per S.S. (Steamship) “Shengli”.

5. We want the goods to be of exactly the same quality as that of those you previously supplied us.

PART THREE

商务电子邮件翻译技巧

Task I

1.

【解析】随着人们生活节奏的加快，商务电子邮件英语逐渐趋于口语化和非正式化。但是，作为一种正式的公函语体，无论是英文还是中文商务电子邮件用词还是要保留其规范正式的特点。因此，商务电子邮件中多用书面语、谦辞、敬语等，翻译时要尽可能使用庄重规范的词汇，体现商务公函规范正式、公事公办的特性。因此，我们在分析以下几组句子的时候要把握用词庄重规范的特点。

第一组：句子（2）更符合商务电子邮件的用词规范。商务英语电子邮件经常以意思相同或相近的书面词汇取代口语和非正式词汇，如以 in accordance with 代替 according to，以 inform 或 advice 代替 tell，以 dispatch 代替 send，以 otherwise 代替 or，以 therefore 代替 so，以 as for、in connection with、in respect to 代替 about 等。

第二组：句子（2）更符合规范。Thinking of 是比较口语化的表达。

第三组：句子（1）更符合规范。商务英语电子邮件中还经常使用 here、there 和 where 加上 after，by，under，to，with，from，in 等组成复合副词，如 hereafter，hereby，herewith，herefrom，thereafter，thereby，thereunder，thereto 等古体词。虽然在口语中极少用到，但在外贸英语函电中会经常出现。（1）句中的 hereof 等于 of the quotation sheet。将这些古体词翻译成汉语时，也要对应使用一些正式词汇。一般要重复 here 或 there 代表的名词，如此句可译为：随邮附上报价单，所有报盘和销售均应以**本报价单**背面所印条款为准。

2.

（1）独家代理 （2）成交价 （3）发盘 （4）还盘
（5）接受 （6）许可方 （7）货运代理 （8）商业发票
（9）支付货币 （10）预付货款 （11）交货点
（12）成本、保险加运费价（cost, insurance & freight）
（13）成本加运费（cost and freight） （14）离岸价（free on board）

（15）付款交单（document against payment）

（16）承兑交单（document against acceptance）

（17）毛重（gross weight）

（18）净重（net weight）

（19）销售确认书（sales confirmation）

（20）信用证（letter of credit）

（21）盈亏（profit and loss）

（22）电汇（telegraphic transfer）

3.

（1）海损有两种：一种是共同海损，另一种是单独海损。

（2）中国丝绸在欧洲深受欢迎。我们愿同你方合作在美国及南美销售。

（3）我们将发函询问他们广告项目的最高费用，然后相应做出预算。

（4）我们想知道贵方对我方报价是否满意。

4.

（1）翻译正确。“claim”在此为“索赔”之意，而非“声称、断言”。

（2）翻译错误。“Open Policy”在商务英语中是“预约保单”之意，而不能根据字面意思将其译成“开放政策”。

（3）翻译不够准确，原句的意思是交货日期不包括 9 月 10 日，而翻译中用了 by，则将时间扩大到包括 9 月 10 日。因此，把 by 改成 before 将更准确地表达原句的意思。

（4）翻译不够准确，“over US$ 150”并没有包括 150 美元，因此，应改为：The market here for this product is active, and the best price we can offer is US$ 150 or over per ton.

Task II

【解析】第一组：商务电子邮件属于正式文体，主要为书面语，常用复杂句。状语从句、分词短语插入语、同位语、独立主格结构在商务信函中也频繁使用。由于商务电子邮件里常要表示某些条款相互成立、互为条件，或对一连串具有因果关系的事件进行叙述，比起短句，长句能更准确地表达这种多层次的复杂逻辑关系。对于这种复杂冗长的句子，只要对原文进行仔细分析并灵活应用各种翻译技巧进行翻译，就能恰当地翻译原文，准确传递原文含义。具体分析如下：

1. 此句虽然较长，但是思路清晰、结构严谨。此句可译为：我们和你们已有多年的业务关系，希望对我们的询价报最低价。否则，我们就不得不向他处订货了。

2. 此句是由 and 连接的两个分句，前一个分句有一个目的状语，后一个分句是一个从句，翻译时可以把结构打散，再重新组合。可译为：为了满足这位重要客户提前交货的要求，我们已作特殊安排。现通知贵方，全部货物将于 5 月初交运。

3. In our trade with merchants of various countries, we always adhere to the principle of equality and mutual benefit; therefore, it is our hope to promote, by joint efforts, both trade and friendship to our mutual advantage. 译文使用了长句，同时使用了介词短语（如 In our trade with merchants of various countries）、插入语（如 by joint efforts）从而使译文更符合英文商务电子邮件的句式规范。

第二组：公文写作的结构相对固定，因此有些表达方式在使用中逐渐形成固定的套语。中文和英文商务电子邮件中都有其固定的句式，因而在翻译实践中要注意将其翻译成对应的套语。例如：

● 商务电子邮件首段首句常见套语有：Thank you for your e-mail of...; We are in receipt of your e-mail of...等。翻译时可套用中文邮件，直接译成“×月×日来邮收到，不胜感谢，兹回复如下”。

● 表示通知对方时常用：We are pleased to inform you ...，对应中文译成“特此奉告……”。

● 随邮附上某物时常用英语表达有 Attached please find/We are attaching...等，译成符合汉语习惯的“随邮附上……”。

● 请求对方做某事的汉语句式为“请……将不胜感激”，商务信函常用：We would appreciate; It would be appreciated 等。如 It would be appreciated that you could quote your prices of CIF Shanghai for the computers.（请报电脑的上海到岸价，将不胜感谢）。We are looking forward with interest to your reply. Your early reply will be highly appreciated 等。邮件结尾译成“盼复”等常用套语。

4. 兹告知贵方，由于外汇的波动，报价随时可能变化，不另行通知。

5. 如能告知中国皮鞋的其他详情，将不胜感激。

6. In order to give you a general idea of the Cotton Piece Goods now available for export, we enclose a brochure and a price list.

7. We are pleased to confirm our e-mail of shipping advice for today, and inform you that we have shipped you 5,000 tons of iron scrap per M/S Pacific leaving here on May 20. 原句中的“兹确认”是中文信函套语，可以套用英语“We are pleased to”，这是非常规范的处理方法。而且原句较长，英语译文也使用长句的处理方式。

Task III

1. 对比以下每组内的两个句子，判断哪个句子更符合商务电子邮件的语气要求。

【解析】商务电子邮件注重传达礼貌、得体的语气。礼貌和委婉的用语可以使阅读方获得好感。委婉礼貌用语可以在拒绝对方的要求或条件时显得婉转而易于接受，而不至于破坏双方的贸易关系。由此，不难得出这三组句子都是第（2）句的语气更符合商务电子邮件的语气要求。

2. 翻译以下句子，注意保持原文的语气。

【解析】在国际商务电子邮件中，委婉礼貌的语气还用在表达感谢、快乐、满意、道歉等的语句中。要达到语句委婉，可以采用情态动词、被动语态、虚拟语气、please、疑问句等来表达。因此在翻译中，也要注意采用这些方式来保持原句的语气和口吻。

（1）Thank you for your e-mail of June 6 and we attach our Order No. 2245 for lady's shoes.

（2）With reference to your e-mail of May 6, we are pleased to place an order for the following.

（3）如能接受 275 美元的价格并寄送形式发票，我方即开立 1 000 套的信用证。

（4）贵方 5 月 12 日来邮询问之事，我们很遗憾地奉告，我们的全棉运动服最大号为 18 号。

PART SIX
商务电子邮件翻译实践

Task I

1. 本公司若能及早获知贵方准备供货的条款则感幸甚。

2. 我们已看到贵公司在《商业世界》上刊登的广告，希望得到你们 KV-180 打印机的目录和价格单。

3. 随邮件附上我方产品的详细规格，请查收。

4. 为了今后的业务，我方同意不用即期信用证，而改用即期付款交单方式。

5. 很抱歉通知贵方，您方所列的付款方式与我方通常的贸易做法不符。

6. 请将第 45379 号合同项下第一批货物装上 7 月 5 日左右启航的“无锡”轮。

7. 给贵方造成极大不便，对此我方深感歉意。

8. 若不是我们的友好关系，我方是不会报这个价格的。

9. 贵方价格与我方市场行情不符，请贵方按国际市场行情调整一下。

10. 按合同条款，6 月 20 日前应交货，我们最迟需在 25 日前拿到提单。

11. The form and the quality of packing which you offer must be entirely in accordance with our requirements.

12. In order to extend our export business to your country, we wish to enter into direct business relations with you.

13. We look forward to receiving your order and meanwhile enclose a copy of our catalogue as we feel you may be interested in some of our other products.

14. We thank you for your enquiry of July 5 for the captioned goods.

15. The L/C has to reach us not later than September 1st for arranging shipment.

16. Thank you for your e-mail of March 4 and we regret that we have dispatched the wrong goods and will do something for compensation.

17. If you think our offer meets your requirements, please let us have your order at an early date, as supplies are limited.

18. Thank you for the samples which you sent to us on October 11. We are pleased to place an order as specified on the enclosed order sheet.

19. Please send your remittance to our account No. 14236538 with Bank of China Guangzhou Branch in favor of the XYZ Corporation (Guangzhou).

20. The goods will be shipped by Vessel “Dongfeng” Voyage No. 183, which is due to arrive at Copenhagen on October 31. Please book the shipping space immediately and confirm that the goods will be ready in time.

Task II

1.

主题：蓝牙音箱

执事先生：

我公司是 BM 轿车和大客车的生产商，是得克萨斯州休斯敦的 BM 公司的子公司。我们正寻求车载蓝牙音箱的新供货商。据我们所知，贵公司在我国没有本地分销商。

随信附上我方需求的产品的详细规格。

需求数量：2 500 台

交货期：2023 年 4 月 20 日前（包括 20 日）

请报贵方最优惠的 CIF 拉雷多到岸价，并告知产品详细规格。

我们需要你们蓝牙音箱的样品，供实验室检验之用，然后才能下订单。

对于新供货商，我们的付款方式一般是保兑的、不可撤销的即期信用证，以美元支付。

如贵方产品的实验室测试令人满意，并且贵公司能够提供优惠的价格和良好的服务，我们很高兴在今后经常性地向贵公司大量订货。

期待贵方对我方的询盘早日做出答复。

采购部经理　约翰 • 罗杰斯

谨上

2.

敬启者：

5 月 6 日电悉，贵方已接受我方 2 000 打衬衫的订货。

现我方喜复第 7634 号保兑的、不可撤销信用证已于今晨由东京商业银行开出，金额为 17 000 美元。烦请贵方收到后，立即为我们所订货物安排船运。另据悉“无锡”号货轮定于 5 月 28 日从你处开往我港，我们希望由该轮装运此批货物。

若我方客户满意此次试购的产品，我们保证今后继续大量订购。

我们对贵公司在这方面的密切合作深表感谢，同时盼望贵方的装运通知。

谨此

贸易部　彼得 • 约翰逊（签名）

3.

Dear Sirs,

Your inquiry of September 10 has received our attention, and thank you for your interest in our leather shoes and handbags.

Enclosed please find our illustrated catalogue. All the goods we supply are made of leather of superior quality. The bright color and elegant designs together with the super workmanship can meet the requirement of a fashion trade such as yours.

A representative of our company is now in Hong Kong. He will be pleased to call you next week with a full range of samples of our hand-made lines. He is authorized to discuss the terms of order with you or to negotiate a contract. We shall be most grateful if you give him the benefit of your advice and assistance.

Yours truly,

4.

Dear Mr. Jones,

We accept your counter-offer of March 8 and are pleased to confirm having concluded the transaction of the captioned goods with you. Our factory has informed us that they can, at present, produce 30,000 bags per week. Thus you may rest assured that your order of 50,000 for shipment next month will be fulfilled as contracted.

However, we would like to emphasize that your L/C must reach here by the end of this month. Otherwise, shipment has to be delayed.

We attach with this e-mail our Sales Confirmation No. 03M15 in duplicate. Please countersign and return us one copy for file.

We appreciate your cooperation and trust that our products will turn out to your satisfaction.

Sincerely yours,

×××

Sales Manager

第十二单元　国际商务合同翻译

参考译文与解析：

PART TWO

热身练习

Task I

外贸销售合同

编号：

日期：

签约地点：
卖方：
地址：　　　　　　　　　　邮政编码：
电话：　　　　　　　　　　传真：
买方：
地址：　　　　　　　　　　邮政编码：
电话：　　　　　　　　　　传真：
买卖双方同意按下列条款由卖方出售，买方购进下列货物：
1. 货号：
2. 品名及规格：
3. 数量：
4. 单价：
5. 总值：
6. 生产国和制造厂家：
7. 包装：
8. 唛头：
9. 装运期限：
10. 装运口岸：
11. 目的口岸：
12. 保险：
13. 付款条件：
14. 单据：
15. 装运条款：
16. 品质与数量、重量的异议与索赔：
17. 人力不可抗拒因素：
18. 仲裁：
19. 备注：
卖方：　　　　　　　　　　买方：
签字：　　　　　　　　　　签字：

Task II

1. 承兑人	2. 付款交单
3. 条款	4. 以下称
5. 国际贸易合同	6. 以此为证
7. 依照，根据	8. 主营业地
9. 上述的，前述的	10. 执行合同

Task III

1. 本合同用英文和中文两种文字写成，一式四份。双方执英文本和中文本一式两份，两种文字具有同等效力。

2. 对于利益损失、延误、商誉损失或任何特别或间接的损害赔偿，不论何种原因引起，卖方概不承担责任。

3. 买方向卖方订购下列商品，条件如下。

4. 基于此，应依照本合同第四条第六款调整资金账户。

5. 本合同签字之日 1 个月内，即不迟于 12 月 15 日，乙方须将货物装船。

PART THREE

国际商务合同的语言特点与翻译技巧

Task I

【解析】在商务合同中，有些格式和句式是几乎每份合同都要用到的，这些格式和句式往往约定俗成、大同小异。格式化是商务合同的特征之一。因此，熟悉各种商务合同的格式和句式是合同翻译者入行的最基本要求。翻译者应善于积累，学会套用，从而在翻译时能够触类旁通，收到事半功倍的效果。参考译文如下：

1. 本合同于_________年_________月_________日由_________（以下简称甲方）为一方，与_________（以下简称乙方）为另一方签订。

2. 本合同于_________年_________月_________日在_________（签约地点）依_________（国家名称）法律成立的、营业地点在_________（公司地址）的公司_________（以下简称甲方）和按_________（国家名称）法律注册成立、营业地点在_________（公司地址）的公司_________（以下简称乙方）共同签订。

Task II

【解析】在本书第一单元，我们讲到商务英语的主要特征之一是正式性，国际商务合同正是商务英语正式性的具体体现之一。现具体分析如下：

1. 该条款中使用的“amicable consultation”为正式用语，意为“友好协商”。另外，“have entered into，abide by，in accordance with”都属于正式用语，英文合同起草者习惯使用这些正式用语来体现合同条款的严密性。译文为：根据国家有关旅游事业管理的规定，甲乙双方经协商一致，并签订本合同，共同信守执行。

2. 基于大陆法系对英美法系的影响，英文商务合同的外来词主要是法语和拉丁语。一些合同的起草者习惯使用这些外来词来突出合同等法律文本的庄重性。例如本句中的“pro rata”的意思是“按比例”。译文为：补贴应按每单位售价的 2%计算并从购价中按比例扣除。

3. 商务合同文本的庄重性也体现在句型的选择上。在英文合同中以 where 引导的条件状语比使用 if 或 when 引导的条件句显得更为正式，常译为“……的”。译文为：外资企业为有限责任公司的，外国投资者对企业的责任以其认缴出资额为限。

Task III

【解析】无论中文还是英文合同，其语言都必须简洁、准确、到位，不得有任何含糊其词的地方。

1. 译文 2 比译文 1 更能准确反映合同的原意。在译文 1 中有两处译得不够准确：其一，discrepancy 在说明货物质量时，应译为“异议”；其二，after the arrival of the goods at the port of destination 译为“在货物到达目的港之后”，所指范围过大，应译为“货物到达目的港之日起”。

2. 译文 2 比译文 1 更为简练，也更为准确。译文 1 翻译腔比较浓厚。准确性本身就是合同的语言特征之一。它体现在数字、日期方面准确无误。

Task IV

【解析】第 1 小题中“调整”的中文意思是指重新调配，使适应新的情况和要求，内涵上既包括增加也包括减少。译文 1 将其译为“be increased”显然是以偏概全，不够严谨。译文 2 的“be adjusted”则准确表达了“调整”一词的全部含义。

第 2 小题的译文 1 和译文 2 的意思完全一样，但译文 1 省略了括号中的大写部分，导致合同的严谨性不够。如果合同一方故意改动数字，则会带来很大的合同纠纷，而译文 2 则完整规范、无懈可击。

Task V

【解析】通过对比原文和译文，可以发现译文中的“goods in bond”和“Bonded Goods”都是指“保税货物”。很显然，这种错误并不是由于译者的疏忽而为，而是译者为了追求译名的多样化刻意而为。这样，读者就不得不揣测不同词语的法律意思，从而影响了合同的精度。

Task VI

【解析】英语和汉语相对而言，英语使用被动语态的频率大大高于汉语。因此，在商务合同中，英语大量使用被动语态，而汉语则使用主动语态。翻译时需要根据实际情况进行语态之间的转换。本句中“be reached，be rejected”都翻译成了主动语态，这样更符合汉语的表达习惯。参考译文为：当事人双方必须达成协议，同意将纠纷提交仲裁解决。如无此协议，任何仲裁人都不能受理仲裁申请。这种协议可在纠纷发生之前或之后达成，即由双方当事人签订书面仲裁协议，当事人在向仲裁人申请时，必须提交包含仲裁条款的合同或临时仲裁协议，否则仲裁机构不予受理。

PART SIX

国际商务合同翻译实践

Task I

【解析】

就合同的标题而言，英汉合同在表达及格式上主要有如下两点不同：(1) 英文合同在标题部分经常叠用同义词，如：made and concluded，by and between，terms and conditions 等，比汉语更为正式；(2) 在当事人地址的表达上，汉语是“从大到小”的顺序，英文是“从小到大”的顺序。参考译文如下：

Export Contract

Contract No.: <u>SZ0207426</u>

Conclusion Date: <u>October 10, 2023</u>

Conclusion Place: <u>White Swan Hotel</u>

<u>Guangzhou, P. R. China</u>

The Seller: <u>Jianli Group</u>

ADD: 38, Tiansha Street, Guangzhou,
Guangdong, P. R. China
TEL: ____________
FAX: ____________
TELEX: ____________
The Buyer: AFG Trading Co., Ltd. USA
ADD: 126, New York, N.Y., U.S.A.
TEL: ____________
FAX: ____________
TELEX: ____________

This Contract is hereby made and concluded by and between the Seller and the Buyer and the Seller whereby agrees to sell and the Buyer agrees to buy the undermentioned commodity under the terms and conditions specified as follows.

Task II

【解析】商务英语与通用英语不同之处在于其专业化，国际商务合同中的普通词汇也具有专业性词汇的含义。具体分析如下：

1. 该条款中“cover”“settlement”，均为普通词汇，但在经贸英语中却分别为“投保”“付款结账”之意。译文为：买方应投保一切险。

2. 该句中“concern”若按照其字面意思翻译为“有关的”，则语义会显得模糊笼统，不够严谨，有违这些词汇在法律背景下的特殊含义。根据合同内容可以看出，运输机构和合同货物之间的关系是“承运”关系，因此，应将它翻译为“承运”。具有特殊专业意义的普通词汇在英文经贸合同中起着相当重要的作用。因此，译者在翻译这些词汇时，要根据语境，结合相关经贸专业知识，认真领会，仔细推敲其语用特征。译者还应对经贸知识有相当了解，唯有如此，译者才能准确把握这些普通词汇在经贸英语中所表达的专业术语意思。译文为：由承运机构所开具收据的日期即被视为交货日期。

3. 该句中“acceptance”与“offer”是法律词汇，属于合同法中的两个重要的法律术语，其准确、规范的译文应分别为“承诺”和“要约”。前者是指受要约人对要约内容表示同意，而后者则指一方希望与另一方订立合同的意思表示。译文为：要约一旦承诺，合同即行成立。

4. 该句中“damage”与“damages”两者的意思有很大的区别：damage 仅为普通词汇，有“损害，损失”之意。而原文中的 damages 则已作为法律词汇，并应理解为“损害赔偿金，损害赔偿”。译文为：一方违约的损害赔偿金包括因其违约而使另一方遭受损失的金额，含利润损失。

5. 两个同义词“null and void”被视为一个整体，通过并列使用两个具有相同含义的词语，排除了一词多义的现象引起的歧义，体现了经贸合同的严谨性和正式性。译文为：此类后果往往是合同被宣布无效。

6. 本句中的“modification or alternation”可被译为“修改或变更”。这是因为“modification”与“alternation”两个单词的意思是有细微差别的，前者是指对原文合同的进一步完善和改进；后者则可能是对合同内容的实质性变动，因此在这里，出于法律角度考虑，应将其分别译出。作为译者，在遇到翻译这类近义词或同义词并用现象时，要特别谨慎，仔细斟酌两者之间的细微差别，并在汉语中找出相应的词给予表达。译文为：任何对本合同的修改或变更都应经双方同意。

7. 在国际商务合同中，采用较为正式的、古体惯用副词的现象常有所见，因国际商务合同属于法律性公文，使用古体词可体现其严肃性，也体现法律公文的结构严谨、逻辑严密、言简意赅等特征。古体词常由“where，here，there”等副词分别加上“after，by，in，of，on，to，under, upon, with”等介词构成合成副词。古体词的使用是经贸英语合同的特征之一，译者在翻译时应保持这一文体特征。译文为：本合同由 3A 公司（以下称“卖方”）和 3B 公司（以下称“买方”）于 2022 年 1 月 10 日在北京签订。

8. 两个同义词“null and void”被视为一个整体，体现了合同文本的严谨性。译文为：本合同以中英文书写，一式两份，双方各执一份。本合同自双方代表签字之日起生效。自本合同签订后，以前有关的信件、电传文件均为无效。

Task III

1. 甲方应于 2022 年 7 月 28 日将该货物交给乙方。
2. 甲方应于 2022 年 7 月 28 日（含 28 日）前将该货物交给乙方。
3. 甲方应于 2022 年 7 月 28 日前将该货物交给乙方。
4. 普通译法：装船：2022 年 2 月 28 日前装船。
   专业译法：装船：2022 年 2 月 28 日前（含 28 日）装船。
5. 普通译法：余款在货物到达目的港后结算。
   专业译法：余款应在货物到达目的港后即行支付。
6. 普通译法：总价：5 200 000 美元。
   专业译法：总价：5 200 000.00 美元（大写：伍佰贰拾万美元整）
7. 合资公司的注册资本为________（大写：________美元），甲方和乙方各出资百分之五十（50%），计________（大写：________美元），双方将按上述投资比例分享利润，分担亏损和风险。
8. 投资金额增加了 0.5 倍，即从原来的 100 万美元增加到现在的 150 万美元。

Task IV

The Sellers shall advise the Buyers by telex, and simultaneously advise the buyers' shipping agent at the loading port, 30 days before the contracted time of shipment, of the Contract No., name of commodity, quantity, loading port and expected date of arrival of the goods at the loading port, enabling the buyers to arrange for shipping space. Absence of such advice within the time specified above shall be considered as sellers' readiness to deliver the goods during the time of shipment contracted and the Buyers shall arrange for shipping space accordingly.

Task V

1. 译文：如迟交技术资料和软件超过六个月，引进方将有权终止合同。在这种情况下，让与人必须将引进方已支付的全部金额加上年利率为 12%的利息，一起退还给引进方。

2. 译文：采购合同将被授予按照本投标邀请函的条件和规定做出响应且标价最低的

投标人。但是规定，该投标人的标价是合理的，且符合联合国人口基金会的利益。

3. 译文：凡属于本章规定检查范围内的任何档案，如无书面形式，则不予接受检查要求，除非公司自费将此档案制成书面形式。

4. 译文：凡在制造或装船运输过程中，因不可抗力致使卖方不能或推迟交货时，卖方不负责任。

5. 译文：此项贷款可支付当地费用的 85%。但此项费用必须由英国承包商直接支付，并须在合同预付款的幅度内，即最高不得超过合同金额的 15%。

6. 译文：卖方交付的货物必须与合同所规定的数量、质量和规格一致，并按照合同所规定的方式装箱或包装。

7. 译文：中国 A 公司和英国 B 公司，根据《中华人民共和国中外合作经营企业法》及其他有关法律、法规的规定，本着平等互利的原则，通过友好协商，同意在中华人民共和国广东省广州市，共同合作经营企业，特订立本合同。

8. 译文：如买方在 2023 年 8 月 1 日或在此之前未向卖方发出装运须知，则卖方可自行决定取消本合同，并要求买方赔偿因未发出装运须知而使其蒙受的一切损失。

第十三单元　技术术语翻译

参考译文与译例分析：

PART TWO

热身练习

Task I 略

Task II 参考译文如下：

1. 终端	2. 探测传感器	3. 阿罗星系
4. 格里年	5. 南岛	6. 儿童安全包装
7. T-plate	8. V-belt	9. X-ray
10. autocontrol	11. semi-metal	12. FM

Task III

【解析】B 组的技术翻译相对 A 组而言更为成功。

音译就是译成读音与原词相同或相近的汉字。这种方法通常用于翻译人名、地名计量单位及新材料的名称。考虑到译名的规范化和通用性，用词要大众化，读音应以普通话的发音为标准。

（1）新发现的自然现象。例如：gene（基因）、quark（夸克）

（2）计量单位名称。例如：Hertz（Hz）赫兹（频率单位）、Erg 尔格（能量单位）、Lumen 流明（光通量单位）、Gilbert 吉伯（磁通势单位）、Maxwell 麦克斯韦（麦磁通单位）、Calorie 卡路里（热量单位）、Var 乏（无功功率）、Amp 安培（电流单位）

（3）新材料的翻译。例如：copy（拷贝）、genome（基因组）、clone（克隆）、aero-train

（悬浮火车）、nanotechnology（纳米技术）

但有些专业术语随着历史的发展已为人们所熟悉或掌握，其音译的效果不及意译，往往会导致人们理解的混乱。因此，现在逐渐由音译转变为更加明确易懂的意译。例如：valve（凡而—阀门），washer（华司—垫圈），flange（法兰—凸缘）等。

A 组中 Vitamin（维他命）、Cartoon（卡通）、Penicillin（盘尼西林）仍然采用音译的方法，容易导致人们理解的混乱。如果采用意译的方法，将 Vitamin 译成维生素，Cartoon 译成动画片，Penicillin 译成青霉素，这样的翻译会使人们的理解更加明确。

B 组中 Microphone（话筒）、Engine（发动机）、Motor（电动机）采用的是明白易懂的意译方法，更容易为人们所熟悉和掌握。

PART THREE
技术术语翻译技巧

Task I

技术术语的语音特征和翻译技巧。

第一组 beer（啤酒）、card（卡片）、jeep（吉普车）、carbine（卡宾枪）的翻译都采用了一部分原来英文的语音，再在音译后面加用一个表示特点的汉字。Beer 的英语发音和中文翻译“啤”非常接近，但是如果只用一个“啤”字，有点意思不明，在“啤”字后面添加一个“酒”字，就兼顾了发音和意义。card 的英语发音和中文翻译“卡”非常接近，“卡”这个字在中文中有多种意思，如果只用一个“卡”字，有点意思不明，在“卡”字后面添加一个“片”字，就使意思明确多了。jeep 的英语发音和中文翻译“吉普”非常接近，但是如果只用“吉普”这两个字，让人不明白所指的是什么事物，在“吉普”后面添加一个“车”字，就立刻使意思变得很明确了。carbine 的英语发音和中文翻译“卡宾”非常接近，但是如果只用“卡宾”这两个字，令人不明白所指的是什么，所以在“卡宾”后面添加一个“枪”字，人们自然就明白了。

第二组 neon sign（霓虹灯）、motor-cycle（摩托车）既采用了一部分音译，也采用了一部分意译的方法，是音译和意译方法的完美结合。在 motor-cycle 中，motor 和中文翻译“摩托”发音相近，而 cycle 则采用了意译的方法翻译成“车”。同样，neon sign 的前半部分采用音译的方法翻译成“霓虹”，后半部分则采用意译的方法翻译成“灯”，音译和意译结合的方法使意思更加明确。

第三组 servo（伺服系统）、typhoon（台风）、bandage（绷带）结合以上两种方式的优势，这样的翻译不仅体现出英语的发音，而且在汉语中反映出确切的含义。

Task II

1. B　2. A　3. D　4. C　5. B　6. C　7. A　8. D

Task III

【解析】技术翻译的目的是达到译文与原文的意思表达等同或者近似，使读者了解和认知科学技术，从而造福于生活。技术翻译技巧归纳如下：

翻译第 1 组技术用语时采用了意译法。意译法是最常用的翻译方法，它能使读者直接了解术语的含义。就英语而言，有不少专业术语是由派生词或复合词构成的，必须确切了解原文术语的构词手段及含义，才能译成相对应的汉语术语。

翻译第 2 组技术用语时采用音译法，技术英语中某些由专有名词构成的术语、单位名称、新型材料的名称等，在翻译时都可采用音译法。考虑到译名的规范化和通用性，用词要大众化，读者应以普通话的发音为标准。

翻译第 3 组技术用语时采用了音意结合法。这种译法就是在音译后加上一个表示特点的汉字，或是一部分采用音译，一部分采用意译，使词义比单纯音译更容易理解。

翻译第 4 组技术用语时采用了形译法。某些产品或材料的外形与某个字母形状相似，并以该字母定名时，可译成相应的字或用与该字母字形相近的汉字进行翻译。在以某个字母代替某种概念时，可直接将字母译出。

翻译第 5 组技术用语时采用了创造新词的方法。随着科学技术的发展，特别是由于化学和核物理学的研究，发现新的元素和新的粒子的命名，在翻译时一般可根据原文中包含的某个音或所代表的某个概念来创造新词。

参考译文如下：

1. （1）半金属 （2）二极管 （3）数字计算机 （4）空气压缩机
（5）输入 （6）输出 （7）全息摄影术 （8）半导体
（9）monopole （10）multiplexer （11）bandwidth （12）radioactivity
（13）blue print （14）gear box （15）work-piece
2. （1）牛顿 （2）瓦特 （3）摩尔 （4）赫兹
（5）伏特 （6）克隆 （7）基因 （8）纳米技术
（9）尼龙 （10）卡路里
3. （1）啤酒 （2）多普勒效应 （3）摩尔斯电码 （4）罗氏硬度
（5）绷带 （6）帕拉橡胶
4. （1）工字钢 （2）U 型钢 （3）工字梁 （4）十字钻头
（5）环形圈 （6）V-belt （7）T-square （8）twist bit
（9）X-ray （10）cross-road
5. （1）碳 （2）铀 （3）苯 （4）醚
（5）氡

PART SIX

技术术语翻译实践

Task I

1. D　2. A　3. B　4. C　5. F　6. E　7. H　8. G　9. J　10. I

Task II

1. 防火墙　2. 胶原纤维　3. 肤质　4. 肌密配方
5. 紧致啫喱　6. 代谢精华　7. 凡士林　8. 代谢活化剂
9. 机能保湿霜　10. D 形阀　11. 天然保湿因子　12. 分贝

13. 软化皮肤　14. 更新面膜　15. 逻辑电路

Task III

1. coat　2. activation toner powder　3. elasticity　4. collagen
5. composition　6. anti-aging ingredients　7. epidermis　8. dermis
9. tube　10. function　11. gentle cleansing　12. revitalize skin
13. neck contour　14. bright complexion　15. skin microcirculation

Task IV

1. B. 借用人体器官名称的专业术语。　2. A. 借用动物名称的专业术语。
3. B. 借用物品名称的专业术语。　4. A. 借用物品名称的专业术语。
5. A. 借用动物名称的专业术语。　6. A. 借用人体器官名称的专业术语。

Task V

1. BCT-4D 紧肤疗法是从恢复人体皮肤与生俱来的自然自愈能力，从改善细胞机能层面，令真皮层胶原蛋白大量自我生成。

2. 今天，除了在中国和其他一些地区，实际上每个社会成员都受到石油与天然气的供给及其价格的影响：直接受影响的是家庭使用及运输方面，间接受影响的是关系到就业和国民经济的许多别的方面。不论国民经济状况是否良好，都是如此。

3. 紫外线、辐射、空气污染和其他因素每天都在损害我们的皮肤。随着年龄的增长，皮脂膜变得越来越薄，并且不像以前那么健康，这很容易导致一些有毒和敏感的物质侵入皮肤。

4. 修复表皮，重建皮脂膜，恢复皮肤的天然保护屏障。

5. 无妆胜有妆。

6. Instant and lasting face lift shapes your features, giving you a smoother and firmer appearance.

7. Witness the miracle, as if years never leave traces on your skin.

8. The designer must have access to stock lists of the materials he employs.

9. Combination of precious platinum liquor and Switzerland top stem cell technology, re-create youthful skin for you.

10. Generative adversarial networks (GANs) are a type of artificial intelligence technique that can generate realistic images, text, and music.

第十四单元　商务报告翻译

参考译文与解析：

PART ONE
认识商务报告与商务报告翻译

Task I 略

Task II

这是一份相对比较简单的工作进展报告。尽管篇幅较短，但紧扣主题，内容全面，句子结构严谨，报告中不乏专业术语。参考译文如下：

致总经理约翰·安德鲁先生：

墨西哥湾钻探情况报告

刚开始两到三英尺的钻探工作相当容易，但钻过一层白垩（石灰岩的一种）后，我们遇到了第一层坚硬的玄武岩。这一阶段，我们必须更换钻头。因此，钻探速度慢下来了。钻探坚硬岩层时，我们必须经常停歇，确保钻头不会过热。

第三阶段的钻探情况变化无常。有时是坚硬的岩石或卵石；有时又是松软的白垩。尽管第三层比第二层普遍松软一些，但我们无法加快速度，因为松软层并不厚，更换钻头需要很长时间。

最后一层是更为坚硬的岩石，很多时候钻头过热。然而，机械工人耐心细致，技术熟练，我们最终钻到了石油矿层。

张飞

工程部经理

PART TWO
热身练习

Task I

1. 目前，中国约有果汁生产商 6 000 家，其中 1 000 多家具有相当的产能。中国的果汁市场分为三股力量：其一是中国大陆著名企业，如汇源和娃哈哈；其二为台湾企业，如统一企业和康师傅；其三为大型跨国企业，如可口可乐和百事可乐。

2. 中国国家统计局数据显示，多数果汁生产企业位于华南和华东地区。具体而言，华南地区产量为 359 799 吨，占全国产量的 22%；而华东地区产量达 476 562 吨，占全国产量的 29%。

Task II

本报告根据家电制造企业的销售量对前 50 名进行排名。

报告中所分析的公司，其总营业额大约为 5 870 亿欧元，包括本报告中涉及价值 1 250 亿欧元的常用电器：冰箱、冷柜、洗衣机、烘干机、洗碗机、抽油烟机、烹饪器具、微波炉、空调和吸尘器。

从公司总部所在国来看，中国有 11 家，美国和意大利各有 6 家，欧洲其他国家有 14 家，日本、韩国、新西兰和印度共有 13 家。

本报告介绍了 50 家电器制造商的公司背景、历史与现状、基本数据（包括过去两年的营业额、白色家电营业额、白色家电占总产量的份额、员工人数及人均营业额，有些还提供了已售电器的数量），并按公司、产品和地域对销售进行细分，还包括产地、品牌、部门、控股公司以及子公司的办公地址和联系方式。(《全球电子家电品牌价值 50 强报告》)

PART THREE
商务报告翻译技巧

Task I

【解析】本部分只列举了典型商务报告中的典型段落，因此，这里不讨论商务报告本身应该具备的普遍特征，如完整性、正确性，而侧重探讨其语言特征。这几题虽不能完全代表各类商务报告的特征，但也可对商务报告的语言特征窥见一斑。通过对这些商务报告的研究，我们可以将商务报告的语言特征归纳如下：

第一，准确性（Accurate）：商务报告必须准确无误，用词准确，数据无误，不允许有任何含糊不清或数据矛盾的地方，如“China's total import and export from Jan. to Dec. in 2009 amounted to US$ 2.207,27 trillion，down by 13.9% on a year-on-year basis.”数据必须有真凭实据或来自官方的统计数据，尽量避免使用“about, approximately”等比较模糊的词语。

第二，简洁性（Brief）：商场如战场，忙碌是永恒的主题，商务报告如果语言累赘、啰嗦，会耽误领导的时间，延误决策的制定，从而影响公司的业绩。因此，商务报告必须简洁明了，言简意赅，如“Of which export was US$ 130.72 billion, up by 17.7%, and import was US$ 112.29 billion, up by 55.9%.”，这里用“up”一个词表示增幅，而没有用“with an increase of”或者“representing an increase of”，可见，商务报告惜字如金。

第三，清晰性（Clear）：商务报告每个部分必须结构合理、条理清晰、逻辑清楚。摘录的三段都能围绕主题，思路清晰，表达清楚，如“In general the demand for home appliances has shown the biggest increase for many reasons. Especially there has been a sharp increase in our sales in rural areas in the west regions.”先综述需求增长，然后指出特别之处，符合人们认识事物的逻辑规律，清晰易懂。

第四，客观性（Objective）：商务报告必须客观公正，不掺杂任何个人感情。其数据通过调查统计得出，商务报告中尽量少用“I think, We think”之类的语言，即使是有关建议可能具有一定的主观性，但这些建议是基于调查研究的客观基础之上提出的合理建议，本身就具有客观性，如：“Through comparison and analysis, it is recommended that the price of our products should be lowered by 3%～5%.”表面看，数据不是十分精确，但这确实是经过调查比较得出的客观结果。

Task II

【解析】商务报告是典型的应用型文体，具有一定的说明性，与文学翻译相比，商务翻译留给译者的发挥空间往往比较小，所以，通常情况下采用直译法。比如第 1 小题“Combined, these 43 brands account for 85% or more of our sales and profits”翻译成“这 43 个品牌的销售额和利润超过公司销售总额和利润的 85%”，直接翻译其含义即可。当然，报告中的某些词汇或者短语可以适当意译，如“ensure proper, effective and efficient use of the HKSAR's support funds”中的三个形容词“proper, effective, efficient”可以直接译成“恰当的、有效的、高效的”，但跟上下文结合起来，语言不够通顺。根据语境，“proper”表示“恰当使用”，也就是把钱花在刀刃上，即“用得其所”，“effective, efficient”分别表示“有效的和高效的”，这里转换为“效果好、效率高”。

本部分参考译文如下：

1. 持续加强全球领先品牌的地位。我们的产品组合包括 23 个品牌，年销售额超过 10 亿美元，并且 20 个品牌的年销售额约为 5 亿美元或更多。这 43 个品牌合并起来占据了我们 85%或更多的销售额和利润。这些品牌是未来创新的平台，将推动销售增长。（宝洁 2009 年年度报告）

2. 在中国，果蔬饮料含有水果和蔬菜汁。果蔬汁直接由新鲜或冷藏水果和蔬菜制成。果蔬饮料通过向果蔬汁中添加水、糖液和制酸剂等制成即饮饮料。在中国，果蔬饮料的果汁含量应不低于 10%，否则它们属于其他类别的饮料。（中国果蔬饮料行业研究报告，2010—2011）

3. 经过前期比较和分析，我们提出了以下关于西门子业务战略调整的建议，涉及价格水平和售后服务。我们应该将目前的报价降低 3%～5%，以使西门子的价格与中国家电市场的平均价格水平持平或略低。只有这样，西门子的报价才能更具竞争力。我们应该将免费保修期延长至 1 年以上，甚至更长，以向客户展示我们对售后服务的重视，并增强客户对我们公司的信心。

4. 香港特别行政区在四川地震灾区的重建工作进展顺利，项目资金根据工作进展进行了释放。接下来，我们将重点关注项目资金的管理，以及项目的管理、监督和审计等工作，以确保香港特区的支持资金得到正确、有效和高效的利用。（香港特别行政区在四川地震灾区重建工作进展报告）

5. 四川省政府高度重视重建项目的监控，并发布了一系列监管文件，明确规定了工作模式和责任。四川方面还加强了内部责任和监督机构。在省、市（州）和县级别建立了协调机制，明确了项目实施管理和监督责任。（香港特别行政区在四川地震灾区重建工作进展报告）

Task III

1. 促成并购包括跨国并购上扬的主要因素是发达国家利率低、利润增长和资产价格回升。并购的价值飙升 28%，达 3 810 亿美元。在许多产业，尤其是在发达国家产业持续重组和合并进程中，这些交易发挥了重要作用。（《2005 年世界投资报告》）

2. 企业健康俱乐部将帮助员工改变他们的行为模式并选择更为健康的生活方式，以此来降低公司的医疗费用，提高工人的生产效率。医疗费用将有所降低，原因是医疗保险金、缺勤率、补缺率将降低，工人索赔和工作拖拉现象将减少，住院时间将缩短。

3.《2007 年贸易与发展报告——区域合作发展》建议，发展中国家应加强与其他发展中国家的区域合作，但对南北双边协议和区域特惠贸易协定要谨慎推进。这些协定可以在市场准入方面带来收益，也可提高外商直接投资，但它们也可能限制国家的政策空间，而国家政策在优势产业中长期发展方面起重要作用。相比而言，发展中国家加强区域合作可以加快工业化和结构调整的步伐，使其容易融入世界经济。然而，为了达到这一目的，贸易自由化并不够，积极的区域合作应拓展到政策领域，这些政策能挖掘经济发展与结构调整的潜力，包括货币与金融安排、大型基础设施项目和知识生成项目以及工业政策等。

Task IV

1. 舒适、卫生、设计优良的内衣销路看好，而**质量不高的**产品会退出市场。

2. 尽管中国人口众多，中国果汁饮料消费量很低。2009 年，人均果汁消费量**不到** 10 升。

3. **宝洁公司是世界上对消费者研究和市场研究投资最多的公司。**我们每年与近 60 个国家的 500 万消费者开展互动，每年在理解消费者方面投资达 3.5 亿美元。这些活动让我们能够洞见创新机会在哪里，如何服务顾客以及如何与顾客沟通交流。

4. 青岛海尔集团是中国最大的空调和冰箱制造商。该集团报告认为，由于价格更高的节能产品销售量增长了，2009 年集团利润增长了 50%。公司得益于去年中国将家电下乡补贴项目推向全国范围，以促进包括电视机、冰箱、洗衣机、手机和电脑的**销售**。财政部统计数据表明，截至今年 12 月 15 日，政府已经支付了 63 亿元补贴，今年预算超过去年两倍，高达 152 亿元。

5. 另外，研发被认为是经济活动中**最不可能“分解”**的活动，因为它涉及的知识对于公司具有战略意义，也因为开展研发经常需要在局部地区的集群内开展使用者和生产者之间的密集知识交流（其中相当部分是默契性的）。

Task V

参考译文如下：

中国服装市场八大发展趋势

根据目前中国服装产业的状况，未来相当长一段时间内，下列八大发展趋势在中国服装市场占主导地位。

人们追求漂亮、舒适又能体现其个人品位的新款西服，传统西服也会稳步增长。面料高档、设计时尚、做工一流的产品将会占据重要的市场份额。

公司制服日益受到欢迎。自 1998 年以来，许多公司把制服当成企业形象的一部分，其需求日趋上升，尤其是具有独创设计的产品。

成熟消费者市场持续增长。45 岁以上人口达 3 亿人，这一市场潜力巨大。为了开发这一市场，品味高雅已成为流行词。

对高质量的内衣需求呈增长趋势。随着生活水平的提高，人们越来越重视内衣。舒适、卫生、设计优良的内衣销路看好，而质量不高的产品会退出市场。

童装的消费模式和童装设计会发生翻天覆地的变化。过去，人们很少注重童装的设计和健康因素。如今，人们更关注年轻一代的生理、精神和心理发展，简单、适用、漂亮的童装（包括中小学校服）需求强劲。

随着中国加入世界贸易组织，服装市场中女装首当其冲受到冲击，这是因为国内制造的女装在面料、配饰、设计和工艺方面远远落后于世界水平，必须采取行动取得新突破。

运动服依然大受欢迎。受健康意识提高和全国范围健身浪潮的影响，运动服成为衣柜中必不可少的衣物。今天的运动服强调舒适和实用，低端产品没有任何市场。

量身定做服装市场继续增长。由于人们越来越追求完美体现其品位和个性的服装，批量生产的成衣不再满足他们的需求。可以预测，高档精品服装和定制正装的专卖店会迅猛发展。（香港贸易发展局网站）

PART SIX 商务报告翻译实践

Task I

1. 根据工厂设备处的建议，检查小组于 2023 年 7 月 15 日对车间进行了实地考察。

2. 中国对美国、日本和欧盟成员国的出口占出口总量的 53.6%，但大多数中国企业并不熟悉国际标准。

3. 近年来，中印两国贸易增长较快，贸易额持续快速增长。双边贸易从 2000 年的 29.14 亿美元增长到 2005 年的 187.03 亿美元，年均增长 45%。

4. 教育让人们选择他们期望的生活，使他们在人际关系、社区和工作中自信地表达自我。但是，对 1.15 亿失学的小学适龄儿童而言，这一人权被剥夺了。他们多数人来自贫穷家庭，他们的母亲也没有接受过正规教育。（《千年发展目标报告》，2005）

5. 1998—2006 年，发展中经济体实际出口额翻了一番以上，而七国集团增长了不足 50%。在发展中地区，尽管其贸易条件有所恶化，东亚和南亚显然最成功地实现了出口增长（以数量计），增长率约为 160%。在其他发展中地区，出口数量增长较为缓慢，接近于七国集团，但从贸易条件中获得的利益提升了购买力，进而促进了进口。总体而言，发展中国家在全球贸易中所占的份额从 1996 年的 29%增加到 2006 年的 37%。（《2007 贸易与发展报告》）

Task II

中国水果资源丰富。2009 年，中国水果产量大约为 1.2 亿吨（不含瓜类），在全世界名列前茅。尽管中国人口众多，中国果汁饮料消费量很低。2009 年，人均果汁消费量不到 10 升。根据市场调查，中国 2009 年果汁饮料生产量为 1 347 万吨，比 2008 年增长 14.2%；市场规模约为 575 亿元人民币，同比增长 15%。

市场调查显示，在中国果汁市场，100%浓缩果汁仅为 5%到 6%，而绝大多数果汁为低浓度果汁（果汁含量不超过 25%）。这主要是消费者购买力和消费行为所导致的。

至 2009 年年底，中国目前拥有果汁生产商 1 000 余家，但大型厂家寥寥无几。除了像汇源、可口可乐和百事可乐几家企业的产品畅销全国外，其他大多数企业仅在某个区域的市场上销售。受融资能力和营销渠道的限制，这些区域性企业无法在国内市场运营。从长远看，它们可能成为果汁市场上大公司的收购对象。通过收购，大公司可以提高区域市场份额，建立本土化的生产基地。

2008 年爆发的全球金融危机严重打击了中国果汁出口。2008 年，中国果汁出口总量为 794 000 吨，出口总值为 12.6 亿美元，同比分别下降了 30.4%和 7%。国际金融危机严重影响了中国果汁出口市场。2009 年，中国果汁出口总量为 897 000 吨。但是，由于出口价格下降，出口总值降到了 7.624 亿美元，同比下降了 39.4%。2010 年第一季度，中国果汁出口继续下降。

中国果汁市场大部分为低浓度果汁，仅有小部分为高价格、高浓度的果汁。通常情况下，消费者没有降低果汁饮料方面的开支。因此，全球金融危机并未对国内的果汁市场造成巨大的损失。

根据对世界饮料市场发展的调查，人均国内生产总值达到 3 000 美元时，居民会更重视补充维生素饮料。2009 年，中国人均国内生产总值超过 3 000 美元。据预测，2010—2014 年，中国果汁市场会持续增长，人均果汁消费量会快速增长。未来几年，中国果汁市场可能成为国内外企业的竞争焦点。

Task III

理论上，研发活动进入发展中国家的这种国际化既在意料之中，也在意料之外。在意料之中有两个原因。第一，由于跨国公司不断扩大在发展中国家的生产，可以预见，有些研发活动（调整适应型）会随之跟进。第二，研发活动是服务活动的一种形式，与其他服务一样具有“分解性”，其中某些部分放在实施效果最好的地方。实际上，贸易与发展会议和罗兰·贝格咨询公司在 2004 年对欧洲大公司开展的一次调查发现，所有服务功能——包括研发——现在都有可能在境外得到满足。在意料之外是因为，研发活动是技能、知识和辅助需要等要求很高的一种服务活动，过去一向只在具有强大创新体系的发达国家进行。另外，研发被认为是经济活动中最不可能“分解”的活动，因为涉及的知识对于公司具有战略意义，也因为开展研发经常需要在局部地区的集群内开展使用者和生产者之间的密集知识交流（其中相当部分是默契性的）。

显而易见，到目前为止，参与研发国际化进程的仅有少数发展中国家和转型经济体。但是，它们中有些国家和经济体已经对极为复杂的研发活动具有吸引力。这一事实表明，发展中国家有可能发展并具备与跨国公司全球研发体系接轨所必要的各种能力。从东道国的角度看，研发国际化不仅为转让在其他地方开发的技术打开了大门，而且也为技术开发进程本身打开了大门。这有可能帮助一些东道国提高自己的技术和创新能力。但是，这也有可能加大没有与全球创新网络衔接的国家的落后差距。(《2005 年世界投资报告》)

第十五单元　商务文摘翻译

PART ONE
认识商务文摘及商务文摘翻译

Task

【解析】商务文摘浩如烟海，涉及面非常广泛，主要涉及商务、经济、贸易等方面的内容，其中有许多各行各业的专有名词和行业术语，译者需要谨慎处理。本部分参考译文如下：

1. 在过去几年中，中国政府的主要目标是减少农产品的出口比例，同时增加工业产品和矿产品的出口比例。目前，各种各样的工业品出口海外，中国的资本设备被许多发展中国家用于各个领域的建设项目，如农业、林业、轻工业、食品加工业、储水、运输与通信业等领域。

2. 在纪念品市场上，亚洲无疑是所有地区中潜力最大的。全球纪念品市场的确切规模很难估计。纪念品是一个大致的概念，包括从历史人物到现代名人的签名和艺术品，而买家则形形色色，从热诚的追随者到更理性的投资者，等等。业内人士估计，每年纪念品交易额约为 5 000 万美元，这因拍卖物品而异。所谓的“绩优股”在任何指定的年份都会促进销售，“绩优股”也就是与世界偶像（如麦当娜或卓别林）或具有重要历史意义的人物（如丘吉尔）等有关的物品。

3. 据大部分业内人士说，亚洲的纪念品市场远远落后于西方。尽管近几个月富有的亚洲买家开出了创纪录的价格，以获得稀有的葡萄酒、珍贵的艺术品、珍稀邮票等拍卖品，这一地区的纪念品市场却尚未带来像西方市场那样的影响。主要拍卖行苏富比拍卖公司、佳士得和宝龙的亚洲分支机构在该地区没有纪念品专家，需要把涉及这类市场的问题转给伦敦、纽约或洛杉矶的办事处。

PART TWO
热身练习

Task

【解析】报刊文摘具有时效性，具有新闻英语简洁、准确的特点，翻译时需要关注日常事件以及报刊文摘的常用词汇和短语。本部分具体分析如下：

1. 报刊文摘中常用现在时态，翻译成汉语时往往可以忽略时态方面的问题，因为汉语是一种很少使用时态的语言。建议翻译为：中国是世界上网民最多的国家，其电子商务和移动支付交易额名列前茅。

2. 报刊文摘往往习惯使用一些固定句型和说法，如本句中“It’s estimated that…”是被动语态里面的特殊句型，可译为“据估计”；类似的例子还有“It is reported（据报道），It is hoped（大家希望），It is expected（大家希望），It is believed（大家相信），It is said

（据说）”等。另外，该句中有一个商务术语，“venture capital”，是风险资本的意思。建议翻译为：据估计，过去 20 年中，有 3 000 多家公司（包括非技术公司）在其发展的某个阶段曾获得过风险资本。

3. 本句中“woke up to”不能直译为“醒来”，它是指“认识到，意识到”，但翻译成“启动”一词能更好地与后面的“全新的货币”搭配，也更加生动。原文中的两个被动句“were distributed”和“were undertaken”都译为主动句式，更符合汉语的表达习惯。建议翻译为：2002 年 1 月 1 日，欧洲 12 国共同启动了一种全新的货币，并将在以后两个月内逐步取消各国原有的货币。在这个雄心勃勃的前所未有的货币改革行动中，超过 145 亿的纸币和 560 亿的硬币在这 12 个国家发行。为了使这一巨大变革得以顺利进行，各地举行了大规模的宣传活动。

4. 商务文摘的句子结构比较灵活，翻译时需要根据目的语表达习惯进行调整。本句需要把最后部分调整到句首才符合汉语的表达习惯。建议翻译为：中国高层智囊团的高级研究员周六表示，中国明年 GDP 增幅大约为 9%，但中国经济面临劳动成本增长、流动资金问题和难以保持长期快速发展等挑战。

5. 商务文摘紧跟时代脉搏，翻译时可适当使用新词。本句中的“donate his entire fortune to charity after his death”字面上是“死后将全部财产捐出”，其实就是我们常说的“裸捐”，英文中也可以用 all-out donation 来表示。建议翻译为：一位中国著名企业家和慈善家（陈光标）已承诺“裸捐”，成为中国第一位响应比尔·盖茨和沃伦·巴菲特慈善捐助活动的富豪，他们将于不久后来华宣传慈善。

PART THREE

商务文摘翻译技巧

Task I

1.

（1）分析人士说，快餐每年产业规模为 1 020 亿美元，但最近其增长速度放缓了，这是由于同食品零售店的竞争更加激烈，也由于人民更加富裕，愿意尝试新东西，愿意多花一些钱。

（2）据报道，中国的风投主要集中于数码领域，主要投向如大数据、人工智能，及金融科技等数码科技。尤其值得一提的是，中国在虚拟现实、自动驾驶汽车、机器人及无人机等方面的风投位居前三名。

（3）根据最近对全国汽车经销商的调查显示，多数面临财务困境，今年甚至有可能破产。一家独立调查公司联新公司说，该公司对 21 个国内外品牌的 1 252 个汽车经销商进行了调查。2008 年，大多数汽车经销商没有盈利，约 60%处于亏损状况。

2.

（1）据报道，该国的失业率已经达到百分之七。

（2）当然，正如许多企业领导指出的那样，全球销售并不意味着全球品牌。

（3）美国贸易代表罗伯特·佐利克对与会者说：“我相信随着新世纪时间的推移，当人们回顾今天的时候，他们一定会认为允许中国加入世界贸易组织是加强全球经济贸易体系的一个关键性的举措。”

（4）调查显示，17.3%的汽车经销商对他们的财务状况“满意”或者“比较满意”，超过70%的人说他们利用了利息更高的私人融资方式。

（5）根据一项新的报告，科学家们认为未来将有可能记录下人类的梦境并加以解释。他们称已经发明了一套可以记录大脑高级活动的系统。

（6）人才服务公司德科集团美国分部在一项民意调查中发现，美国的经济衰退拉近了老板和雇员之间的关系，只有30%的员工希望能得到老板那颇具压力的职务。这一调查与10月中旬的“全国老板日”有关。然而，调查也发现，在市场形势严峻的情况下，有些人愿意更加努力，以求保住自己的工作。

3.

（1）“失业乐活”用于形容在意外失业之后因享受空闲而感到的快乐。“欧猪五国”则是首字母合成词，指欧洲主权债务危机最严重的葡萄牙、意大利、爱尔兰、希腊和西班牙五国。

（2）“破裂社会”或“社会衰退”描述的是人们可以察觉到的道德价值观败坏的状况。“鬼宅”一词也进入了词典，它指的是因经济衰退而停工的未建成的住宅区。

（3）《中国广告法》修订建议的重点之一就是要让明星代言人要对他们所代言的产品担负更多的责任。这些修订是为了加强对名人代言和名人广告的管控。

4.【解析】商务报刊文摘中，简单句和复合句常常交错使用，并伴有大量的介词短语、插入语、同位语等，使语句结构更严密，细节更突出。特别是在新闻报道文体中，插入语的使用可对报道事件进行补充说明，为读者提供更多的背景资料。例如：本题各句中的斜体部分就属于插入语。另外，从时态看，商务文摘多用现在时或者将来时，对过去事件的描述也采用一般过去时；从语态来看，商务文摘常用被动语态。本部分参考译文如下：

（1）在一切几乎从零开始的经济特区，只要中国政府认为对国家有益，外国人可对任何项目进行投资，例如出口货物的生产或私人住宅的房地产开发。

（2）尽管美国疲软的需求导致了短期美元利率急剧下跌，但对于发展中国家的发展是积极的，它也导致商品价格下跌超过6%，世界贸易增长率下跌了3%。

（3）由于在21世纪的头10年，（与中国相比）美国经济年平均增长率低了大约七点五个百分点，假设这一趋势继续下去，且人民币汇率年均升值3%（这是相当合理的），那么只需11年时间，中国经济就会变得比美国更强大，这意味着到2020年，中国将成为第一大经济体。

（4）需要生产更多的产品以创造更多的就业机会和利润。

Task II

【解析】商务文摘标题往往三言两语，简明扼要地阐明文章的内容。翻译时不能片面地仅仅忠实于标题，而往往需要联系文摘全文内容，通盘考虑，灵活进行处理。就翻译方法而言，第1—5小题采用直译法，第6—7小题采用意译法，第8—9小题采用增译法，第10题采用套译法，同时也采用了增译法。具体分析如下：

1. 卷起竹幕

——中国政府允许外商在其沿海投资

2. 经济衰退让老板和员工走得更近

3. 香港是美国蛋类出口的最大市场

4. 国际易货贸易的复苏

5. 经济困境笼罩着新市场前景

6. “三不”一代（NEET 是指 people not in education，employment or training 的首字母缩写，指的是一群“不上学，不工作，也不参加培训的年轻人”。文章讨论了目前在日本和英国的年轻人中存在的 NEET 现象并探讨这种现象的社会根源。首字母缩写不仅使文章标题显得简洁，而且因为是作者新造词，很容易引起读者的兴趣。）

7. 西点军校东山再起（题目翻译必须具有吸引力，否则读者不会继续阅读文摘内容，这里的 comeback 不能简单地翻译成“回来”，而应该是“东山再起，重塑雄风”的意思。）

8. 世博即将谢幕 下一站米兰（gear up 原意为“加速驶向某地”的意思，这里是指上海世博会即将结束，米兰即将做好准备，所以翻译成“下一站米兰”。如果仅仅这样翻译而不提供任何背景信息，读者可能以为是“体育比赛的下一站”，这里增加了背景知识“世博即将谢幕”，使标题意义非常明确。）

9. 山姆大叔的帝国逻辑（该文摘一开始就尖锐地指出“布什因为一个国家蔑视国际法就对其发动战争的逻辑有点可笑。布什自上台以来，美国政府撕毁的国际条约和违背的联合国协议比世界上其他国家过去 20 年内的总和还多。”原标题用“empire”来暗指美国是因为“9 • 11”后西方世界已越来越多地将美国与曾在公元前辉煌一时、因穷兵黩武遭人怨恨、最后衰落垮台的古罗马帝国相比，认为美国是 21 世纪的罗马帝国。如果直译为“帝国的逻辑”易使中国读者联想到一切西方帝国主义，但冠以“山姆大叔”则使译文标题与原标题一样立场鲜明，并不乏调侃。（郎芳，2009）

10. 巾帼不让须眉　女性领导能力优于男性（本标题如果按照字面含义翻译，“女性领导力优于男性”就可以了，但是为了增强标题的吸引力，翻译时套用了汉语习语“巾帼不让须眉”，使其标题及全文含义跃然纸上。）

Task III

1. 目前还没有关于国际收支的无形贸易项目官方统计资料，但是 2005—2010 年间的有形贸易顺差规模以及公布的旅游收益增加表明，在过去的几年中经常项目一直是顺差。

2. 顾客退休时，必须结清欠款，随后账户可转为信用贷款，收取约百分之五的利息。

3. 分析人士说，去年年底实施的货币紧缩政策使许多公司尤其是私营公司陷入困境。有报告指出，沿海地区成千上万的中小企业由于难以从银行获得贷款而倒闭了。人民币快速升值，劳动力和原材料成本上涨也是造成这种局面的主要原因。

4. 广告直接有助于把货物以合理的价格分销出去，因此可以使公司建立一个稳定的国内市场，同时也使公司有可能以具有竞争力的价格出口产品。

Task IV

贸易壁垒

第三个特殊的问题是贸易壁垒。由于种种原因，所有国家对通过它们边境的某些商品都设有贸易壁垒。有一些贸易壁垒是直接和出口有关的，例如在美国，未经政府批准，战略军事物资是不允许出口的。不过大多数贸易壁垒是用来限制进口的。最常见的两种进口壁垒是配额和关税。

配额

配额是用数量或价值表示的数额限制。例如，从欧洲进口的 A 级小商品每年不得超过 50 000 件的配额是一种以数量表示的限制。而对某种日本玻璃器皿的进口规定每年不得超过 100 万美元的限制则是一种以价值表示的配额。

关税

关税是对进口到一个国家的商品所征收的税额或费用。这类关税有两种：收入关税和保护关税。收入关税是为增加政府税收而征收的。这种关税一般较低，通常每件或每磅商品征收低于 25 美分的关税。保护性关税是为了限制外国企业将某种商品在该国销售而征收的，其基本目的是阻挠可能以低于本国产品价格出售的商品进口。由于这个原因，保护性关税通常是相当高的，从而迫使外国企业提高其价格以偿付关税。

Task V

亚洲，成本过高

国际货币基金组织刚刚预言，亚洲的经济繁荣在未来几年中还要持续下去。索尼公司刚刚宣布，它将不再从日本出口电视，因为它没有可能把其价格定得更有竞争力。就这两条信息，亚洲的企业应该注意其中的哪条呢？

听听索尼的吧。即使在一个不断扩大的市场上，成本仍起着关键的作用，而对许多企业来说，亚洲正开始使它们的成本变得过高。

亚洲的经济奇迹可以精彩地概括为史无前例的削价抢生意。亚洲经济增长是因为，它是西方渴望的最廉价的低技术消费产品的来源。韩国并未发明新的或更高效的生产技术，它们只不过通过低工资赢得其市场份额。

PART SIX

商务文摘翻译实践

Task I

建议改译为：

市场只是某种产品或劳务交易双方所进行的相互联系的总和。它可以像纽约证券交易所、福尔顿鱼市场或芝加哥商会那样正式组织起来且地理位置集中，也可以不是这样。鞋市和钢架市场都没有经过正式组织，无法在地图上的某个具体地点找到它们。市场仅仅是交易双方的互动过程，通过这一过程确定成交的价格和数量。

Task II

1. 他说，不同年代员工的职业期望和就业价值观不同，这是一个难以弥合的鸿沟。

2. 贸易是如何进行的？如果一个美国人从佛罗里达购买桔子，他自然要用美元付款。桔农也希望收取美元，因为，它们的开销和日常生活费用都是用美元结算的。在一个国家内，经济交易显得很简便。

3. 根据顾客提供的样品来生产产品，同时大力鼓励补偿贸易。由此国外的供应商提供原材料和设备并收到由其提供的设备生产出来的制成品作为回报。补偿贸易在某种程度上不同于易货贸易和反向贸易，因补偿贸易中，国外提供的设备和制成品有直接的联系。

4. 香港蛋类市场的主要供货方正努力增加产品的竞争力，为的是保住或扩大市场份额。为了推销中国蛋，中国蛋类及蛋产品公司最近举行了一次“幸运抽奖”——香港的流行促销活动——为获胜的零售商发金奖。他们设计出引人注目的广告，推销中国鲜蛋和咸蛋。

5. 圣诞购物节极其重要，对零售商而言不成功则成仁。随着节日渐进，由于消费者手头紧、支付能力下降，寻求最划算的物品，零售商们面临激烈竞争。对整个零售业而言非常艰难，但根据多数零售商报告显示，赢家多过输家。

Task III

1. In the period from the first 1851 World Exhibition held in Britain to 1999, humanity suffered two World Wars. The brutal reality and the bloody lessons of mechanized war aroused people's hopes for peace. With these aspirations of people for a happy life, scientific and technological revolutions have brought about unprecedented advances and economic growth, vigorously boosting productivity, the economies and societies of all countries.

2. According to International Monetary Fund statistics, about 64.8 percent of the world's foreign exchange reserves were denominated in US dollars at the end of 2000. Euro holdings amounted to 12.7 percent. Yet there are more practical reasons for central banks to hold dollars, such as a country's exchange rate regime. After the Asian financial crisis of 1997–1998, most governments adopted floating exchange rate regimes. However, many central banks have continued to target a core rate against the US dollar. Dollar holdings are essential to trim currency movements.

参考文献

R. Quirk, et al. A Grammar of Contemporary English [M]. London: Longman, 1973.
澳大利亚图标：http://www.overseasstudy.cn/australia/gb/article/2005-7/3935-1.htm，2010-09- 01.
百度百科：http://baike.baidu.com/，2010-09-30.
北京市人民政府外事办公室：http://www.bjfao.gov.cn，2009-08-18.
常玉田. 国际商务英语写作 [M]. 北京：中国商务出版社，2005.
常玉田. 经贸英译汉教程 [M]. 北京：外文出版社，2005.
陈海彬. 商务英语单证翻译失误分析 [J]. 湖南医科大学学报，2010（5）：224-225.
陈建平. 经贸合同英语词法特征及其翻译 [J]. 中国科技翻译，2006（2）：30-33.
陈建平. 经贸合同英语的语言特征及其翻译 [J]. 中国翻译，2005（7）：80-84.
陈欧. 外贸英语的语义辨析 [J]. 中国科技翻译，2002（4）：28-31.
陈苏东，陈建平. 商务英语翻译（英译汉）[M]. 北京：高等教育出版社，2003.
陈小慰. 翻译功能理论的启示——对某些翻译方法的新思考 [J]. 中国翻译，2000（4）：10-13.
陈秀桃. 商务英语写作 [M]. 北京：对外经济贸易大学出版社，2008.
陈亚利. 英文商务写作——案例分析与实践 [M]. 天津：天津大学出版社，2004.
辞海编辑委员会. 辞海 [M]. 上海：上海辞书出版社，2000.
崔立红. 商标权及其私益之扩张 [M]. 济南：山东人民出版社，2003.
丁衡祁. 翻译广告文字的立体思维 [J]. 中国翻译，2004（6）：77-82.
范武邱. 实用科技英语翻译讲评 [M]. 长沙：湖南科技出版社，1998.
方梦之. 英汉翻译基础教程 [M]. 北京：中国对外翻译出版公司，2008.
凤凰财经网：http://finance.ifeng.com/jigou/stockcom/helanyinhang.shtml，2010-09-09.
付慧平. 论企业外宣翻译的“信息突出——经济简明策略”原则 [J]. 考试周刊，2010（9），235-237.
郭贵龙，张宏博. 广告英语文体与翻译 [M]. 上海：华东师范大学出版社，2008.
贺川生. 商标英语 [M]. 长沙：湖南大学出版社，1997.
贺雪娟. 商务英语翻译教程 [M]. 北京：外语教学与研究出版社，2007.
洪明. 排偶修辞在商业广告翻译中的美感功效 [J]. 上海翻译，2006（1）：38-41.
胡昌宇. 经贸英语的语体特点与翻译 [J]. 淮北煤师院学报，2002（2）：95-96.
胡庚申，王春晖，申云桢. 国际商务合同起草与翻译 [M]. 北京：外文出版社，2003.
胡鉴明. 商务英语函电 [M]. 北京：中国商务出版社，2006.
胡开宝. 英语网站、网络名称的构成及翻译 [J]. 科技英语学习，2004（9），45-48.
胡克明，胡志伟. 英语广告词精品 [M]. 北京：北京大学出版社，1999.
胡晓姣. 名片中姓名及称谓的英译 [J]. 高等教育与学术研究，2006（1）：35-38.
沪江英语：http://tr.hjenglish.com/page/92042/,2010-10-10.

黄国文. 语篇分析的理论与实践——广告语篇研究［M］. 上海外语教育出版社，2001.
黄友义. 坚持“外宣三贴近”原则，处理好外宣翻译中的难点问题［J］. 中国翻译，2006（4）：27-28.
黄忠廉，李亚舒. 科学翻译学［M］. 北京：中国对外翻译出版公司，2004.
贾文波. 应用翻译功能论［M］. 北京：中国对外翻译出版公司，2004.
贾秀花. 浅谈商务英语中缩略语的使用［J］. 商场现代化，2008（6）：219.
金焕荣. 商务英语翻译［M］. 苏州大学出版社，2007.
郎芳. 标题书名翻译的审美标准［J］. 海南师范大学学报（社会科学版），2009（6）：141-144.
李本现. 国际商务诸“单”的英译［J］. 中国科技翻译，1998（3）：14-16.
李波阳. 商务英语汉英翻译教程［M］. 北京：中国商务出版社，2005.
李德荣. 商务英语基础教程［M］. 上海：华东理工大学版社，2005.
李克兴，张新红. 法律文本与法律翻译［M］. 北京：中国对外出版公司出版社，2006.
李太志. 商务英语言语修辞艺术［M］. 北京：国防工业出版社，2006.
李永红. 目的论视角下的企业外宣资料英译［J］. 文教资料，2007（2）：157-158.
连淑能. 英汉对比研究［M］. 北京：高等教育出版社，1993.
梁为祥，李岗. 新理念商务英语专业翻译教程［M］. 上海：复旦大学出版社，2008.
林宗豪，等. 中国企业简介的网页英译问题调查及应对策略［J］. 通化师范学院学报，2010（1）：90-94.
刘法公. 商贸汉英翻译评论［M］. 北京：外语教学与研究出版社，2004.
刘法公. 商贸汉英翻译专论［M］. 重庆：重庆出版社，1999.
刘季春. 实用翻译教程［M］. 广州：中山大学出版社，2007.
刘宓庆. 文体与翻译［M］. 北京：中国对外翻译出版公司，2007.
刘伟奇. 国际商务单证的作用及种类［J］. 对外经贸实务，2005（3）：61-62.
卢立程. 企业对外宣传材料翻译中的语篇重构［J］. 肇庆学院学报，2007（3）：53-56.
路甬祥. 科学与中国［M］. 北京：北京大学出版社，2006.
吕和发. 公示语的功能特点与汉英翻译研究［J］. 术语标准化与信息技术，2005（2）：22-27.
吕和法，单丽萍. 汉英公示语词典［Z］. 北京：商务印书馆，2009.
罗建华. 涉外文秘写作［M］. 广州：广州高等教育出版社，2009.
马会娟. 商务英语翻译教程［M］. 北京：中国商务出版社，2004.
马会娟. 商务英语翻译教程［M］. 中国商务出版社，2004.
梅德明. 中级口译教程［M］. 上海：上海外语教育出版社，2003.
潘红. 商务英语英汉翻译教程［M］. 中国商务出版社，2004.
潘立，谢建平. 汉语公示语的语言特点及语用翻译策略［J］. 浙江理工大学学报，2009（3）：466-469.
潘敏. 人无我有，人有我精——评孙致礼《新编英汉翻译教程》［J］. 外语界，2003（4）：77-79.
潘文国. 公共场所英语标识语错译解析与规范［M］. 上海：上海外语教育出版社，2010.
彭萍. 实用商务文体翻译［M］. 北京：中央编译出版社，2008.

秦荻辉. 科技英语语法［M］. 北京：外语教学与研究出版社，2007.
沈炜艳. 从外宣资料英译中的常见错误看译者应具备的素质［J］. 东华大学学报（社会科学版），2007（4）：287-290.
石定乐，蔡蔚，王纯琳. 实用商务英汉互译［M］. 北京：北京理工大学出版社，2006.
宋德文. 国际贸易英文合同文体与翻译研究［M］. 北京：北京大学出版社，2006.
宋天锡. 翻译新概念——英汉互译使用教程［M］. 北京：国防工业出版社，2009.
孙亮，翟年祥. 广告词典［K］. 成都：四川人民出版社，1997.
唐莉玲，姚玲. 浅谈产品介绍书的英译［J］. 桂林航天工业高等专科学校学报，2005（3）：57-60.
陶博. 法律英语［M］. 上海：复旦大学出版社，2004.
陶全胜. 从翻译目的论看企业外宣资料汉英翻译原则［J］. 合肥工业大学学报（社会科学版），2005（4）：124-128.
王寅. 英汉语言宏观结构区别特征［J］. 外国语，1990（6）：36-40.
王建国. 功能翻译理论与我国的翻译教材建设［J］. 语言与翻译（汉文），2004（2）：58-60.
王静. 外宣资料的功能性编译法探讨［J］. 上海翻译，2010（3）：40-42.
王妮. 浅谈外贸英语单证的英语缩略语［J］. 科技信息，2007（16）：444-445.
王青. 论外宣资料的编译［J］. 淮海工学院学报（社会科学版），2010（4）：86-88.
王伟. 外宣类文本翻译初探——以成都锦江宾馆简介翻译为例［J］. 大众商务，2010（6），230.
王增文. 商务英文合同的句式特点及翻译［J］. 商场现代化，2007（5）：5-6.
韦晓萍，刘明忠. 企业英语网站翻译策略研究［J］. 社科纵横，2009（7）：167-169.
翁凤翔. 当代国际商务英语翻译［M］. 上海：上海交通大学出版社，2006.
吴建兰，盛芝义. 省略和倒装在科技英语中的应用［J］. 河北理工学院学报，2004（4）：193-195.
吴伟. 从语篇分析角度浅谈语篇和语篇翻译［J］. 湖北广播电视大学学报，2008（8）：121-122.
吴希平. 英语广告修辞种种［J］. 中国翻译，1997（5）：24-25.
项红梅，何小群. 浅谈名片翻译的原则及方法［J］. 西南民族大学学报（人文社科版），2007（12）：79-81.
肖姗. 语篇分析与翻译［J］. 法制与社会（教育文化版），2008（3）：225-226.
谢金领. 世纪商务英语翻译教程（第三版）［M］. 大连：大连理工大学出版社，2009.
徐华，等. 纺织品外贸实务英语［M］. 北京：中国纺织出版社，2007.
许建平. 英汉互译实践与技巧［M］. 北京：清华大学出版社，2007.
许明武. 科技英语句层信息功能研究［M］. 北京：中国社会科学出版社，2007.
杨大亮. 大学商务英语翻译教程［M］. 北京：北京大学出版社，2003.
杨婷. 浅谈英语缩略语的翻译［J］. 浙江万里学院学报，2007（20）：15-16.
尹雪艳. 外宣文本翻译的关联性信息和价值［J］. 文教资料，2010（1）下旬：30-33.
于关炎. 进出口单证翻译中的“信息灵活对等”［J］. 对外经贸实务，2004（6）：16-17.
余富林. 英汉缩略语的比较与应用［M］. 北京：清华大学出版社，2002.

余富林，等. 商务英语翻译（英译汉）[M]. 北京：中国商务出版社，2003.
袁建军，梁道华. 国际经贸英文合同的语言特征与翻译 [J]. 重庆交通大学学报，2009（10）：126-129.
曾庆元. 目的论视角下的招商外宣英译——以滨海新区招商外宣英译为例 [J]. 职业时空，2010（6），160-162.
张聪义，戴聪腾. 科技英汉互译技巧比较研究 [J]. 长沙大学学报，2008（4）：101-103.
张海琳. 论英文经贸合同的语言特征及其翻译 [J]. 洛阳大学学报，2004（9）：67-69.
张新红，李明. 商务英语翻译（英译汉）[M]. 北京：高等教育出版社，2003.
章咏. 常用名称术语英文缩写中文速查手册 [M]. 北京：中国财政经济出版社，2005.
赵军峰. 商务英语口译 [M]. 北京：高等教育出版社，2003.
赵萱，郑仰成. 科技英语翻译 [M]. 北京：外语教学与研究出版社，2006.
中国日报：http://language.chinadaily.com.cn/chineseterm.shtml?ty=a，2010-09-30.
中国日报英语点津：http://www.chinadaily.com.cn/language_tips/news/2010-11/01/.
中华人民共和国国家标准——服装术语 GBT 15557—2008 [M]. 北京：中国标准出版社，2008.
中华人民共和国商务部：http://english.mofcom.gov.cn/.
周领顺. 试论企业外宣文字中壮辞的英译原则 [J]. 上海科技翻译，2003（3），59-60.
周燕，廖瑛. 英文商务合同长句的语用分析及其翻译 [J]. 中国科技翻译，2004（11）：29-32.
邹力. 商务英语翻译教程 [M]. 北京：中国水利水电出版社，2006.